Celebrating the First 100 Years of The Carnegie in Pittsburgh 1895 • 1995

Agnes Dodds Kinard

"Carnegie built thousands of libraries, here and all over the world, but this Carnegie Institute, with a museum of natural history, a museum of art, a music hall, and an adjoining library, this is unique. Carnegie built only one of these — here, in Pittsburgh."

— James A. Fisher, 1981
Life Trustee

This illustration by Henry Koerner, previously appeared on the cover of Celebration of Carnegie, *published in 1982.*

Identified as a Pittsburgh artist Henry Koerner was a familiar figure on his bicycle as he went about painting scenes of this city and it's many bridges. He was born in Vienna, Austria in 1915 and left in 1938 as Hitler's troops marched in, escaping the fate of his parents who died in the Nazi Holocaust. Coming to America, he became an American citizen and served in the United States Army. The artist came to Pittsburgh and taught at Chatham College where he met and married Joan, one of his students. Koerner may also be more widely remembered for the 54 portraits of famous personalities he painted for the covers of Time Magazine from 1955 to 1967. The 44 cover subjects published included John Fitzgerald Kennedy and Maria Callas, the Opera star linked with Aristotle Onassis before he married the widowed Mrs. Kennedy.

Each summer the Koerners returned to Vienna where Henry continued to bicycle out to paint each day until he was struck by a hit and run driver. He lingered, unconscious and died on July 4, 1991.

Table of Contents

An Introduction 11
Foreword, *The Carnegie*, by Ellen S. Wilson 15

Carnegie Institute Historical Perspective

Views of Carnegie Institute: 1905, 1950, 1980 and 1994 16
Andrew Carnegie, Founder 18
    Pittsburgh in Carnegie's Day 28
Carnegie Institute is Dedicated 29
Presidents of Carnegie Institute 1896 to Present 30
Original Officers and Board of Trustees 30
1994 Board of Trustees 31
Chronology of the Building 33
    The Noble Quartet 35
    Cornice of the Carnegie 36
    The Names on the Cornice (Glossary page 249) 248
The Carnegie Library 38
The Music Hall 42
Foyer of the Music Hall 45
Second Century Fund Campaign 47

The Carnegie Museum of Art

Directors of the Museum, 1896 to Present 48
Paintings in the Rotunda of the Music Hall 48
Paintings in the Music Hall Foyer 49
Painters with a Pittsburgh Connection 49
Architecture Hall 54
Hall of Sculpture and Balcony 55
The Heinz Architectural Center 58
    Architecture Exhibitions 58
Great Staircase Hall 64
    Alexander Murals 64
Ailsa Mellon Bruce Galleries and
    Collection of Decorative Arts, 1994 65
The Scaife Galleries 74
    Sculpture Court: Collection of Sculpture 76
Carnegie *International Exhibitions* 80
    First Prize Winners and *International* Works in the Collection 97
Development of Collection of Paintings 105
    Collection of Prints and Drawings 116
    Collection of Photographs 119
Department of Film and Video 122
Museum of Art Exhibitions in Addition to the *Internationals* 126
The Women's Committee, Museum of Art 134
The Patrons Art Fund 143
The Fellow's Art Fund 146
    The *Man and Ideas* Lectures, 1969-1994 147
    Carnegie Institute's Art in the Community —
        The Three Rivers Arts Festival 148
        The Associated Artists of Pittsburgh 151
    Pittsburghers' Support of the Arts
        Pittsburgh Art in Other Cities 154
        Cubism in Pittsburgh, 1913 158

The Carnegie Museum of Natural History	Directors of the Museum, 1896 to Present	160
	Establishing the Collections	160
	Collections Rated Outstanding	166
	Carnegie Museum of Natural History Library	168
	Publications	169
	Powdermill Nature Reserve	170
	Bird-Banding and Other Research	170
	Andrew Carnegie's Dinosaurs	171
	Dinosaur National Monument	173
	Field Expeditions: Paleontology Research	176
	Geologic Time Scale	177
	Cenozoic Hall	177
	Paleozoic Hall	178
	The Natural History Exhibition Gallery	178
	Nature Portraits — Netting Collection	180
Behind the Scenes	Division of Education	182
	Division of Exhibit and Design Production	185
	Division of Earth Sciences	
	Section of Vertebrate Paleontology	186
	Section of Invertebrate Paleontology	190
	The Bayet Collection	190
	Section of Paleobotany	193
	Division of Life Sciences	
	Section of Amphibians and Reptiles	194
	Section of Botany	196
	Section of Birds	199
	Section of Mammals	201
	Section of Invertebrate Zoology (Entomology, Insects and Spiders)	203
	Division of Anthropology	205
	Includes Archeology, Ethnology	
	Section of Conservation	209
	The Council, Museum of Natural History	210
	The Benedum Hall of Geology	212
	The Discovery Room	213
	Mellon Hall of North American Mammals	214
	Hall of African Wildlife	215
	The Hillman Hall of Minerals and Gems	217
	Polar World: The Wyckoff Hall of Arctic Life	220
	Walton Hall of Ancient Egypt	221
The Carnegie Science Center		223
The Andy Warhol Museum		230
About Carnegie Institute	Maintaining Carnegie Institute	244
	Glossary to the Names on the Cornice	249
	Bibliography	256

List of Illustrations and Photographs

Celebration of Carnegie in Pittsburgh illustration, Henry Koerner ...	3
Life is a Passing Shadow, Yaacov Agam	13
Views of Carnegie Institute* (1994 View by Robert Ruschak)	16
Cottage on Moodie Street*	18
Andrew Carnegie with brother Tom*	19
Adam and Eve, Albrecht Dürer	21
Skibo Castle *	22
Carnegie Golf Outing*	22
Carnegie Hero Medal*	23
Mr. and Mrs. Carnegie, Farewell to Pittsburgh*	24
Andrew Carnegie and his Library*	26
Gazette Times Cartoon*	29
Founders-Patrons Day*	31
Carnegie Institute*	33
Noble Quartet*	35
Carnegie Library Storymobile, photograph by Barbara Hart-Sturges	38
Library Restoration*	38
Twin Towers Music Hall*	42
Interior of the Music Hall, courtesy of *Carnegie Magazine*	44
Foyer of the Music Hall, photograph by Photosynthesis	45
Panther Hollow, Pittsburgh, John Kane	49
Concert for Two Harps, photograph by Harold Corsini	54
View of Architecture Hall*	56
Tongue of the Cherokee, Lothar Baumgarten	57
Entrance to The Heinz Architectural Center, photograph by	
Joanne Devereaux	58
Dormer Window, photograph by Joanne Devereaux	59
Twin Bridges Project for Point Park, Pittsburgh, Pennsylvania,	
Frank Lloyd Wright	60
Great Staircase*	64
Ailsa Mellon Bruce, Philip de Laszlo	65
Paul Mellon , William F. Draper	65
Long Case Clock	67
Side Chair, Christian Herter	68
Side Chair, Giles Grendey	68
Side Chair, American, New York	68
Armchair, Louis Majorelle	68
Rocking Chair, Charles Rohlfs	69
Chair, Frank Lloyd Wright	69
Child's Chair, Gerrit Rietveld	69
Armchair, Ludwig Mies van der Rohe	70
Long Chair, Marcel Bruer	70
Chair, Wharton Esherick	71
Armchair, Pittsburgh Plate Glass Company	71
Chair for R.A. Miller, Beverly Buchanan	71
Chair and Ottoman *Little Beaver*, Frank Gehry	71
Two-handled Cup, Cover, and Stand	72
Sacrifice of Iphigenia on her Wedding Day, Rudy Autio	73
Night, Aristide Maillol	75
The Tightrope Walker, George Segal	76
Reclining Figure, Henry Moore	77
Lost Objects, Allan McCollum	78
Elegy II (Opus 134), Barbara Hepworth	78
Head of a Boy, Pablo Picasso	78

Unless otherwise noted, photographs listed were provided by the Museum of Art
* *Indicates photograph from Carnegie Library of Pittsburgh, Pennsylvania*
** *Indicates photograph from Carnegie Museum of Natural History*

Victory, Augustus Saint-Gaudens 79
Panathenic Procession, Phidias 81
Portrait of a Boy, John Singer Sargent 83
Woman VI, Willem de Kooning 87
Ten Men, Susan Rothenberg 88
Landscape, Francis Bacon 89
Divine, David Hockney 90
Untitled 2, Brice Marden 91
Recover, Ross Bleckner 92
Arrangement in Black: Portrait of Señor Pablo de Sarasate,
     James Abbott McNeill Whistler 98
Eve After the Fall, Auguste Rodin 99
Portrait of Mrs. Chase, William Merritt Chase 99
The Old King, Georges Rouault 100
Man Walking, Alberto Giacometti 101
Don't Be Cruel, Elizabeth Murray 103
Cell II, Louise Bourgeois 104
Dem Unbekannten Maler, Anselm Kiefer 106
Nymphéas (Water Lilies), Claude Monet 110
Still Life with Brioche, Edouard Manet 111
Sailing, Edward Hopper 115
Le Stryge (The Vampire), Charles Meryon 116
Japan Bridge in the Rain, Utagawa Hiroshige 116
Time Exposed, Hiroshi Sugimoto 119
Dog Star Man, Stan Brakhage 123
The Sleep of Reason, Bill Viola 124, 125
Oh Fearful Wonder of Man, Henry Koerner 129
Carnegie, Richard Serra 133
The Heart of the World, René Magritte 134
Past Presidents, Women's Committee of The Museum of Art,
     photograph by Andy Starnes 135
Girls and Flowers, Aristide Maillol 136
Still Life with Strawberries, Levi Wells Prentice 137
Gate of Adobe Church, Georgia O'Keeffe 138
Die Verspottung (The Mocking), Georg Baselitz 138
Pittsburgh Memories, Romare Bearden 141
Young Women Picking Fruit, Mary Cassatt 142
Two Models, One Seated on Floor in Kimono, Philip Pearlstein 146
Andrew W. Mellon, *Carnegie Magazine* 154
Man with Pipe, Jean Metzinger 158
Dr. William J. Holland* 161
Butterfly Exhibit** 161
*Camel Driver Attacked by Lions*** 162
"George" Exhibit** 163
Least Bittern** 170
New York Journal, November 1898** 171
*Diplodicus carnegii*** 172
Mural of *Tyrannosaurus rex*, Ottmar von Fuehrer** 174
*Tyrannosaurus rex*** 175
Early Ancestry of the Dog** 179
Showy Lady's Slipper, Andrey Avinoff** 181
Museum on the Move** 184
Moon Rise, Zabriskie Point, Death Valley, CA, Kerik Kouklis 185
Chinese Letter Stamp** 187

Unless otherwise noted, photographs listed were provided by the Museum of Art
*   *Indicates photograph from Carnegie Library of Pittsburgh, Pennsylvania*
** *Indicates photograph from Carnegie Museum of Natural History*

**List of Illustrations
and Photographs**
Continued

Skull of *Triceratops brevicornus*** 189
Python Skeleton** 195
*Centrosema virginianum*** 197
*Tadarida brasiliensis*** 201
Carnegia mirabilis, Dr. John Rawlins** 204
Firefly beetle, Dr. John Rawlins** 204
Handmaiden Moth, Dr. John Rawlins** 204
Native American Boy** 205
Miss Kochi** 207
Fall of the Sky, Hone 208
Night on the Nile Invitation 211
Invitation for the Council for The Musuem of Natural History 212
Time Tower ** 213
Rocky Mountain Elk** 214
Rhinoceros** 215
Santens Brothers Taxidermy** 216
Calcite** 217
Beryl, Harold & Erica Van Pelt** 217
Rhodochrosite, Debra Wilson** 219
Polar World Exhibit** 220
The Offering Diorama** 221
Carnegie Science Center 223
Carnegie Science Center 224
The Discovery Hive, Carnegie Science Center 227
USS Requin, Carnegie Science Center 229
Andrew Carnegie, Andy Warhol 230
Andy Warhol Museum, Paul Rocheleau 231
Marilyn, (Three Times), Andy Warhol, Photograph
    by Richard Stoner 234
Joseph C. Fitzpatrick* 235
Jackie, Andy Warhol, Photograph by Lockwood Hoehl 239
Andy Warhol, The Andy Warhol Museum 242
Floor plans for The Carnegie, Courtesy The Carnegie's Public
    Relations Department 247
*Das Ende des 20. Jahrhunderts (The End of the Twentieth
    Century)*, Joseph Beuys 255

Unless otherwise noted, photographs listed were provided by the Carnegie Museum of Art
*   *Indicates photograph from Carnegie Library of Pittsburgh, Pennsylvania*
** *Indicates photograph from Carnegie Museum of Natural History*

An Introduction

This, my tribute to "The Carnegie," Andrew and his *Palace of Culture*, which now reaches across the city to include The Carnegie Science Center and The Andy Warhol Museum, is an "update" on my book of 1982. *Celebration of Carnegie in Pittsburgh*, known as the "Gold Book," was also a labor of love, written at a time when Andrew Carnegie was less recognized, less appreciated as the practical visionary and benefactor we now applaud.

It is astonishing how much has changed in those intervening 12 years, from the mundane to the remarkable. Typewriters and carbon paper have given way to computers and fax machines, and giant corporations such as Gulf Oil and Koppers Company (both established by Andrew W. Mellon and his brothers) have vanished from the Pittsburgh scene. Steel, the giant on whose shoulders our economy rested, has been shaken to its knees. No longer is Pittsburgh the corporate headquarters it used to be. The venerable Horne's Department Store, founded in 1849, which served the elite of the area for more than 100 years, and where the young Andy Warhola was a window dresser, was sold into oblivion in 1994. On the plus side, and underground, Pittsburgh now boasts a subway, albeit a very short one — just 1.1 miles from Grant Street to the Point — which opened July 3, 1985.

In addition to these visible, physical changes, there are other, more subtle developments. The Carnegie now considers entertainment, in addition to education, as a factor in developing exhibitions, programs, and workshops to attract the public. For the first time, to coincide with the All-Star baseball game held in sports-wild Pittsburgh in 1994, The Museum of Art presented an exhibit of its own vintage collectors baseball cards and related drawings, and The Carnegie Science Center opened a new permanent exhibition *The Science of Baseball*.

There is a new sensitivity, mandated by law in 1991, relating to Native American artifacts which were originally obtained from burial sites. Subtle changes have also been afoot in The Museum of Natural History in the way tribal customs are exhibited for enhanced public understanding of cultural differences.

I miss the volatile, vibrant Henry Koerner, the distinguished "Pittsburgh artist," who gave me his impressionistic drawing for the cover of the Gold Book. He died July 4, 1991, after being struck by a hit and run motorist, while bicycling out to paint in his native Vienna. Another loss, mourned by the community at large, was the death April 4, 1991, in an airplane accident, of Senator H. John Heinz, III, trustee and benefactor of The Carnegie and all aspects of our area.

But The Carnegie, and its parent Carnegie Institute, has prospered mightily, thanks to the foresight of former president Robert Wilburn and the dedicated efforts of the Second Century Fund Committee under the leadership of past president James Mellon Walton, and fellow trustees Henry Hillman and Thomas O'Brien. The facade of The Carnegie complex on Forbes Avenue has been cleaned and restored, and a much-needed parking garage added. The Carnegie Library has also been cleaned and refurbished. Endowments for The Museum of Natural History and for The Museum of Art have been greatly increased, conservation departments have been established and endowed. Five new natural history halls have been created, and many important works of art have been acquired for the renewed galleries. Four *Carnegie International Exhibitions* have been held, and dinosaurs have continued to attract crowds of children and grown-ups alike.

Meanwhile the Buhl Planetarium became a part of The Carnegie and then of the new Carnegie Science Center, while Pittsburgh became the home of The Andy Warhol Museum as an adjunct of The Carnegie.

Celebrating the First 100 Years is a compendium of facts and figures, presented with a frankly Pittsburgh bias, intended to be dipped into from time to time, perhaps with nostalgia. It is a compilation of gleanings of "ephemera," from the multitude of articles, brochures, catalogues, reports, and publications issued by the Institute, plus contemporary news articles about its activities. The richest source of all is *Carnegie Magazine*, published by the Institute over more than 50 years. R. Jay Gangewere, long-time editor, keeps it lively, interesting, and reliable, and I thank him for his accessibility and generous spirit. His suggestion led me to Ellen S. Wilson, who graciously granted me permission to use her words from *The Carnegie*, published by the Institute in 1992, as a foreword here.

Echoing her words, "How, then, can there be a book about The Carnegie? Any authoritative summary can be quickly outdated . . . The best that can be done is a snap shot — here is the institution at one chosen moment in its history."

All of these facts and figures were carefully chosen from authoritative annual reports or articles published over the years by or for The Carnegie through its vairous departments.

Although there is an emphasis on art, an effort was made to be "even-handed' in the selection of material for this collection of "snap shots." My regrets are offered readers whose orientation may be more toward the scientific. Even in the field of art, some of the activities, as for instance those of the important Department of Education, have not been treated in depth due to the limitation of space. That department includes responsibility for the Childrens' Room, the tours for school children, the Docents' tours and lectures as well as the information for various publications of the Museum of Art. The funding sponsors of these activities are many and varied, all appreciated.

Celebrating the First 100 Years is a backward glance over those historic decades. Looking ahead to a second century of service and delight to a larger audience, The Carnegie officially inaugurated the 1995-1996 Centennial with plans for an unforgettable extravaganza. Eclipsing the 1985 festivities which observed Andrew Carnegie's 150th Birthday, this celebration again collaborated with the Pittsburgh Symphony Orchestra in programs commemorating their shared Centennial.

Recalling the 1993 non-stop, weekend entertainment which opened The Andy Warhol Museum, The Carnegie launched the year-long program with a commuter promotion on Friday, October 6, 1995 at 5 pm which ran non-stop, with music, dancing and films shown throughout the night — until 9 pm Saturday, October 7th . . . enjoyed fleetingly against the backdrop of the more lasting exhibitions and displays, especially prepared by the Museum of Natural History and the Museum of Art.

The Carnegie Library of Pittsburgh and each of the components of The Carnegie featured special exhibits and events. The Museum of Natural History, as befits its seniority, highlighted its expeditions, research and collections; the Museum of Art, in addition to opening The Carnegie *International* of 1995, exhibited art from the collections which have appeared over the span of the *Internationals*. There were also special attractions at the more contemporary Carnegie Science Center and The Andy Warhol Museum.

All events "Free to the Public" would have gladdened the heart of the founder, Andrew Carnegie. Perhaps he would be pleased, too, that an official delegation traveled to Centennial observances in Scotland, and were overnight guests at Skibo Castle, Mr. and Mrs. Carnegie's very own Highland retreat.

Life is a Passing Shadow, 1970, by Yaacov Agam, Israeli;
Gift of Mr. and Mrs. Harold J. Ruttenberg, 1974.

Acknowledgements

When I look again at my acknowledgments from 1982, I must include first here, my appreciation to Carole Long Kamin, who, with taste and flair, for 20 years managed the shops for The Museum of Art and The Museum of Natural History. She, "held the faith" as to the value to visitors to The Carnegie of an informal, easy to read book. Dolly Kacsuta Parks, principal, Kacsuta Parks Design, undertook the design of the Gold Book, and I marvel again at her vision, meticulous artistry, and her patience with my tendency to keep adding more nuggets of information to the copy.

Now, in thinking of The Carnegie Centennial and the many persons to whom I extend my warm acknowledgment for their help, I hope I am not overlooking anyone, if so, my sincere apologies along with my unspoken thanks.

I am glad that Lu Damianos, president of the Women's Committee in 1993, welcomed my gift to the committee through The Museum of Art, as an expression of my appreciation of the tremendous contribution this group of talented, energetic women make to the cultural life of the city. My thanks go to Elizabeth Schoyer of the committee for her overview of that section, and to Bege Galey for information about the early years. And, looking ahead, the enthusiasm of President Janet Krieger plus the combined efforts of Jane Thompson and Joan Kaplan in bringing the book to the readers will be most important.

I was pleased that the president of The Carnegie, Dr. Ellsworth Brown, as a fellow historian, thought this a worthwhile volunteer project and offered the help of Lorene Vinski and volunteer Barbara Barkett from his office, which I happily accepted. Marilyn Holt, head librarian of the Pennsylvania Room at the main library and her assistant Gil Piachuck led me to the rich lode of early photographs of Andrew Carnegieana.

Paul Mellon, the quintessential patron of the Arts and special patron of The Carnegie, graciously arranged for the inclusion here of his portrait by William Draper, who also painted Robert Wilburn the immediate past president of The Carnegie. By courtesy of Jeffrey Fleming, computer magic made it possible to include the dramatic portrait of The Carnegie Science Center. Robert Ruschak also kindly granted permission for inclusion of his photograph.

I especially thank Phillip Johnston, director of The Museum of Art for his openness to the idea and his helpfulness in making my copy as correct and complete as possible, given the limitations of time and format. He generously added his own assessment of some of the most important exhibitions the museum has shown during his regime as director. Sarah Nichols, curator of Decorative Arts, couldn't have been more painstakingly helpful as to my material concerning the collections in her domain. Vicky A. Clark, through her articles, provided insight into the more recent *Carnegie Internationals.* While Richard Armstrong, curator of Contemporary Art provided specific information about the 1995 *International Exhibition.* Other busy curators who found time to check my copy, and improve it, were Bill Judson, of the Department of Film and Video and Christopher Monkhouse of the Heinz Architectural Center. Rebecca Scuillo of the Heinz Center located the photographs I needed, as did Diane Becherer, director of Public Programs and Services. Registrar Cheryl Saunders and her assistant, Rachel Rampa, of The Museum of Art cheerfully sent page after page of computer print-outs which helped determine who gave what and when. Elissa Curcio, Publications Assistant, quickly produced the considerable number of photographs requested from The Museum of Art.

Juliette Grauer, volunteer arranger, informed me about the long history of The Carnegie Travel Adventure film series. Robert Croneberger, Director of The Carnegie Library of Pittsburgh gave of his time to review the chapter on Andrew Carnegie's beloved legacy. Thomas N. Armstrong, III had not yet become Director of The Andy Warhol Museum nor had Seddon L. Bennington been appointed to head The Carnegie Science Center at the time my work on each of those chapters was complete, based on other sources deemed reliable. I am grateful to Dan Verakis for his help in locating the photos of The Science Center.

In The Museum of Natural History, Dr. James Richardson, curator of Anthropology and Grete Evans of the Netting Collection assisted in locating elusive photographs. A quick course in Entomology was given to me by curator Dr. John Rawlins, while suggesting slides of beautiful insects to include here. The Director, Dr. James A. King, personally proofread much of the text dealing with the scientific divisions and curatorial sections in the museum, for which I am indeed grateful. He also facilitated

my obtaining a number of natural history photographs with the help of Ellen Moore, his assistant. But most of all I am thankful to Dr. King for giving me an office hideaway in which to work. Now, when I see a yellow door, I feel a warm glow.

When I am in the marble halls it is always a pleasure to encounter the cheerful presence of Guard James Graziano who long ago delivered our mail and now loves being at The Carnegie as do I.

Beyond The Carnegie, I think of Donald Miller, whose articles on art are always full of information and insight. Patricia Lowry, writer about architecture, formerly for *The Pittsburgh Press* and now with the *Post-Gazette,* helped locate a special photograph with an article she wrote years ago about the Women's Committee of The Museum of Art, and I thank Andy Starnes for his permission to use the picture.

Appreciation is due also to Walter Rutkowski, Executive Vice President of The Carnegie Hero Fund for supplying the recent statistics about the Carnegie civilian heroes.

In the early days of this undertaking, Elizabeth Brown and Kathy Rogulin, both of Carnegie Mellon University, assisted me with my intractable computer.

My son, Allan Dodds Frank, whose editorial ability was honed at *Forbes* Magazine, suggested improvements to my text and my husband, James P. Kinard, always encouraged me even when he hated to see me leave to go to my office. Both are in my thoughts, with special affection.

My hope is that readers will enjoy *Celebrating the First 100 Years* as much as I have enjoyed writing about Pittsburgh's revered treasure, The Carnegie.

— *Agnes Dodds Kinard*

Foreword

"It is the mind that makes the body rich."
— Andrew Carnegie

Two years after Carnegie Institute opened to the pubic in 1895, it was too small. What started as Andrew Carnegie's benevolent impulse in 1890, to build a library with art galleries, a museum, and a concert hall, has been growing ever since. In 1907, the expanded Library and Institute was opened. That building, with thirteen and a half acres of floor space, contained 165,000 square feet of cut sandstone on the exterior, and 6,000 tons of marble inside. In 1956, The Museum of Natural History gained a biological field station in the Laurel Highlands. In 1974, The Museum of Art opened the Sarah Scaife Gallery, bringing the Institute's floor space close to seventeen acres and opening new cultural opportunities for visitors to the museum. Buhl Science Center joined The Carnegie in 1987, leading to the opening of The Carnegie Science Center in 1991. The new Andy Warhol Museum brings another dimension to this vital institution.

How, then can there be a book about The Carnegie? Any authoritative summary can be quickly outdated with a gift from a benefactor, or a good idea from one of its 2,300 staff members and volunteers. The best that can be done is a snapshot — here is the institution at one chosen moment in its history.

Cultural institutions are, in their way, a series of snapshots, and none more so than The Carnegie. The building itself, in all its various pieces, is an example of architectural style throughout a century. The names of famous men engraved on the entablature reflect the heroes of the turn of the century. The mission of The Museum of Art was, from the beginning, to concentrate on contemporary art, and its galleries are now full of classics that may have been shocking in the 1930s and 40s. The Museum of Natural History shows not only the evolution of life but the evolution of scientific thought in its collections and the way they are exhibited. The Carnegie Library of Pittsburgh has changed from repository of history to community activist as it keeps up with the needs of the neighborhoods it serves, but the history is still there for those who seek it.

It is impossible to make a culture freeze a moment for study, but that is what these great collections do. And the collections themselves never stop growing, enlarging their mission the way Andrew Carnegie kept enlarging his original gift until even he was shocked and pleased by what he had helped to create. This book is a glimpse of an institution that is still evolving, a freeze frame of a cell in mitosis. Like any concrete representation of an idea, it is intended to lead the reader to what cannot be captured on paper.

— *Ellen S. Wilson*

Views of The Carnegie — 1905, 1950, 1980 and 1994

Approaching the Institute towards the library, over a
bridge now buried. Music Hall is at left. The towers
were removed in the expansion of 1905.

Photographs from Carnegie Library of Pittsburgh, Pennsylvania

Looking toward Carnegie Institute and Carnegie Mellon
University, from the University of Pittsburgh, pre-Scaife
Gallery, about 1950.

Aerial View of Carnegie Institute with the Scaife Gallery
in foreground, Forbes Avenue diagonally to right, about
1980.

Photograph from Carnegie Library of Pittsburgh, Pennsylvania

The Carnegie, viewed from the University of Pittsburgh,
1994.

Photograph by Robert Ruschak

Andrew Carnegie . . .
"The Star Spangled Scot"
1835-1919
Founder of Carnegie Institute

Boyhood

Andrew Carnegie was born on November 25, 1835 in Dunfermline, the ancient capital of Scotland from 1060-1650. Andrew was the first of the two sons of William and Margaret Morrison Carnegie (a sister died in infancy). In the cottage on Moodie Street, the father's looms were on the ground floor and the family lived above.

As Andrew Carnegie reminisced in *My Own Story*, he and his brother Thomas, his junior by eight years, were nurtured on tales of Scottish independence, industriousness, tenacity, and courage. Their mother, Margaret Morrison Carnegie, was the daughter of a prosperous maker of leather shoes, and their father, a weaver by hand of damask table cloths. As a boy Andrew's daily duty was to fetch buckets of water for the household from the well at the head of the street. He was allowed to keep rabbits when he devised a way to provide them with food. His boyhood chums helped gather the necessary grass in return for the simple privilege of having one of Andrew's rabbits named for them.

The family lived comfortably near the ancient Pittencrieff Castle, Glen and Abbey until the introduction of textile weaving machinery ruined Mr. Carnegie's trade. Although living nearby, the family was barred from the Glen by the Laird because the Carnegie and Morrison men were radical liberals, politically and religiously. They repudiated the privilege of royalty and the rigid constraints of Calvinism and were outspoken leaders of the weavers. (Carnegie himself in affluent later life became the Laird when he purchased Pittencrieff Castle and turned it over to the public as a park free to everyone.)

Family Emigrates to America

Andrew had only four years of schooling when the family was forced by poverty to emigrate to America. After their looms and household goods were sold, it was still necessary to borrow 200£ sterling for the balance of their passage across the Atlantic. Departing May 17, 1848, it took seven weeks by the sailing ship *Wiscasset* to reach New York and an additional three weeks by barge through the Erie Canal to reach Pittsburgh. The Erie Railway was then under construction. Joining the mother's relatives in Allegheny, now the North Side of Pittsburgh, the Carnegie family lived in two rooms over a small weaver's shop at 336-1/2 Rebecca Street. The area was known as, "Slabtown."

Work and Opportunity

Thirteen-year-old Andrew went with his father to work from dawn to after dark in The Blackstock Cotton Mill as a bobbin boy for $1.20 per week. Andrew figured that $25 per month would keep the family without being dependent

Cottage on Moodie Street, Dunfermline, Scotland where Andrew Carnegie was born, November 25, 1835.

Photograph from Carnegie Library, Pittsburgh, Pennsylvania

on others. Margaret Carnegie worked at home for Henry Phipps, a local cobbler, making and mending shoes as she had learned in her father's shop. Young Tom helped by waxing the leather threads. Later Andrew recalled that, in spite of the long hours of labor, many a Saturday midnight found his mother washing and ironing his one suit, to have it fresh for Sunday church. The boy was released from the mill drudgery when offered a job as errand boy for the telegraph operator in Pittsburgh, at a raise to $2.50 per week. He taught himself the Morse code by listening to the operators sending telegraphic messages concerning traffic on the railroad and train accidents.

Andrew Carnegie, age 16, with his brother Thomas.

Photograph from Carnegie Library, Pittsburgh, Pennsylvania

Access to Colonel Anderson's Library

In night school he learned basic accounting and on Saturday afternoons as a, "working boy," he had the privilege of borrowing a book from the 400-volume library of Colonel James Anderson. A prosperous manufacturer of iron, the colonel was a philanthropist who personally attended his library each Saturday afternoon.

(In his honor, Carnegie later commissioned a tribute to the colonel by the artists who created the memorial to President Lincoln in Washington, D. C. The work, completed in 1904, was a bronze sculpture *Statue of Labor* by Daniel Chester French, as the centerpiece of a monumental, curved, high-backed bench in marble, an exedra, by Henry Bacon.)

In those early days, management of the rail traffic through Pittsburgh involved constant use of the telegraph, especially when train wrecks obstructed the line. When young Andrew arrived at the office one morning, he discovered that such an accident had occurred, paralyzing rail traffic in both directions. Knowing that no trains would move without direct orders from the superintendent who might not arrive for some time, he ascertained the position of each train, issued orders in superintendent Thomas Scott's name, and soon had orderly rail traffic restored. Later, Scott confided to an associate, "Do you know what that little white-haired Scotch devil of mine did today? I'm damned if he didn't run every train on the division in my name, without the slightest authority."

Thomas Scott rose to the presidency of the Pennsylvania Railway, taking five-foot-three-inch Andrew with him with each promotion. At the time of the Civil War, president Lincoln called Scott to Washington, D. C. to head the Union's railway. Young Carnegie was charged with establishing the telegraph system. In that capacity he was present at the battle of Bull Run but not as a soldier. After a few months Carnegie returned to Pittsburgh as superintendent. He was exhausted and had suffered, "what seemed to be a mild sunstroke" which left him with a lifelong aversion to the heat of our American summers and with doctor's orders to avoid them.

First Investments

William Carnegie died October 2, 1855 the month before his elder son's 20th birthday. A few years later, Mr. Scott offered Andrew the opportunity to invest $500 in Adams Express Co. Andrew's widowed mother borrowed $500 by mortgaging their little house, on which they had just completed payment of $500 of the $700 total cost of it, and this became Andrew's first capital investment, on which he received a monthly dividend of $10. In 1862 he was able to afford his first trip back to his beloved homeland, and by 1863, Carnegie, at age 28, had an income of $47,000, of which only $2,400 was from the railroad. For Carnegie the transition from railroading to the steel business was natural. On one of his trips back to Scotland he met and conferred with Sir Henry Bessemer, inventor of an advanced process for making steel. It was a logical progression from an early investment in the building of railroad sleeping cars (1/8 interest in the Woodruff Co. for $500), to sensing the profit to be made in supplying the materials for those cars and for rails and bridges. As a result, in 1863, he established the Keystone Bridge Co. and, in 1866, the Pittsburgh Locomotive Works and the Union Iron Mills. Soon he formed The Carnegie Corporation for the manufacture of iron and steel, which proved so successful that he left the railroad and devoted his energies to his own businesses.

Builds Steel Mills

Pioneering in the application of chemistry to the making of steel, and in the use of cost accounting in the running of this business, Carnegie built the Edgar Thomson Steel Works. Strategically located between the rail lines of the Baltimore and Ohio and the Pennsylvania Railroads, the plant was named for a president of the latter.

During the excavating for the building, "there on the field of Braddock's defeat many relics of the battle were found . . . bayonets, swords and the like." Artifacts of American Indians were also unearthed. Perhaps these discoveries stimulated Carnegie's interest in natural history.

(In 1865 the newly affluent Carnegie had given his hometown of Dunfermline a public bathhouse, there being no indoor plumbing at the time. A relic of that era may be seen in 1995 in Pittsburgh, on Fifth Avenue, near the Birmingham Bridge, the "Public Baths" building still stands although it is no longer in use as such.)

Move to New York — Philanthropic Ambitions — Libraries

By 1867 Andrew Carnegie was headquartered in New York City, with an income of $50,000 per year. When he was 33-years-old he wrote a memo planning early retirement and life of culture instead of money-making. (In an article in the *North American Review* of June, 1889 he wrote, "The man who dies thus rich, dies disgraced." Later his treatise on the *Gospel of Wealth* presaged his giving away 90% of his wealth.) Recalling his father's early efforts in Dunfermline to create a small library by banding together with friends to share their few books, Carnegie resolved to give libraries, "free to the public." Before his death he had given 2,500 communities free libraries. The first was to Dunfermline, with the cornerstone laid by his mother, next he gave a library and recreation center to his workmen and their families in Braddock, Pennsylvania. As early as 1890 Carnegie had offered to build a library for Pittsburgh, but it was not until 1895 that the building was completed. Part of the delay was due to the need to repeal the Pennsylvania law which until 1887 prohibited the collection of taxes to support libraries. To the original library and music hall building, he added a natural history museum and an art gallery, making the complex one of the first in the country. It cost an estimated $25 million in 1907.

Adam and Eve by Albrecht Dürer, 1504, German. The Museum of Art, Carnegie Institute, Pittsburgh; Gift of Andrew Carnegie in 1895 and bequest of Charles J. Rosenbloom, 1974.

Special Gift to Pittsburgh

The Carnegie Institute was a very special gift to "Dear Old Smoky Pittsburgh," and was Andrew Carnegie's first large-scale, personal philanthropic endeavor. Carnegie scrutinized every detail of the construction, even the draping used for modesty on the copies of Greek and Roman statuary. When the committee deciding on the notables whose names would be engraved on the cornice around the building agreed to honor Rudyard Kipling but not Bobbie Burns, Mr. Carnegie objected but did not prevail! Omitted too were such personages as Dante, Cervantes, Vivaldi, Byron, Whitman, Blake, Plato, Dostoevsky . . . were any women even considered? (Those chosen are listed in the

Glossary to *Carnegie's Cornice*, page 249 from the award-winning article in *Carnegie Magazine*, mentioned elsewhere in this text.)

Andrew Carnegie also took a personal interest in the art obtained for the collections of The Museum of Art, giving the famous *Adam and Eve* copper engraving by Albrecht Dürer, 1504, and many other works.

He established the *Carnegie International Art Exhibitions* at the Institute with the idea that the museum could select from the best in contemporary art to establish a permanent collection for Pittsburgh. Carnegie arranged for the, "museum" (as The Carnegie Museum of Natural History was then called) to obtain the finest specimens of dinosaur fossils by purchase or expedition. Eventually the museum became the source of replicas of these creatures displayed in many of the capital cities of the world. The museum today has branched into many scientific areas as a natural history research center, in addition to being a place of natural history exhibits. It has been much loved by generations of Pittsburghers.

Skibo Castle in Scotland

Andrew Carnegie remembered the pangs of poverty and professed not to be an elitist, although he rose to the company of presidents and kings whom he entertained royally at Skibo Castle. It was a many-thousand-acre, ancient manorial estate of the Roman Catholic Bishops of Caithness, Scotland. When Carnegie acquired it from the then owner, George Dempster, for 85,000£ sterling in 1898, the ancient buildings were in ruins. For $4 million, Carnegie built his own castle where he enjoyed the cool summers with his baby daughter and his wife, at whose request he had bought the retreat in the Highlands of Scotland. Even there, he kept a sharp eye on his business, but found time to write numerous articles for magazines and newspapers. He campaigned for the adoption of a system of simplified spelling. Meanwhile, he carried on a

Skibo Castle in the Highlands of Scotland — built by Andrew Carnegie as a retreat from the heat of American summers.

Photograph from Carnegie Library, Pittsburgh, Pennsylvania

voluminous correspondence, maintaining friendships with literary personages like Mark Twain. (In their letters they addressed one another as St. Mark and St. Andrew.)

Establishes Pension Funds — Founds Technical School

"St. Andrew" established pension funds for the railroad and steel workers, and with $15 million provided a fund for aged teachers. He preferred to give to small, struggling colleges rather than to prestigious ones. Giving $600,000 to Tuskegee Institute, Carnegie stated that it was a rare privilege to know Booker T. Washington whom he called, "a man compounded of all virtues." He founded the Carnegie Institute of Technology, naming the school for home economics in honor of his mother, Margaret Morrison Carnegie.

Blame for Homestead Steel Strike

Andrew Carnegie was infinitely loyal to family, friends, and business partners. In appreciation of his own good fortune, he sought to share his wealth with those who had helped him to his success. Many of his boyhood chums became his associates and were, "Carnegie millionaires." Carnegie was not without detractors, however. Some newspaper cartoons of the day depicted him, trowel in hand, frantically building a brick wall, each brick a library, in an effort to achieve immortality. He had received in the press some of the opprobrium heaped on his associate Henry Clay Frick because of the brutality with which the Pinkertons, the company's armed police, put down the strikers at the Homestead steel plant in 1892, thereby breaking the union. While Carnegie was summering in Scotland, Frick was in charge. (In 1992 the Centennial of the infamous strike, the drama was reexamined in tragic detail by a voracious media, as discussed on page 25.)

Carnegie enjoys golfing with friends.

Photograph from Carnegie Library, Pittsburgh, Pennsylvania

Carnegie Hero Fund

The Carnegie Hero Fund Commission for the United States and Canada was established by Andrew Carnegie in 1904. Headquartered in Pittsburgh's Oliver Building, the fund is administered by a small staff and 21 members of the Commission. Carnegie felt that civilian courage should be awarded as well as military bravery. He was impressed with the daring of two would-be rescuers who gave their lives trying to save the 178 men and boys who died in a disaster in the Harwick mine near Pittsburgh. With $5 million, Carnegie established the Commission by a formal document which bears the signature of his wife, Louise Whitfield Carnegie, as the sole witness.

In 1993, the Commission awarded 92 Carnegie medals, bringing the total to 7,787 of the more than 68,000 rescue acts reviewed. The medal carries an award of $2,500 with additional assistance for continuing support of widows, widowers, other dependents, and disabled heroes. From 1904 through 1993 more than $12,235,000 was granted in monetary awards for support while scholarship assistance and medals totaled about $8,250,000. Thus, more than $20.6 million has been granted, rewarding remarkable acts of bravery by men, women, and children who have sought to save others from death by drowning, burning, or attack, by runaway vehicles or trains, or other hazards. During 1993 fourteen of the heroes lost their lives, bringing that total to 1,590. In 1992 an awardee was one of only four individuals in the Commission's history to have been granted the medal twice, almost 20 years apart.

Andrew Carnegie established separate Hero Funds in France, Germany, Norway, Switzerland, The Netherlands, Sweden, Scotland (Dunfermline), Denmark, Belgium, and Italy, in that order, in the period of 1909-1911. In 1974, *Carnegie Magazine* carried a review of an engrossing book about the Heroes of the Carnegie Award. Entitled *A Walk on the Crust of Hell* by

Medal of the Carnegie Hero Fund established by Andrew Carnegie in 1904.

Photographs from Carnegie Library, Pittsburgh, Pennsylvania

Jack Markowitz, it was published by the Stephen Greene Press, 1975, Brattleboro, Vermont.

Early Advocate of League of Nations

Andrew Carnegie was a man of peace. As president of the Peace Society of New York, he worked for the abolition of war. As early as 1907, in an address, he advocated the creation of a league of nations, namely Britain, the United States, Germany, Russia, and France. He established the Carnegie Endowment for Peace, in New York, and The Carnegie Institution of Washington, D.C. He built the Palace of Peace in The Hague, Holland, The Pan American Building in Washington, and the Central American Court of Justice in Cartago, Costa Rico. Until the outbreak of World War I in 1914, he had lived a vigorous outdoor life, according to his wife, Louise Whitfield

Carnegie, but the outbreak of war was too much for him, his health and his natural optimism suffered.

Private Life of the Carnegies

When Andrew Carnegie and Louise Whitfield met on New Year's Day 1880, he was 44 and she 23. Louise became the preferred of a number of young ladies squired by bachelor Carnegie in New York, but she considered him, "too rich." She wanted to be a helpmate for her husband and felt that he would not need her. When they became engaged in 1883 the pledge was called off after eight months, and when reaffirmed the following year was kept secret, due to Andrew's reluctance to leave his strong-willed and possessive mother. But when Andrew was ill, after losing both his mother and only brother Tom to typhoid within a few days of one another, Louise visited him, and in a few months they married. They had one child, a daughter Margaret, born in 1897, ten years after their marriage. In a foreword to *My Own Story by Andrew Carnegie*, published in 1920 after his death, Mrs. Carnegie wrote, "The world disaster was too much. His heart was broken." Andrew Carnegie died in 1919, at age 84, survived by Mrs. Carnegie and Margaret, Mrs. Roswell Miller. Mrs. Carnegie continued to spend summers at Skibo until 1939. The outbreak of World War II forced her to leave, carrying her gas mask, on September 1, never to return. Daughter Margaret summered there also until Skibo Castle was sold as an exclusive hunting lodge, ending a Carnegie era.

Celebration of Carnegie's 150th Birthday

In 1985, in honor of the 150th anniversary of Carnegie's birth, there was a city-wide celebration involving principally the Carnegie Institute, the Pittsburgh Symphony Orchestra, and Carnegie Mellon University. The University assembled a stellar group of graduates of the School of Drama in a variety of special

Mr. and Mrs. Carnegie wave goodbye to Pittsburgh as they return by rail to their home in New York.

Photograph from Carnegie Library, Pittsburgh, Pennsylvania

performances including, "Carnegie Salutes Carnegie" at the Civic Arena, launching their most ambitious fund raising drive in the University's history. *Carnegie Mellon Magazine*, Vol. 4 No. 1, Fall 1985 featured on its cover the University's bronze bust of Andrew Carnegie by J. Massey Rhind.

Inside Andrew Carnegie was the lead article by Peggy Farrar subtitled, "A Psychohistorian's Point of View." The author also had an article in *The Pittsburgh Press* November 17, 1985, *Carnegie on the Couch*. Even after a, "psychoanalysis" of Carnegie she admitted, "Based on his subconscious motivation, Carnegie defies categorization as either an altruistic hero or a self-serving egotist," but the article does have some interesting insights into the character of this most complex individual.

The magazine *Pittsburgh*, April 1985, carried an article, *The Gospel According to Andrew*, by Victoria Kohl which was illuminating concerning Carnegie's philanthropic philosophy and attitudes toward organized religion. In his

Gospel of Wealth, published in 1900, the steel magnate had set forth his suggestions for worthy beneficiaries which did not include hospitals and churches. His religious convictions were kept more private but his wholehearted agreement with his literary friend Herbert Spencers' defense of the Darwinian theory of evolution put him at odds with religious hierarchies. One of the rare reports of Carnegie's humor is contained here. Born a Presbyterian but a nondenominational Christian since his father had left the church, Carnegie quipped that he "might have been a Baptist but you know the water is pretty cold in Scotland."

In observance of the anniversary, The Pittsburgh Symphony, billed as "The Pittsburgh Orchestra," gave three anniversary concerts: in Heinz Hall, in the Carnegie Library in Carnegie, Pennsylvania, and in Pittsburgh's Carnegie Music Hall. The program in the Music Hall, November 25, 1985, opened with the dedication march written by Pittsburgh composer Adolph Foerster for the opening of Carnegie Institute November 7, 1895. The work was designed to highlight the notes A and C, the founder's initials. The program continued with Scottish Dances by Malcolm Arnold and a work by Victor Herbert, Andrew Carnegie's favorite composer, which had its world premier in 1900 conducted by the composer. The concert, under the baton of Conductor-in-Residence Michael Lankester, continued with a piece by Richard Wagner which had been performed by the Pittsburgh Orchestra in its inaugural concert in the Music Hall, in 1896. It was the overture to the opera Rienzi, *The Last of the Tribunes*. The Pittsburgh Symphony continued its celebration by performing in Carnegie's honor at The Edinburgh Festival in Scotland on its European Tour during the summer. Exchange programs were arranged between the tiny museum in the cottage in Dunfermline where Carnegie was born and counterparts in his vast museum complex in Pittsburgh.

In the presence of Mayor Richard Caliguiri, Governor Dick Thornburg, Senator H. John Heinz, III, and G. I. Tankersley, president of the Pittsburgh Symphony Society, the program in the Music Hall that evening continued with the appearance of A Special Guest. In the right side box, beaming and cordially waving to the audience there was Mr. Carnegie himself! It was a delightful touch, apparently the idea of his great grandson, Kenneth Miller, then a 36-year-old software developer from New York. Winding up the evening was a birthday party and preview of *Mr. Carnegie's Museum*, a major exhibition chronicling the life and Pittsburgh legacy of the Scotsman and the development of his museum of natural history.

In addition to mounting this exhibit, The Museum of Natural History had undertaken the remounting of the fossil skull of a mastodon, an early gift of Andrew Carnegie to the museum. The Carnegie observance also involved The Museum of Art and the Library, each with a special tribute. The Museum of Art staged *The 1985 Carnegie International* and organized an exhibition of drawings and watercolors which traveled to Edinburgh, Scotland. The Library offered many displays and numerous activities, joining with the Institute in *The Carnegie Family Fling*, a community birthday celebration for Andrew Carnegie. In December the traditional Christmas trees in Architecture Hall were decorated by the Women's Committee of The Museum of Art to depict our Scottish connections to Andrew Carnegie.

Homestead Steel Strike Recalled

The glow of the 150th Birthday celebration was dampened, if not extinguished, in 1992 by the centennial observances of the infamous Homestead Steel strike. There was a renewed outpouring of bitterness and blame on both Carnegie and Frick. On New Years Day 1992, an inch high headline in black ink in the *Pittsburgh Post-Gazette* trumpeted, "CARNAGE OF BATTLE

RELIVED Homestead Steel Strike of 1892"
. . . As reported by Jim McKay on the 100th anniversary of those events of July 5 and 6, 1892,
the story continued, "The bloody battle that
pitted workers and townspeople of Homestead
vs. Pinkerton detectives hired by the Carnegie
Steel Company, had become legend in labor
history. That confrontation, the occupation by
state militia, and the attempted assassination
of industrialist Henry Clay Frick, who managed
Carnegie's Homestead plant, were the most
sensational events in a year that ushered in a
dark era of industrial labor relations."

Frick survived two bullets and stabbings
by anarchist Alexander Berkman and lived to
break the union. Carnegie, summering in Scotland to avoid the hot weather as his custom, was
branded a coward, hypocrite, and traitor to his
workmen. A century later, the bitterness was
intensified by the fall of the mighty steel industry, bringing unemployment, decay, and despair
to formerly proud and prosperous Pittsburgh
neighborhoods. In retrospect, the absent Carnegie was judged in the light of 20th century
workers' rights and by the ethical standards of
the 1990s and was found wanting. Never mind
that in those early days there was no instant
communication, no airborne travel, no air
conditioning, and, alas, no framework for labor
negotiations on a democratic basis.

One hundred years after the doomed
strike there was graphic media coverage and a
three-day symposium for historians from around
the country held in Andrew Carnegie's Homestead Library. The Bost Building, an old hotel
which had been the strike headquarters, was
purchased as a future labor museum. A documentary film *The River Ran Red*, produced
by a former electrician's apprentice at USX's
Clairton Works, was released and widely viewed.
(USX formerly the United States Steel Corporation). *The Homestead Strike of 1892*, a book by
reporter Arthur Burgoyne, and other critical
reviews of the infamous strike, were widely read.

Andrew Carnegie, 1835-1918. Giver of Libraries,
Founder of Carnegie Institute, Pittsburgh.

Photograph from Carnegie Library, Pittsburgh, Pennsylvania

Exclusive Fishing and Hunting Club
The Johnstown Flood

A year earlier, *The Pittsburgh Press*, March 3,
1991, featured a story about an exclusive, "un-
mercifully short-lived oasis created in the late
1800s by some of Pittsburgh's biggest tycoons."
The membership of the South Fork Fishing and
Hunting Club, according to the article, included
Andrew Carnegie, Andrew Mellon, Henry Clay
Frick, Secretary of State Philander Knox, transportation magnate Charles Clarke, and others
of the richest families in Pittsburgh. For a cool
summer retreat they had bought hundreds of
acres of land in the hills 14 miles above Johnstown and built elaborate cottages around Lake
Connemaugh. The lakes' waters were held back
by an old earth dam to which repairs were not
made, despite warnings to the club's president
that the dam was unsafe. On May 31, 1889,
under torrential rains, the earthworks burst
sending 450 acres of water, 200,000 tons a

minute, in a tidal wave in some places 70 feet high, roaring down on Johnstown. In a space of ten minutes 2,209 persons perished in that Pennsylvania disaster. Secrecy shrouded the causal link between the club, its members, and the flood until the roster was included in a centennial story in *The Pittsburgh Press*, February 19, 1989. It indirectly triggered the 1991 story which featured idyllic photographs taken by Louis Clarke as a youth which were discovered in an attic by his daughter, the great-granddaughter of Charles Clarke. She had never heard of Lake Connemaugh, or of the role it played in the flood, until cousins in Pittsburgh sent her the 1989 clipping about the South Fork Fishing and Hunting Club Historical Preservation Society. And so, more than 100 years after the fact, more opprobrium is heaped on the so-called, "robber barons." Recording these tragic events were the Academy Award winning documentary films *The Johnstown Flood* by Charles Guggenheim and the expanded version *The American Experience* which aired on PBS, Public Broadcasting System. The host was Pittsburgh-born historian David McCullough, author of the book, *The Johnstown Flood*.

Carnegie's Foresight

On a more positive note of hindsight, around the turn of the century Carnegie had purchased 5,000 acres of land on Lake Erie bordering Pennsylvania and Ohio. When he sold his steel interests to J. P. Morgan and associates for $480 million in 1901, the land was included. In the 1960s the merged U. S. Steel Company had plans to build a massive modern steel mill on the Erie property, but the economic downturn by 1985 resulted in the entire parcel being for sale at a multimillion dollar price. The Western Pennsylvania Conservancy in 1991 negotiated a complex transaction under which the Richard K. Mellon Foundation purchased 3,131 acres of the Pennsylvania portion of the land from USX for $6.5 million. It was then deeded,

as the David M. Roderick Wildlife Reserve, to the Conservancy which sold to the Pennsylvania Game Commission for $3 million . . . a maneuver of which Carnegie could have been proud, especially since the Corporation retained the 1,869 acre Ohio portion, the balance of the 5,000 acres, for future economic development.

In the 1989 preface to his definitive biography, *Andrew Carnegie*, reprinted by The University of Pittsburgh Press, Joseph Frazier Wall wrote . . . "the paradoxical Scot was full of ironies. He was a pacifist, yet made steel plate for the American Navy; was a professed friend of labor, yet outraged workers by his absence during the Homestead strike; and declared himself the enemy of privilege, yet lived like Scottish royalty." Andrew Carnegie had intended to complete his autobiography in the summer of 1914 but the war intervened. Earlier he had been inspired . . . "a book of this kind, written years ago by my good friend Judge Mellon of Pittsburgh, gave me so much pleasure . . ."

My Own Story by Andrew Carnegie
Andrew Carnegie by Joseph F. Wall,
reprinted by The University of Pittsburgh Press, 1989

Carnegie Magazine: March-April 1989
The Return of the Carnegie Story
January-February 1992 — Dunfermline
Editorials by R. Jay Gangewere

Pittsburgh in Carnegie's Day

When Andrew Carnegie arrived in Pittsburgh in 1848 the town was just emerging from the devastating fire of 1845, which had destroyed the entire business portion of the city. (The Museum of Art owns two eyewitness views of the disaster painted by the English-born artist, William Coventry Wall, older brother of artist Alfred S. Wall, an original trustee of Carnegie Institute.)

1850, Population: 40,000

As Andrew Carnegie later recalled, by 1850 the population in and around Pittsburgh was not more than 40,000. The business section did not extend as far as Fifth Avenue, "a very quiet street, remarkable only for having the theater on it." Telegrams to the manager of the theater were delivered free, and the delivery boys were allowed to view the plays from the balcony without charge. This is how 14-year-old Andrew Carnegie acquired his taste for the theater. Young Andrew also delivered many a telegram to General Robinson, who was the first white child born west of the Ohio River . . . (The last Indian uprising had been subdued in 1794.)

Carnegie saw the first telegraph line extend from the East into the city, and later, the first locomotive, which was brought by canal from Philadelphia. Travelers to that city faced a three-day journey by canal and rail. In Pittsburgh, the event of the day was the arrival and departure of the steam packet to and from Cincinnati, for daily communication had been established.

Smoky, in 1860

As Pittsburgh became industrialized, the smoke and soot increased to the point that Carnegie, describing the atmosphere of 1860, said that any accurate description would be set down as the grossest exaggeration. "The smoke permeated and penetrated everything . . . if you washed face and hands, they were as dirty as ever in an hour. The soot gathered in the hair and irritated the skin." Andrew, fair of hair and skin, reacted by moving with his widowed mother and brother to Homewood, where, "there were country lanes and gardens in abundance." Even in 1901 soot and smoke were hazards. Dr. W. J. Holland, director of the Carnegie Museum, in his first annual report stated: "The preservation of such collections in good condition necessarily involves considerable labor in a city in which the importance of the consumption of smoke is not as thoroughly appreciated as we trust it will ultimately be."

Schenley Park

Despite the smoke-filled atmosphere, the area between the Carnegie Institute and Centre Avenue remained largely farmland, with cows grazing where the Cathedral of Learning now stands. In 1893, three years after the opening of the Library, the Schenley Hotel, nearby on Forbes Avenue, was built by Franklyn F. Nicola, the real estate entrepreneur and visionary. He had visited many great European cities and dreamed of a civic center of which Pittsburgh could be proud. Backing Nicola in this enterprise was a group of leading citizens including Andrew Carnegie, who acted also as trustee for Mary Croghan Schenley, absentee owner of most of the real estate in the area.

Schenley Park had been established on 300 acres given to the city by Mrs. Schenley, heiress, through her mother, to the large O'Hara estate in Pittsburgh. At age 15, she had eloped from boarding school in New York with the headmistress's brother, dashing, 43-year-old, twice-widowed Captain William Schenley. Their married life was spent in London, England, where she died in 1903, having survived her husband by 20 years. Although most of her life was spent in England, in her will she identified herself as being, "of Pittsburgh." The Schenley estate was approached by Mr. Nicola who headed a group which for $250,000 purchased an additional 120 acres. He then convinced the commissioners of Allegheny County to erect the Soldiers and Sailors Memorial Hall.

Mrs. Schenley's portrait was painted by a trustee of The Museum of Art, Martin Leisser, and hangs in the nearby School for the Blind. Among Mrs. Schenley's many generous gestures was her gift of the historic Block House at the Pittsburgh Point, to the Daughters of the American Revolution, which no doubt saved it for Point State Park.

Carnegie Institute of Technology

It was at a dinner in the Schenley Hotel in November of 1900 that Andrew Carnegie informed the trustees of Carnegie Institute of his offer, by letter to Mayor William Diehl of Pittsburgh, to build and endow a technical school. (The mayor's granddaughter, Joan, became the mother of the late U. S. Senator H. John Heinz, III.) The trustees agreed to add it to their responsibilities for The Carnegie Museum, Music Hall, Library, and Department of Fine Arts. The city in 1903 purchased 32 acres adjacent to Schenley Park, constituting the campus of Carnegie Institute of Technology, now Carnegie Mellon University. Andrew Carnegie's letter to the Mayor had concluded with the phrase, "My heart is in the work," which was included in the emblem of Carnegie Tech until the merger with Mellon Institute in 1967. Mellon Institute was founded in 1913 by Andrew W. and Richard B. in memory of their father Judge Thomas Mellon who, as a banker, established the family fortune.

Carnegie Institute is Dedicated

The *Gazette Times*, predecessor of the *Pittsburgh Post-Gazette*, Wednesday, April 10, 1907 ran as the lead story, the arrival of Andrew Carnegie for the dedication of his gift, Carnegie Institute, to the city. Top center of the front page of the newspaper was a cartoon showing the area bounded by the three rivers as framing a profile sketch of The Laird of Skibo . . . Carnegie's Pittsburgh.

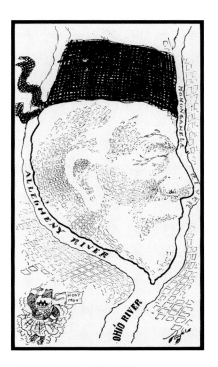

The town begins to look like this.

After one of the worst snow storms of the winter, the Carnegies had slipped out of New York unbeknown to their 35 honored out-of-town guests who, with 160 pieces of luggage, would follow them to Pittsburgh for the ceremonies. Mr. Carnegie wanted a private preview, since he had steadfastly refused to see even a photograph or sketch after approving the final plans for the enlarged building; in fact, he had not visited Pittsburgh for six years. Even through the final

24 hours, the edifice was being readied for the opening. The space where the temporary building had stood was being transformed into lawn. One of the great bronze groups which now adorns the front of the building, delayed in some manner, was rushed in by express, with no thought to expense. A complete test of the electric lighting of the Institute was made and found satisfactory.

The Music Hall was the scene of the formalities, with the distinguished participants arriving by dignified procession from the Schenley Hotel. Dr. Hammerschlag, director of the Carnegie Technical Schools, led the escort, composed of the faculty of the schools marching through rows of Carnegie students lining the way. Then came Dr. W. J. Holland, director of Carnegie Museum of Natural History, with John W. Beatty, M. A., director of the Department of Fine Arts, followed by A. H. Hopkins, librarian of the Pittsburgh Carnegie Library, with Emil Paul, director of the Pittsburgh Orchestra, and Charles Heinroth, the new city organist of Pittsburgh. Ten paces after them marched Andrew Carnegie and William N. Frew, president of Carnegie Institute. Then came the foreign guests of note, distinguished Americans, the trustees, the Episcopal and the Roman Catholic bishops, Mayor Guthrie and members of the Carnegie Hero Fund Commission. Closing the procession was the student body of the Carnegie Technical Schools, uniformed in the colors of the schools and carrying the Carnegie plaid. On arrival at the Music Hall, the dignitaries proceeded to their seats on the platform, and the students were permitted free access to the Institute with a good hour to make an inspection before the doors were opened to the public. "The trustees had been compelled to make stringent rules with regard to holders of tickets . . . some 300 tickets have been issued to persons entitled to standing room . . ." These dedication ceremonies were the highlights of three days of festivities in honor of the occasion.

Presidents of Carnegie Institute 1896-1995

Serving with dedication and distinction have been:

William Nimick Frew
January 2, 1896 to April 28, 1914

Samuel Harden Church
April 28, 1914 to October 11, 1943

William Frew
October 26, 1943 to January 31, 1948

James Moorhead Bovard
February 20, 1948 to December 31, 1967

James Mellon Walton
January 1, 1968 to August 15, 1984

Robert Charles Wilburn
August 15, 1984 to August 14, 1992

Ellsworth H. Brown
March 15, 1993 to Present

Carnegie Institute Board of Trustees of the Carnegie Fine Arts and Museum Collection Fund 1896-1898

W. N. Frew, *President*
Robert Pitcairn, *Vice President*
H. C. Frick, *Treasurer*
S. H. Church, *Secretary*

Albert J. Barr
Edward M. Bigelow
John A. Brashear
John Caldwell
Thomas M. Carnegie
Samuel H. Church
George H. Clapp
Josiah Cohen
Robert H. Douglas
Edward M. Ferguson
Hon. Henry P. Ford
William N. Frew
Henry C. Frick
Reverend William J.
   Holland *
George L. Holliday
John G. Holmes
James T. Hudson
John McM. King
Reverend A. A. Lambing
George A. MacBeth

Hon. Christopher L.
   Magee
William A. Magee
Andrew W. Mellon
Charles C. Mellor
David McCargo
Thomas J. McClure
William McConway
Dr. William H. McKelvey
Henry Phipps, Jr.
Robert Pitcairn
H. Kirke Porter
Dr. John P. Sterrett
A. Bryan Wall
Samuel D. Warmcastle
David T. Watson
Joseph R. Woodwell

*
*Resigned March 1898 to assume
the directorship of the museum.*

Founders Day, Carnegie Institute, Pittsburgh, Pennsylvania, May 2, 1910.

Seated, left to right: William N. Frew, President William Howard Taft, and Hon. Philander C. Knox; Standing, left to right: Capt. A. W. Butt, Count Johann Heinrich Von Bernstorff, Rev. John R. Ewers, Samuel Harden Church, and Count Conrad De Buisseret.

Photograph from Carnegie Library of Pittsburgh, Pennsylvania

The Carnegie Boards of Trustees

After 87 years of operation under the original by-laws, on May 3, 1983, the Board of Trustees of Carnegie Institute adopted totally new by-laws and articles of incorporation. A new class of, "Term Trustees" includes 18 persons serving for three years and eligible for a second three-year term. The 18 members of the Board of Carnegie Library of Pittsburgh have always served ex officio on the board of the Institute, along with the 18 "Life Trustees" who are successors to the original museum trustees nominated by Andrew Carnegie at the founding of the Institute. A decade earlier the board had faced the facts of economic life and reluctantly instituted a suggested museum contribution of $1.00 for non member adults . . . in 1994 the "suggestion" was $5.00.

Chronology of the Building of Carnegie Institute — The Carnegie

1881 • Andrew Carnegie offered Pittsburgh $250,000 for a library, free to public.

1887 • Pennsylvania enacted necessary legislation.

1890 • Carnegie increased offer to $1 million; building to include library, music hall, art gallery, museum, and accommodation for learned societies.

1892 • Cornerstone of original building laid.

1895 • Dedication of building to the public; $1 million endowment added by Andrew Carnegie.
   • *Architects:* Chosen by competition entries. Longfellow, Alden, and Harlow, architects associated with Henry Hobson Richardson in Boston. Pittsburgh office had been established when Alden came with Richardson for the building of the Allegheny County Courthouse and Jail, a masterpiece in 1888 and still toward the year 2000.
   • *Style:* Renaissance with twin Venetian towers.

1896 • Creation of Carnegie Institute to develop Andrew Carnegie's art and natural science interests.
   • First *Carnegie International Exhibition.*
   • Excavation of Indian Mounds at McKees Rocks by Carnegie archeologists.
   • Pittsburgh Symphony Orchestra begins performing at Music Hall.

1902 • Carnegie Library building to be enlarged. (The Carnegie Library of Pittsburgh is now a separate institution, with its main branch still in the same building.)

1907 • Dedication of Carnegie Museum and Art Gallery, with new Foyer to The Music Hall. Three days of ceremonies, with heads of state from around the world, guests of Mr. Carnegie.
   • *Architects:* Alden and Harlow engaged to redesign building. Beaux Arts tradition. Twin Venetian towers removed. Expansion along Forbes Avenue.
   • *Material:* 6,000 tons of marble, interior: 165,000 square feet of cut stone, exterior: Grey sandstone backed by brick over steel.
   • *Roof:* Red tile, (replaced by cooper in 1907. In 1957 copper roof removed, replaced with green Alodine aluminum, now grey.)
   • *Sculpture:* The architectural sculpture adorning the exterior of the Institute was executed by John Massey Rhind (1858-1936), who like Andrew Carnegie, was a Scot. Mr. Carnegie chose and supervised all.
   • *Cost:* Estimated at $25 million but total is unknown as Andrew Carnegie supplied much of the structural steel from his own mills without charging the trustees. It was delivered at the job before the builders required it.
   • *Dimensions:* 460' frontage on Forbes Avenue, 640' frontage on Schenley Park Plaza side. 138' from basement to top of dome. Originally five acres on the ground, now with the Scaife Galleries approximately 17 acres floor space.

1957 • Free Bookmobile service inaugurated by Carnegie Library.

1974 • Addition of the Scaife Galleries, Museum of Art.
   • *Architect:* Edward Larrabee Barnes, of New York; builder also of the Walker Art Center, Minneapolis.
   • *Design:* Conceived as a separate entity as well as an organic extension of the original structure.
   • *Style:* "Contemporary Urban Monumental."

- *Material:* Emerald Pearl Norwegian granite and glass, interior walls of glass, 40' high.
- *Added:* Twelve galleries for display of permanent collections, galleries for changing exhibitions. Offices and library and other facilities for The Museum of Art, a café, art shop, children's room, and theater.
- *Added:* 155,000 square feet of interior space, with an additional 16,000 square feet in the open Sculpture Court, connected to the old building by two bridge galleries.
- *Cost:* $12 million, on time, and within budget. Endowed by the Scaife Family. Volunteer staff organized.

1975
- Renovation of Museum of Art Galleries in old building. Creation of the Heinz Galleries for special exhibitions. Gift of Mr. and Mrs. H. J. Heinz, II, endowed by the Howard Heinz Endowment.

1976
- Reconstruction of a section of the old building. Creation of the Ailsa Mellon Bruce Galleries for Decorative Arts. Endowed by the Andrew W. Mellon Foundation, Inc., New York, New York.

1979
- Installation of Data Processing Center, Carnegie Museum of Natural History by grant from the Richard King Mellon Foundation.
- Acquisition of the Annex, at 5800 Baum Boulevard, Pittsburgh, adding 33,000 square feet additional space for The Carnegie Museum of Natural History.

1980
- Renovation of the Annex, adding classrooms, lab, etc. The city of Pittsburgh provided $485,000 to make Carnegie Institute more accessible to the handicapped.
- Hillman Hall of Minerals & Gems, Carnegie Museum of Natural History. Endowed by the Hillman Foundation and Henry L. Hillman.
- Geology Hall, with gifts from Mr. and Mrs. G. Albert Shoemaker and Consolidation Coal Company.

1981
- Section of Conservation, Museum of Art, established.
- Estate Planning Program inaugurated.
- Renovation of original building continues. Grants from city of Pittsburgh, $500,000 and from The Kresge Foundation, $250,000.

1982
1983
- The *Carnegie International Exhibition* returns to its original format.

1986
- School of The Carnegie formed.

1988
- Announcement of the Second Century Fund campaign, with goal of $125 million by 1995.
- Opening of Benedum Hall of Geology.
- Opening of Martin Luther King, Jr. Center of Carnegie Library.

1990
- Installation of modern climate control at The Carnegie.
- Restoration and cleaning of building facade, improved lighting.

1991
- Opening of Walton Hall of Ancient Egypt.
- Opening of The Carnegie Science Center with Rangos Omnimax Theater.
- Construction of parking garage with 485 spaces, designed by Wiliam Trebilcock Whitehead. Cost $6 million.

1992
- Opening of Natural History Exhibition Gallery.

1993
- Opening of Hall of African Wildlife.
- Ellsworth H. Brown appointed seventh president.
- Opening of Heinz Architectural Center in The Museum of Art.

1994
- Opening of The Andy Warhol Museum.

1995
- Centennial Celebration.
- Opening of the Alcoa Hall of Native Americans.

1996
- 100th anniversary of *Carnegie International.*
- 100th anniversary of Carnegie Institute.

Background dates and events to consider:

World War I, 1914-1918
The stock market crash, 1929
The great Depression, 1939
World War II, 1939-1944

The Noble Quartet and Company

Shakespeare

Michelangelo

Bach

Galileo

Personifying the highest human achievements the four heroic bronze figures, "anchoring" The Carnegie's building on Forbes Avenue are: Shakespeare for Literature, Bach for Music, Michelangelo for Art, and Galileo for Science. With every meaningful detail skillfully depicted, they are masterworks of John Massey Rhind, Carnegie's fellow Scot. They were sculpted in clay by the artist in his New York studio and shipped to Europe to be cast in bronze, then returned to Pittsburgh in time for the dedication of the building.

All are seated on ancient Greek-style chairs, indicating their classical status, and each is accompanied by the special tools of his craft. Appropriately Shakespearean are the pen in hand, open book, and masks of tragedy and comedy. Bach is at the keyboard with a musical manuscript nearby. Michelangelo, with mallet and chisel, has a replica of his famous work *The Dying Gaul*. For Galileo, Atlas holds a globe circled by astrological figures upon which the scientist's compass rests.

The great earthbound figures are male, representing corporeal life while, in the conventional 19th Century Victorian symbolism, the female figures above, represent the higher form of the life of the spirit. These four groups of three allegorical figures each, indicate the ideals, as distinguished from achievements, in the arts and sciences. Each also has symbolic items such as a small lamp of learning, a quill pen and paper of papyrus or parchment, for literature. Cymbals, pipe, and lyre connote music and, for art, a flower, a compass on paper and a palette daubed with paint. For science an armillary sphere with circles of the celestial sphere, a chemist's flask, and a bone symbolize The Carnegie's fame in finding and analyzing fossil bones.

When the monumental sculptures adorning the facade and roof line of The Carnegie were lowered to earth in 1991 for repair and reinforcement, the viewer could recognize the skill of the artist in adjusting his design to allow for the distortion of perspective due to the intended viewer being almost 100 feet below.

What the Muses Hold by R. Jay Gangewere in *Carnegie Magazine*, January/February 1992.

Photographs from Carnegie Library of Pittsburgh, Pennsylvania

Cornice of The Carnegie

The special issue of *Carnegie Magazine*, January/February, 1982 was a veritable mini-encyclopedia concerning the pantheon of names carved on the cornice (fascia) of Andrew Carnegie's Institute, completed in 1907. While announcing that the magazine would henceforth have a new enlarged look, and be issued as a bimonthly for the first time since its beginning in 1927, editor R. Jay Gangewere took a new, in-depth, look at the names of those immortalized on the cornice of the massive building. As a person-in-the-street guide, a glossary gave a brief biography of all 110 male individuals and it is included here on page 249. For the erudite analyses reference should be made to the articles by the scholarly experts: *Antiquities*, by Professor Jerry Clack of the Classics Department of Duquesne University; *Science*, by John E. Guilday, of the Section of Vertebrate Paleontology, Carnegie Museum of Natural History; *Music*, by Roland Leich, Professor Emeritus of Music at Carnegie Mellon University; *Art*, by David G. Wilkins, Associate Professor of Fine Arts at the University of Pittsburgh; and *Literature*, by Donald G. Adam, Associate Professor of English at Chatham College and the Glossary (page 249), compiled by Robin Mager.

The specialized articles follow the overview by editor Gangewere who recognized that the names of the masters of art, natural history, science, literature, and music carved on the exterior of Carnegie Institute and Carnegie Library of Pittsburgh have intrigued passers-by since the turn of the century. Debates continue over the relative importance of those included, versus those candidates omitted. The first requirement was that they be male and, the second, preferably, dead. (Donald Adams in his article observed that, in 1892, "Tennyson had the good fortune to die.")

The decision as to those chosen was the responsibility of a committee, so independent that it ignored the sentiments of Andrew Carnegie which he wrote in a letter, October 24, 1894, to President William N. Frew, "Some of the names have no business to be on the list. Imagine Dickens in and Burns out." Carnegie did not win that one but proceeded with his wish to honor Burns by erecting, and personally unveiling, a statue of the poet in 1914, at a prominent place in Schenley Park. Three years later a flagpole designed by Sylvian Salieres, the French medalist, was placed at the northwest corner of the Institute. Departing from the original concept of considering only traditional European names and symbolism, four bronze tablets at the base of the flagpole depicted aboriginal figures (including a Native American) representing "Primitive Language," "Primitive Construction," "Primitive Drawing," and "Primitive Music."

Andrew Carnegie's more general views were expressed in a letter February 2, 1896 to President Frew, ". . . unless the institution be kept in touch with the masses, and therefore popular, it cannot be widely useful." The names of the scientists, including inventors and explorers, reflect an applied, practical interest. The young men at Carnegie Tech were expected to travel across the new Schenley Park Bridge to the library where the scientific literature was kept. The original museum was facing Panther Hollow and that is where the names of the scientists are seen. Authors were grouped on either side of the library's entrance. To the left of the library were the names of artists, near the location of the art galleries within the building. The names of composers were incised on the north facade, circling The Music Hall on Forbes Avenue. Early drawings of 1893-94 indicate three different treatments of the exterior of the building, including even some names which were never carved.

With the addition to the Institute by Alden and Harlow in 1907, the original north and east side walls of the building were covered, necessitating recarving the names on the new facade or adding new names to the list. (Part of the original cornice for The Music Hall still exists but is buried behind structural steel and stonework for the addition.) By 1907, explorers Magellan and Columbus qualified, as did architect Wren and Photographer Daquerre (1787-1851), indicating that the selection of names is a story of cultural relationships as well as of architectural changes to the building.

A look at the "men of science" reveals that the preponderance of them were inventors or discoverers such as Gutenberg or Newton. In addition there are nine zoologists, five astronomers, four botanists, four explorers, two geologists, and one chemist. From another angle, all men of the West: 12 Britons, 10 Americans, four French, four Germans, three Italians, one Pole, one Portugese, one Swede, and one Swiss. All were men of ability, drive, and above all, great curiosity.

Of the 110 names selected, there are 11 "ancients," 39 men of science, 30 composers, 16 literary figures, and 14 artists. This was an increase of 10 artists over the original four, namely Leonardo, Raphael, Michelangelo, and Titian, all of the Italian Renaissance. The addition of Donatello, Bramante, Veronese continued that tradition, bringing the Italian representation to half of the total number of artists. Four ancient Greeks: Ictinus, Phidias, Praxiteles, Scopas, and English architect Wren, who continued the classical mode, were added, plus two painters from the 17th century, Rembrandt and Velasquez. The dominance of the Italian Renaissance is based on the Victorian idea of Carnegie's day, that this period epitomized the dignity of man and the glorification of individual accomplishment.

Each of the modern experts in the four categories: Science, Music, Literature, and Art enumerated candidates they felt worthy of inclusion although not chosen. Some were alive at the time of the selection process and presumably ineligible. Others were simply passed over. Here is an abbreviated list of the missing worthies: Aeschylus, Hippocrates, Plato and Socrates; Balboa, Bering, and Marco Polo; Bellini, Monteverdi, and Vivaldi; Dürer, Giotto, Goya, Palladio, and Manet; Balzac, Cervantes, Dante, Dostoevsky, and Wordsworth. This is just a sample of possible candidates for the cornice, but as Professor Adam put it, "criticizing a committee is like cheating at solitaire, too easy to satisfy." It is interesting to note, however, that, even among the four 20th century scholarly articles the only female names mentioned as possibilities were Sappho, Curie, and O'Keeffe.

Carnegie's cornice has room for some additional names, but not enough to hold all those who should be included . . . what a challenge for a new committee!

The Carnegie Library of Pittsburgh
A Separate Legal Entity

One of two Storymobiles which belong to *Beginning with Books* located in the Homewood branch of the Carnegie Library. Photo courtesy of Joan B. Friedberg, co-director, *Beginning with Books.*

Photograph by Barbara Hart-Sturges

also for The Andy Warhol Museum and The Carnegie Science Center. Specific administrative and physical services are shared and the members of the board of the library are ex-officio members of the board of the Carnegie Institute. In addition to the Oakland facility, there are 18 branch libraries, eight of which are located in buildings donated by Andrew Carnegie prior to 1919.

There is also the Library for the Blind and Physically Handicapped, several reading centers in the public housing communities, and a district film library, part of the Allegheny Regional Library, a branch library on the North Side. Four bookmobiles, funded by the county, serve the county areas which have no public libraries. Two Storymobiles belong to *Beginning with Books*, a separate organization located in the Homewood branch, with affiliation to the library. Funded by Bell of Pennsylvania, Buhl

Pittsburgh's Carnegie Library is unlike any other major public library in the United States. The others are departments of government. Andrew Carnegie believed so strongly in the value of "book learning" to improve the life of the working man that he felt libraries should be supported by the communities they serve. As early as 1890 Andrew Carnegie had offered to build a library for Pittsburgh, but it was delayed pending action by the Pennsylvania legislature repealing the law, which until 1887 prohibited the collection of taxes to support a library. When he built the library in 1895 to be "free to the people" he required the city to provide $40,000 annually for its operation. By 1993 the budget of the entire Carnegie Library of Pittsburgh was $15 million or 375 times the $40,000 of 1895. Although sharing the same building with The Carnegie's Museums of Art and Natural History, the library is legally and financially separate from the Carnegie Institute, which is the umbrella

Before and After — The library and facade of The Carnegie, cleaned and restored.

Photograph from Carnegie Library of Pittsburgh, Pennsylvania

Foundation, the Howard Heinz Endowment, and the Richard K. Mellon Foundation, the Storymobiles go into the neighborhood like modern Pied Pipers to spellbind the children.

Library Not Endowed

Although Carnegie gave more than $56 million for the construction of over 2,500 public libraries to cities and towns across the country he did NOT endow them. This was true even for the library in old Allegheny, Andrew's first home in America. Exceptions were the Braddock Library, which he established for the families of the workmen in his own steel mill and endowed with $1 million, and the Carnegie and Homestead Library and recreation centers for his workers. From the beginning there was recognition of the importance of bringing reading and books to children. Reading clubs were organized in schools, churches, stores, even in homes and alleys if 12 children were gathered to hear a volunteer read or tell them stories. This was also a way the children of immigrant families could learn to speak the new language well.

Carnegie's Monument to Colonel James Anderson

Although the city of Allegheny was merged into Pittsburgh in 1907, the library there remained independent until 1956. In the intervening years it deteriorated through neglect and lack of funds. The librarian for many years complained bitterly about the deplorable conditions, even in the sanitary facilities which were used by undesirables. When finally the place was closed for a complete overhaul, the monument Andrew Carnegie had erected in honor of his patron, Colonel James Anderson, was destroyed. Only the bronze statue of the seated workman, reading, and the bust of Colonel Anderson were saved. Under the caring eyes of architect Sylvestor Damianos, the library on the North Side was rehabilitated and the music hall section became the home of the Pittsburgh Public Theater. And through the indomitable effort of Ann Wardrop, life trustee and member of the Women's Committee of The Museum of Art, $120,000 was raised to rebuild the Anderson-Carnegie exedron. It is appropriately placed near its original location.

Shrinking Tax Base

The Carnegie Library of Pittsburgh also suffered a decrease in funding in the late 1980s because of the decline of the steel industry and the demise of such civic-minded corporations as Gulf Oil Corporation, the Koppers Company and others which formerly augmented the city's tax revenues. By the time of retirement for Anthony Martin, director for 16 years, the central library clearly needed a physical updating and a new direction as its use had gradually declined. Robert Wilburn, president of The Carnegie (1984-1992) as a former Pennsylvania Secretary of Education, understood the importance of bringing the functions of the library up-to-date. He brought Robert Croneberger, a native Pennsylvanian, here to bring the library's mission in line and on line with today's technological realities and social needs.

New Director . . . New directions

Director Croneberger, the ninth in almost a century of service, in May, 1986 joined a tradition of distinguished librarians at The Carnegie. Especially notable was Ralph Munn, director from 1928-1964, designer of the library system for Australia and New Zealand. The present director has overseen the installation of the Internet system of databases and networking computers. Community information such as schedules of events, news of educational programs, and activities will be freely available to library users via the Freenet computer programs. Modern computer technology has replaced the old card file system, offering instant access to the files via title, author, topic etc., *Caroline* is the apt name of the main new reference system.

Meanwhile the library's interior of that era was also refurbished and renewed, brightened and lightened but maintaining the early aura. Century-old murals, some hidden for years under white paint, were rediscovered due to the painstaking efforts of conservator Christine Dalton. During the closing for rearrangement of some of the departments, a selection of 3,000 volumes was housed in a Bookmobile parked in the Schenley Plaza for the convenience of the public.

There was a flurry of public protest when it was suggested that for reasons of economy the Business Branch would be moved from downtown to the North Side. (It had been moved from the Frick Building across Grant Street to One Mellon Bank Center.) The outcry had a beneficial result as it attracted additional funding, and the decision to move was reconsidered. A public/private partnership developed between The Carnegie Library and Point Park College and its library, resulting in the establishment of The Library Center in the old Warner Theater on Fifth Avenue, formerly the Bank Center.

Director Croneberger forged a revived relationship with the University of Pittsburgh's Library School (which had its origin at Carnegie Institute of Technology) and also in 1987 entered into partnership between an academic and a public library by agreement with the Community College of Allegheny County. When the Public Library Association held its National Convention in Pittsburgh in 1988, Robert Croneberger headed the committee for arrangements, and in 1991 he was a delegate to the White House Conference on Libraries and Information Services.

The Library Serves the Community

In the main library the hours of service are 69 hours during the winter months, including Sunday openings, and 65 hours the rest of the year, better than the 60 hours per week required by the legislature. The branch library hours vary from a high of 56 to a low of 35 hours. Even so, a number of new programs were instituted to better serve the needs of the public. With many people losing their jobs because of the downsizing of local businesses and industries, job-seeking skills became a high priority and the library provides the guidance and help required. In 1986 Mediation Centers were established in several neighborhood branches to give people a forum for settling differences without expensive and prolonged litigation — funded by a United Way Agency.

Ten years earlier February was designated Black History Month and each year special activities are planned around this theme. In 1988 Pittsburgh's August Wilson, the nationally acclaimed playwright, was the featured speaker at the *Man and Ideas* lecture. Wilson, a school dropout, has been called "a graduate of Carnegie Library." The Martin Luther King, Jr. Reading Center, established in the Hill District in 1988, is dedicated to Dr. King's memory and the Civil Rights Movement in the United States. The year 1988 also marked the sesquicentennial of the establishment of The Carnegie Library with a celebration exhibition of photos, posters, and drawings in recognition of Andrew Carnegie's library building accomplishments.

In 1991 a longtime Carnegie trustee was honored when the library's Rare Book Room was renamed the William R. Oliver Special Collections Room . . . in recognition of his being a "leading force" since 1951 until his death at age 94 in March of 1994. Traditional annual observances are the Fall Festival of Children's Books and National Library Week, each accompanied by a burst of inspiring, educational, and entertaining events.

Because contributions to cultural organizations also seriously declined, the library established the Foundation Center in 1993, to assist non-profit groups by providing a centralized source of information about how and where to seek grants to fund their activities.

The Library's Needs

The library itself was in need of help and in 1989 The Friends of the Library was formed to assist with fundraising, membership and to be the library's advocates before legislative groups. This is crucial as The Carnegie Library faced a 1994 budget deficit of some $1.7 million and The Friends turned out in full force at City Council hearings. Lester Becker, past president of the Pittsburgh Bibliophiles presides over The Friends of the Library. (50 years ago, "Friends of the Music Library" flourished and 30 years ago there were informal Friends of some of the branches.)

Of the financing, the city of Pittsburgh has supplied 40%, Allegheny County 40%, and the Commonwealth of Pennsylvania 20%. The city's contribution since 1990 remained at $5.5 million, exceeded for the first time in 1993 by the county's contribution. For 1994 the figures are: from the city, $5,786,408; from the county, $5,922,398; and from the state $2,559,656. Passage of the legislation establishing the Regional Assets District, effective December 22, 1993, gave The Carnegie Library a share in the proceeds of a 1% increase in the sales tax, with the result that the library will receive a total in public funds approximately 12 times that received by The Carnegie itself. Within the city of Pittsburgh, the population in 1990 was 369,879 and within Allegheny County, excluding the city of Pittsburgh, the population served is more than one million. The many public services provided by Carnegie Library of Pittsburgh make it a central resource for Western Pennsylvania. It is in the forefront of bringing the latest advance information technology to its patrons for the benefit of the entire Pittsburgh region.

Meeting Special Needs

The Regional Library for the Blind and Physically Handicapped is at 4724 Baum Boulevard in the Leonard Staisey Building, so named in 1990 in honor of the retired legislator and judge who died just days before the official dedication. Despite his own handicap of blindness, he had helped make it possible for The Carnegie to buy the building it had rented for 20 years. This library is funded by the Commonwealth of Pennsylvania. Tapes and cassettes of requested titles are mailed to homebound persons without charge, truly a great service, sponsored by the Federal Government through the Library of Congress.

The book collection of the Carnegie Library includes more than 2,260,700 volumes, and the non-book collections contain slides, musical and spoken records, cassettes, 8-mm films, and more than 3,000 periodicals. Carnegie Library is known for the strength of its collections in such specialized fields as technology, art, music, business and finance, and Western Pennsylvania history. The library has traditionally reached a broader cross-section of the public than the Carnegie Institute by providing advice and assistance to people needing help in starting a business, finding a job, or resolving a crisis. Helping people to educate themselves is the library's most important mission in the community, which echoes Andrew Carnegie's original idea.

In the Pittsburgh Photographic Library the city has one of the unique photographic resources of any major city, and its sponsorship of the *International Poetry Forum* assists one of the major poetry centers in the country. Founder and president of the Forum, Pittsburgh's Samuel Hazo in 1993 was named the first official poet of Pennsylvania.

Among the sources for this material:
The Pittsburgh Post-Gazette:
1986, by Donald Miller
May 9, 1988, by Sally Kalson
December 5, 1993, by Bob Hoover
Three Rivers News: Winter 1990
The Pittsburgh Press:
March 8, 1992, by Thomas Buell, Jr.

The Carnegie Music Hall in Pittsburgh

The Building . . . Organ Recitals . . . and Gifts

Famous throughout the area, The Carnegie Music Hall, with its grand entrance through the gilt-encrusted marble foyer, is the one section of the massive Carnegie Institute which has remained substantially as it was built in 1895. Its elegant white, gold, and old rose decor has been freshened, and the pipe organ, one of the world's largest, has been renewed, but the old world ambiance still pervades. Seating approximately 2,000, The Carnegie Music Hall is one of the most perfect concert halls in the world in terms of acoustics. There are 8,600 pipes in the organ, the largest, 32 feet long, weight 1,000 lbs., while the smallest is only a fraction of an inch long. It would cost more than $100,000 to replace this organ today.

Of the more than 7,000 pipe organs given by Andrew Carnegie during his lifetime, the first was to the Swedenborgian Church in Allegheny. His father had been one of the congregation numbering fewer than 100. In addition to the original organ for The Music Hall, Carnegie also gave a fine instrument to St. Paul's Roman Catholic Cathedral nearby.

Andrew Carnegie's wish that The Music Hall provide an opportunity for the general public to become acquainted with good music led him to establish the post of Municipal Organist of the City of Pittsburgh.

The position of hall organist was one of the most coveted musical positions in the city. Among the organists who held the post were Frederick Archer, 1895-1901; Charles Heinroth, 1906-1932; Marshall Bidwell, 1932-1962. Paul Koch, whose father Dr. Casper Koch served as organist at North Side Carnegie Library for many years, has been organist at Carnegie Music Hall, since 1974, and at St. Paul's Cathedral on Fifth Avenue. Free organ recitals were given weekly from 1895, and after 1966, monthly from October to March. Over 4,600 recitals have been given, complete with concise, interesting annotations. The concerts have been broadcast over radio station WLOA.

"The two towers, rather tame but pleasant versions of the Campanile of San Marco at Venice, were the dominant vertical accents in the general composition. . . These ornamental campanili whose belfries sheltered neither bell nor watchman ceased to enliven the Oakland scene after 1904. . ." James D. Van Trump, *An American Palace of Culture*, 1970.

Photograph from Carnegie Library, Pittsburgh, Pennsylvania

The Pittsburgh Symphony, 1896 to 1910

When Carnegie talked about his dreams for The Music Hall, one of the Pittsburghers who listened was George Westinghouse, founder of Westinghouse Electric Corporation. He and other industrialists decided that Pittsburgh should do more than just flex its industrial muscle, and in 1896, only one year after the doors opened, Westinghouse and colleagues put an orchestra in the house that Carnegie built. The Pittsburgh Symphony flourished there from 1896 to 1910, including four years under famed composer-conductor Victor Herbert, 1901-1904, who wrote *Babes in Toyland* while in Pittsburgh.

Notable Appearances

Among the famous musicians who appeared with The Pittsburgh Symphony, there were composers Edward MacDowell, Richard Strauss, and Sir Edward Elgar. In 1896, MacDowell, then America's foremost composer, appeared as soloist in his *Piano Concerto No.1.* In 1904 guest conductor Strauss introduced his *Till Eulenspiegel* to Pittsburgh. And in 1907 Sir Edward led the orchestra in his own *Enigma Variations* at the dedication of The Music Hall's foyer.

Guest soloists with the orchestra included such legendary performers as cellist Pablo Casals and singer Mme. Schumann-Heink. The finest American musical groups also came to The Carnegie Music Hall stage. Walter Damrosch and the New York Philharmonic were there for three concerts during the week the hall opened in 1895. The Chicago Symphony came in 1896; the Metropolitan Opera in 1909. By 1910, however, interest in The Pittsburgh Symphony waned. For 16 years the city was without a symphony, until 1926 when concerts by the reestablished orchestra were performed in the larger hall of nearby Syria Mosque. (In 1971 the Orchestra moved downtown to Heinz Hall, the elaborately refurbished former Penn Theater, a movie house. Syria Mosque was demolished in 1991 and the site is now owned by the University of Pittsburgh which plans to erect a building on the plot.)

Distinguished Guests

In 1919 there was a reception in Carnegie Music Hall for the king and queen of Belgium. In 1927 President Calvin Coolidge spoke for a Founder's Day program. In 1950 Dwight Eisenhower, then president of Columbia University, was the speaker.

Among the long list of cultural royalty who through the years have played Carnegie Music Hall: Ferruccio Busoni, Percy Grainger, Mary Garden, Dame Myra Hess, Geraldine Farrar, Enrico Caruso, Eugene Ysaye, Fritz Kreisler, Jascha Heifetz, Nathan Milstein, Gregor Piatigorsky, Rosa Ponselle, John McCormack, Paul Robeson, Kirsten Flagstad and Princess Grace of Monaco, who appeared for the International Poetry Forum. In 1938, pianist Sergei Rachmaninoff was so furious to learn that some of the overflow crowd had been seated on stage, he refused to perform. Cooler heads prevailed however, and he went on. A few years back, tenor Luciano Pavarotti had no such qualms about playing Carnegie Music Hall with the overflow crowd seated on stage. When Ezio Pinza sang at the hall in 1940, the 1,000 persons in the audience sat horrified when a piece of plaster fell from the ceiling onto the stage. Pinza smiled and kept singing.

Two of the most widely traveled performers in the arts, dancer Jose Greco and guitarist Carlos Montoya, who for many years played the hall regularly, stated that the decor and acoustics in the hall had no equal among the halls they had visited in this country.

The Second Century Fund provided several million dollars for refurbishing the elegant interior furnishings of The Music Hall, improving the back stage amenities, modernizing the lighting, while preserving the acoustical purity of the hall.

Memorable Events

In 1993 alone there were 250 individual events in the Music Hall including awards ceremonies, high-school graduations, and corporate gatherings, so the charm of Carnegie Music Hall has obviously not diminished to this day. Available for rental by other groups, the hall has been home to meetings of the Composers Forum, the International Poetry Forum*, the *Man and*

Ideas lectures, the Mendelsohn Choir, The Pittsburgh Chamber Music Society, the River City Brass Band, and the distinguished Y Music Series; the Three Rivers Lecture Series and performances of the Pittsburgh Opera Theater, as well as other civic events. It is also a perennial location for the showing of The Carnegie's popular Travel Adventure Film series for members and guests, which celebrated its 46th season in 1993. The series, from October through March, presents 15 films, each with commentary by their producer, attracting some 100,000 visitors annually. The programs have been selected, arranged and introduced for more than a decade by Juliette Grauer, a volunteer.

In addition to the activities in The Music Hall, the Performing Arts Department, formed in 1986, presents popular performances in a variety of other settings within The Carnegie.

The summer, "Jazz Happy Hours," "Sunset Concerts," and "Vectors On Tap" are held in the outdoor Sculpture Court. There are performances by the "Mellon Jazz Festival Student Jazz Spectacular," the "Back Door Concert Series," "Music with the Masters," the Pittsburgh Early Music Ensemble and many more. The Three Rivers Shakespeare Festival in 1993 presented *The Children's King Lear* in the Hall of Architecture for the 56th annual holiday season.

*The *International Poetry Forum* was founded in Pittsburgh in 1966 by Dr. Samuel Hazo, a noted poet, and the late Theodore L. Hazlett, Jr., the final director of the Pittsburgh-based A. W. Mellon Education and Charitable Trust. The Forum has brought hundreds of poets from the U. S. and abroad to Pittsburgh to read their works, bringing the city world recognition as a center for poetry.

The interior of Carnegie Music Hall.

Photograph courtesy Carnegie Magazine

The Foyer, Carnegie Music Hall

The Foyer of Carnegie Music Hall with statue of Andrew Carnegie, by fellow Scot James Massey Rhind, whose sculptures also accent the facade of the building. The statue was the gift of the Carnegie Veteran's Association, in 1916, as "testimonial of esteem for their founder by his fellow members of the Association."

Photograph by Photosynthesis

". . .the grandest and most spectacular is undoubtedly the foyer of The Music Hall, which is one of the most splendid examples of Edwardian display in America . . ."

James D. Van Trump, 1907-1995
An American Palace of Culture, 1970

Dedicated in 1907 by Andrew Carnegie to the people of Pittsburgh in three days of official ceremonies, the foyer of The Music Hall is monumental and magnificent. Stretching across the entrance to The Music Hall, the handsome mosaic patterned marble floor is 135' long and 60' wide. The room is French in style, of the Edwardian era, yet an impressive example of the power of the American capitalistic dream, as it became real in the opulent pre-income tax period ended forever by World War I.

The ornamental plaster work throughout the foyer was at the time a branch of sculpture. All details of the ceilings were molded and cast in a studio set up in the building. A superintendent came from Philadelphia to supervise the work of 85 plasterers whose skills included casting, moldmaking, and molding. Most of the casters were Italian, and their two moldmaking bosses were French. They worked for $4.20 per day for a 44-hour week, liberal pay for those days. Cost of the ceiling plaster work has been estimated at $14,000 (1905-06), but it surely must have taken longer than 6-7 weeks, and so that estimate is open to question.

A veritable "International," marble of six nations was used in the construction of the foyer. Columns and pillars are from marble quarried in Greece. The walls are of French eschallion with the inlays making a colorful mosaic. Other marbles include Verde antico, red Verona and Siena from Italy and Royal Irish green Connemara marble from Galway, Ireland. The flooring contains English white marble; the smoking room, African varieties. Surrounding the hall are 24 huge Vert Tinos marble pillars, soaring 28' to carry the balcony, beneath the carved and gilded ceiling, which is 45' above the floor. Each pillar was made in three pieces and is said to weigh six tons.

On the Forbes Avenue side of the balcony is the Green Room, now the headquarters of the Women's Committee of The Museum of Art. It, too, has a handsome marble floor and simpler carved ceiling. In the early days this was the ladies' withdrawing room where they could smoke in privacy. The gentlemen retired to the basement to smoke their cigars in a handsome room with red marble pillars; it is now a classroom for painting classes of The School for The Carnegie.

In the fall of 1981 approximately 25,000 visitors viewed the exhibit, *Pioneer Cars At Carnegie*, sponsored anonymously through the Carnegie Institute. Twenty-one classic automobiles dating from 1898 to 1913, the Carnegie era, were displayed in the marble hall. To permit the cars to enter, the bronze doors, weighing 1,800 pounds, had to be removed for the first time since they were installed in 1907.

Andrew Carnegie's presence, sculpted in bronze, presides over one end of the foyer. A massive fireplace with the seal of the city of Pittsburgh on the chimney breast is at the other. Elaborate banquets, elegant receptions, and disco dancing for Fashion Show crowds have filled the hall. It has even been transformed into a street scene for a colorful Medieval festival. Special exhibitions and musical entertainment such as the 1990 *Vienna in Concert* have been held here. The foyer provides the perfect backdrop for the wares of 40-some dealers in the Antiques Show, presented annually since 1993 by the Women's Committee of The Museum of Art.

The foyer is not only the grand entrance to The Music Hall, but it also leads to the Carriage Entrance lobby and Architecture Hall and is the link to the Scaife Galleries of The Museum of Art. The foyer also serves as a display area for the works of a number of artists with a Pittsburgh connection, discussed in a subsequent chapter.

The Carnegie Second Century Fund

Launched in 1988 by Carnegie's president Robert C. Wilburn with co-chairmen trustees Henry L. Hillman, Thomas H. O'Brien, and James M. Walton, and a steering committee of 16, the Second Century Fund set forth to prepare the institution for its 1995 centennial and another century of service. The goal was to raise $125.5 million to: secure the physical plant, create and refurbish exhibitions, increase endowment funds, build a new science center, add a parking garage to the main building, and sustain ongoing operations during the campaign. At the five-year mark, the Second Century Fund had accomplished many of these goals through projects that touch nearly every area of, and every visitor to, The Carnegie. The fund as a whole received 51 Leadership gifts, 22 of which were contributions of $1 million or more, for a total as of September 13, 1993, of $130,689,322 of which $16 million was allocated to The Carnegie Museum of Natural History and $20 million to The Museum of Art for acquisition and conservation of works of art. (This stellar achievement was all the more remarkable considering the fact that The Carnegie had faced a deficit of $526,000 in 1985.)

A goal of $8 million was set for Program Endowment for the outreach programs offered through the School of The Carnegie, which was established in 1986 as the umbrella for the education programs offered by The Museums of Art and Natural History, The Andy Warhol Museum, and The Science Center. (The Tam O'Shanter series of art classes attended by Andy Warhola, Philip Pearlstein, and other well-known artists taught by Professor Joseph Fitzpatrick, is now called Art Connections.)

The dream of a new science center was fulfilled in 1991, and early in 1993 The Carnegie Science Center welcomed its one millionth visitor. For the thousands who visit The Carnegie's Oakland facility at any particular time, the parking garage has made access to the museums far more convenient. The Hall of Sculpture in The Museum of Art received a new lighting system that left it brighter and better suited for display. The casts in the Hall of Architecture were cleaned and the walls repainted (for the first time in 40 years) in the original pastel colors.

The Museum of Natural History opened four new exhibition halls since the start of the campaign: Benedum Hall of Geology, Walton Hall of Ancient Egypt, Natural History Gallery, and the Hall of African Wildlife and the children's Discovery Room.

Many Pittsburghers remember Andrew Carnegie's building as sooty and dark, but future generations will identify The Carnegie by its white sandstone facade after the cleaning that washed away 95 years of industrial grime. Less visible but equally important to the vitality of the institution has been the building of the endowment funds to support ongoing programs, exhibits, and staff, as well as renewed conservation efforts within The Museum of Art and The Museum of Natural History.

While working to fund these and other improvements identified at the onset of the campaign, donors have initiated additional projects at The Carnegie. Two of the most significant of these include the creation of The Heinz Architectural Center in The Museum of Art (opened November 1993) and the installation of Digistar technology in the Henry Buhl, Jr. Planetarium & Observatory at The Science Center. The Andy Warhol Museum, as a vital part of The Carnegie stands alone as a triumphal achievement in tribute to Pittsburgh's most famous contemporary artist.

The Carnegie Museum of Art Directors from the Founding to the Present

John W. Beatty
1896-1922

Homer Saint-Gaudens
1923-1950

Gordon Bailey Washburn
1950-1962

Gustave Von Groschwitz
1963-1968

Leon Anthony Arkus
1969-1980

John R. Lane
1980-January 1987

Phillip M. Johnston
Acting Director, January 1987-May 1988
Director, May 1988-Present

Paintings in the Rotunda of The Music Hall

Renowned artists have painted the distinguished persons who have presided over the Carnegie Institute since its inception. A number of these portraits are on view in the rotunda of Pittsburgh's Carnegie Music Hall.

In the central position there is the portrait of the founder, Andrew Carnegie, by Anders Zorn of Sweden (1860-1920), portraitist of Sweden's royalty. Samuel Harden Church, president of the Institute 1914 to 1943, was painted by Sir William Orpen of Ireland (1878-1931). The distinguished area-artist Malcolm Parcell portrayed William Frew, president 1943-1948. James M. Bovard, president 1948-1967, was painted by Everett R. Kinstler, the artist whose portrait of Mrs. Alan Scaife hangs at the entrance to the display areas of the Sarah Scaife Gallery of

The Museum of Art. Homer Saint-Gaudens, director of The Museum of Art, was portrayed by George Luks in a painting which also hangs nearby. The portrait of president 1968-1984, James M. Walton, by Aaron Shikler Tickler, painter also of Jaqueline Kennedy Onassis, is a striking and colorful likeness. The painting of Robert Wilburn, president 1984-1992, a graduate of the U. S. Airforce Academy was fittingly portrayed by William F. Draper, an official Navy Combat Artist in World War II. Among his credits are portraits of Admirals Nimitz and Halsey, murals for the United States Naval Academy, portraits of U. S. Presidents Kennedy and Nixon and Mr. Paul Mellon, patron of the National Gallery in Washington, D.C. and the Carnegie Institute in Pittsburgh. Dr. Stewart's portrait was by Johanna Hailman, Pittsburgh artist, daughter and granddaughter of local artists.

Portraits of several of the directors of The Carnegie Museum of Natural History may also be seen in the rotunda of The Music Hall. Dr. Holland was wearing his medal and decorations when painted by American artist Leopold Seyffert. Doctors Avinoff and Jennings were both portrayed by the Russian-born Elizabeth Shoumatoff, the artist who was working on the portrait of President Franklin Delano Roosevelt when he died at Warm Springs, Georgia in 1945. (Mrs. Shoumatoff died in early December 1980, aged 92.) The British artist, Bernard Hailstone, painted the portrait of Dr. Netting, looking relaxed with pipe in hand.

Paintings in the Foyer of The Music Hall, and Galleries

Painters with a Pittsburgh Connection
Scalp Level Painters

The paintings grouped in The Music Hall Foyer are mainly by artists with a Pittsburgh connection. Artists now deceased, who were born in Pittsburgh or if born elsewhere, whose major work was accomplished here . . . and whose work is in the collection of The Museum of Art, Carnegie Institute. Some of the artists connected with this city were famous in life and now are almost forgotten. Others whose work was unsung in life achieved posthumous recognition. Illustrative of the former category is **John White Alexander** whose murals around the Grand Staircase Hall are discussed in some detail in that section. Alexander was born in Allegheny in 1856 and was orphaned when he was seven-years-old. Like Andrew Carnegie he became a telegraph messenger, then went to New York where he worked as an office boy. His art career began as an illustrator for *Harper's Weekly*. By the turn of the century, Alexander was one of America's most popular artists. In 1901 he became a Chevalier of the French Legion of Honor. Although self-taught, by 1893 he was recognized by the prestigious art groups of his day, becoming a member of 20 and president of several. Alexander's painting *Aurora Leigh* was included in the *International* of 1904 and came to The Museum of Art in 1940 by gift of C. Bernard Shea.

Panther Hollow, Pittsburgh, c. 1933-34, by John Kane, American; Mr. and Mrs. James F. Hillman Purchase Fund, 1963.

John Kane, also self-taught but "primitive" was 67-years-old when his painting *Scene from the Scottish Highlands* was accepted in the *Carnegie International* of 1927. He made his living as a construction worker and house painter. The Museum of Art owns more than a dozen of his paintings of local scenes, the hills and valleys, houses, mills, and bridges of Pittsburgh. An addition in 1981 to the museum's collection of Kane's work is his *Bloomfield Bridge*, c. 1930, one of the many gifts to the Institute by Mr. and Mrs. James H. Beal. Two of Kane's paintings were of scenes close to The Carnegie, *The Cathedral of Learning*, 1930, and *Panther Hollow*, Pittsburgh, 1933-4, perhaps the last he painted before his death in 1934.

Mary Cassatt was born in 1844 in Allegheny, which is now the North Side of Pittsburgh. Although her father was mayor of Allegheny for a time, Mary Cassatt did not claim it as a place of her affections. She did, however, consider herself American, even though Paris became her home some time between 1868 and 1874 and remained so until her death in 1926. The Museum owns a sizable collection of her work, including prints and drawings as well as the painting *Young Women Picking Fruit*. This painting is related to her mural, commissioned for the 1893 Columbian Exposition, which showed women and children picking fruit. Friend of Degas, Cassatt exhibited with the Impressionists and adopted their color range in her tender groupings of women and children. This painting was the first acquisition of the Patrons Art Fund, newly created in 1922. (Additional information about the successive purchases from the fund to 1940 is included in that section.)

Another painting in the permanent collection which has a Pittsburgh connection through Mary Cassatt is the *Toilet of Venus* by Simon Vouet. A Frenchman, born in 1590, he studied in Rome, was influenced by the works of Michelangelo and Caravaggio. He returned to Paris as court painter to King Louis XIII and died in 1649. His style had a strong influence on French painting. This canvas, painted about 1630, was once owned by Madame DuBarry, mistress of Louis XV. It was sold at Versailles in 1777, three years after the death of the king. His mistress died under the guillotine in 1792. *The Toilet of Venus* was bought by Mary Cassatt in 1905, for her brother. It was inherited by her niece, Mrs. Horace Binney Hare, of Radnor, Pennsylvania, who gave it to Carnegie Institute in 1952.

Another artist born in Pittsburgh, in 1895, who lived and died in Paris, 1937, was **Henry Ossawa Tanner** who was noted for his paintings of religious subjects. After his family moved to Philadelphia, Tanner studied with Thomas Eakins and in Paris with Constant and Laurens. Tanner's paintings were exhibited in several *Internationals*. The Museum acquired his *Judas* from the 1899 *Annual Exhibition*, but traded it for his *Judas Convenanting with the High Priests* from the 1905 show. This, in turn, was exchanged for his *Christ at the Home of Mary and Martha* from the 1907 exhibition, a work that has remained in the collection but is not currently on view. In 1973 the U. S. Postal Service issued a stamp honoring Tanner in its American Arts Series of Commemorative Stamps. The occasion was marked with appropriate ceremonies in the foyer, sponsored by the Selma Burke Art Center and the A. W. Mellon Educational and Charitable Trust.

An artist who was born in Pittsburgh, 1871, who died here in 1958 was **Johanna Knowles Woodwell Hailman**. The daughter and granddaughter of artists, she was taught painting at an early age by her father Joseph R. Woodwell, who had studied in France with the early Impressionists. Although she painted many subjects, she is best known for her paintings of gardens and flowers. Her *American Beauties* may be seen in the foyer of The Music Hall. The museum owns a number of her oils, including a posthumous portrait of Douglas Stewart, director of Carnegie Museum of Natural History, 1922-26. It was commissioned in 1926 by the Fine Arts Committee and dated 1928. Many of her paintings came to the museum by her bequest as did those of her father, **Joseph R. Woodwell** (born in Pittsburgh, 1842, died here in 1911) who was well-known as a painter, particularly of landscapes. He studied in Paris and came to know Renoir, Pissaro, Millet, and Monet and was a companion of Sisley. Returning to Pittsburgh in 1867, he painted with a group of artists at **Scalp Level**, a village in the Allegheny Mountains near Somerset during the 1870s and 1880s. He was a trustee of Carnegie Institute and a member of the Fine Arts Committee, 1896-1911. The Museum of Art owns *A Portrait of Joseph R. Woodwell* by Thomas Eakins, of Philadelphia, "the great American master of realism." Four of the ten oil paintings by Joseph R. Woodwell which the museum owns are hanging in the foyer to The Music Hall. His *Magnolia* and *Little Guard Harbor* are in the Scaife Galleries.

Joseph R. Woodwell's father was **Joseph Woodwell**, a woodcarver in Pittsburgh, who had as apprentice **David Gilmour Blythe**. Blythe was born in 1815 in East Liverpool, Ohio, coming at age 15 to Pittsburgh. Although he had no formal training, he worked as an itinerant portrait painter, in East Liverpool and in Uniontown, Pennsylvania. He is, however, most admired for his works of social and political satire, which for the most part were painted during his residence in Pittsburgh from 1854 until his death in 1865. Of the 25 oils listed for Blythe in the museum's catalogue (1973), *Post Office*, c. 1862-75, hangs in the Scaife Gallery, and *Prison Scene* is in the foyer of The Music Hall.

Although The Museum of Art, Carnegie Institute is the major repository of Blythe's paintings, the 1981 traveling exhibition, *The World of David Gilmour Blythe* (1815-1865), was organized by the National Museum of American Art. The exhibit was sponsored locally by Pittsburgh National Bank, Pittsburgh being "the city that fired Blythe's imagination during his years of residence" here. Included in the show were paintings, sculpture, and works of art on paper by "America's foremost 19th century satirist."

Blythe's employer, Joseph Woodwell, the woodcarver, also owned a painting called The *Captives*, 1858, by **Isaac Eugene Craig** who was born near Pittsburgh in 1830. He was a painter of portraits, and religious and historical subjects. He lived in Pittsburgh, Philadelphia and Europe and was working in Florence, Italy, before his death sometime after 1878. This canvas was successively owned by Woodwell, his son, and his granddaughter before coming to The Museum of Art.

One of the artists who was in the group painting at the colony of **Scalp Level** was **Jasper Holman Lawman**, born in Xenia, Ohio in 1825. He was a scene painter in the old Drury Theater in Pittsburgh before going to Paris in 1859 to study painting. In 1887 he did the canvas referred to as *Scene on Paint Creek Near Scalp Level*. It hangs in the foyer with the work of some of his colleagues. Lawman died in Pittsburgh in 1906.

Scalp Level is also the title of a painting done in 1875 by **Martin B. Leisser**, who was born in Pittsburgh in 1845 and died here in 1940. He studied art in Munich and Paris and became head of the Pittsburgh School of Design and later headed the art department of the Pennsylvania College for Women, now Chatham College. He was a trustee of Carnegie Institute, 1910-1915 and is credited with persuading Andrew Carnegie to include a school of art in his new Technical School close by. Two of the six of his oils owned by the Institute hang in the foyer: *Bearded Man*, 1886, and *Franciscan Church of Rothenburg, Bavaria*, 1912. A full length portrait of Mary Croghan Schenley by Leisser hangs in the School for the Blind in nearby Oakland. (Leisser was the teacher and mentor of Pittsburgh born John Covert, 1882-1960, younger cousin of Walter Arensberg, patron of the Philadelphia Museum of Art. Covert's painting *Model and Painter*, 1916-1923, which is elsewhere in the museum, was the gift in 1986 of the artist's uncle and aunt, Mr. and Mrs. Charles Covert Arensberg.) The Leisser Art Fund continues to provide additions to the collections of The Museum of Art.

George Hetzel was born in France in 1826 and came with his parents to Pittsburgh in 1828. After study in Germany his early work was in portraits and still life but his greatest fame came with landscapes of Western Pennsylvania. Five of his oils are owned by the museum, one titled *Little Paint Creek* and another *Woodland Path*, 1868, which hangs in the foyer. He died in 1899 in Somerset, Pennsylvania.

A member of the original Board of Trustees of Carnegie Institute was **Alfred S. Wall**. Born in Mount Pleasant, Pennsylvania in 1825 he, too, was a member of the colony of artists at **Scalp Level**. He was a landscape painter and art critic and teacher of his son, A. Bryan Wall, who was born in Mount Pleasant about 1861. The work of the father is represented by five canvases in the museum, one of which, *Mountain Brook in Autumn*, may be seen in the foyer. Another, entitled *Woodland Scene*, c. 1883, is inscribed on the back, "Presented to **John W. Beatty**, 1883." Beatty was himself a painter, and lifelong Pittsburgher, 1851-1924. He studied at the Munich Academy of Fine Arts. His painting *The Wood Gatherer*, 1894, is also in the foyer. In 1896 he became the first director of the Department of Fine Arts, (now The Museum of Art), Carnegie Institute, and organizer of the first *International Exhibition*, serving until 1922. He died in 1924.

Going back even before the beginning of Carnegie Institute is the work of **William Coventry Wall**, older brother of Alfred Wall. Born in England in 1810, he was educated at Oxford and became a portrait and landscape painter. He is best remembered here for his two paintings of Pittsburgh after the fire of 1845 which devastated the city. One was done two days after the fire, from Birmingham, now South Side, and the other next day, from Boyd's Hill. These views of the ruins bring to mind the painting by J. M.W. Turner, *Burning of the Houses of Parliament*, London, 1834.

A pair of portraits, one of Benjamin Darlington and the other of Henry Clay (1832), illustrate the work of **James Reid Lambdin**, who was born in Pittsburgh in 1807. After studying art in Philadelphia, he opened a portrait studio here, but three years later returned to Philadelphia where he died in 1889. *Henry Clay* is in the Scaife Gallery.

Women and Children, with Indian Massacre in the Background is the work of **Trevor McClung**, who was born here and who died here, 1816-1893. He studied abroad, then became known for his many portraits, but he also painted genre scenes. A contemporary, **William Louis Sonntag**, was born in East Liberty in 1822. He, too, studied abroad, and became associated with the Hudson River School. He is known for his landscapes, of which the museum has two: *The Susquehanna Near Bald Eagle Mountain*, 1864, and *Fall Landscape*.

Francis Raymond Holland was born in Pittsburgh in 1886. He specialized in seascapes and landscapes which included a series of impressions such as *Panther Hollow, Pittsburgh*, 1918. He died in New York in 1934. Another artist, **William Baziotes**, was born in Pittsburgh in 1912 and died in New York in 1963. While with a WPA Federal Grants Project from 1938 to 1941, he was influenced by Surrealism, and he developed an abstract style based on biomorphic forms. His painting *Black Knight*, 1954, hangs in the Scaife Gallery.

Just 30 years old at his death in 1918, **Frederick A. Demmler** of Pittsburgh was represented until recently among the canvases in the foyer by *Vera*, 1916, now in the Scaife Gallery. The Museum also owns an earlier work, *The Black Hat*, 1914, by the same artist, donated by Oscar Demmler, his brother. **Aaron Harry Gorson** was born in Latvia in 1872. He painted in Pittsburgh from 1903 to 1921 and is noted for his nocturnal views of the steel mills and the industrial life of the city. Examples of these themes are *On the Monongahela* and *Steel Mills*. Another Gorson painting is *Lower Allegheny*, 1909, donated to the museum in 1978 by Senator and Mrs. H. John Heinz, III. Gorson left Pittsburgh for New York City hoping, unsuccessfully, to find a better market for his works, but Pittsburghers were his best patrons, and he died, almost penniless in New York in 1933. Since his death, Gorson's paintings have increased in value as the great steel mills have been dismantled and disappeared from the scene. Ironically, at an auction held in Pittsburgh in 1992 of the art of the bankrupt H. K. Porter Company, formerly owned by Thomas Mellon Evans around 1975, eight works by Gorson were sold for a total of $125,000.

Gorson had studied with **Thomas Anschutz** at the Pennsylvania Academy of Fine Arts and in Paris with Constant and Laurens, as did Tanner. In 1979 the Director's Discretionary Fund provided the museum with Gorson's pastel *Man at the Forge*, c. 1928. A painting by Anschutz, which is of special interest locally, is *Steamboat on the Ohio*, c. 1871, in the Scaife Gallery. Anschutz studied with Thomas Eakins at the Pennsylvania Academy, and Anschutz's pupils include some of the most important innovators in American art: Marin, Henri, Sloan, Glackens, and Demuth, of whom Henri and Glackens are listed in the 1973 catalogue of the museum.

In 1978 *The Spirit of the Hills* by **Augustus Vincent Tack**, was donated by friends and family of Henry Oliver, Jr., trustee of Carnegie Institute. Tack was born in 1830 to Mary Cosgrove and Theodore Edward Tack, a family prominent in the oil business in Pittsburgh. Tack's works were exhibited in the *Internationals* in the early 1900s. Most of his abstract paintings are in the Duncan Phillips Collection in Washington, D.C.

American Paintings and Sculpture to 1945 in The Carnegie Museum of Art, 1991, by The Carnegie Museum of Art, contains a wealth of information concerning the **Scalp Level*** artists and others, "with a Pittsburgh connection."

Also see the *Catalogue of Painting Collection, Carnegie Institute 1973*. The attribution of each work is there stated, and each annual report mentions all the benefactors of the particular year. The art public is indebted to all the donors, too numerous to list here. In acknowledging this debt, this study by reference incorporates all their names.

———————————

* See also *Carnegie Magazine* cover story, September/October, 1984.

Architecture Hall

"About twenty museums once had rooms like this. Now the Hall of Architecture in The Museum of Art is the lone survivor and is considered a 'treasure.'"

— *The Pittsburgh Press*
November 15, 1981

Recalling the Tomb of King Mausolus, 353 B.C.

The visual and psychological impact of the Hall of Architecture on most visitors does not depend on recognizing it as a re-creation of the tomb of King Mausolus of Halicarnassus in Asia, built in 353 B.C., once one of the Seven Wonders of the World. Its ruins were excavated in 1856 by Sir Charles Newton of Britain. Using actual measurements and classical literary descriptions, architects were able to develop adaptations of the plan. This vast square, 125' x 126', lit by a skylight 76' above the marble floor, awes by its majestic dimensions and by the congregation of architectural presence assembled here. Twenty-eight Ionic columns surround the room, somewhat lost among the many design elements represented.

Plaster Casts for Hall of Architecture Opening in 1907

At the turn of the century museums in capital cities of the world relied on plaster casts of great architectural elements for their displays. As world travel became more available to the general public, art critics tended to disdain the use of plaster casts in art museums. Many museums, therefore, dismantled their displays of classic architecture, and even Architecture Hall in Carnegie Institute has had to resist that trend, which now seems to be reversed. When the Institute opened in 1896, it was accepted practice that life-size plaster reproductions of the great architectural and sculptural treasures of the past would be ordered from the Italian firm

Concert for two harps, Lucile Johnson Rosenbloom and Marcela Kozikova, Architecture Hall, Museum of Art, Carnegie Institute.

Photograph by Harold Corsini

specializing in them. The facade of the 12th century Romanesque Church of St. Gilles du Gard was not in the catalogues however, and because of its size it presented quite a challenge. Special permission was obtained from the French government to make molds of the facade from impressions taken directly from the structure. Under the direction of a chief of studio of the Trocadero, a French museum, the work was done for about $8,000, plus an unspecified donation to the municipality and the cost of the transatlantic shipping. As the casts were made from the molds, they were packed in crates for shipment. A French workman came to Pittsburgh to assist in the erection of the facade. A special framework of timber and wire was constructed on which the sections were carefully mounted and joined so as to give the impression of a unified whole. Completed in time for the opening of the Institute in 1907, it was one of the most spectacular sights of that grand occasion.

Casts Teach Development of Architecture from Ancient Times

Also in the Hall are reproductions of other architectural monuments, 144 in all, which illustrate the development of architecture from ancient times through the Renaissance period: the Gothic Portal of Bordeaux, the Eastern doors of the Baptistery of St. John by Ghiberti, and other replicas.

There is a complete replica, reduced in size, of the Parthenon of Athens as it looked in its original state before its roof was blown off by a Venetian cannonball, which hit an ammunition cache that the Turks had set in the Parthenon. Inside was the statue of Athena Parthenos (Athena, the Virgin), dressed in her drapery of pure gold, which in its actual form had constituted the treasury of Athens. When the ancient Athenians wished to add to their treasury, goldsmiths would melt the additional gold and cast it as new folds to Athena's large and expanding robe. On a smaller scale there are casts of many of the items discovered when the layers of lava from Mt. Vesuvius were cleared away from the ruins at Pompeii and Herculaneum. Art critics in recent decades found Architecture Hall lacking in artistic merit, but the public over the years has found it exciting and special. Financial constraints probably saved the hall from being disassembled during its period of twilight. Now, in 1994, it is viewed as a historical treasure. The casts have been cleaned, the ceiling repaired, the hall repainted in its original colors, with improved, updated lighting, all as a project of The Carnegie's Second Century Fund.

Activities in the Hall

The Hall has provided an inspiring backdrop for the Saturday art classes for hundreds of school children, as well as for seasonal displays such as the Italian Nativity scene and the great trees decorated for Christmas. Dinners, receptions, ballet and other dance presentations, and a Dinosaur Ball have been held here, and many musical events of which one of the most fitting was an intimate concert of music for two harps. Memorable also were the nationality dinners preceding guided tours to related collections in The Museum of Art. The Three Rivers Shakespeare Festival in 1993 presented *The Children's King Lear* . . . and in December the Hall of Architecture rang again with the sounds of ethnic music, for the 56th annual holiday season celebration.

The Hall of Sculpture

Patterned after the fabled Parthenon, the Temple to Athena on the Acropolis in Athens, the Hall of Sculpture incorporates Pentelic marble from the same quarries that supplied the material for the Parthenon in Greece. The original of the frieze, or decorative band, was carved under the supervision of Phidias, the Greek sculptor, in the 5th century B.C. Around the walls here is a plaster reproduction of the sculptured frieze which adorns the outside of the Parthenon. The 524-foot frieze depicts the procession that inaugurated the annual festival of Athena, the virgin goddess, protectress of Athens. It was given by Andrew Carnegie in 1898, along with many other pieces.

When the hall opened in 1907 the majority of these 69 casts of ancient sculpture, dating from about 3600 B.C. to about 15 A.D., were displayed here. Casts of some of the great works of Greek and Roman antiquity are still an important presence among the colonnades which support the balcony. Other heroic classic figures appear on the balcony.

Overhead, on the skylight ceiling, there is a work from the 1988 *International* by the German artist Lothar Baumgarten (b. 1944). *The Tongue of the Cherokee* presents the Cherokee alphabet, which was formulated early in the 19th century. There is a philosophical connection in the influence of the classic Greek

View of Architecture Hall.

Photograph courtesy of Carnegie Magazine

culture on American thought at the beginning of the 20th century, contrasted with the current recognition of the role of the Native Americans in our history.

The marble floor of this skylit area now is a main display space for contemporary art, especially large works from the *Carnegie Internationals*. Shown here to advantage in 1994 was *Fallen Timber*, by Carl Andre (b. 1935). The work is a series of 24 waist-high, squared columns of wood, arranged in military-style formation, giving a changing perspective as the viewer circles the installation. As an occasional alternative to the exhibition of set art pieces in the hall, there are special performances by dancers and musical groups.

A small gallery between the Hall of Sculpture and Architecture Hall is devoted to a series of tiny rooms displaying the Sarah Mellon Scaife Collection of scaled miniature furniture, silver and porcelain in settings which reproduce Mrs. Scaife's French-style bedroom, her library, and Georgian dining room at Penguin Hall in Ligonier.

The balcony is visually part of the hall itself. In the stairway area to the balcony from the hall are objects from the Art Nouveau/Deco periods, including a set of four Tiffany stained glass windows taken from the Richard Beatty Mellon house which stood off Fifth Avenue, in what is now Mellon Park, across from the present location of the Ellis School.

A number of artists have chosen portions of the balcony as staging areas for their site-specific works for the *Carnegie Internationals.* Decorative Arts objects — principally glass, ceramics, and metalworks, including silver, that may range in date from the 18th century to the present, are also displayed around the wall of the dramatic balcony of the Hall of Sculpture.

The balcony now provides the main entrance to the Heinz Architecture Center which opened in 1993. The center and the Frank Lloyd Wright office displayed there are discussed in detail in the following chapter.

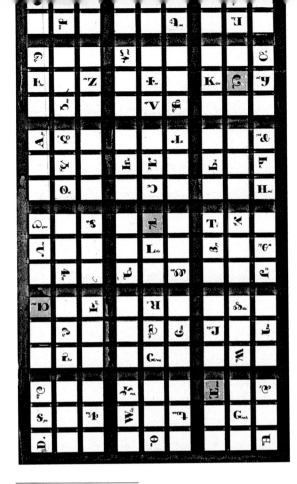

Ceiling, Hall of Sculpture, The Museum of Art, Carnegie Institute. Overhead, the glass on the skylight ceiling has been etched with letters, symbols of the Cherokee alphabet. The work by Lothar Baumgarten is *The Tongue of the Cherokee* obtained from the *International* of 1988 by a $50,000 grant from the Women's Committee of The Museum of Art.

The Cherokee alphabet, or *The Tongue of the Cherokee*, was created by Sequoyah, who was born in a village in Tennessee a few years before the American Revolution. He was the son of a full-blooded Cherokee mother and Nathaniel Gist, a Dutch trader with the Indians. When the father abandoned the family, the boy was raised by his mother in the tribal culture and tradition, although in later life he sometimes was known as George Gist. He became fascinated by the white man's "talking leaf," the paper with written or printed words, and he resolved to create an Indian "talking leaf." Sequoyah devoted 12 years of his life (1809-1821) to the development of a syllabary, which led to the Cherokee being able to read and write in their own language, able to pass on their accumulated wisdom to the yet unborn. Sequoyah remains the only one in history to develop an alphabet completely on his own.

Entrance to The Heinz Architechtural Center from the Hall of Sculpture Balcony.

Photograph by Joanne Devereaux

The Carnegie Museum of Art
The Heinz Architectural Center

Survey of Architectural Exhibitions in Pittsburgh

The Heinz Architectural Center opened on November 7, 1993 as an artistically separate but physically integrated entity within The Museum of Art of The Carnegie. The Drue Heinz Foundation's $10 million gift to establish the center honors the memory of her husband, the late Henry J. Heinz, II, his interest in architecture and devotion to the city of Pittsburgh. The location on the second floor was chosen by Mrs. H. J. Heinz, II and Museum of Art Director Phillip Johnston. The rectangular gallery had been renovated 20 years ago as part of the Heinz Galleries for temporary exhibitions and remains a viable exhibition space.

Scholarly Christopher Monkhouse, former Curator of Decorative Arts of the Rhode Island School of Design, was appointed Curator of the Heinz Architectural Center and is credited with establishing the initial collection.

The Pittsburgh Connection

Native Pittsburgher Ann Kalla, a Carnegie Mellon University graduate, and her partner Pietro Cicognani were the architects awarded the $4.5 million challenge of creating The Heinz Architectural Center. The architects' brilliant solution was the three-story, 19,000 square foot interior addition. The drama of the three-story entrance hall is heightened by two bridges and the rays from the daylight above. Now it glows with brilliant color, vibrant red, blue, and ochre walls embellished with fragments of architectural elements: boiseries from the Richard Beatty Mellon collection, and a fragment of the original copper cornice designed by John Massey Rhind for Carnegie Institute, removed when the building was enlarged in 1907.

The Hall of Architecture became the centerpiece of the new addition with 144 casts of architectural elements from ancient Egypt, the Acropolis in Greece, and from other world famous buildings. The adjacent Hall of Sculpture echoes the interior of the Parthenon in Athens, and it is from the balcony of that Hall that the visitor reaches the Heinz Architectural Center.

The logo of The Heinz Architectural Center is the copper dormer window from the former Andrew Carnegie mansion, which is now the Cooper-Hewitt Museum, The Smithsonian Institution's National Museum of Design. Two of the windows came to The Carnegie as a gift from Pittsburgher Nicholas Lardas whose firm, NIKO Contracting Co., replaced the 1901 Carnegie roof in New York with a new copper roof.

The San Francisco Office of Frank Lloyd Wright (1867-1959)

Frank Lloyd Wright used this office during the final decade of his life. The partitions and furniture designed by Wright were acquired for the center by a generous grant from the Women's Committee of The Museum of Art. Cicognani Kalla Architects faithfully reinstalled the two

The Heinz Architectural Center Dormer Window from Carnegie Mansion in New York.

Photograph by Joanne Devereaux

6'10" high partition walls set at a 120 degree angle in the 900 square foot office. This plan was originally the work of Wright's younger associate Aaron Green, a former Taleisin fellow, with detailed adjustments specified by Wright. Fitted into this compact space in San Francisco were kitchenette and toilet facilities as well as the reception area, drafting room, consultation, and utility rooms shown in Pittsburgh. The office was at 319 Grant Avenue in a modest four-story building near the gateway to San Francisco's Chinatown.

Frank Lloyd Wright and the Pittsburgh Kaufmann Family

"No architect has captured the imagination of the American public like Frank Lloyd Wright,"

avers Richard Cleary, associate professor of Architecture at Carnegie Mellon University. Generally acknowledged as Wright's masterpiece is *Fallingwater* at Bear Run, 70 miles east of Pittsburgh. The house was commissioned in 1935 by Edgar Kaufmann, president of Kaufmann's department store in Pittsburgh. At the same time he commissioned Wright to design his office at the store. After Mr. Kaufmann's death in 1955, the office was dismantled and moved to nearby Grant Street to the charitable trust he had established. From 1963 to 1972, the dismantled office was stored, until Edgar Kaufmann, Jr. offered it to the Victoria and Albert Museum in London so there would be a complete work of Wright's on display in Europe. However, due to lack of funding, two decades passed until, finally, the Kaufmann Pittsburgh office was permanently installed in England's Victoria and Albert Museum within a year of the installation of Wright's San Francisco office in Pittsburgh.

Edgar Kaufmann, Jr.'s lifelong interest in architecture was sparked by his boyhood admiration for the reproduction of the facade of the Abbey Church of St. Gilles du Gard in Carnegie Institute's Architecture Hall, one of the many casts commissioned by Andrew Carnegie and, incidentally, the largest in the world. Kaufmann, Jr. became professor of Architectural History at Columbia University and after his parents' deaths he gave *Fallingwater* to the Western Pennsylvania Conservancy for public use and inspiration. (Another private home by Wright is at Chalk Hill in the Laurel Mountains, *Kentuck Knob*, commissioned by Mr. and Mrs. I. N. Hagan of Uniontown in 1954.)

Best known perhaps of Wright's many major public works is the Guggenheim Museum (1943) in New York. Other works by Wright commissioned by Kaufmann, Sr. for Pittsburgh, but not built, were a civic center at the Point, an apartment building on Mount Washington, a downtown parking garage, and a dramatic

*Twin Bridges Project for Point Park, Pittsburgh,
Pennsylvania,* 1947, by Frank Lloyd Wright, American;
Museum purchase: gift of Women's Committee,
Carnegie Treasures Cookbook Fund, 1986.

design, *Twin Bridges Project for Point Park,
Pittsburgh, Pennsylvania,* 1947.

Wright is reported to have said about the
prospect of improving Pittsburgh that it would
be cheaper to tear it down! The pencil and ink
drawing entered the museum's collection by
purchase gift proceeds from *The Carnegie Treasures Cook Book,* a project of the Women's Committee of The Carnegie Museum of Art.

Early Architectural Exhibitions in Pittsburgh

Designs by Alden & Harlow for the $5 million
expansion of Carnegie Institute were displayed
in 1900 in an impressive exhibition staged by
The Pittsburgh Architectural Club. The club
also held exhibitions in 1903, 1905, 1907,
1910, and 1913. In 1903 the nearly 700 exhibits included work of the New York firm of Israel
& Harder. Shown were front and rear elevation
of a monument in Washington, D.C., memorial
to the founder of homeopathic medicine,
Christian Friedrich Samuel Hahnemann. Cru-
sader for this accomplishment was Dr. James
H. McClelland of Pittsburgh. His donation, in

1897, of the original architectural model to
Carnegie Institute in effect laid the cornerstone
for the collection of architectural models by
The Heinz Architectural Center nearly a century
later. (Dr. McClelland's house, "Sunny Ledge,"
on Fifth Avenue, designed by famed Alden &
Harlow, was a veritable house museum of early
1900s medical practice from a residential base.
Dr. McClelland's artist daughter, Rachel Sutton,
inherited his house and at her death sought to
leave it intact, medical instruments and all, to
posterity, but that was not to be — and in
1993, alas, the collection was dispersed at auction by the new private owners of the red brick
dwelling.)

In 1905 the Pittsburgh Architectural
Club's exhibition was on a reduced scale due
to the construction for the addition to Carnegie
Institute. Of the 413 works shown, the competition drawings for the design of the campus
for Carnegie Technical Schools (now Carnegie
Mellon University) were featured, including
those of the winner, Palmer & Hornbostel of
New York.

The Pittsburgh Club's show of 1907 was one of the most significant architectural shows held in the United States in the 20th century. This first exhibition in the Alden & Harlow addition to Carnegie's art galleries included "1,508 works, making it twice as large as any architectural exhibition ever held in America," according to *The America Architect*. Viewed by 88,000 visitors, the *Modern Movement* highlighting Frank Lloyd Wright's prairie school architecture was a hit of the show. This was the first Pittsburgh exhibit of his work. The catalogue of the 1910 exhibition of the Pittsburgh Architectural Club included as a permanent record three of the installation photographs from the 1907 show. Wright's work was shown again in 1913 in the Architectural Club's eighth exhibition, which attracted over 20,000 visitors in two weeks.

The 1907 show had exhibited modern American and German architecture together. It thus was a forerunner of *The International Style* exhibition organized by The Museum of Modern Art in New York 25 years later, with Edgar Kaufmann, Jr. as guest curator. By contrast, Carnegie Institute in 1936 exhibited drawings and photographs of buildings erected before 1860 in Western Pennsylvania. This comprehensive survey was supported by a grant to the Pittsburgh chapter of the American Institute of Architects through the Buhl Foundation. It also published *The Early Architecture of Western Pennsylvania* by Charles Stotz, chairman of the survey. Liberally illustrated with measured drawings and photographs by Stotz and his Pittsburgh colleagues, including Robert Schmertz, this remains the standard reference book.

Architectural Exhibitions from the 1940s through the 1980s

In the 1940s, '50s, and '60s, a number of exhibitions of architectural photographs were mounted in the galleries at Carnegie Institute, often with the support of Henry J. Heinz, II who was an accomplished architectural photographer in his own right. The Department of Fine Arts at Carnegie Institute of Technology organized an exhibition entitled *A Study of Architecture through Structure* in 1955. Two major traveling exhibitions to come to Carnegie Institute were: *The New Spirit*, an exhibition of the work of Le Courbusier in architecture, and city planning, printing, and writing arranged by the Walker Art Center in Minneapolis in 1946. Two decades later, in 1966, *The Architecture of Louis I. Kahn* was exhibited in Pittsburgh through the auspices of the Museum of Modern Art, with the cost underwritten by the Women's Committee of The Carnegie Museum of Art. In 1972, the museum showed a traveling exhibition organized by the Metropolitan Museum of Art entitled *The Rise of an American Architecture*. Guest curator was Edgar Kaufmann, Jr. who praised Pittsburgh's Evergreen Hamlet which had been developed in 1851-52 by William Shinn.

Late in 1983 and early in 1984, *Great Drawings from the Collection of the Royal Institute of British Architects* were exhibited at The Carnegie Museum of Art, funded in part by Mr. and Mrs. H. J. Heinz, II. This was the beginning of an Anglo-American architectural exchange program which has flowered since 1992 with the collaboration of The Heinz Architectural Center and the Royal Academy of Arts in London. Working together on exhibitions, publications, and programs of mutual interest helps expand and strengthen the capabilities of each.

International Exhibition Organized
Architecture in a Well-Ordered Universe: Lord Burlington's Villa at Chiswick and Thomas Jefferson's Grounds at the University of Virginia — October 29, 1994 - January 8, 1995
This combination of two exhibitions was the first international exhibition organized by The Heinz Architectural Center. It was the first collaboration in what promises to be a series with

the Royal Academy in London. In this instance, the Center and the Academy joined with a third collaborator, the Canadian Centre for Architecture.

Chiswick Villa, built from 1725 to 1729 on a suburban site outside London, was one of the most influential private houses in the history of architecture. Its owner and architect, Richard Boyle, 3rd Earl of Burlington (1694-1753), is the leading representative of a peculiarly English phenomenon, the nobleman or land-owner who practiced architecture as might a professional. At a moment when classical architecture was being re-assessed, Burlington designed a sequence of magisterial buildings between 1720 and 1730 that established him as the pioneer in the making of a new architecture. These included his own villa at Chiswick, the York Assembly Rooms, General Wide's house in London, and the astonishing designs for Houses of Parliament in 1733 that were twenty years in advance of their time.

The exhibition included approximately 120 works: paintings, drawings, watercolors, plans and elevations, as well as books and prints. Sources of inspiration deriving from works by Palladia in 16th century Italy to those of the 17th century British architect Inigo Jones illustrated the evolution of Chiswick Villa's design from preliminary schemes to finished plans and drawings. Included were the rare garden studies by William Kent and topographical views by a host of painters, including P.A. Rysbrack, Jacques Rigaud, John Rocque, John Donowell and George Lambert. The vast majority of works displaying the history of the creation of this "Arcadian Villa" have never before been shown to the public.

The second exhibition focused on one of America's great architectural landmarks, Thomas Jefferson's University of Virginia. Thomas Jefferson, third President of the United States, is America's foremost representative of the gentleman architect — very much in

Burlington's tradition. And, like Burlington, he studied and drew upon classical Renaissance precedents, for the creation of his designs. The University of Virginia, constructed from 1817 to 1826 in the royal town of Charlottesville, as the summation of Mr. Jefferson's architectural endeavors. Moreover, it reflects his educational philosophy. Its importance to him is expressed in his request to have it included on his grave marker as one of only three of his many accomplishments: "Author of the Declaration of Independence/of the Statute of Virginia for Religious Freedom/and Father of the University of Virginia."

This exhibition was organized by the Bayly Art Museum at the University of Virginia and grows out of the University of Virginia's celebration of the 250th anniversary of Thomas Jefferson's birth. The exhibition draws upon the extraordinary collection of his papers at the University of Virginia, including many drawings from his hand.

Chiswick was the manifestation of an architectural ideal, the perfect setting in which to live a life guided by reason. For Jefferson, the "Academical Village," his phrase for the University of Virginia, was the ideal place where citizens might be trained to continue the great experiment in democracy which he helped shape. Each saw his design as the architecture of a well-ordered universe and considered his project among his greatest achievements.

Retrospective Exhibitions

The work of Bartram Grosvenor Goodhue, architect of Pittsburgh's First Baptist Church close by in Oakland, had been frequently shown in the exhibitions of the Pittsburgh Architectural Club. In 1929, in a retrospective, the School of Architecture at Massachusetts Institute of Technology made it possible for more than 100 of his original drawings to be exhibited at Carnegie Institute.

The opening of the Scaife Galleries in 1974 provided the ideal occasion for mounting a retrospective exhibition of the work of its architect, Edward Larrabee Barnes. The opening of The Heinz Architectural Center in 1993 was likewise the occasion for a retrospective, titled *Aedificare*, of the works of its architects, Pietro Cicognani and Ann Kalla. From *Cassas to Heinz* was the title of the address given at the opening of the center by John Harris, former curator of the drawings collection of London's Royal Institute of British Architects (RIBA). Tracing the history of exhibiting architecture, beginning with Louis François Cassas in Paris in 1806, the speaker paid tribute to the founding in 1972 by Mr. and Mrs. Heinz of the Heinz Gallery for Drawings at RIBA. In just over 20 years, nearly 10 exhibitions have been presented there.

The Drue Heinz Foundation and Other Benefactors

The preview dinner featured New Yorker Tom Wolfe, critic of architecture and author of *Bonfire of the Vanities,* the choice of Mrs. H. J. Heinz, II. The inaugural exhibition *The Shock of the Old: Architectural Drawings from Frank Lloyd Wright to Robert Adam* showed architectural drawings from 1947 by Frank Lloyd Wright to Robert Adam c. 1780-1790. About 50 drawings by British architect Sir Edwin Lutyens ranged from churches to country houses to commercial buildings and furniture. Of the 99 drawings shown, 64 were acquired by funds provided by the Drue Heinz Foundation. The two Adam's drawings were acquired through the Charles J. Rosenbloom Fund. Several of those loaned came from the archives of Carnegie Mellon University and from Pittsburgh Historical & Landmarks Foundation, the Historical Society of Western Pennsylvania, Dollar Bank, Allegheny County, and several architectural firms. The gifts included one from Mrs. John F. Walton and a number from J. L. Hillman Simonds. The two autographed draw-

ings on display came as gifts from architects Richard Neutra and Paul Schweikher in the early 1960s. Leon Arkus, then assistant director, had written to 18 important architects asking for drawings for an exhibition. Most replied that their drawings were not suitable, but Schweikher responded as did Neutra who sent the two exhibited plus four others.

In honor of the opening of the center, a concurrent exhibition *Artists and Architecture* was mounted in the Scaife Special Exhibition Gallery. The theme was illustrated by the multitude of architect-designed examples, especially of furniture, throughout the Scaife and Bruce Galleries.

Overall, the collection of The Heinz Architectural Center focuses on "the art of architecture" through more than 4,000 drawings and fragments and includes sketches, models, schematics, and construction plans for "everything from churches to skyscrapers to monuments and even a 1932 gas station." Now, for the first time, the center's own works may form the basis of future exhibitions, reversing the previous need for The Museum of Art to rely on loaned works or traveling exhibitions. The center surveys the history of Western Pennsylvania architecture and seeks to place it in a national and international context. Designed to fit into its home at The Carnegie Museum of Art, the Center brings to completion the tradition of Architectural study and exhibition begun with Carnegie's Hall of Architecture in 1907.

Information from: Christopher Monkhouse and the brochure published by The Carnegie for the opening of The Heinz Architectural Center; *Carnegie Magazine* November/December 1993 and January/February 1994; *Pittsburgh Post-Gazette:* November 5, 1993, by Donald Miller; December 12, 1993, by Patricia Lowry.

View up the Grand Staircase of The Carnegie Museum of Art, lined with the murals of John White Alexander.

The Great Staircase Hall
The Alexander Murals

The Great Staircase Hall, added a decade after the original building of 1896, symbolizes Andrew Carnegie's monumental gift to his be-loved Pittsburgh. The Hall leads directly into The Carnegie Museum of Natural History and connects eastward to the Scaife Galleries, added in 1974. To the west is The Hall of Architecture. The staircase leads up to the second floor galleries of The Museum of Art. Massive marble pillars encasing steel support the great staircase which rises three stories, from one patterned marble floor to the next. The sculptured bronze doors of the elevators complement the elaborately worked grilles of the balustrades which incorporate less marble and more metal as the stairs ascend from the second to the third floor.

The Murals — The Crowning of Labor
Softening the effect of stone and metal is a series of large murals called *The Crowning of Labor,*

which winds its way around the walls of the staircase. These murals were the masterpiece of John White Alexander who was born in Allegheny City, now North Side, Pittsburgh, in 1856. (More about Alexander in the chapter *Painters with a Pittsburgh Connection.*) Forty-eight of the Institute's panels were painted in his New York studio, but Alexander died in 1915 before he could finish the scheme of 69 canvases, to cover more than 5,000 square feet. It was the largest mural commission ever given to an American artist, for which Alexander was paid $175,000, the highest sum any artist had ever received for a single project.

As art critic Donald Miller wrote in *Carnegie Magazine,* for years there had been speculation as to the identity of the Knight of Labor in black armor, and it has now been established that it was a self-portrait of Alexander. The knight personifies the City of Pittsburgh as his breastplate bears the crest of the city, derived from William Pitt, Earl of Chatham. The knight is rising from the cauldron of iron and steel to be crowned by a goddess. The fluidity of his painting has been likened to that of John Singer Sargent. Influenced by the work of Whistler, Alexander, too, was partial to compositions dominated by monochromes. His studies of the half-nude steelworkers in the panels on the first floor of the Institute have been called vigorous, but today's critics consider his a second-rate talent. This assessment may be changing as indicated by the fact that Alexander's painting *Aurora Leigh,* which until 1980 hung in the Foyer to the Music Hall, has been elevated to the Scaife Galleries in The Museum of Art.

John White Alexander, handsome and jovial, loved Pittsburgh, serving as a juror at many of the *International Exhibitions.* He was an original member of the Pittsburgh Art Commission formed in 1895, deliberating on much of the city's sculpture until his death. Among his many works is the outstanding portrait of Walt Whitman in the Metropolitan Museum of Art, New York. In 1916 Carnegie Institute mounted a memorial exhibition of Alexander's work which traveled to 11 art-oriented organizations.

The Museum of Art, Carnegie Institute Collection Handbook, 1985, includes Studies for The Crowning of Labor 1906-07, a four panel oil on linen sketch, 18-1/2 x 47 inches. The panel appears again in American Paintings and Sculpture to 1945, issued in 1991 by The Carnegie Museum of Art, but is there titled Apotheosis of Pittsburgh: Studies for Carnegie Institute Murals.

The artist was not known to rely on sketches, preferring to work directly on the canvas. This panel, however, was Alexander's gift to William N. Frew, president of the Board of Trustees of Carnegie Institute, 1896-1914. It was Mr. Frew's idea to have a mural by Alexander for the staircase. The panel was successively owned by Mr. Frew's son William Frew, Carnegie president 1943-1948, and by Haugh & Keenan Storage Co., who gave it to the museum in 1948.

The Carnegie Museum of Art
The Collection of Decorative Arts

Department Established in 1953

The Department of Decorative Arts was established in 1953 with a $75,000 grant from the Sarah Scaife Foundation. It "came of age" in 1956 when the Foundation pledged $20,000 annually, for three years, for acquisitions, conditional on $10,000 being committed each year, in cash or works of art, from other sources. Actually the first step came in 1951 under the tenure of Director Gordon Bailey Washburn when a group of decorative arts objects was transferred from The Museum of Natural History to The Museum of Art. Until that time European and American decorative arts were included in the anthropological collections of the "Department of the Museum," the original turn-of-the-century title.

The Ailsa Mellon Bruce Galleries, 1976
The Bruce Collection, 1970

An important new dimension was added to The Museum of Art in Pittsburgh with the opening in 1976 of the Ailsa Mellon Bruce Galleries, funded and endowed by the Andrew W. Mellon Foundation, Inc. These galleries were renovated and reinstalled in 1988. Four spacious rooms, entered from the Grand Stair Hall, display the museum's growing collection of furniture and decorative art objects, pre-circa 1830, of which Mrs. Bruce's collection (originally over 2,800 pieces) is a major part. Andrew W. Mellon, Secretary of the U. S. Treasury under Presidents Harding, Coolidge, and Hoover, was Mrs. Bruce's father. When he was appointed Ambassador to Great Britain, Mrs. Bruce accompanied him to London and served as his official hostess in 1932 and 1933.

The collection formed by Ailsa Mellon Bruce was divided at her death among three American museums. Her Impressionist paintings now belong to the National Gallery in Washington, which was founded by her father,

Ailsa Mellon Bruce, by Philip de Laszlo. National Gallery of Art, Washington D.C.; Gift of Ailsa Mellon Bruce.

Paul Mellon, by William F. Draper. National Gallery of Art, Washington D.C.; Paul Mellon Collection.

Photographs courtesy of Mr. Mellon

who declined to have it bear his name. The gold, silver, and porcelain boxes and some other works of decorative art were given to the Virginia Museum of Art in Richmond, Virginia.

Most of Mrs. Bruce's extraordinary collection of English silver, furniture, and porcelain, French furniture and decorations, Continental European and Asian porcelain, formerly in her homes, came to The Carnegie Museum of Art in her native Pittsburgh. This great gift in 1970 was through the good offices of Mrs. Bruce's brother, Paul Mellon.

In addition to Mrs. Bruce's collection of English and French furniture, the Bruce Galleries contain the museum's 17th century and American furniture collections displayed to illustrate the evolution of furniture style and fine craftsmanship from the 17th to the early 19th century. Shown together with the furniture are tapestries, carpets, and other contemporary textiles, mirrors, chandeliers, engravings, paintings, silver, ceramics, and sculpture.

Tapestries

The walls of the first of the four Bruce Galleries, the Medieval and Renaissance Gallery, are high and windowless to re-create a feeling of the enclosed fortress-like life led by Europe's upper classes in the 15th, 16th, and most of the 17th centuries. They are hung with four important tapestries, one of which illustrates Alexander entering Babylon in triumph, from *The Life of Alexander*, a series designed by Charles Le Brun (1619-1690). These tapestries are only part of the larger collection featured in *Carnegie Magazine*, December 1981. The cover story, a discussion of The Museum of Art's collection of tapestries by a consultant to the Metropolitan Museum of Art, documented for the first time the entire collection of the museum. Art historian Edith A. Standen summed up the purpose of tapestry as that of looking splendid at a distance and being full of delightful surprises near at hand. These tapestries bear out this obser-

vation and constitute an unusually varied and interesting small collection. Chronologically, they extend from the late Middle Ages to near the end of the 18th century. Though most were woven in Brussels, there are examples from the Gobelins manufactory in Paris and some even from England. The subjects run from religious allegory to classical myth to genre scenes, and the dimensions from a huge wall-covering to a small screen panel.

Illustrative of the entertaining qualities of tapestry is the detail of winter from *The Seasons of Lucas*, showing a lusty scene, almost the focal point of the complete tapestry. This is one of two tapestries given The Museum of Art by the Hearst Foundation, in 1954.

Other Collectors, Other Objects

Including the splendid collections of Mrs. Bruce, the museum possesses more than 15,000 decorative art objects, not all of which are on exhibit at any one time. The collection of fine porcelain includes a selection of German early 18th century Meissen pieces from the famous *Swan Service*, and a Meissen covered beaker from the Böttger period. Especially notable was the purchase, in 1988, of the pair of porcelain French vases (caisses a Fleures Carrees) made in 1754 in the Vincennes Factory. Founded in 1738, the factory moved from Vincennes to Sevres in 1756 and is still operating today, in the mid-1990s.

European works of art in the museum's collection from various other sources include terra cotta 17th-18th century models, enameled 11th-18th century pieces, carved wood and ivory figures, and 15th-16th century armor from the Hearst collection. In the early 1980s a significant new direction was set for the collecting of decorative arts. The museum began to acquire objects that would complement eras and areas already well-represented in the paintings collection, namely American and European works from around 1850 to the present.

Miniatures

The museum's collection is rich in small objects, particularly those made of porcelain and precious metals. Objets de vertu include a collection of 18th century European gold boxes and European and American miniature portraits. An early mainstay of the museum's holdings was the Herbert DuPuy collection of miniatures and other small precious objects, given in 1927. (The DuPuy Fund continues to aid acquisitions.)

Sarah Mellon Scaife's miniature scaled reproductions (1 inch equals 1 foot) of her French-style bedroom, her library, and Georgian dining room at Penguin Court, her Ligonier home, display her collection of miniature furniture, silver and porcelain. The series of tiny rooms of Mrs. Scaife, Mrs. Bruce's cousin, may be closely viewed in a display area between the Halls of Sculpture and Architecture. Each Christmas season a larger "miniature," the ever popular 18th century Neapolitan Christmas *presepio* is featured in the Holiday display in Architecture Hall (discussed in the section on the Women's Committee of The Carnegie Museum of Art.)

In the spring of 1994 a dazzling miniature room, styled after *The Salon of the Four Seasons* in the Chateau de Breteuil, France was installed in the Bruce Galleries. The salon was the gift of Ruth McChesney of Sewickley, an internationally known miniaturist, widow of a Pittsburgh industrialist. Mrs. McChesney researched 18th century chateaux to discover one with the period furnishings essentially intact. She designed the overall scheme for the miniature room as well as making the petitpoint carpet, inspired by an 18th century Savonniere at Versailles. Mrs. McChesney engaged a number of other artists, two of whom were also from Sewickley. Jean Wickware made the flowers for the pair of console commodes and Richard Smith painted the portrait of Baron de Breteuil, the fire screen, and the four-panel floor screen from the original in the Getty Museum. The room provides a

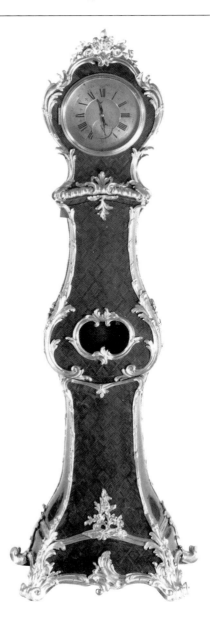

Long Case Clock (Regulateur), c. 1750, by Joseph de Saint-Germain, French; king and other veneers on oak with silvered and gilded bronze; Museum purchase: gift of the Women's Committee and Paul Mellon, 1987.

context for viewing the museum's collection of French furniture of the period.

Furniture

The furniture on display in the Bruce and Scaife Galleries includes representations of English, American, and Continental European pieces. There are: a fine German secretaire-medaillier, from around 1780-90, attributed to David

Roentgen who in 1783 was called "undoubtedly the best cabinet-maker this century;" a superb English rococo-style chest of drawers, attributed to William Gomm (c. 1698-1780) and a magnificent tea table from Portsmouth, New Hampshire, attributed to Robert Harrold (active 1765-1792).

The museum in 1993 acquired an important neo-classical, semi-circular commode, c. 1778 by Thomas Chippendale, (1718-1789) who designed it for Denton Hall in Yorkshire, England. (Chippendale also made other furniture for the Scottish architect/designer Robert Adam, 1728-1792). The purchase was made possible through the Ailsa Mellon Bruce Fund and the Berdan Memorial Trust Fund. These two funds along with other contributions were instrumental in the museum's acquisition of a number of other important additions to the collections. These include a rosewood veneer breakfast table, American, New York c. 1815, acquired in 1987; and a cabinet on stand, Dutch

(**1**) *Side Chair*, c. 1882

(**2**) *Side Chair*, c. 1740

(**3**) *Side Chair*, c. 1740-50

(**4**) *Armchair*, c. 1900

c. 1690-1700, walnut veneer and various inlaid woods and ivory on oak, acquired in 1988. The previous year, through a gift by the Women's Committee and Paul Mellon, the furniture collection was enriched by a long case clock (regulateur), c. 1750 in oak with other wood veneers, silvered and gilded bronze, by Joseph de Saint-Germain (French, master in 1750).

During the early 1980s the museum's holdings of furniture were greatly enhanced by the 25-piece collection of Western Pennsylvania furniture, the gift of Mr. and Mrs. James A. Drain. Included are a fine locally made chest of drawers dated 1799 and a desk and bookcase by Henry Shallenberger of Fayette County, c. 1826, from the Drain's superb collection of late 18th and early 19th century decorative arts.

When the curator of The Carnegie's Department of Decorative Arts, Sarah C. Nichols, was interviewed in June of 1993 by Donald Miller of the *Pittsburgh Post-Gazette*, he noted that "she was surrounded by literally dozens of chairs . . . But she wouldn't sit on them." Enumerating the "dozens" in the collection is beyond the scope of this article but mention may be made of a select few: one of the most elaborate is a side chair, designed by Christian Herter in gilded maple, with mother-of-pearl inlay and embroidered silk upholstery. (1) It was made around 1882 by the Herter Brothers for the New York mansion of William H. Vanderbilt and came to the museum in 1983. In complete contrast is the *Child's Chair*, c. 1920,

———

(2) *Side Chair*, c. 1740, by Giles Grendey, English; walnut, walnut veneer and needlework; Ailsa Mellon Bruce Fund, 1983; (3) *Side chair*, c. 1740-50, American, New York; walnut, walnut veneer on maple; Gift of the Women's Committee in memory of Mrs. John Berdan, 1983; (4) *Armchair*, c. 1900, by Louis Majorelle, French; walnut with original leather upholstery; Decorative Arts Purchase Fund, 1984; (5) *Rocking chair*, 1901, by Charles Rohlfs, American; oak, leather; DuPuy Fund, 1984; (6) *Chair*, c. 1904, by Frank Lloyd Wright, American; oak and leather; Decorative Arts Purchase Fund, 1982.

(5) *Rocking chair*, 1901

(6) *Chair*, c. 1904

(7) *Child's chair*, c. 1920

(7) designed in wood and leather by the Dutch architect, Gerrit Rietveld (1889-1964) and purchased through The Fellows Fund in 1990. Two other chairs designed by architects are the plywood *Long Chair* of 1936 by Marcel Breuer (1902-1981) (9) and corrugated cardboard *Little Beaver with Ottoman*, 1991 by Frank Gehry (b. 1929) (13). Also in the collection is a glass chair, made by the Pittsburgh Plate Glass Company (now PPG Industries) (11) around 1939. A New England "lolling" chair was acquired through the Berdan Fund and the famous DCM chair by Charles Eames was given by Herman Miller, Inc. There are also the chairs designed by Frank Lloyd Wright which may be seen in his San Francisco office now installed in the Heinz Architectural Center of The Museum of Art.

With the founding of The Heinz Architectural Center in 1990, the Decorative Arts Department formalized and pursued with new vigor a collection direction which had existed previously, namely, objects designed by architects. A number of other pieces designed by distinguished architects were acquired, notably a beautiful Hall Settle, 1899, of oak, pewter, brass, and mirror glass designed by the English Arts and Crafts architect Charles Voysey (1857-1941); and a massive desk in red oak, the work of the architect of Pittsburgh's acclaimed Court House, Henry Hobson Richardson, for the Court of Appeals in Albany, New York (1880-1884). Both pieces were purchased by the museum in 1992 through the Berdan Memorial Trust Fund.

---

(8) *Armchair*, designed 1927, made c. 1927-30, by Ludwig Mies van der Rohe, German, designer, and Lily Reich, upholstery designer; chromed steel and cane; DuPuy Fund, 1982; (12) *Chair for R.A. Miller*, c. 1989, by Beverly Buchanan; wood; Patrons Art Fund, 1992.

(8) *Armchair*, c. 1927-30

(9) *Long chair*, c. 1936

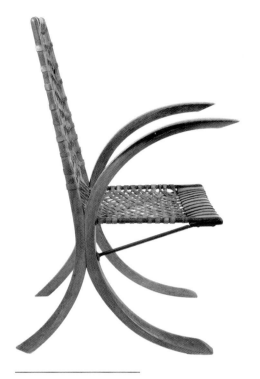

(10) *Chair*, c. 1939

A more ephemeral appearance in the museum was *The Modern Chair: Ideal and Real*, an exhibition in the Forum Gallery, (formerly the Entrance Gallery), July 23 - October 2, 1994. The curators selected eight chairs from the museum's collection to show the ways 20th century artists, architects, designers, and craftsmen have addressed the functional, symbolic, and stylistic aspects of the chair. Works by the aforementioned Rietveld and Gehry joined those of Pennsylvania craftsman Wharton Esherick (10), and contemporary artists Beverley Buchanan and Richard Artschwager. Six red granite chairs, 1500 pounds each, from the collection of Mellon Bank, on view beside the museum's Forbes Avenue fountains, complemented the exhibition. Called *Chairs for Six*, the work of Scott Burton, these chairs were first shown at The Museum of Art in the 1985 *Carnegie International.*

(11) *Armchair*, c. 1939

(12) *Chair for R. A. Miller* c. 1989

(13) *Chair and Ottoman, "Little Beaver,"* 1991

Large-scale Special Exhibitions
of Decorative Arts

Courts and Colonies: The William and Mary Style in Holland, England, and America was the first large-scale international decorative arts exhibition to be organized by The Carnegie Museum of Art. It was mounted in collaboration with the Cooper-Hewitt Museum, which is housed in Andrew Carnegie's New York mansion. The Carnegie's director, Phillip M. Johnston, served as curator of the American section of the exhibition and contributed an essay discussing the William and Mary style in America to the catalogue. The exhibit celebrated the 300th anniversary of the Glorious Revolution of 1688, which brought William III and Mary II to the English throne. It was the first single exhibition to treat the William and Mary style from the viewpoint of all three countries.

In addition to the exhibitions the museum has organized in recent years, it should be noted that other important exhibitions of decorative arts produced in the last decade traveled to Pittsburgh. Included were: *The Machine Age in America 1918-1944* (1987) and recently two significant exhibitions of African Art organized by the Center of African Art in New York City, *Art/Artifact, African Art Through Western Eyes* (1989) and *Africa Explores: 20th Century African Art* (1992). Other major exhibitions of decorative arts have been *The American Craftsman and the European Tradition 1620-1820* (1990) and *Silver in America, 1840-1940: A Century of Splendor* (1995).

Silver

A 17th century German silver sculpture of Hercules and Antaeus was among the first substantial purchases for the department made by the first curator, Herbert P. Weissberger. The silver of the Ailsa Mellon Bruce collection comprised nearly 200 examples of early French, Irish, and English work. More than half of them, 103

Two-handled Cup, Cover, and Stand, 1659; silver; Women's Committee Acquisition Fund and John Berdan Memorial Fund, 1990.

pieces, were made in London, and constituted an important collection in themselves. This London silver represents the high quality of craftsmanship and the variety of English taste from the 17th and 18th centuries to the reign of William IV in the second quarter of the 19th century. Examples include two early silver double-handled, lidded cups 1681, 1683-84; the one photographed, 1659-60; and a double-handled cup with stand, 1658-60, purchased by the museum in 1990.

Two pieces of silver with Western Pennsylvania connections came to the museum in 1980. A mug, c. 1817-1833, by Joseph Lownes, with O'Hara family history was donated by George S. Ebbert, Jr. and Mr. and Mrs. James K. Ebbert in memory of Mrs. James M. Schoonmaker, Jr. An important 1848 water pitcher retailed by the Pittsburgh silversmith James B. McFadden, inscribed to Mrs. Charles Avery, wife of a 19th century Pittsburgh cotton merchant, was the gift of Mr. and Mrs. Michael Malley, Jr.

One of the earliest examples of American silver in the collection was made about 1750 by Jacob Hurd of Boston (1702-1758). The silver *Caster*, for sugar or pepper, was given to the museum in 1987 by Mr. and Mrs. Edward Holyoke Schoyer, descendants of the original owner Dr. Edward Augustus Holyoke (1728-1829).

The museum received a piece of Pittsburgh history by gift from James O'Hara Denny IV in 1988. The Denny silver service for tea and coffee was made by Baldwin Gardner in 1817 for Elizabeth, daughter of General James O'Hara, wife of Harmer Denny, whose father, Ebenezer Denny, was the first Mayor of Pittsburgh. (The O'Hara heiress, Mary Croghan Schenley, gave 300 acres of her estate to the city of Pittsburgh for Schenley Park.)

In 1993 the museum acquired *Fruit Stand*, in silver, designed by the English artist Charles Ashbee (1863-1942) who had trained as an architect. It was made in 1905 by the London Guild of Handicraft which was founded by Ashbee in 1888 and held a royal warrant as a guild of jewelers and silversmiths to Queen Alexandra, wife of Britain's King Edward VII. The floral designs of the piece reflected the English Garden Movement of the early 20th century.

Ceramics

Ceramics is the topic of this section but first a note about glass. The O'Hara and Craig factory, founded in 1797, was Pittsburgh's first glasshouse in what was to become a thriving industry. The Bakewell Company was a prominent manufacturer as was R. B. Curling & Sons, Fort Pitt Glass Works, which was founded in 1827. The Historical Society of Western Pennsylvania holds a comprehensive collection of Pittsburgh glass from the early days of the city's heyday as an important glass-making center in America. The Carnegie Museum of Art has in its decorative arts collection a distinguished example of the earliest surviving glass produced by the Curling factory . . . a pair of decanters made in 1828. They were given to Robert Curling's daughter Martha to celebrate her marriage to George

Albree and were a gift to the museum from Alice B. Albree in 1946.

Since 1982 the museum has had an active interest in contemporary ceramics and in that year the museum was the recipient of eight examples of the work of the distinguished ceramist Adelaide Alsop Robineau (1865-1929) given by her grandson, Dr. Dana Robineau Kelley. The artist's porcelains had won grand prizes at international expositions in Turin, Italy in 1911 and at the Panama-Pacific at San Francisco in 1915. The Metropolitan Museum in New York honored her work with a retrospective exhibition after her death. *The Urn of Dreams*, 1921, is the most recent of the works here, the earliest dates to 1905.

Sacrifice of Iphigenia on her Wedding Day, 1983, by Rudy Autio, American; porcelain; Decorative Arts Purchase Fund, 1984.

Also in 1982 a collection of primarily 18th century Black Basaltes Ware, a medium perfected by Josiah Wedgwood (1730-1795) and made by his company in England from 1769 to the present, came to the museum. This collection of Black Basaltes and Jasper Ware was assembled by the late Tillie S. Speyer and was given in her memory by her children.

Contemporary Ceramics and the Vessel Aesthetic was the title of an article in the January/February, 1986 issue of *Carnegie Magazine* by Sarah Nichols, then assistant curator of Decorative Arts. The work of a number of artist/teachers was discussed and illustrated, including Rudy Autio's *Sacrifice of Iphigenia on her Wedding Day*, 1983, which the museum acquired in 1994, along with works by Wayne Higby, Susanne Stephenson, Betty Woodman, and Adrian Saxe, all American artists, born from 1930 to 1943. Several of these and other contemporary ceramics are displayed on the balcony of the Hall of Sculpture.

In the spring of 1991 the works of contemporary ceramicist Warren MacKenzie were exhibited (March 3-June 2) and discussed in *Carnegie Magazine*, March/April issue of that year. The collection of Mr. and Mrs. Charles H. Carpenter in 1995 brings the museum the *Rainforest Table* by contemporary furniture maker Edward Zuzza, a 17th century Sunflower Chest from Connecticut, and a rare Tiffany punch bowl of 1906, designed by Louis Comfort Tiffany.

The Decorative Arts Department is also responsible for the small collections of non-Western objects, from Africa, Asia, and the South Pacific, in The Museum of Art. The gift in 1973 of the Asian collection of Walter Read Hovey, chairman of the Art Department of the University of Pittsburgh, aided by selective purchases, significantly increased the scope of the museum's collection. It includes sculpture, ceramics, and bronzes, as well as the Chinese and Japanese ivories of the Henry J. Heinz

collection. In the 1970s the museum formed a small but interesting collection of African art. This was augmented in 1993 with the gift from Gareth Griffiths and Drs. Helen and Robert Overs, relatives of Walter Overs, Bishop of Liberia from 1919-1922, of his vast collection of African objects.

Benefactors

In addition to Mrs. Bruce, Mrs. Scaife, and Mr. and Mrs. Drain, individual donors to the collection of decorative arts of The Museum of Art, Carnegie Institute, have historically included Mrs. John Berdan, Mrs. J. Frederic Byers, Mr. and Mrs. Charles Denby, Mr. Herbert DuPuy, Mr. and Mrs. Aleon Deitch, Mrs. Paul B. Ernst, Mrs. Fred C. Foy, Mr. Howard Heinz, Mrs. Vira I. Heinz, Mr. and Mrs. James H. Heroy, Dr. Walter Read Hovey, Mr. Jay C. Leff, Mr. and Mrs. Alan G. Lehman, Mr. and Mrs. Edward O'Neil II, Mr. and Mrs. John F. Walton, Jr., and Mrs. Thomas C. Wurtz. Among more recent benefactors are: Mr. and Mrs. Samuel Bell, Mr. and Mrs. Stanley Gumberg, Joan B. Lappe-Bowman, Donald C. McVay, and Mr. and Mrs. Alexander Speyer III, and others whose names have been and are to be recorded in the annual reports of Carnegie Institute.

The Carnegie Museum of Art
The Scaife Gallery

Less than ten years after the opening of the Ailsa Mellon Bruce Galleries, The Museum of Art opened the monumental Scaife Gallery presented in memory of Sarah Mellon Scaife, first cousin to Mrs. Bruce. This magnificent addition to Carnegie Institute, to Pittsburgh and the region, was given and endowed by the Scaife family and the Scaife Foundation. Completed in 1974, the gallery provides: 12 galleries for display of The Museum of Art's permanent collections of paintings, drawings, prints, and sculpture; the administration offices; the Café, Art Shop, Forum Gallery, Department of Film and Video, Children's Room, Museum of Art Theater, and a cloakroom which adjoins the old part of the building. Architect Edward Larrabee Barnes conceived the Scaife both as a separate building and as an organic extension of Carnegie Institute. The emerald pearl granite from Norway and the 40-foot-high glass curtain walls of the new building are a perfect complement to the weathered grey sandstone exterior of the original structure.

Night, 1939, by Aristide Maillol, French; bronze; Gift of the A. W. Mellon Charitable Trust, 1960.

As a part of the Institute, the Scaife Gallery amplifies and extends the general plan and circulation. Much of the ground floor is built of stone as an extension of the exterior. The effect is of a rugged, street-like quality, excellent for the display of large sculpture. When the

Scaife opened, the first work commissioned in honor of the occasion was *The Free Exchange*, 1973-1974, a large-scale red, white, and blue, electrically driven sculpture by the French master Jean DuBuffet, the gift of the Scaife family. It enlivened the space for which it was commissioned, the entrance corridor of the Scaife Gallery, until some time after the death of the artist May 12, 1985.

As a gallery of The Museum of Art, the Scaife has its own existence, its own controls, and two entrances: the Fountain entrance from Forbes Avenue and the Sculpture Court entrance from the parking area and garage. Serving as a meeting place for patrons of the Café is Dan Graham's *The Heart Pavilion* in two-way mirror, glass, and aluminum, from the 1991 *Carnegie International.*

The Sculpture Court entrance to the Scaife Gallery is dominated by a single work of art. The *Tightrope Walker*, a realistic figure in plaster by sculptor George Segal, balances high above with great dramatic effect. In contrast to the ground floors, the galleries above are designed to show the paintings lit by the soft light of the changing sky. The ascent to these galleries is up the broad, gradual staircase flanking the 40-foot glass wall of the Sculpture Court. Entrance to the 12 Scaife galleries is through a small sitting area in memory of Sarah Mellon Scaife, whose portrait by Everett Raymond Kinstler hangs there.

The Scaife galleries were refurbished and the collection reinstalled in 1984 in observance of the 10th anniversary of the opening of the new gallery of The Museum of Art. The Founders-Patrons Day that year featured an exhibition of Mark Rothko's *Works on Paper* 1925-1970.

Across from the galleries for the permanent collection to the right are the Heinz Galleries for special exhibitions. These constitute a bridge, making it possible to circulate in the new and old areas of the building without a change in ambiance. The Heinz Galleries arrive in the center of the Institute building at the Grand Staircase Hall, on the other side of which are the Ailsa Mellon Bruce Galleries for furniture and the decorative arts.

The spacious Heinz Galleries provided the area for an internal expansion of The Museum of Art with the creation of The Heinz Architectural Center which opened in 1993. Entered from the balcony of the Hall of Sculpture, the center is the gift of the Drue Heinz Foundation in memory of H. J. Heinz II. (A separate chapter is devoted to The Heinz Architectural Center.)

In 1994, for their 20th anniversary, the 12 Scaife Galleries were completely renewed and redesigned by Richard Gluckman, "the alchemist of light" who transformed the Frick & Lindsay building into the stunning Andy Warhol Museum. Under the guidance of Director Phillip Johnston, the curators reorganized and reinstalled the paintings and art objects with an "international" philosophy: that is, in chronological progression, showing, for instance, works from America contemporaneous with those in England, France or elsewhere, highlighting their relationships. The $140,500 undertaking was funded by the Scaife Family Foundation in memory of Sarah Scaife whose generosity during the 1960s, continued by her family into the 70s, made it possible for the museum to acquire many works by the great Impressionists and Post-Impressionists.

The Scaife Gallery was the first major expansion of the Carnegie Institute since the early 1900s. It contains 155,000 square feet of space and encloses an additional 16,000 square foot outdoor Sculpture Court. With the addition, at a cost of $12.5 million, the Institute has 800,000 square feet, about twice the size of the 40-story IBM Building in New York City. A remarkable accomplishment in 1974 was the completion of the building on time and under budget by architect Barnes and the Turner

The Tightrope Walker, 1969, by George Segal, American; Fellows Fund and National Endowment for the Arts, 1970.

Construction Co. Andrew Carnegie would have been pleased.

The Carnegie Museum of Art Sculpture Court Collection of Sculpture

The outdoor Sculpture Court, added with the Scaife Gallery in 1974, links the new and old sections of Carnegie Institute. Between the massive elements of the building, honey locust trees and a cascading waterfall provide a serene garden-setting for experiencing the quality of the sculpture. Architect Edward Larrabee Barnes used a dramatic double zig-zag pattern of tiers of steps which, seen from below, merge visually yet permit sculpture to be positioned on the different levels. The sculpture may be viewed from another perspective from the stairway to the Scaife Galleries.

As of 1994 the works exhibited in the Sculpture Court include: *Reclining Figure*, 1957, by Henry Moore (the sole work relocated to accomodate the 1995 *International*); *Shutter*, 1974, by Anthony Caro; *Tropical Garden's Presence*, 1974, by Louise Nevelson; *Three Forms*, 1970, by James Rosati; *Blue Parallel*, 1967, by Duayne Hatchett; *Figure 1964 (Opus 357)*, by Barbara Hepworth; *Two Slender Lines*, 1981, by George Rickey; and, near the waterfall, the seated nude, *Night*, 1939, by Aristide Maillol. Upon entering the Scaife Gallery from the parking area one is aware of George Segal's *The Tightrope Walker*, 1969, overhead, pervading the entire space with its presence.

The Hall of Architecture contains plaster casts of architectural and sculptural treasures from antiquity. The Hall of Sculpture incorporates *Panathenic Procession* as an interior frieze, the original of which was carved under the supervision of Phidias, the 5th century B.C. Greek sculptor. Around the balustrade of the balcony there are other reproductions of heroic Greek and Roman figures. Occupying the vast marble floor of the hall in 1994, however, was the contemporary work *Fallen Timber* 1980, by Carl Andre, b. 1935. Twenty-four squared columns of wood arranged in military-style formation, gave a changing perspective as the viewer circled the installation. The hall awaits new large works from the 1995 *International*. They will join several other contemporary sculptures which entered the collections after being exhibited in the *Internationals*. On the Forbes Avenue side of the building, near the fountain entrance to The Museum of Art is Richard Serra's towering *Carnegie*, created especially for the site and the *International* of 1985. It was given by Mrs. William R. Roesch in memory of her husband, president of United States Steel Corporation. The 40-foot sculpture is of four giant vertical panels of weathering

Reclining Figure, 1957 by Henry Moore, American, won the $1,500 second prize in the 1958 *International Exhibition of Contemporary Painting and Sculpture*. It was purchased by Mr. and Mrs. G. David Thompson and given to The Museum of Art in memory of his son David.

steel, leaning inward to touch at their top corners, leaving a small passage below which can be entered to glimpse a patch of sky. Just inside the museum is the *Heart Pavilion*, by Dan Graham, b. USA 1941, created for the 1991 *International*. It is a heart-shaped construction in two-way mirror, glass, and aluminum, which the viewer may enter to enjoy the reflected images. One contemporary sculpture remembered in that main entrance hall, not on view in 1994, but bears mention. It is the colorful, kinetic *Free Exchange* 1973-74 by the French artist Jean DuBuffet, who died in Paris May 12, 1985, aged 83. The first work of art created to celebrate the opening of the Scaife Gallery in 1974, it was the gift of the Sarah Scaife Foundation.

Many works of sculpture are dispersed among the paintings and decorative arts displayed in the Scaife and Bruce Galleries: *Great Winged Creature*, 1963, by Alicia Panalba; *Khajuraho*, 1979, by Jack Youngerman; *Pisthetairos in Ipse*, 1965, by Eduardo Paolozzi;

Pink Leaf, 1956, by Louise Nevelson; Jean Arp's *Sculpture Classique,* 1964; and a portrait bust of *George Bernard Shaw,* 1934, by Jacob Epstein (1880-1955). The polished steel sculpture *Chinese Sleeve No. 2,* 1960-72, by Isamu Noguchi, is derivative of origami, the Oriental art of folded paper. Giacometti's 1961 *International* prize-winning *Man Walking* is there, as is Marini's *Horse and Rider.* Equally impressive is *St. John the Baptist,* c. 1878, by Auguste Rodin, other examples of whose work are also owned by The Museum of Art. *Walking* by Alexander Archipenko was given by the artist's wife. *Aizian* (In the Wind), 1958, is an early piece by Eduardo Chillida, co-winner of the 1979 Andrew W. Mellon award of the *Pittsburgh Carnegie International.* Another work shown in that exhibition is *Large Torso,* 1974, a powerful bronze sculpture by leading Abstract Expressionist Willem de Kooning. Several sculptures by other contemporary artists have been

Elegy II (Opus 134), 1946, by Barbara Hepworth, English; Gift of Ruth H. Jackson in memory of Alexander H. Jackson, 1982.

Head of a Boy, 1906, by Pablo Picasso, Spanish; Museum purchase: gift of Howard Heinz Endowment, 1966.

Lost Objects, 1991, by Allan McCollum, American; enamel on cast concrete, *Carnegie International,* 1991.

added to the collection. Some of them are: *Bird,* a limestone sculpture by William Edmondson (American, c. 1883-1951); *Nautilus,* 1962, an iron and concrete sculpture by James Wines; and *Elegy II (Opus 134),* 1946, by Barbara Hepworth. Nine works by the noted Pittsburgh-born sculptor Mary Callery, 1903-1977, were bequeathed in her estate and came to the museum in 1981.

From the 1985 *International,* a large (181" h x 155" w x 207" d) site-specific sculpture *Promised Land,* by Bill Woodrow, b. 1948, England, was acquired through the Mrs. George L. Craig, Jr. Fund. (It consists of steel office cabinets, car hoods, enamel paint, and men's clothes, including 36 jackets.) Another, completely different type of work acquired from the 1985 *International* is the fabricated neon sculpture *Having Fun/Good Life/Symptoms,* by Bruce Nauman, b. 1941 USA. It was the gift of the partners of the law firm, Reed Smith Shaw & McClay.

The 1988 exhibition brought the museum *Dos Nones,* 1988, a work in iron, polymethyl methacrylate sheeting, by Susana Solano, b. 1946 in Barcelona, Spain. From the 1991 *International* several other sculptures entered the collection: *Unreadable Humidity* by Huang Yong Ping, b. 1954, China; two works exhibited together, titled *Offerings* by Ann Hamilton, b. 1956 USA; *Cell II,* by Louise Bourgeois, b. 1911 USA, from the Heinz Family Fund; and *Supplement #7 Seychelles 7/8,* by Christopher Williams, b. 1956 USA, gift of the Luhring Augustine Hetzler Gallery, Santa Monica gallery.

A work of historical interest is *Victory,* c. 1912, by Augustus Saint-Gaudens, 1848-1907. The sculptor was born in Ireland, the son of a French shoemaker, and was brought to America before his first birthday. At the peak of his career he had a virtual monopoly on major sculptural projects in the United States through his friendship with noted architect, H. H. Richardson and others. Carnegie's

Victory, c. 1912, gilded bronze, by Augustus Saint-Gaudens, American, b. Ireland; Museum purchase, 1919.

Victory is a reduced version of the monumental tribute to General Sherman, victor of the Civil War, which is on the Grand Army Plaza at the entrance to Central Park in New York City. The full-scale version was cast in 1902 and, after the death of the sculptor in 1907, his widow authorized the casting of several reduced versions, including this one of about 1912.

A bas-relief by Saint-Gaudens, 1882, of his son Homer (second director of The Museum of Art, 1923-50), was given by General and Mrs. Henry L. Jones, II in memory of Samuel Harden Church (president of Carnegie Institute 1914-1943). The museum also received an elegant fiberglass work *Khajuraho,* 1979, by Jack Youngerman, given by Mr. and Mrs. Sidney M. Feldman in memory of Richard Mace Feldman. The museum's first motor powered op-art work is *Tuning Forks,* by Wen Ying Tsai, meant to be seen under strobe-light illumination. It was given by Professor and Mrs. William Mullins.

A number of other artists, as well as the European and American, are represented in the sculpture collection, including: Arp, Andre, Barnard, Barye, Bloomer, Bourdelle, Braque, Buchanan, Butler, Caro, Carpeaux, Corbero, Cronin, Dalou, Dioda, Duff, Epstein, Flannagan, Gerhard, Hiltmann, Ipousteguy, Kelley, Lassaw, Laurens, Manship, Nadelman, and Ubac. Although the collection has concentrated on the work of European and American artists, there is a small but choice group of Ancient, Eastern, and African art as well. They range in age and nationality from the Roman sarcophagus of 225 A.D., given by Baronness Cassel van Doorn in 1953, to the 13th century's Chinese goddess and bronze Shiva from India. From Africa there is a Nigerian chief depicted on a relief plaque of copper alloy dating from the late 16th to the early 17th century which was purchased in 1958. These works and a Japanese ivory, 1880-1900, from the H. J. Heinz collection, are pictured in the *Collection Handbook* of The Museum of Art, 1985.

Although the Court is the focal point for the sculpture of The Museum of Art, there are many outstanding works placed throughout the galleries, the Institute and, indeed, the city of Pittsburgh. Outside the public television station WQED on Fifth Avenue is *Tower Iron No. 5* by Joseph Goto, the first sculpture of The Museum of Art to be put into the community on loan. *Forest Devil,* by Kenneth Snelson, was shown at the Three Rivers Arts Festival in 1977, and is now in Mellon Square in downtown Pittsburgh. It was acquired by gifts from the people of Pittsburgh through the efforts of the Women's Committee, Museum of Art. Alice Snyder, of that committee, was also instrumental in the selection of a number of works placed in The Allegheny Landing Sculpture Park on the shores of the Allegheny River. Ned Smyth's two-part architectonic sculpture dominates Pittsburgh's first public sculpture park. *Piazza Lavoro,* four large facades surrounding a column, sits like an acropolis above the slope to *Mythic Source,* a column in the center of a mosaic pavement on

the river's edge. The monumental work establishes the central axis of the park, where three other sculptures are sited as well: *The Builders,* a realistic bronze, by Georges Danhires; *Pittsburgh Variations,* a playful, colorful environment, by George Sugarman; and *The Forks,* abstract forms, by Isaac Witkin. All were site-specific works commissioned to interpret the theme of this city's industrial and labor history. The work by Smyth, (American, b. 1948) was the gift of the Allegheny Conference on Community Development, commissioned by the Heinz family and the H. J. Heinz Company in 1984.

This brief introduction can only mention some of the sculptural riches in the collections of The Carnegie Museum of Art.

The Carnegie Museum of Art

The Pittsburgh International Exhibitions *of Contemporary Art, 1896-1994*

Carnegie International Exhibition

"That the *Internationals* spread goodwill among nations through art understanding is to be affirmed by the popularity of the Prix Carnegie abroad. It has probably brought more fame to Pittsburgh than any other civic activity."

— *Leon Anthony Arkus*
Catalogue of Retrospective Exhibition
December 5, 1958-February 8, 1959

In celebration of the opening, in 1890, of the Carnegie Library in Allegheny, Andrew Carnegie subsidized the first large exhibition of European paintings in Western Pennsylvania. This success led him to invite the Art Society of Pittsburgh to arrange another show in 1895 to inaugurate the opening of the Carnegie Library in Schenley Park. In the exhibition were

Panathenic Procession, frieze by Phidias of Greece, Hall of Sculpture, The Carnegie, 1907.

325 canvases, some by American but most by European painters. Andrew Carnegie provided financially for the succeeding exhibitions, reasoning that the Institute would thereby have the opportunity to choose from the best of the contemporary work in building a fine permanent collection. The Andrew Carnegie Fund continues to be an important source of support for acquisitions for the collection of The Museum of Art.

Catalogue of the *First Annual Exhibition*, 1896

In 1896 the *First Annual Exhibition* was formed by John W. Beatty, art director of the newly organized Carnegie Institute, and was juried by the Fine Arts Committee of the Institute. (The term *International* was not used until 1920.) The time between the organization of the Carnegie Fine Arts and Museum Collection Fund and the opening date of the exhibition was so limited that many of the invited painters found it impossible to send their works. The catalogue was augmented by paintings on loan by their collector-owners, and the director acknowledged indebtedness to the generosity of: H. C. Frick, A. M. Byers, John Caldwell, Mrs. William Thaw, Jr. of Pittsburgh, Charles L. Freer of Detroit, Alexander Reid of Glasgow, art dealers in Paris, London, and M. Knoedler of New York, as well as to the Academy of Fine Arts, Philadelphia.

The catalogue included photographs of the artists as well as of some of the paintings. Winslow Homer's *The Wreck* was number one. After the information about the paintings and the artists, there was a detailed and glowing description of the museum's 15 reproductions of, "the greatest pieces of sculpture in the world," the originals of which were said to be in the Vatican and museums in Rome, Florence, and Naples in Italy, as well as in the Louvre in Paris, and the British Museum in London. As a crescendo there was a colorful description of the 524-foot frieze by the Greek sculptor Phidias, from the time of Pericles, titled the *Panathenic Procession*, which graces the walls of the Hall of Sculpture. Lastly, there was an explanation of the reproduced panels of *Lucia Della Robbia*, created about 1431-1440 with the theme of boys dancing and angels singing.

In 1896, 60 artists from the United States were represented, plus 54 from France, 16 from Scotland, 11 from England, 10 from "Bavaria," and one each from Italy, Canada, and Sweden. Among the United States group were 30 artists from Pennsylvania, including 11 women. Of the women, Cecilia Beaux, of Philadelphia, received third prize in 1896 when the jury was composed of the Fine Arts Committee of Carnegie Institute. The following year Miss Beaux served on the Jury of Award, and in 1899 her painting *Mother and Daughter* was awarded first prize. The Museum of Art owns her portrait of Mrs. Andrew Carnegie.

One exhibitor in the 1898 *International* was Anna Elizabeth Klumpke (1856-1942), represented by her portrait of the famed French painter of horses, Rosa Bonheur. Klumpke had received many awards for her work prior to her meeting in 1889 with the French artist, 34 years her senior. The two kindred spirits lived and worked together in a chateau south of Paris until Bonheur's death in 1899, leaving Klumpke as her beneficiary. On the occasion of the centennial of the birth of Bonheur in 1922, the American artist presented the portrait to The Metropolitan Museum of New York which already owned Bonheur's masterpiece *The Horse Fair*. Mrs. William Thaw, Jr. acknowledged as a lender of art in the catalogue of the first *Carnegie International*, was also the subject of a portrait painted in Pittsburgh in 1897 by Klumpke. Years later, when World War I broke in 1914, Klumpke turned the chateau which she had inherited from Bonheur into a hospital for French soldiers, and Mrs. Thaw was a major contributor to its upkeep.

Juries of Award, to 1922

After 1896, until 1922, the Juries of Award consisted of ten painters elected by the contributing artists; two jurors to be European. Artist members of the jury have included such well-known figures as Henri Matisse, Thomas Eakins, Edward Hopper, Marcel Duchamp, William Merrit Chase, and Louise Nevelson. Starting in the '30s some museum directors were appointed as well; they included Alfred H. Barr, Jr., Perry Rathbone, James Thrall Soby, James Johnson Sweeney, and Seymour Knox. In later years the jury consisted of two artists and two critics, involving art historians such as Lionello Venturi, Lawrence Alloway, Adelyn Breeskin, and Roland Penroe. Actor and collector Vincent Price was a member in 1958. Screening committees were appointed in London, Munich, Paris, and The Hague to accept works for the exhibitions from those submitted in their individual cities. The committees were comprised of artists such as American expatriates John Singer Sargent, Mary Cassatt, and James McNeill Whistler as well as Maurice Denis, Augustus John, and John Lavery.

The International, *Single Largest Art Event in the United States*

From its beginning in 1896, *The Pittsburgh International Exhibition of Contemporary Art* became the single largest art event in the United States and through most of its history has been one of only three or four comparable exhibitions in the world. It is the second oldest, the Venice Biennale having preceded Pittsburgh's first by a few months. In 1958 the *Pittsburgh International* was its 41st such exhibit while the Venice Biennale of that year was the 29th in the series. The New York Times reviewing the 1982 Biennale characterized it as, "the sick man of the international exhibition circuit . . . illness dates . . . from 1968 . . ."

The Carnegie Museum of Art, is virtually the nation's oldest museum of modern art. The first purchase made by The Museum of Art from the first *International* were *The Wreck* by Winslow Homer, 1896, winner of the gold medal and $5,000 prize. The record of works Homer exhibited at the *Internationals* is an impressive one: he submitted to the first eight and to the tenth (1896-1901, 1903-1904, 1907) and he never had a work rejected. In 1898 a special exhibition of Homer's watercolors was held at Carnegie Institute as part of the third *International*, and in 1908 a retrospective loan show of 22 of his greatest oils was included as a part of the 11th *International*.

Homer Saint-Gaudens

Portrait of a Boy by John Singer Sargent, 1890, from the first *International* was also purchased by the museum in 1932. The boy portrayed was Homer Saint-Gaudens, director of the Carnegie Institute's Department of Fine Arts, now The Museum of Art, from 1923 to 1950. In 1981, The Museum of Art received a bas-relief portrait-sculpture of the boy Homer, created by his father, famed sculptor Augustus Saint-Gaudens, in 1882, almost a century earlier. As director, Homer Saint-Gaudens selected the works for the

Portrait of a Boy, 1890, by John Singer Sargent, American b. Italy; Patrons Art Fund, 1932.

Portrayed is Homer Saint-Gaudens, Director of The Museum of Art, 1923-1950.

annual *Pittsburgh International Exhibitions* and reformed the unwieldy jury system from an elected to an appointed group of fewer members. In 1924, Saint-Gaudens instituted the Popular Prize, an award based on the public's response to the works of art.

The International *Changes Format*
In 1902 the exhibition was a singular departure from the first six, returning in effect to the earlier plan of showing a major number of works from collectors in the Pittsburgh vicinity. As many as 155 masterworks from the previous 300 years were borrowed from public and private collections in the United States and included works by Eugene Delacroix, Anthony Van Dyck, Rembrandt, Peter Paul Rubens, Frans Hals, and Edouard Manet.

The following year only American artists living in the United States were invited, and the record attendance of 138,000 gave proof to its popularity. However, the international scope was revived in 1904. For that exhibition and for 1905, a temporary brick building was erected near the construction site of the addition to the original building. The first hiatus in the annual exhibits occurred in 1906 due to preparations for the opening of the enlarged Carnegie Institute building.

New Galleries for the 11th International in 1907
The eleventh *International* in 1907 inaugurated the new art galleries with the largest exhibit, 515 paintings, and attracted more than 142,000 visitors, a new high in attendance. With the 1908 exhibition, the inclusion of one-man shows as part of the *International* was initiated with 22 canvases by Winslow Homer. This was followed by individual shows of the work of Alfred East, Frederick Childe Hassam, J. Alden Weir, John Lavery, Lucien Simon, Paul Dougherty, and Emile René Menard.

The Carnegie Museum First to Buy Work of Frederick Childe Hassam
The artist honored with a one-man show in connection with the *International* of 1910 was Frederick Childe Hassam, who had 38 works exhibited. Beginning with the *International* of 1896 and ending with that of 1935, 90 of Hassam's paintings were included, winning awards in 1898 and in 1905. The artist served on the Jury of Award in 1903, 1904, and in 1910. The Museum of Art was the first to buy the work of Childe Hassam with the purchase, from the 1899 *International*, of his famous *Winter on Fifth Avenue*, 1892. From the *International* of 1909, the museum acquired Hassam's *Spring Morning*, 1909.

War Causes Suspension of the International Exhibitions

World War I, 1914-1918, caused the suspension of the *International Exhibitions*. In 1920 they resumed annually as the *International Exhibition* in which a special exhibition of bronzes by Auguste Rodin was included, the only sculpture shown prior to the 1958 *International*. Financial difficulties increased, however, until a grant in 1927 from the Honorable Andrew W. Mellon and Mr. Richard B. Mellon, both Trustees of Carnegie Institute, made it possible to continue the *Internationals* for a few years. In 1931 the attendance was a record of 161,747, possibly because of the controversy concerning the prize-winning painting, *Suicide in Costume*, by Franklin C. Watkins, who was not claimed as a relative by the Pittsburgh Watkins family.

Depressed economic conditions and lack of funds caused cancellation of the exhibit in 1932, but the *Internationals* resumed in 1933. The 1935 exhibition, called the "Mail Order Exhibition," was unusual in being assembled through correspondence between Director Saint-Gaudens and 12 assistants in Europe who helped in the selection process. Financial difficulties precluded transatlantic travel. In 1937, through the Patrons Art Fund, the museum acquired Edward Hopper's *Cape Cod Afternoon*, one of the 42 paintings sold from that exhibition. The *International Exhibitions* continued through the 1939 show which included a group of émigré artists displaced by the fighting in Europe, but World War II finally brought the *Internationals* again to a halt.

Throughout the '20s and '30s, the exhibitions provided the occasion for critics' battles in which the advance of modernism into America, especially modernist abstraction, was met with fierce resistance in the press. When Braque's *The Yellow Cloth* won first prize in 1937, the *New York Herald Tribune* critic wrote:

"A more purposeless jumble I have never seen, and there is nothing in the smallest degree interesting about it. The composition, as I have indicated, is weak, so is the drawing, and the color has no charm or 'quality' whatever. Why *The Yellow Cloth* received the first prize remains a mystery, unless it is to be explained on the hypothesis that the jury desired to make a gesture toward the left."

Survey of American Painting, the Exhibition in 1940

In 1940 the Institute offered, instead of the exhibition of international art, a *Survey of American Painting*, retrospective in viewpoint. The following year the exhibition was entitled *Directions in American Painting*, which was said to be forward-looking, involving exclusively the participation of living American artists whose paintings had never appeared in a *Carnegie International*. The show consisted of 302 paintings selected by the Jury from 4,812 canvases submitted by artists, citizens of the United States. Twenty-eight of the artists were from Pennsylvania, among them Robert Lepper of Carnegie Tech in Pittsburgh and N.C. Wyeth of Chadds Ford. Sixty-some of the paintings accepted were the work of women.

The Internationals *in the 1950s*

In 1950, with a gift of $225,000 from the A. W. Mellon Educational and Charitable Trust, the next three *Internationals* were paid for in advance commencing with the 38th *International*. Organized by Homer Saint-Gaudens, who then became director emeritus, it marked the close of the annual exhibitions. The first prize of $2,000 went to Jacques Villon, the second to Lyonel Feininger, the third to Priscilla Roberts. An additional prize was described: "Garden Club Prize, $300". . . to Leon Devos.

Serving as associate director under Saint-Gaudens was John O'Connor, Jr., author of *The History of Pittsburgh Internationals at Carnegie Institute 1896-1952*.

In 1950 Gordon Bailey Washburn was appointed Director of the Department of Fine Arts which was renamed The Museum of Art. When he took over the direction of the *Internationals* in 1952 he opened them more vigorously to European and Abstract Art and included the first works from the Eastern Hemisphere.

After 1952 the Exhibit was Held on a Triennial Basis

The catalogue to the 1955 *International* featured a forthright Abstract Expressionist cover design attributed to, "Afro, a member of the 1955 *International* Jury of Award." Included were works by Helen Frankenthaler, Richard Diebenkorn, Jackson Pollock, Ad Reinhardt, Robert Motherwell, Sam Francis, Stuart Davis, Larry Rivers, William Baziotes, Alberto Burri, and Andrew Wyeth (son of N. C. Wyeth who was included in the exhibition of 1940).

During the Washburn years, the world view reflected in the exhibition catalogues steadily expanded. In 1952, for example, Washburn wrote about Andrew Carnegie; in 1958 he quoted Werner Heisenberg, Rainer Marie Rilke, Henry Miller's *The Creative Process,* and Alan Watts' *The Way of Zen.* The crucial 1958 *International* had an especially sensitive finger on the pulse of change and emergence, with Marcel Duchamp as a member of the Jury of Award, and a prize given to Jasper Johns for *Grey Numbers.* Also in the exhibition were works by Joseph Cornell, Robert Rauschenberg, Allan Kaprow, Ellsworth Kelly, and Michael Snow, alongside works by Rothko, Newman, and Reinhardt. In a still deeper layering were works by Picasso and Ben Shahn, both perennial inclusions in *Internationals.*

Alexander Calder Invited to Create Sculpture for 1958 Show

Just eight months prior to the opening of the 1958 *International Exhibition*, which for the first time was extended to include sculpture, Gordon Washburn invited Alexander Calder to enter a major work to hang over the Grand Staircase of the Carnegie Institute. Calder came, surveyed the scene, measured the space (66' high by 35' square) and created a masterpiece. His mobile *Pittsburgh* is constructed of delicately balanced iron rods and aluminum fins, materials appropriate for this city. Dominating the stairwell space *Pittsburgh* became literally and figuratively the centerpiece of the 1958 *International Exhibition of Contemporary Painting and Sculpture* for which Calder was awarded the $3,000 first prize. Second place and $1,500 went to Henry Moore for his *Reclining Figure*, 1957.

Both works were purchased by the late G. David Thompson. Thompson, along with Ben Shawn and Perry T. Rathbone, represented the United States on the Jury of Awards for the *Carnegie International* of 1955, of which the *International* of 1958 was the immediate successor. In memory of his son David, Thompson gave Moore's *Reclining Figure* to The Museum of Art and Calder's mobile to Allegheny County. No longer "mobile," repainted in sports colors green and gold, condensed in size, and motor driven, Calder's masterpiece hung for 20 years in the lobby of the former Pittsburgh International Airport. In 1978, restored to its original black and white, it came on loan to The Museum of Art, to float again for a decade over the Grand Staircase. When the new, greatly enlarged airport was built, the Calder mobile was returned to the county, and it now welcomes air travelers to Pittsburgh.

Statistics, Sales

In the course of the first 40 Pittsburgh *Internationals* (1896-1955), 13,623 paintings were exhibited, representing 3,138 artists from 38 countries. The 1,024 works sold brought a total of $909,569. Approximately 2,500,000 persons viewed the exhibitions. Complete records on the net costs of the various *Internationals* have not been available. However, the 1896 *International* was budgeted at about $7,000, by 1952 the cost had increased to $71,699, and by 1995 was well over $1 million.

In pre-Depression 1923, a record was set when 23 paintings brought $78,687. The greatest number of paintings sold was from the 1955 *International*, 83 works, more than one-third of the saleable paintings, for a total of $70,425. In 1961 sales amounted to $227,451. On Patron's Day alone in 1964 sales came to $167,145. The 1970 *International*, which included works by 12 "Masters in Their Own Time," sold 58 pieces of art for an impressive $294,480. The twelve artists are listed later.

The Pittsburgh Bicentennial in 1958, Retrospective

The *Internationals* had been limited to the medium of painting until the dramatic innovation in 1958 of the addition of contemporary sculpture. That year's exhibition also included a retrospective of winners of previous *Internationals*. These two art exhibits were the major events of the *Pittsburgh Bicentennial Celebration* of that year. Leon A. Arkus, assistant director at the time of the 1958 *International and Retrospective Exhibition of Paintings from Previous Internationals, Carnegie Institute*, writing in the catalogue for that exhibition, acknowledged a debt to John O'Connor, Jr. for much of the material. Arkus made some interesting assessments concerning *The Merits of Juries and Awards*, (both Renoir and Monet had works refused!), *Inclusions and Omissions* (Toulouse-Lautrec, Rodin, Cezanne, Gaugin, Rousseau, and Modigliani were entirely omitted as of 1958), *Criticism and Public Reactions* ("The presentation of first prize to Franklin C. Watkins in 1930 for his *Suicide in Costume* precipitated more controversy than any other award."). Included were records of all the winners of prizes and honorable mentions as well as the names

of the distinguished jurors, impossible to include in this brief overview.

A note about jurors: William Merritt Chase served 11 times, Elmer Schofield eight, Cecilia Beaux seven, John White Alexander seven, Robert Vonnoh six, and Thomas Eakins served five times.

The article *Collecting from the Internationals*, by Vicky A. Clark, in *Carnegie Magazine* September 1982, states that not only were artists of the stature of Matisse, Braque, and Kandinsky belatedly included in the exhibition, but that the *International* ignored several current movements of 20th century art such as Fauvism, German Expressionism, Cubism, and de Stijl. Also listed were a number of prize-winning paintings which were acquired by museums other than The Carnegie Museum of Art, which, by hindsight, would have been valuable additions to the collection at The Carnegie.

Director Washburn also revived the idea of one-artist shows within the larger exhibitions. In 1961 he gave this honor to seven artists: David Smith, Grace Hartigan, and Richard Diebenkorn from the United States; Reg Butler and Alan Davie from England; Pierre Alechinsky from Belgium; and Carl-Henning Pedersen from Denmark.

Continuing triennially, the *Internationals* were held in 1961, 1964, and in 1967. Gustave von Groschwitz, successor to Washburn, organized the 1964 and 1967 *Internationals*. The 1967 version included works from 34 countries, a dramatic increase over the five countries represented in 1896.

Individual Exhibitions, 1970 -1982: Prints and Drawings

"Masters in Their Own Time" — 12 over 70. From 1970 until 1982, the *International Exhibitions* were replaced by one-person exhibitions of the work of older, established artists — Chillida, Alechinsky, de Kooning.

Woman VI, 1953, by Willem de Kooning,
American, b. The Netherlands; Gift of G. David
Thompson, 1955.

Ten Men, 1982, by Susan Rothenberg, American; Museum purchase: gift of Mr. and Mrs. Anthony J. A. Bryan and A. W. Mellon Acquisition Endowment Fund, 1983.

The last of the renowned series appeared in 1970 when Director Leon Arkus announced that "the archaic prize system has been abandoned." The *Pittsburgh International* of 1970 reduced the number of artists represented to fewer than one-third of those shown in earlier exhibitions but enabled each artist to show three or more works. Arkus presented 267 works by 101 artists and added prints and drawings for the first time. In addition, there was a special group of 12 "Masters in Their Own Time," all of whom were over 70 years of age. Included were Joseph Albers, Alexander Calder, Sonia Delaunay, Max Ernst, Naum Gabo, Henri Michaux, Joan Miro, Henry Moore, Louise Nevelson, Pablo Picasso, Mark Tobey, and Bram van Velde.

Revised Format in 1977, Andrew Mellon $50,000 Prize

Inflation boosted the skyrocketing costs of crating, insuring, and transporting over great distances the contemporary larger and heavier works of art, causing consideration of changes in the format of the *Internationals*. Replacing the original *Pittsburgh International Exhibition of Contemporary Art* was a new series, sponsored by the A. W. Mellon Educational and Charitable Trust of Pittsburgh. Beginning in

1977 the *Pittsburgh International Series* concentrated on the work of individual artists rather than on the broad spectrum of Contemporary Art. In addition to the honor of being selected by the distinguished *International* Awards Advisory Committee, with the trustees and director of The Museum of Art, there was the Andrew W. Mellon prize of $50,000. (One of the principal designers of the format for the new series was John Walker — graduate of Shadyside Academy, Pittsburgh — former director of the National Gallery of Art, Washington, D.C., of which Andrew Mellon of Pittsburgh was the founder.)

Selected to receive this signal honor, deemed to be a "Nobel Prize in the Arts," inaugurating the new series of *Internationals* in 1977 was Pierre Alechinsky of Belgium. An artist of international stature at age 50 in 1977, Alechinsky had exhibited in every *Pittsburgh International* since 1952, and his work is represented in more than 65 leading museums in Europe, U. S., Canada, Asia, and Latin America. The Awards Advisory Committee recommending selection of Alechinsky included James Johnson Sweeney, former director of three prestigious museums: the Guggenheim and the MOMA in New York and the Fine Arts in Houston. As early as 1955 Mr. Sweeney had

Landscape, 1952, by Francis Bacon, English; Gift of Edgar Kaufmann, Jr., 1956.

admired and acquired Alechinsky's work and in 1961 Director Gordon Washburn had included Pierre Alechinsky in a one-man show at the *Pittsburgh International.*

The Museum of Art, Carnegie Institute, on the occasion of the 1977 *Pittsburgh International*, issued an impressive, all-inclusive book, plus catalogue, entitled *Alechinsky Paintings and Writings*, with foreword by Leon Arkus, Director of The Museum of Art, and introduction by playwright Eugene Ionesco. Loaded with color photographs of the paintings, the catalogue listed 134 paintings, mostly in acrylic after 1965, and 35 drawings and watercolors, "collection of the artist."

Two Artists Share Mellon Prize in 1979-1980 Exhibition

Sharing the $50,000 prize of the 1979-1980 *Pittsburgh International* were, Willem de Kooning, painter, Holland-born, citizen of the United States, and Eduardo Chillida, sculptor, of Spain, both of whom had been represented in the exhibition of 1958. That same year Chillida also won the Sculpture Prize at the Venice Biennale. He has shown in every *International* in Pittsburgh from 1958 to 1979. De Kooning's work has been represented in the *Internationals* of 1952, 1955, 1958, 1961, 1964, 1970, and 1979. More than 250 works of the two artists were exhibited in the *Pittsburgh International* of 1979-1980, attracting one of the largest audiences since World War II.

The 1982 International Reverts to Traditional Role

With funding provided by the A. W. Mellon Educational and Charitable Trust, the 1982-83 *International* was under the directorship of John R. Lane, who succeeded Leon Arkus in 1980. (It was in 1980 that the Pittsburgh-based Trust, with the encouragement of Paul Mellon and Institute Trustee Adolph W. Schmidt, made a terminal grant to endow the perpetuation of the *Carnegie International Exhibitions.*) This 48th *Carnegie International* was planned to revert to its traditional purpose as a broad-based forum for what is new and of special interest in International Contemporary Art.

The exhibition included 63 artists, each represented by three works dating since the preceding *International* of 1979. Gene Baro, adjunct curator of Contemporary Art, chose the selections on his visits to some 25 different countries. This was the first *International* not directly reflecting the vision of the director of The Museum of Art. The qualifications for this *International* were: objects by artists showing promise; recognized artists at a creative peak; senior contemporary masters continuing to make artistic contributions. There were to be no prizes or jurors. Only three of the artists had been seen in previous *Internationals.* There were 12 Americans, one of whom, David Schirm, working in California, was originally from Pittsburgh. The youngest artist, Adir Sodre de Sousa of Brazil, was 19; the eldest, Jean DuBuffet of France, 80. Seven of the artists were women.

The 1982 International's *Artists,*

Dates of Birth, Countries of Origin . . .
United States, with 12 artists: Rackstraw
Downes, 1939; Red Grooms, 1937; David Izu,
1951; Lee Krasner, 1908 (widow of Jackson
Pollock); Terence LaNoue, 1941; James
McGarrell, 1930; David Schirm, 1945 (Car-
negie Mellon graduate); Albert Stadler, 1923;
David Stoltz, 1943; Christopher Wilmarth,
1943; Isaac Witkin, born in South Africa, 1936;
and Stanford Wurmfeld, 1942.

England, six artists: Bernard Cohen, 1933;
Jennifer Durrant, 1942; Nigel Hall, 1943;
David Hockney, 1937; John Hoyland, 1934;
and Patrick Jones, 1948. Spain, five artists:
Sergi Aguilar, 1946; Chema Cobo, 1952; Louis
Gordillo, 1934; Jose Maria Iglesias, 1933; and
Antoni Tapies, 1923. New Zealand, four artists:
Jeffrey Harris; Colin Lanceley, 1938; Milan
Mrkusich, 1925; and Greer Twiss, 1937. Japan,
four artists: Yoshio Kitayama, 1948; Yoshishige
Saito, 1904; Kishio Suca, 1944; and Kakuzo
Tatehata, 1919. France, three artists: Christian
Bonnefoi, 1948; Jean DuBuffet, 1901; and
Pierre Nivollet, 1946. And two artists from each
of the following: Argentina, Jorge Demirjian,
1932 and Felipe Carlos Pino, 1945. Brazil:
Antonio Sergio Benevento, 1945 and Adir Sodre
de Sousa, 1962. Canada: Wendy Knox-Leat,
1950 and Judy Singer, 1951. Finland: Jukka
Makela, 1949 and Ernst Mether-Borgstrom,
1917. Netherlands: Armando, 1929 and Jan
Riske, 1932. Mexico: Fernando Garcia Ponce,
1933 and Susana Sierra, 1942. West Germany:
Gotthard Graubner, 1930 and Erwin Heerich,
1922.

One artist each from the following coun-
tries: Australia, Michael Shannon, 1927; Austria,
Karl Prantt, 1923; Chile, Claudio Bravo, 1936;
Colombia, Fernando Botero, 1932; Eire,
Michael Warren, 1950; Greece, Theodore
Manolides, 1944; Italy, Piero Dorazio, 1927;
Israel, Buky Schwartz, 1932; Korea, Jin-Suk-
Kim, 1946; Norway, Jacob Weldermann, 1923;

Sweden, Olle Kaks, 1941; Switzerland, Max
Bill, 1908; West Berlin, Johannes Geccelli,
1925; South Africa, Illona Anderson, 1948;
and Yugoslavia, Milos Saric, 1927.

A gift of $100,000 from Alcoa Founda-
tion augmented the income of the exhibition's
own endowment and also supported the showing of the exhibition at the Seattle Art Museum
in 1983. Alcoa of Australia was to sponsor the
tour to three Australian museums, the first time
that the *Carnegie International* would have
been shown abroad, but unfortunately, unfavorable reactions of the art critics forced the cancellation of the tour.

Divine, 1979, by David Hockney, English; Gift of
Richard M. Scaife, 1982.

Untitled 2, 1986, by Brice Marden, American; Edith H. Fisher Fund, 1987.

Director of Museum of Art, Co-curator in 1985

The adverse critical response to the 1982 showing had led to a thoughtful analysis of how best to fashion the 1985 exhibit. John Caldwell, Curator of Contemporary Art, and Carnegie Director John R. Lane co-curated the 1985 *International*, with an advisory committee including Linda L. Cathcart, Rudi Fuchs, Kasper Konig, Hilton Cramer, Nicholas Serota, and Maurice Tuchman. Selected were 150 works of 45 artists from Denmark, Germany, Holland, Britain, and the United States.

The 1985 exhibition catalogue took the form of a critical anthology and for the first time, in terms of the *Pittsburgh International*

Exhibitions, essays on Minimalism and Conceptualism acknowledged the cognitive element in art to exist. In a sense, the 1985 *International* showed the coming to age of the exhibition after nearly a century of struggling to accept the sometimes difficult and challenging cultural material that entered the American public sphere by way of the *International*.

The result proved to be a highly praised achievement which, "exposed the heady excitement of the early '80s with Anselm Kiefer, Julian Schnabel, and Susan Rothenberg." Noted and lauded was, "acceptance of the figure and narrative in works by Malcolm Morley, John Ahearn, and Jörg Immendorff and the renewal of penetrating realism by Lucian Freud and Eric Fischl." In the painting of Frank Stella and everywhere there was color, from the density of Brice Marden to the jarring contrasts of Georg Baselitz and the jewel-like intensity of Howard Hodgkin. The works in the 1985 *International* were aggressive, big, and spirited, exemplified by Richard Serra's esthetics of confrontation embodied in his 40-foot corten steel *Carnegie*, 1985 which towers over the visitor at the Forbes Avenue entrance to The Carnegie.

The artists whose work was shown in the 1985 *International* are: (born in the United States unless otherwise noted) John Ahearn, b. 1951; John Baledessari b. 1931; Georg Baselitz b. 1938, Germany; Dara Birnbaum b. 1946; Jonathon Borofsky b. 1942; Scott Burton b. 1939; Francisco Clemente b. 1952, Italy; Enzo Cuccchi b. 1950, Italy; Richard Deacon b. 1949, Wales; Jan Dibbets b. 1941, Netherlands; Jeri Georg Dokoupil b. 1954, Czechoslovakia; Luciano Fabro b. 1936, Italy; Eric Fischl b. 1948; Barry Flanagan b. 1941, Wales; Lucien Freud b. 1922, Germany; Howard Hodgkin b. 1932, England; Jenny Holzer b. 1950; Jörg Immendorff b. 1945, Germany; Neil Jenny b. 1945; Bill Jensen b. 1945; Ellsworth Kelly b. 1923; Anselm Keifer b. 1945, Germany; Per Kirkeby b. 1938,

Denmark; Jannis Kounellis b. 1936, Greece;
Sol Le Witt b. 1928; Robert Longo b. 1953;
Markus Lupertz b. 1941, Czechoslovakia;
Robert Mangold b. 1937; Brice Marden
b. 1938; Malcolm Morley b. 1931, England;
Bruce Nauman b. 1941; Sigmar Polke b. 1941,
Germany; Gerhard Richter b. 1932, Germany;
Susan Rothenberg b. 1945; Robert Ryman
b. 1930; David Salle b. 1952; Julian Schnabel
b. 1951; Richard Serra b. 1939; Cindy Sherman
b. 1954; Frank Stella b. 1936; Bill Woodrow
b. 1948, England.

Corporate sponsor of the 1985 exhibition was United States Steel Corporation in
recognition of the 150th anniversary of the
birth of Andrew Carnegie, whose Carnegie
Corporation became the nucleus of the U. S.
Steel Corporation in 1901.

Tradition Continued in 1988

Director Lane and Curator Caldwell continued
the tradition of the *International* in 1988 as an
exhibition of artists they chose with an advisory
committee: Jean-Christophe Ammann (Basel),
Maria Corral (Madrid), Kathy Halbreich
(Boston), Nicholas Serota (London), and Joan
Simon (New York). Dr. Lane joined the advisory
committee after resigning from The Carnegie in
January of 1987 to become director of the San
Franciso Museum of Modern Art.

Despite the inclusion of 13 artists from
the 1985 show, in the 1988 *International* there
was a "hushed, muted, and almost magical
feeling." It showcased the work of 39 artists,
18 of whom created works specifically for the
occasion, in many cases with installations or
pieces made for particular spaces. Eight others
were showing work never before exhibited, and
10 other artists presented pieces that had not
before been seen in this country.

This exhibition reflected the concerns
of the late 1980s, with AIDS as the most
prominent theme because of its devastating
effect on the art world. Also addressed were

Recover, 1988, by Ross Bleckner, American; Gift of
The Hillman Company, 1988.

non-mainstream ideas, cultures, and concerns
that characterize end-of-the-century life.

Artists Represented in the Carnegie International
November 5, 1988 - January 22, 1989
American and European Artists:

Giovanni Anselmo b. 1934, Italy; Siah
Armajani b. 1939, Iran (lives in USA); Richard
Artschwager b. 1923, USA; Georg Baselitz
b. 1938, Germany; Lothar Baumgarten b. 1944,
Germany; Joseph Beuys, 1921-1986, Germany;
Ross Bleckner b. 1949, USA; Anna and Bernard
Blume b. 1937, Germany; Francesco Clemente
b. 1952, Italy; Luciano Fabro b. 1936, Italy;
Peter Fischli b. 1952, Switzerland and David
Weiss b. 1946 Switzerland; Günther Förg b.
1952; Germany; Katharina Fritsch b. 1956,
West Germany; Peter Halley b. 1953, USA;
Rebecca Horn b. 1944, Germany; Anish

Kapoor b. 1954, India; Anselm Kiefer b. 1945, Germany; Per Kirkeby b. 1934, Denmark; Jeff Koons b. 1955, USA; Jannis Kounellis b. 1936, Greece; Wolfgang Laib b. 1950, West Germany; Sherrie Levine b. 1947, USA; Brice Marden b. 1938, USA; Agnes Martin b. 1912, Canada; Elizabeth Murray b. 1940, USA; Bruce Nauman b. 1941, USA; Sigmar Polke b. 1941, Germany; Gerhard Richter b. 1932, Germany; Susan Rothenberg b. 1945, USA; Robert Ryman b. 1930, USA; Julian Schnabel b. 1951, USA; Joel Shapiro b. 1941, USA; Susana Solano b. 1946, Spain; Rosemarie Trockel b. 1952, West Germany; Cy Twombly b. 1928, USA (lives in Italy); Meyer Vaisman b. 1960, Venezuela (lives in USA); Bill Viola b. 1951, USA; Jeff Wall b. 1946, Canada; and Andy Warhol, 1928-1987, USA.

The majority of the works were chosen by the artists in consultation with the curator of the exhibition: Bill Viola and Fischli/Weiss, with William Judson, curator of Film and Video. The exhibition included the Hall of Sculpture for the first time, occupied 40,000 square feet of gallery space designed by Charles B. Froom.

Joseph Beuys and Andy Warhol

Advisory Committee member Jean-Christophe Ammann, suggested Joseph Beuys' *Das Ende des 20. Jahrhunderts* (The End of the 20th Century) 1983-85, for inclusion in the show. If any one work characterized a sense of doom mixed with anticipation, it was Joseph Beuys'. At first glance, it looked like a collection of rocks arbitrarily placed on the floor of the gallery. Upon closer inspection, the majority of the basalt stones seemed to have fallen over while a few remained standing, reminding one of the ruins of ancient temples, Stonehenge, or modern buildings destroyed by earthquakes. The image, echoed Beuys' own description of how he, a combat pilot in World War II, shot down in Crimea, was saved from near death by being covered with fat and felt for warmth, by the nomadic Tartars who rescued him. This double metaphoric collapse of civilization and its possible salvation, gains strength from Beuys' title (photo on page 255).

Andy Warhol, also enigmatic and charismatic, was of immense importance to younger artists. Discussion of Andy Warhol's works for the show had revolved around his late series of self-portraits, one of which was purchased for The Museum of Art by the Fellows Fund in 1986. Beuys' and Warhol's ideas,though dissimilar, relate closely in boldly joining art and life and in questioning the meaning and role of art and artists in our society. While Warhol, the self-created celebrity, resisted political involvement, Beuys, the performer, was a passionate activist. The legacies of both Beuys, 1921-1986 and Warhol, 1928-1987, could be seen throughout the 1988 exhibition and were addressed in a public symposium on that topic. In addition there were lectures by Ross Bleckner, Peter Halley, Agnes Martin, and Joel Shapiro.

The jurors were the advisory committee, with trustees Henry L. Hillman and Konrad M. Weis. The Carnegie Prize was awarded to Rebecca Horn for *The Hydra-Forest*, 1988 performing: Oscar Wilde, consisting of an electrical device, glass, mercury, and shoes.

Funding for the 1988 Carnegie International

Income from the endowment created in 1980 by the A. W. Mellon Educational and Charitable Trust to support the *Carnegie International*, provided approximately half the funds required by the exhibition. Additional funding: The Pennsylvania Council on the Arts, The National Endowment for the Arts, and the Howard Heinz Endowment. The James H. Beal Publication Fund, established in 1987 for The Carnegie Museum of Art was for the first time applied to the publication of the all-color catalogue. A major contribution by The Hillman Company, headed by Museum of Art Trustee Henry Hillman, made the 1988 *Carnegie International* a reality.

The 51st International *1991-1992*
Beyond The Carnegie

Overseen by Phillip Johnston, Director of
The Museum of Art, the 51st *Carnegie International* of 1991, the largest to date, was
organized by Mark Francis, curator of Contemporary Art at The Carnegie and Lynne Cooke,
critic and co-curator, *Carnegie International.*
They were assisted by an advisory committee:
Kasper Honig of Germany, Fumio Nanjo of
Japan, and David Ross, director of the Whitney
Museum of American Art in New York city.
(Phillip Johnston had succeeded to the directorship of The Carnegie Museum of Art in 1988
after serving as acting director on the departure
of John Lane for San Francisco.)

An article entitled "Endangered Species"
by art critic Harry Schwalb in *Pittsburgh Magazine,* January, 1992 stated, "paint and painters
are relevant as ever — in spite of the latest
Carnegie International (one of the finest in
50 years). This sensitively calibrated exhibition
underplayed painting, sculpture and video —
and focused on installation art, on such theatrical site-specific leviathans as Ilya Kabakov's
abandoned Russian orphanage, a soul battering
work worth ever kopeck of its reputed $50,000
construction cost . . . but the *International* was
also making a point . . . it seemed to be saying
that the issues facing humankind at the close
of the millennium require more than formalist
art."

For the first time in its history, the exhibition moved beyond The Museum of Art —
to The Museum of Natural History and other
parts of The Carnegie, to The Carnegie Library, to the Mattress Factory on Pittsburgh's
Northside, to the Richard King Mellon Hall of
Science at Duquesne University, and to a public
park at the intersection of three major streets
near Gateway Plaza in Pittsburgh.

In the selection process, the geographical
palette stretched from the west coast of Ireland
to Ukraine and in the opposite direction as far

as Japan (taking in the west coast of Canada,
the Los Angeles metroplex, and New Mexico).
In an essay in the catalogue the curators observed: "since then, (the 1988 *International*),
a somewhat different art world has emerged:
to take but one example, a kind of painting
quite removed from the expressionistic styles
highlighted in 1988 has developed. More generally . . . the focus . . . has veered away from
painting to other media, to installation and
assemblage, to sculpture, and to photography."

These are the **44 artists, from 13 countries,** whose 219 works were shown: Michael
Asher b. 1943, USA; Richard Avedon b. 1923,
USA; Judity Barry b. 1949, USA; Lothar
Baumgarten b. 1944, Germany; Christian
Boltanski b. 1944, France; Louise Bourgeois
b. 1911, France; John Cage b. 1912, USA;
Sophie Calle b. 1953, France; James Coleman
b. 1941, Ireland; Tony Cragg b. 1949, England;
Richard Deacon b. 1949, Wales; Lili Dujourie
b. 1941, Belguim; Katharina Fritsch b. 1956,
Germany; Bernard Frize b. 1953, France; Dan
Graham b. 1942, USA; Ann Hamilton b. 1956,
USA; Richard Hamilton b. 1922, England;
David Hammons b. 1943, USA; Huang Yong
Ping b. 1954, China; Derek Jarman b. 1942,
England; Ilya Kabakov b. 1933, Ukraine, USSR;
On Kawara, Japan; Mike Kelley b. 1954, USA;
Louise Lawler b. 1947, USA; Ken Lum
b. 1956, Canada; Allan McCollum, b. 1944,
USA; John McCracken, b. 1934, USA; Boris
Michailov b. 1938, Ukraine, USSR; Lisa Milroy
b. 1959, Canada; Tatsuo Miyajima b. 1957,
Japan; Reinhard Mucha b. 1950, Germany; Juan
Muñoz b. 1953, Spain; Bruce Nauman b. 1941,
USA; Maria Nordman b. 1943, Germany; Giulio
Paolini b. 1940, Italy; Stephen Prina b. 1954,
USA; Tim Rollins + K.O.S. b. 1955, USA;
Richard Serra b. 1939, USA; Thomas Struth
b. 1954, Germany; Hiroshi Sugimoto b. 1948,
Japan; Philip Taaffe b. 1955, USA; Christopher
Williams b. 1956, USA; and Christopher Wool
b. 1955, USA.

Members of the Advisory Committee were joined by Museum of Art board members Deborah D. Dodds and Konrad M. Weis to form the Jury of Award for The Carnegie Prize. Winner of that honor was the Japanese artist On Kawara for *Today 1966-1990*.

Additions to the Art Collections from the 1991-92 Exhibition

Through The A. W. Mellon Acquisition Endowment Fund and/or the *Carnegie International* Acquisition Fund, a number of works from the 1991 exhibition were added to the collections of the museum: three paintings by On Kawara, USA b. 1932, (Japan), winner of the 1992 Carnegie Prize for his installation of *Today, 1966-90*; several sculptures: *Heart Pavilion* by Dan Graham, b. 1942, USA; *Unreadable Humidity* by Huang Yong Ping, b. 1954, China; two works exhibited together, titled *Offerings* by Ann Hamilton, b. 1956 USA.

Two other sculptures from the *International* entered the collection: *Cell II*, by Louise Bourgeois, b. 1911 USA, from the Heinz Family Fund and *Supplement #7 Seychelles 7/8*, by Christopher Williams, b. 1956 USA, gift of the Luhring Augustine Hetzler Gallery, Santa Monica. Also acquired was an installation by Louise Lawler, b. 1947 USA, entitled *HAVING ATTAINED VISIBILITY AS WELL AS MANAGING TO CATCH THE EYE OF THE SPECTATOR*. And by gift from Carnegie trustee Milton Fine, five photographs, *Arctic Ocean; Irish Sea: Isle of Man; Aegean Sea: Pilion; Indian Ocean: Bali*; and *Java Sea: Bali*, all from *Time Exposed* by Horoshi Sugimoto b. 1948, Japan.

1995 Carnegie International

The Carnegie's peripatetic curator of Contemporary Art, Richard Armstrong, visited 508 studios outside the United States in 26 countries in selecting the work of 36 artists for the 1995 *Carnegie International*. This prestigious, one-hundred-year-old exhibition will be the artistic highlight of the celebrations for the Centennial of Andrew Carnegie's gift to the city of Pittsburgh.

Truly "international," two-thirds of the artists whose work was chosen are from other countries, with only one-third from the United States. Fourteen are sculptors, 11 are painters, and 9 are video or photographic artists. In age they range from 27 to 81 and 35% are women. Their works have been made since 1991. Of the sculptors, Armstrong has included the work of the late Donald Judd, whom he considers the greatest American sculptor since Alexander Calder and David Smith.

Armstrong met his Advisory Committee of three in Prague after extensive travels to: New York, London, Cologne, Paris, Arnhem, Antwerp, Venice, Vienna, Budapest, Krakow, Warsaw, Rome, Milan, Madrid, Barcelona, Haifa, Jerusalem, Tel Aviv, Moscow, St. Petersburg, Portugal, four cities in Japan, six cities in Canada, and possibly India . . . "There is not enough Contemporary Art being produced in the Islamic world to warrant going there." Armstrong foresaw an, "eclectic exhibition, young artists as well as people with long careers . . . lots of painting and lots of younger sculptors, including women." The cost of the Centennial *International* is estimated to be, "well in excess of $1 million."

Furniture as a metaphor is a recurring theme in the works selected, ranging from cast pieces by Rachel Whiteread of London to the overscale table and 6'9" chair by Robert Therrien of Los Angeles. New Yorker Richard Artschwager's table-derived work is titled *In the Presence of Mine Enemies*, while from Warsaw, Poland, Miroslav Balka schematizes the floor plan and contents of his childhood home.

Richard Tuttle of New Mexico uses lights and banal materials while Robert Gober adapts the urinals (originally featured in Marcel Duchamp's scandalous early 20th century work) in his new work. Rirkrit Tiravanija, a Thai sculptor living in New York, engages the audience, often feeding them.

Judd died in 1994 as did the painter Joan Mitchell who worked at Giverney, France deriving inspiration from the same landscapes as Monet. Their inclusion follows the 1991 precedent of showing works by Andy Warhol and Joseph Beuys. Germany's Sigmar Polke and Georg Baselitz are represented, Baselitz with enormous impasted paintings. In contrast, colorful and cheerful are the folkloric floral compositions by Beatriz Milhazes of Rio de Janeiro.

Doris Salcedo of Bogata, Colombia, expresses her concern over the tortured killings in her South American country by covering her niche compositions of shoes with cow bladder, evoking the image of violence. The themes of mortality and death are present also in Cindy Sherman's large photographs.

From Tokyo one of the black paintings of the venerable artist Tomoharo Murakami will be seen, as will the totemic portraits by Chuck Close. The three-dimensional film of Stan Douglas and that of the video artist Tony Oursler will be on view as well as works by the Canadian photographer Angela Grauerholz.

Here are the artists represented in the 1995 *Carnegie International*: Chantal Akerman b. 1950, France; Nobuyoshi Araki b. 1940, Japan; Richard Artschwager b. 1923, USA; Miroslaw Balka b. 1958, Poland; Stephan Balkenhol b. 1957, Germany; Georg Baselitz b. 1938, Germany; Rob Birza b. 1962, Netherlands; Chuck Close b. 1940, USA; Stan Douglas b. 1960, Canada; Leonardo Drew b. 1961, USA; Marlene Dumas b. 1953, Netherlands; Louise Fishman b. 1939, USA; Robert Gober b. 1954, USA; Angela Grauerholz b. 1952, Canada; Gary Hill b. 1951, USA; Craigie Horsfield b. 1949, Great Britain; Christina Iglesias b. 1956, Spain; Donald Judd, 1928-1994, USA; Per Kirkeby b. 1938, Denmark;

Guillermo Kuitca b. 1961, Argentina; Moshe Kupferman b. 1926, Israel; Thomas Locher b. 1956, Germany; Agnes Martin b. 1912, USA; Beatriz Milhazes b. 1960, Brazil; Joan Mitchell, 1926-1992, USA; Tomoharu Murakami b. 1938, Japan; Sigmar Polke b. 1941, Germany; Tony Oursler b. 1957, USA; Doris Salcedo b. 1958, Colombia; Cindy Sherman b. 1954, USA; Robert Therrien b. 1947, USA; Rirkrit Tiravanija b. 1961, USA; Richard Tuttle b. 1941, USA; Franz West b. 1947, Austria; Rachel Whiteread b. 1963, Great Britain; and Remy Zaugg b. 1943, Switzerland.

The artists included were selected by the curator, Richard Armstrong, formerly of the Whitney Museum in New York, with an advisory group of three: Bice Curiger, editor-in-chief of *Parkett Magazine* in Zurich, Switzerland; Mark Rosenthal, curator of 20th century art for the National Gallery of Art in Washington, D.C.; and Vicente Todoli, curator of the Instituto Valenciano de Arte Moderne in Spain. In May of 1995, the group met for three days in Lake Como, Italy. Carnegie Trustees Lea Simonds and Milton Fine join the advisory committee in the vote selecting the winner of the Carnegie Prize. More than 40% of the artists in the exhibition have work in The Carnegie Museum of Art in Pittsburgh. The corporate supporter of the 1995 *International* is PNC Bank with support also by the A.W. Mellon Foundation and the National Endowment for the Arts.

For the 100th anniversary of the *International* in 1996, curated by Vicki A. Clark, the museum will mount a retrospective of works from past *Internationals*, providing a kaleidoscopic review of a century of developing trends in art.

Curator Richard Armstrong and his secretary, Lynn Corbett, were helpful in supplying information about the 1995 *Carnegie International Exhibition*.

The Carnegie Internationals
1896-1994, First Prize Winners

1896 John Lavery, Scottish, *Lady in Brown*
Winslow Homer, American, *The Wreck*
Chronological Medal awarded

1897 James J. Shannon, English, *Miss Kitty*

1898 Dwight W. Tryon, American,
Early Spring in New England

1899 Cecilia Beaux, American,
Mother and Daughter

1900 Andre Dauchez, French, *The Kelp Gatherer*

1901 Alfred H. Maurer, American,
An Arrangement

1903 Frank W. Benson, American,
A Woman Reading

1904 W. Elmer Schofield, American,
Across the River

1905 Lucien Simon, French, *Evening in a Studio*

1907 Gaston La Touche, French, *The Bath*

1908 Thomas W. Dewing, American, *The Necklace*

1909 Edmund C. Tarbell, *Girl Crocheting*

1910 William Orpen, Irish,
Portrait of the Artist (Myself and Venus)

1911 John W. Alexander, American, *Sunlight*

1912 Charles Sims, English, *Pastorella*

1913 Glyn W. Philpot, English, *The Marble Worker*

1914 Edward W. Redfield, American,
The Village in Winter

1920 Abbott H. Thayer, American,
Young Woman in Olive Plush

1921 Ernest Lawson, American, *Vanishing Mist*

1922 George W. Bellows, American,
Eleanor, Jean, and Anna

1923 Arthur B. Davies, American,
Afterthoughts of Earth

1924 Augustus John, English, *Madame Suggia*

1925 Henri Eugene Le Sidaner, French,
Window on the Bay of Villefranche

1926 Ferruccio Ferrazzi, Italian,
Hortia and Fabiola

1927 Henri Matisse, French, *Still Life*

1928 Andre Derain, French, *Still Life*

1929 Felice Carena, Italian, *The Studio*

1930 Pablo Picasso, French,
Portrait of Mme. Picasso

1931 Franklin C. Watkins, American,
Suicide in Costume

1933 Andre Dunoyer de Segonzac, *St. Tropez*

1934 Peter Blume, American, *South of Scranton*

1935 Hipolito Hidalgo de Caviedes, Spanish,
Elvira and Tiberio

1936 Leon Kroll, American,
The Road from the Cove

1937 Georges Braque, French, *The Yellow Cloth*

1938 Karl Hofer, German, *The Wind*

1939 Alexander Brook, American, *Georgia Jungle*

1950 Jacques Villon, French, *The Thresher*

1952 Ben Nicholson, English, *December 5, 1949*

1955 Alfred Manessier, French, *Crown of Thorns*

1958 Painting: Antoni Tapies, *Painting*
Sculpture: Alexander Calder, *Pittsburgh*

1961 Painting: Mark Tobey, *Untitled*
Sculpture: Alberto Giacometti, *Man Walking*

1964 Painting: Ellsworth Kelly,
Blue, Black and Red
Sculpture: Jean (Hans) Arp,
Sculpture Classique

1967 Painting: Josef Albers, *Deep Signal*
Francis Bacon,
Three Studies for Portrait of Lucian Freud
Joan Miro, *Queen Marie-Louise of Prussia*
Victor de Vasarely, *Alom*
Sculpture: Eduardo Paolozzi,
Pisthetairos in Ipsi
Arnaldo Pomodoro, *The Traveler's Column*

**1970-
1971** "The archaic prize system has been
abandoned."
Twelve *Masters in Their Own Time*

1977 Pierre Alechinsky, Belgium
$50,000 Andrew Mellon prize

**1979-
1980** Willem de Kooning, Holland-born
painter/U. S. citizen, and Eduardo Chillida
of Spain shared $50,000 Andrew Mellon
Prize

1982 No prize awarded

1985 Anselm Keifer, *Midgard Vitgard*,
$10,000 prize
Richard Serra, *Carnegie*, $10,000 prize

1988 Rebecca Horn, *The Hydra-Forest*, 1988
performing: Oscar Wilde,
The Carnegie Prize

1991 On Kawara, *Today, 1966 to 1990*,
(21,483 days to October 19, 1991)
The Carnegie Prize

Past International *Works in the Permanent Collection as of 1982*

"Collecting from the *Internationals*," an article by Vicky A. Clark, in *Carnegie Magazine*, September 1982, considered the subject in depth. Since 1896 The Museum of Art, Carnegie Institute, had acquired approximately 320 works from the *Internationals*. In the early years, Associate Director John O'Connor, Jr. stated in 1952, "most accessions and almost all purchases came from the *Internationals* and thus reflect their content."

The last number of each entry is the "accession number" indicating the year the museum acquired the work, omitted when acquired by purchase the same year as the *International Exhibition*.

The Museum of Art

1896 **Theobald Chartran**
Portrait of Andrew Carnegie, 1895
Presented by Henry Clay Frick (96)

Johanna Knowles Woodwell Hailman
American Beauties, n.d.
Bequest of Johanna K. W. Hailman (59)

Winslow Homer
The Wreck, 1896

James Abbott McNeill Whistler
Arrangement in Black: Portrait of Señor Pablo de Sarasate, 1884

1897 **Pierre Puvis de Chavannes**
A Vision of Antiquity—Symbol of Form, c. 1885

James Jebusa Shannon
Miss Kitty, 1897

John Singer Sargent
Portrait of a Boy, 1890

1898 **Alfred Sisley**
Village on the Shore of the Marne, c. 1881
Purchase (99)

Elihu Vedder
The Keeper of the Threshold, 1897-98
Purchase (01)

Arrangement in Black: Portrait of Señor Pablo de Sarasate, 1884, by James Abbott McNeill Whistler, American; Purchase, 1896.

1899 **Mary Cassatt**
Young Women Picking Fruit, 1891
Patrons Art Fund (22)

Childe Hassam
Fifth Avenue in Winter, c. 1892
Purchase (00)

Henry Ward Ranger
An East River Idyll, 1896
Purchase (00)

Joseph R. Woodwell
The Gorge, 1899
Purchase (16)

1900 **Edwin Austin Abbey**
The Penance of Eleanor, Duchess of Gloucester, 1900
Purchase (02)

Camille Pissaro
The Great Bridge of Rouen, 1896

1904   **John White Alexander**
Aurora Leigh, 1904
Presented by C. Bernard Shea in memory
of Joseph B. Shea (40)

1907   **John Henry Twachtman**
River in Winter

1909   **William Merritt Chase**
Portrait of Mrs. Chase

      Bruce Crane
November Hills

      Childe Hassam
Spring Morning, 1909

Portrait of Mrs. Chase, c. 1890-95, by William
Merritt Chase, American; Purchase, 1909.

Eve after the Fall, cast 1913, by Auguste Rodin, French;
Purchase, 1920.

1910   **Robert Henri**
The Equestrian, 1909

      Sir William N. M. Orpen
Portrait of the Artist, 1910

1920   **Auguste Rodin**
Eve After the Fall, 1881

      Auguste Rodin
Head of Sorrow (Eleanora Duse), 1882
Exchange with G. David Thompson (55)

      Auguste Rodin
St. John the Baptist, 1878

      John Singer Sargent
Venetian Interior, c. 1882

1921   **Ernest Lawson**
Vanishing Mist, c. 1916-21

1925   **Sir William N. M. Orpen**
Portrait of Samuel Harden Church, 1924
Carnegie Institute Commission (24)

      Leopold Seyffertt
Portrait of Dr. William Jacob Holland, 1925
Carnegie Institute Commission (24)

Asterisks below indicate Patrons Art Fund Purchases

1927 Arthur Bowen Davies
At the Chestnut Root, c. 1910 (30)*

Charles W. Hawthorne
Portrait of a Portuguese Gentleman,
c. 1926 (28)*

1935 Leon Kroll
Morning on the Cape, (36)

1936 Oskar Kokoschka
Portrait of Thomas Garrigue Masaryk,
1936 (56)

1937 Edward Hopper
Cape Cod Afternoon, 1936 (38)

1938 Cornelis T. M. van Dongen
Portrait of E. Berry Wall, 1938 (39)*

James Ensor
Temptation of St. Anthony, 1894
John Henry Craner Fund (58)

1939 Andre Derain
Portrait of an Englishwoman, n.d.
Gift of Charles J. Rosenbloom (40)

Georges Rouault
The Old King, 1916-36 (40)*

The Old King, 1916-36, by Georges Rouault,
French; Patrons Art Fund, 1940.

1952 Alfred Manessier
Games in the Snow, 1951*
(All acquired in 1952)

Samuel Rosenberg
Time Echoes, 1952

Jacques Villon
Portrait of the Artist, 1949*

Fritz Winter
Elevation, 1951*

1955 Afro (Afro Basaldella)
Underwater Hunter, 1955
Gift of Mr. and Mrs. H. J. Heinz, II

Carl Henning
Venetian Landscape

William Baziotes
Black Night, 1954*

Jacques Doucet
Painting No. 47, 1954
Gift of G. David Thompson (55)

Willem de Kooning
Woman VI, 1953
Gift of G. David Thompson (55)

Ben Nicholson
Feb. 18-24 (Azure), 1954
Gift of Mr. and Mrs. William Block (77)

1958 *(All acquired in 1958 except as noted)*

Jean (Hans) Arp
Birth of the Rock, 1958
Leisser Art Fund

Georges Braque
Fragments d'Hesiode, 1930-57*

Alexander Calder
Pittsburgh, 1958
Returned to Allegheny County

Eduardo Chillida
Aizian (In the Wind), 1958
Howard Heinz Endowment Purchase Fund

Emil Cimiotti
Sculpture 6/58, 1958
Gift of the Women's Committee,
Museum of Art

Alan Davie
Target for NO Shooting, 1958
Anonymous Gift (60)

Richard Diebenkorn
A Day at the Race, 1953*
Berkeley No. 37, 1955
Gift of Mr. and Mrs. Charles Denby (61)

Sam Francis
Red, 1958
Gift of Howard Heinz Endowment

Henry Heerup
Self-Portrait, 1955
Howard Heinz Endowment Purchase Fund

Asger Jorn
Incredible Energy, 1957*

Ellsworth Kelly
Aubade, 1957
Richard Mace Feldman Memorial Fund

Franz Kline
Siegfried, 1958
Gift of Friends (59)

Peter Lanyon
Lynmouth, 1957*

René Magritte
The Heart of the World, 1956
Gift of Mr. and Mrs. George L.
Craig, Jr. (60)

Georges Mathieu
Painting, 1957
Gift of Mr. and Mrs. Samuel M. Kootz

Henry Moore
Reclining Figure, 1957
Gift of Mr. and Mrs. G. David Thompson
as a memorial to his son, David (59)

Ronald J. Stein
Homage a Andres Segovia, 1956
Living Arts Foundation Fund and
Patrons Art Fund

Antoni Tapies
Painting, 1958*

1961 **Alberto Giacometti**
Man Walking, 1960

Jose Guerrero
Blue Depths, 1960
Gift of an Anonymous Donor through
the American Federation of Arts

Jean Ipousteguy
David, 1959
Anonymous Gift (62)

Henry Mundy
Device, 1961
William Frew Memorial Purchase Prize

Man Walking, 1960, by Alberto Giacometti, Swiss;
Patrons Art Fund, 1961.

Robert Natkin
The Sleeve, 1960
Gift of an Anonymous Donor through
the American Federation of Arts

Leon Polk Smith
Full White, 1958
Anonymous gift (62)

1964 **Jean (Hans) Arp**
Sculpture Classique, 1964
Patrons Art Fund and John Henry
Craner Fund (65)

Alicia Penalba
Great Winged Creature, 1963
Gift of the Women's Committee,
Museum of Art (65)

Antonio Saura
Imaginary Portrait of Goya, 1963
John Henry Craner Fund (65)

Pierre Soulages
24 November '63, 1963
Gift of Howard Heinz Endowment (65)

1967 **Gottfried Honegger**
Tableau-Relief W. Z. 425, 1966
Mr. and Mrs. James M. Bovard
Purchase Award

Joan Miro
Queen Marie-Louise of Prussia, 1966 (1968)*

David von Schlegell
Traverse, 1965-66
Kaufmann's Purchase Award (68)

1970 *(All acquired in 1970)*

Pierre Alechinsky
Luxe, Calme et Volupte, 1969
Gift of the Women's Committee,
Museum of Art

Joan Mitchell
Low Water, 1969*

George Segal
The Tightrope Walker, 1969
National Endowment for the Arts
Matching Grant and Fellows of The
Museum of Art Fund

Bram van Velde
Composition 1970

Jack Youngerman
March White, 1970
National Endowment for the Arts
Matching Grant and Fellows of The
Museum of Art Fund

(All below, except Daphnis, were acquired by gift
of The Hillman Foundation, Inc., 1970)

1970 **Nassos Daphnis**
5-69, 1969*

Emile Gilioli
Ecstasy, 1968

Gwyther Irwin
Obliquity, 1967

Joan Mitchell
Sans Neige, 1969
Pittsburgh Board of Public Education, the
sculpture is now displayed in the Sculpture
Court of The Museum of The Carnegie

1979 **Willem de Kooning**
Large Torso, 1974
Given by the Family and Friends of Tillie
S. Speyer in her memory (80)
Hillman Library, University of Pittsburgh

. . . .

1985 *International*

"A dozen works will have entered the
collection before the show opens"
                    — *John Lane, Director*

Georg Baselitz
Die Verspottung (The Mocking), 1938
G. B. Washburn & Women's Committee
Memorial Funds

Dara Birnbaum
Will O' The Wisp
Mr. & Mrs. Milton Fine and Carnegie
Acquisition Fund

Gilbert & George
Drunk With God
Richard M. Scaife Fund

Howard Hodgkin
The Cylinder, the Sphere, The Cone
Gene Baro Memorial Fund
Carnegie Acquisition Fund

Anselm Kiefer
Midgard Vitgard, 1980-85
Kaufmann's, Women's Committee
& Fellows Fund
Dem Unbekannten Maler
Richard M. Scaife and A. W. Mellon
Acquisition Funds

Per Kirkeby
Erdbeben
Mr. & Mrs. Stanley Gumberg

Bruce Nauman
Having Fun/Good Life Symptoms
Partners Reed Smith Shaw & McClay
& Carnegie Acquisition Fund

Sigmar Polke
Hochstitz 11, 1941
William R. Scott, Jr. Fund

Susan Rothenberg
Ten Men
Mr. & Mrs. A. F. A. Bryan & Foundations

Robert Ryman
Issue, 1985
Edith H. Fisher Fund

Richard Serra
Carnegie, 1984-85
Mrs. William Roesch

Cindy Sherman
No. 147
Pamela Z. Bryan Fund

. . . .

Bill Woodrow
Promised Land
Mrs. George L. Craig, Jr. Fund

1988 *International*
Ross Bleckner
Recover
The Hillman Company

Lothar Baumgarten
Tongue of the Cherokee
Women's Committee Museum of Art
Patrons Fund

Peter Fischli/David Weiss
The Way Things Go
Mary Jo & James Winokur

Günther Förg
Bleibild 26/88
A. W. Mellon Acquisition

Peter Halley
Two Cells
A. W. Mellon Acquisition

Brice Marden
Untitled 2
Edith H. Fisher Fund

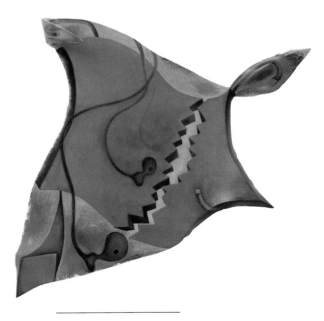

Don't Be Cruel, 1985-86, by Elizabeth Murray,
American; The Henry L. Hillman Fund, 1986.

Elizabeth Murray
Don't Be Cruel
Henry Hillman Fund

Gehard Richter
612-1 Untitled
A. W. Mellon Acquisition

Susana Solano
Dos Nones
Fellows Museum of Art Fund

Bill Viola
The Sleep of Reason
Milton Fine & Gift Fund

Andy Warhol
Self-Portrait
Fellows, Museum of Art Fund

1991 *International*
Judith Barry
ARS MEMORIAE CARNEGIENSIS
Museum Appropriation

Louise Bourgeois
Cell II
Heinz Family Fund

James Coleman
Background
Gift J. L. Hillman Simonds
Foundation
& H. L. Hillman Foundation

Dan Graham
Heart Pavilion
A. W. Mellon Acquisition

Ann Hamilton
Offerings (1)
Table from Offerings(2)
1. A. W. Mellon Acquisition Fund
2. Gift of the artist

On Kawara
19 JUL. 68, APR. 27, 1978, FEB. 29, 1988,
all from the Date Painting
A. W. Mellon & Carnegie Acquisition Funds

Louise Lawler
*HAVING ATTAINED VISIBILITY AS
WELL AS MANAGING TO CATCH THE
EYE OF THE SPECTATOR*
A. W. Mellon Acquisition Fund

Huang Yong Ping
Unreadable Humidity
Carnegie International Acquisition Fund

Tim Rollins + K. O. S.
The Temptation of St. Anthony - The Forms
Women's Committee Museum of Art

Continued. . .

Hiroshi Sugimoto
Arctic Ocean: Nord Kapp, Irish Sea: Isle of Man, Aegean Sea: Pilion,
all from *Time Exposed*
Gift of Milton Fine

Christopher Williams
(Supplement #7)
Seychelles 7/8
Gift Luhring Augustine Hetzler Gallery.

Cell II, 1991, by Louise Bourgeois, American, b. France; Heinz Family Fund, 1991.

The Museum of Art Still Owns over 200 Works from the Internationals

The number of purchases for the museum varied from year to year, from 18 works acquired in 1897 to none in 1933 or 1950. In at least 14 years, the only works purchased came from the exhibitions. The purchases were selected by the Director and the Fine Arts Committee of the museum, and included only 56 of the award-winning works. At least 75 works, primarily from the years before 1950, have been deaccessioned. Despite these losses, The Museum of Art still owns over 200 of the 320 works acquired from the *Internationals*. Approximately one-half are in storage (some for conservation reasons), but about 100 works, or one-third of what was acquired from the exhibitions, are currently on view in the museum galleries. The works range from Winslow Homer's *The Wreck*, the museum's first purchase, coming from the 1896 exhibition, to *Unreadable Humidity* by Huang Yong Ping from the 1991 exhibition.

Many of the works represent key paintings by 19th and 20th century masters. Examples include James McNeill Whistler's *Arrangement in Black: Portrait of Señor Pablo de Sarasate*, 1896, Puvis de Chavannes' *A Vision of Antiquity — Symbol of Form*, 1897, Oskar Kokoschka's *Portrait of Thomas Garrique Masaryk*, 1936, Edward Hopper's *Cape Cod Afternoon*, 1937, Willem de Kooning's *Woman VI*, 1955, Ellsworth Kelly's *Aubade*, 1958, Joan Miro's *Queen Marie-Louise of Prussia*, 1967, and Pierre Alechinsky's *Luxe, Calme et Volupte*, 1970. (Dates here refer to the year of the *International Exhibition.*)

Early acquisitions from the *Internationals* that remain in the collection concentrated on two styles. Impressionist paintings by the French artists Camille Pissarro and Alfred Sisley and by the Americans Childe Hassam, Mary Cassatt, W. Elmer Schofield, and John

Twachtman form the basis of the museum's particular strength in this area. Fashionable portraits by James McNeill Whistler, John Singer Sargent, James Shannon, and William Merritt Chase represent another stylistic trend at the turn of the century.

In the middle years of the *International*, the museum acquired only a few works from each exhibition. These purchases were primarily of works by artists associated with the earlier part of the century such as Oskar Kokoschka, James Ensor, and Georges Rouault. But in more recent years, the purchases reflected contemporary styles. In the '50s, '60s, and '70s, the museum acquired several large scale abstract works by renowned artists such as Richard Diebenkorn, Joan Mitchell, Pierre Soulanges, William Baziotes, and Sam Francis, works which provided the cornerstone of the museum's holdings of art created since 1945.

Since 1896 More Than 100 Works from Internationals *Given to the Museum*

Many of the museum's acquisitions have been gifts. Available statistics indicate that a significant number of works purchased from the *Internationals* have remained in Pittsburgh collections. For instance, in 1955, of 83 works sold, 52 stayed here. In 1967, of the 68 works sold, 42 remained in Pittsburgh. Of the works that remained in Pittsburgh many have entered the collection as gifts at a later date. Examples include John Kane's *Scene from the Scottish Highlands* shown in the 1927 exhibition and given by G. David Thompson in 1959, and René Magritte's *The Heart of the World* shown in 1958 and given by Mr. and Mrs. George L. Craig, Jr. in 1960.

Since the 1896 exhibition the museum has received over 100 gifts of works from the *Internationals*. Henry Clay Frick began the tradition with *Portrait of Andrew Carnegie* by Theobald Chartran in 1896. Many of the museum's friends are included in the list of donors, but the name that shows up most frequently is G. David Thompson, who gave 18 works from the *Internationals* to the museum in the 1950s. Mr. Thompson donated such prize winning works as Henry Moore's *Reclining Figure*, 1957 (Second Sculpture Prize in 1958), Corneille's *Where the Pavement Ends* (First Honorable Mention in 1955), and Cesar's *Animale Organico* (Third Sculpture Prize in 1958). He also gave Willem de Kooning's *Woman VI* (From the 1955 show) as well as works by Alfred Manessier and Joseph Albers.

The Carnegie Museum of Art Development of the Collections Influenced by Directors

The collection of Carnegie Institute's Department of Fine Arts grew more rapidly and more diversely than its founder, Andrew Carnegie, had anticipated in 1895. Seven years later the department had 54 European and American paintings. In another 15 years under the guidance of John Beatty, the first director, it possessed 120 paintings, 13 bronzes, 157 drawings, and 140 Western and non-Western prints. With passing decades the collection diversified still more. In 1991 The Carnegie Museum of Art had in its care approximately 400 American paintings and sculpture dating from the late 18th century to the end of World War II in 1945. It stands today among the nation's dozen or so most significant American art collections.

The *Carnegie International Exhibitions* regularly supplied the Department of Fine Arts with recent American paintings. As the collection evolved, it also came to have a strong contingent of earlier 20th century American Modernism and an extensive group of Western Pennsylvania paintings, including the largest single holdings of works by David Gilmour Blythe and John Kane, both of whom painted in Pittsburgh.

In honor of the sesquicentennial of Andrew Carnegie's birth in 1985, two publications were initiated by John R. Lane, then Director of The Museum of Art since 1980, *Museum of Art, Carnegie Institute Collection Handbook* and *American Drawings and Watercolors in The Museum of Art, Carnegie Institute*. A project initiated by Lane in 1982, but not published until 1992, was a handsome 511 page comprehensive history/catalogue, *American Paintings and Sculpture to 1945 in The Carnegie Museum of Art*.

It was the curator of Fine Arts, Oswald Rodriguez-Roque, who helped obtain a research grant from the National Endowment for the Arts for the publication. Continuing under the successor curator Henry Adams, it was completed by Diana Strazdes with the encouragement of the new director, Phillip M. Johnston, and participation by the members of the art staff. Various stages of the project were funded additionally by the Allegheny Foundation, the Pennsylvania Council on the Arts, James M. Walton, president of Carnegie Institute and Mrs. Walton, the National Endowment for the Humanities, the Luce Fund for Scholarship in American Art (Henry Luce Foundation, Inc.), Sotheby's, and the James H. Beal Publication Fund of The Carnegie Museum of Art.

The Development of a Collection

The collection of American paintings and sculpture to 1945 was built primarily through the purchases of directors whose chief interest was recent art. Only since the 1980s has the collection acquired the relatively protected status of a historical document. Created selectively and deliberately, as a vehicle for public instruction and an embodiment of that public's artistic ideals, the collection has been reshaped repeatedly.

The vicissitudes of The Carnegie's art collection were always interwoven with those of the larger institute of which it is a part, and of the city in which it is. Pittsburgh, fast dominating the nation in steel manufacturing and heavy industry, was acquiring a vast working-class population; this constituency Carnegie Institute was intended to serve. Until 1941 the galleries kept impressively long hours — ten in the morning to ten at night daily and two to six on Sundays — so that all workers in Pittsburgh would be able to visit despite their own long hours.

Dem Unbekannten Maler (To the Unknown Artist), 1983, by Anselm Kiefer, German; Richard M. Scaife Fund and A. W. Mellon Acquisition Endowment Fund, 1983.

For the paintings collection Andrew Carnegie wanted a gallery consisting of two American pictures for each year beginning with 1896, the year of the *First Annual Exhibition*, all hung in chronological order so as to show the progress of art in the United States. Carnegie insisted that no attempt be made to add older paintings to the collection but to concentrate on the acquisition of such modern pictures as are thought likely to become old masters with time. The collection, however, did include 146 photographs of old master paintings, thanks to John Beatty.

John Beatty, Director 1896-1922, and the Collection of American Paintings and Sculpture

In 1896 John Beatty became director of the Department of Fine Arts and served in that capacity until retiring in 1922. He was the city's most distinguished art educator, having been secretary of the Art Society of Pittsburgh and director of the Pittsburgh School of Design. A painter, illustrator, and etcher who had studied in Munich, he was on familiar terms with the European-trained artists of the American mainstream. He served on the advisory committee of the 1893 World's Columbian Exposition in Chicago, organized the exhibition of European art held on the occasion of the opening of The Carnegie Library of Allegheny City in 1890, and mounted the loan show of 321 works held in connection with the opening of Carnegie Institute in 1895.

By 1903 the Department of Fine Arts owned 19 American and 31 European paintings along the lines favored by such collectors as Boston's Isabella Stewart Gardner and Charles Freer of Detroit whose gallery is in Washington, D.C.

In l904 Beatty began to acquire drawings, most of them recent American examples. In 1906 Japanese woodblock prints were added. By 1911 etchings and engravings were about evenly divided between recent etchers such as Charles Meryon, Francis Seymour Haden, James McNeill Whistler, and old master engravers such as Albrecht Dürer, Heinrich Goltzius, and Robert Nanteuil.

A magazine review of 1906 described the annual fund as consisting "only of $50,000, but the director, Mr. John W. Beatty has done wonders with it." By far his most expensive

purchase was George de Forest Brush's *Mother and Child* at $16,500. Regrettably, it was deaccessioned in 1966 and is now in the Metropolitan Museum of Art in New York.

From 1916-1919 the director bought 14 bronzes by such American sculptors as Anna Hyatt Huntington, Abastenia Eberle, Augustus Saint-Gaudens, Frederick Macmonnies, and Hermon MacNeil. In 1919 he added two marbles by George Grey Barnard, and in l920, three bronzes by Barnard's mentor, Auguste Rodin.

The collection was augmented by gifts of paintings such as Pascal-Adolphe-Jean Dagnan-Bouveret's large *Christ at Emmaus* purchased by Henry Clay Frick in 1897, given the following year. James B. Laughlin, another of Pittsburgh's industrialists, also contributed a few smaller works of art at about the same time. Mrs. Charles Homer in 1918 gave 12 small oils by Winslow Homer, but the donations were few and nearly all acquisitions were purchases financed by Carnegie.

Beatty regretted that the permanent collection did not contain "works by some of the great painters of earlier days," such as John Constable and members of the Dutch and Spanish schools of the 17th century, but he did assemble a few "historical" paintings from the 18th and early 19th centuries. He bought two American works, Benjamin West's *Venus Lamenting the Death of Adonis* (1768) and Gilbert Stuart's *Portrait of Henry Nicols* (c. 1810), which continue to be the earliest American paintings in the collection.

When Beatty published his last collection checklist in 1917, the Department of Fine Arts possessed a compartmentalized permanent collection. The ancients were represented by plaster casts and marble copies, the old masters by etchings and engravings, and non-Western aesthetics by Japanese prints, while the moderns held sway over the collections of drawing and painting. The paintings collection had grown steadily to 118 canvases, of which 60 — the largest single national group — were by Americans.

Homer Saint-Gaudens, Director 1923-1950

The second director of the Department of Fine Arts was Homer Saint-Gaudens, the son of the sculptor Augustus Saint-Gaudens, and related on his mother's side to Winslow Homer. With a 1903 Harvard degree in architecture, he became a writer of short stories, a journalist, and for 14 years was stage director for Maude Adams, a famous actress of the day. He later entered the museum field and came to Pittsburgh as John Beatty's assistant in December, 1920. Eighteen months later he succeeded to the directorship, retiring in 1950 at age 70. Saint-Gaudens endured budget crises, an economic downturn, a World War, and aesthetic turmoil more troublesome than his predecessor had faced.

Soon after Andrew Carnegie's death in 1919, gifts of art began to come to Carnegie Institute. Some were American paintings and sculpture, contributed by the artists or their widows. The diversity of collections is noteworthy: ceramics in l920, English silver and American miniatures in 1922, old master drawings in 1923, and old master paintings (mainly Dutch and British portraits) in 1926 and 1929. The range of the collection began to resemble those of other art museums.

By the end of the Beatty administration, even after Carnegie had doubled the annual departmental funds in 1917, rising overhead costs and exhibition expenses had seriously hampered the director's ability to purchase art. In 1922 the Patron's Art Fund, a $130,000 paintings purchase fund, was established by 13 Pittsburgh patrons. Just two years later endowment income barely covered expenses, and the supposedly supplementary Patrons Art Fund became the sole source of revenue for the purchase of art. By 1926 the Department of Fine

Arts was operating at a deficit. Throughout the 1930s the director's annual report tells a tale of the burden of inadequate capital, and economies reluctantly taken. When the Great Depression struck and cancellation of the *Carnegie International* became a possibility, he argued that the exhibition was a "wise extravagance" whose annual cost was "less than half that of an important old master."

The first five or six years of Saint-Gaudens' artistic program were almost indistinguishable from those of Beatty. Carnegie Institute finally had to face the encroachment of modernism. The paintings bought were by American Impressionists (Mary Cassatt, Richard E. Miller, Edward Redfield, Charles Jay Taylor), by recent European painters who varied upon Impressionist conventions (Marius A. J. Bauer, Antonio Mancini, Italico Brass), or by purveyors of turn-of-the-century academic elegance (Alfred J. Munnings, Bernard Boutet de Monvel).

Saint-Gaudens reorganized the *International* so that paintings were arranged by national school. Major Realists won their share of first prizes, and so did major Modernists, Matisse in 1928 (which caused a furor), for example, Pablo Picasso in 1931, and Georges Braque in 1937.

The European paintings purchased were similar to their American counterparts. Saint-Gaudens built his collection around British, Italian, and Spanish painters: Augustus John, Colin Gill, Gerald Brockhurst, Ferruccio Ferrazzi, Felice Carena, Valentin de Zubiaurre, Ignacio Zuolaga, whose names scarcely appear in today's collective memory of 20th century masters.

Saint-Gaudens took an interest in those Americans of the past who could be perceived as predecessors of the Realist revival. The large-scale centennials at Carnegie Institute for Homer in 1936 and for Thomas Eakins in 1945 were expressions of this interest. So, too, were the purchases during the 1930s of Eakins'

Joseph R. Woodwell and John Singer Sargent's *Portrait of a Boy*. Another such purchase was William M. Harnett's *Trophy of the Hunt* (which came from Edith Halpert's Downtown Gallery in 1941, in trade for the 12 small Homer oils given by Mrs. Charles Homer in 1918).

During World War II, 1941-1945, Saint-Gaudens served as a lieutenant colonel and camouflage expert in the War Department, leaving the Department of Fine Arts to the assistant director, John O'Connor. The war also halted the *Carnegie Internationals* because of the disruption of trans-ocean shipping. Exhibitions of American art were mounted instead.

The war years also facilitated the purchase of American art. The savings realized from the suspended *Carnegie International* permitted the purchase, in 1942, of *Noli Me Tangere* by Albert P. Ryder and *Post Office* by David Gilmour Blythe, the latter being the first work in the collection by an artist whom O'Connor described as "one of America's old masters." Thanks to additional contributions to the Patrons Art Fund, O'Connor bought Robert Gwathmey's *Hoeing*, Marsden Hartley's *Young Hunter Hearing Call to Arms*, and Max Weber's *Quartet* in 1943 and Yasuo Kuniyoshi's *Mother and Daughter* in 1945. These four works, like Georges Rouault's expressionistic *Old King*, purchased in 1940, were the most "modern" acquisitions of the Saint-Gaudens era. Circumstances beyond the director's control contributed to the paucity of acquisitions to the permanent collection from 1922 to 1950.

Saint-Gaudens had little use for radical Social Realism and none at all for avant-garde art such as that in the collections of Albert Gallatin of Uniontown (Secretary of the U. S. Treasury, 1801-1814) and Pittsburgh-born Walter Arensberg (whom Fiske Kimball successfully solicited for the Philadelphia Museum of Art during the 1940s). Saint-Gaudens did not accession a single work of Abstract art, even 40 years or more after Abstraction appeared.

The Collection after 1950

Gordon B. Washburn, Director 1950-1962, Saint-Gaudens's successor, headed The Museum of Art, Rhode Island School of Design from 1942 to 1949 and before that, Buffalo's Albright Art Gallery. Washburn was determined to reshape and revitalize Carnegie Institute's art collection and bring the Department of Fine Arts, renamed The Museum of Art, into the ranks of major metropolitan museums. Washburn is best remembered in Pittsburgh as an advocate of Abstract art. His vision fit well with the renewed growth of Pittsburgh, and established the department's direction for the next 25 years.

Funding from the A. W. Mellon Educational and Charitable Trust in 1950 regenerated the *Carnegie International* from its 12-year lapse. Washburn rescheduled it as a triennial, eliminated its previous division into national schools, and rebuilt it as a showcase for international Modernism.

Contemporary Abstraction became the nucleus around which Washburn expanded the permanent collection. By the mid-1950s, as Abstract Expressionism became a prominent feature of the *Carnegie Internationals*, the works of the New York School — including those of Franz Kline, David Smith, Jackson Pollock, Willem de Kooning, and Ellsworth Kelly — began to enter the permanent collection. Equally interested in Abstract Expressionism's European counterparts, Washburn bought for the permanent collection works by such artists as Alberto Giacometti, Carl-Henning Pedersen, Asger Jorn, Afro Basaldella, and Alfred Manessier.

Washburn's purchases of American art prior to 1945 numbered merely 11. Some offered a ruggedly self-taught style (Edward Hicks' *Residence of David Twining*, Ralph Albert Blakelock's *Hawley Valley*, and John Kane's *Larimer Avenue Bridge*), others helped to fill the void in Abstract art (Stanton

Nymphéas (Water Lilies), 1920-21, by Claude Monet,
French; Acquired through the generosity of Mrs. Alan
M. Scaife, 1962.

Macdonald-Wright's *Sunrise Synchrony in Violet* and Patrick Henry Bruce's *Abstract*), and still others presented an American equivalent of Post-Impressionist painterliness, such as William Glackens' *La Villette*, Thomas P. Anshutz's *Steamboat on the Ohio*, and Alfred H. Maurer's *Landscape*.

Washburn also deplored the lack of old master paintings at Carnegie Institute and urged strengthening that part of the collection. The most significant change in Carnegie Institute's collecting history occurred in the last two years of his administration when Sarah Mellon Scaife, Andrew Mellon's niece, offered to purchase important European paintings of distinction for the permanent collection. Bidding unsuccessfully for Rembrandt's *Aristotle Contemplating the Bust of Homer* at auction in 1961, she bought instead Frans Hals' *Pieter Cornelisz, van der Morsch (Man with a Herring)* and Pietro

Perugino's *Saint Augustine with Members of the Confraternity of Perugia*. Purchasing Walter Chrysler's *Nymphéas (Water Lilies)* by Monet in 1962, Mrs. Scaife began a remarkable buying campaign that was continued by her family after her death in 1965 and lasted 17 years. It gave Carnegie Institute 43 mostly European paintings of the late 19th century, including the Impressionist and Post-Impressionist canvases that are now its best-known works. Washburn's purchases with Mrs. Scaife (Perugino, Hals, Edgar Degas, Pierre-Auguste Renoir, Edouard Vuillard, Monet, and Matisse) formed the beginning of a systematic representation of key schools of world art. All were by artists to whom line, color, and form seemed paramount, who, therefore, echoed the concerns of modern art and could be seen as its forerunners.

There is an interesting parallel of events concerning two of the key figures in 19th

practice in Paris. Manet and Dr. Evans met through his beautiful actress mistress who sometimes posed for the artist. When Evans died in 1897 his will endowed the construction of the Thomas W. Evans Museum and Dental Institution of Philadelphia. In 1912 the Institution was absorbed by The University of Pennsylvania and Evan's collection of art disappeared. This work was discovered in 1972 in a storeroom, when the dean of the dental school was looking for something to hang in his office. The first painting by Manet to enter the collection, it came to The Carnegie in 1984 by purchase through the William R. Scott, Jr. Fund.

century French painting: artists Monet b. 1840, and Manet b. 1832. A major work of each artist languished in obscurity for years before coming to The Carnegie. As mentioned above, The Carnegie Museum of Art owns Monet's *Waterlilies*, painted from 1920-21 as part of a project of a series of waterlily panels to be installed in the Orangerie, the former greenhouse in the Tuileries Gardens in Paris. Changes in the plans resulted in the panel remaining in Monet's studio for 30 years after his death in 1926. Through the generosity of Mrs. Scaife, the museum acquired the luminous painting from Walter Chrysler in 1962.

The museum also owns *Still Life with Brioche*, painted in 1880 by Edouard Manet, just three years before his death in 1883. The painting was purchased directly from the artist for 500 francs by Thomas W. Evans an American dentist who had an eminently successful

Still Life with Brioche, 1880, by Edouard Manet, French; William R. Scott, Jr. Fund, 1984.

Gustave von Groschwitz, Director 1963-1968

Washburn was succeeded by Gustave von Groschwitz, formerly senior curator at the Cincinnati Art Museum, who served as director from 1963 to 1968. Von Groschwitz continued to transform the permanent collection along the pattern that Washburn had initiated. Its most visible areas were Abstract art after World War II and French Impressionist and Post-Impressionist paintings. While the collecting of prints, drawings, and non-Western art continued under von Groschwitz, the number of old master paintings and sculpture also grew appreciably. Howard Noble's bequest of 26 old master paintings in 1964 was the most significant single addition. Von Groschwitz's purchases of American art prior to 1945 were negligible.

The problem that The Carnegie's directors of the 1950s and 1960s faced was that the bulk of the American art collection did not fit into reigning standards of museum-worthy art. A logical solution was deaccessioning. As of 1992 only 40 paintings and sculpture remained of the 97 Beatty had acquired for the museum. Of Saint-Gaudens' acquisitions only 60% of the American paintings and sculpture purchased or given during Saint-Gaudens' directorship had been retained.

Leon A. Arkus, Director 1969-1980

Leon Anthony Arkus, who had been Washburn's assistant director and Von Groschwitz's associate director, became director of The Museum of Art in 1969. During Arkus' 11 year tenure, the museum's collections also expanded considerably to encompass Asiatic, African, Meso-American, and Oceanic art, and photography as well. In 1969 a Department of Film was established; a year later a gift of over 2,800 objects from the estate of Ailsa Mellon Bruce greatly enriched the collection of Decorative Arts.

Pittsburgh by the 1960s had transformed itself from a steel town to a corporate capital. The Museum of Art was an example of the remarkable degree to which a city's stature can be correlated with the art owned by its museums. When the elegantly modern Sarah Scaife Gallery opened in 1974, more than 60% of the paintings on view in the "long white vistas" had been acquired in the previous dozen years. During Arkus' tenure, over 120 American paintings that date prior to the end of World War II were either purchased or given to The Museum of Art, a number exceeding Beatty's acquisitions by one-third.

The most visible American art purchases were from the general era of American Impressionism: Hassam's *Northeast Headlands, Appledore*, and Thomas Wilmer Dewing's *Morning Glories.* Maurice Prendergast's *Picnic* was purchased with the proceeds from a memorable "penny campaign" orchestrated by the Women's Committee of The Museum of Art in 1972. Works by several American Modernists entered the collection: John Graham, Georgia O'Keeffe, Augustus Vincent Tack, Arthur G. Dove, John B. Flannagan, and John Storrs. The Blythe and Kane holdings also increased impressively, to the extent that The Carnegie Museum of Art is today the largest single repository of these two artists' work. The representation of Western Pennsylvania artists was also increased.

The largest single addition that Director Arkus made to the collection of American paintings was in what might be called the "American school," mostly landscapes dating from 1845 to 1890, which Arkus built in partial compensation for the Hudson River School paintings that The Museum of Art never had. These purchases, made possible largely through funds established by Howard N. Eavenson, included modest but representative examples of works by such artists as Frederic E. Church, Worthington Whittredge, Martin Johnson Heade, Albert Bierstadt, George Catlin, William Ranney, Bingham, and Ryder. As a result the permanent collection offered for the first time more than a glancing representation of the two generations before Beatty.

John R. Lane, Director 1980-1987

Leon Arkus was succeeded by John R. Lane, holder of advanced degrees in art and business, who served as director from 1980 to 1987. He returned the *Carnegie International* to its historical place as one of the Institute's central activities. He revived the exhibition itself (which had been sidelined by Arkus) as well as the tradition of buying works from it, adding significantly to the museum's contemporary holdings.

Brought from storage were some of the more academic examples of the museum's 19th century paintings, among them Pascal Dagnan-Bouveret's *Christ and the Disciples at Emmaus*, Jules Bastien-Lepage's *Peasant*, Elihu Vedder's *Keeper of the Threshold*, and Edwin Austin Abbey's *Penance of Eleanor, Duchess of Gloucester*. This reflected the strong revived interest in Victorian and French academic painting.

Lane also added 70 works to the collection of American paintings dating to the end of World War II. His most notable addition was the purchase, by the Edith Fisher Fund, of paintings and sculpture by the American Abstract artists of the 1930s and 1940s, among them Burgoyne Diller, Ilya Bolotowsky, Charles Biederman, Harry Holtzman, John Sennhauser, and Gertrude Greene. These were juxtaposed against Leon Kroll's *Morning on the Cape* and a sampling of other Realist works from the 1930s that were retrieved from storage. Lane also set out to regain for the collection some of the aesthetic that typified the early years of the Department of Fine Arts: he purchased Brush's *Blue Madonna*, John LaFarge's *Roses on a Tray*, Richard E. Miller's *Reflections*, and John Sloan's *Coffee Line*, along with works by John Frederick Kensett, John F. Peto, Thomas Crawford, and Hiram Powers that filled other chronological gaps in the permanent collection.

The Carnegie's attitude during the 1980s toward its American paintings and sculpture can be summarized as an enthusiastic rediscovery of the core of the permanent collection. It indicated a new historicism — a desire to accept mutually contradictory past styles, to observe them together, and to present the works as highly valued objects. The publication, initiated by John Lane, of the comprehensive *American Paintings and Sculpture to 1945 in The Carnegie Museum of Art* was a measure of that attitude.

Phillip M. Johnston, Director 1987 to the Present

Phillip Johnston, holder of a master's degree from the University of Delaware through the Wintertur Museum, came from The Wadsworth Athenum in Hartford, Connecticut to Pittsburgh as curator of Decorative Arts. He accepted the directorship in 1987 when Dr. Lane moved to San Francisco to head the museum of art there.

Johnston's in-depth expertise in the field of Decorative Arts, coupled with an extensive knowledge of other areas of art, has made him especially effective in the role of director of the museum. The development of the collections was greatly accelerated in 1988 when the Second Century Fund Campaign established as a major goal the creation of significant endowment funds for acquisitions by The Museum of Art.

A challenge grant of $8 million from the Howard and Vira Heinz Endowments — now the Heinz Family Fund — plus the matching $8 million, has increased the museum's acquisition endowment funds by $16 million. An additional $3 million from the Heinz Family Fund will endow The Museum of Art directorship. Thus, the monies available to purchase works of art have grown from about $200,000 annually in 1984 to about $1 million a decade later. As a result more major works have been added to the collection in the last three years.

Surveying the literally hundreds of acquisitions in the various media since he took office,

Director Johnston was hard pressed to identify the most important for inclusion in this short selection, listed in order of year of acquisition.

Paintings, Sculpture and Installations

Brice Marden (American, b. 1938)
Untitled 2, 1986
Oil on linen
Edith H. Fisher Fund

Gerhard Richter (German, b. 1932)
612-1 Untitled, 1986
Oil on canvas
A. W. Mellon Acquisition Endowment Fund

Lothar Baumgarten (German, b. 1944)
The Tongue of the Cherokee, 1985-88
Painted, laminated and sandblasted glass
Museum purchase: gift of the Women's Committee,
The Carnegie Museum of Art and Patrons Art Fund

Bill Viola (American, b. 1951)
The Sleep of Reason, 1988
Video installation
Museum purchase: gift of Milton Fine

Gioachini Asseretto (Italian, 1600-1649)
Christ Healing the Blind Man, c. 1640
Oil on canvas
Museum purchase: gift of Mrs. Thomas S. Knight, Jr.,
in memory of her mother Mrs. George L. Craig, Jr.

Louise Bourgeois (American, b. France, 1911)
Cell II, 1991
Mixed media
Heinz Family Acquisition Fund

Neil Jenney (American, b. 1945)
North America, 1986
Oil on panel
Heinz Family Acquisition Fund

On Kawara (American, b. Japan, 1932)
Three paintings from the *Today, 1966 – 90* series,
1991
19 JUL. 68, 1968
APR 27, 1978, 1978
FEB 29, 1988, 1988
Liquitex on canvas
A. W. Mellon Acquisition Endowment Fund and
Carnegie *International* Acquisition Fund

Adolph von Menzel (German, 1815-1905)
Departure after the Party, 1860
Gouache and watercolor with gum arabic on paper
Heinz Family Acquisition Fund, 1992

Marsden Hartley (American, 1877-1943)
White Top Mountain, New Hampshire, 1930
Oil on Upson board
Fellows Fund, 1992

Albert Moore (British, 1841-1893)
Acacias, c. 1880
Oil on canvas
Heinz Family Acquisition Fund, 1993

Fernand Khnopff (Belgian, 1858-1921)
Portrait of Madeleine Mabille, 1888
Oil with pencil on mahogany panel
Heinz Family Acquisition Fund, 1993.

Robert Motherwell (American, 1915-1991)
Castile (Espana), 1952
Oil on masonite
Museum purchase: gift of Mr. and Mrs. Charles
Denby, by exchange, 1994

Importance of Individual Collectors

Over the years the role of individual collectors as shapers of the collection has increased. Edward Duff Balken, a print collector and curator of prints under Beatty and Saint-Gaudens, bequeathed a number of Maurice Prendergasts, including the panel painting *Women at Seashore.* Charles J. Rosenbloom, whose old master print collection is now the highlight of the museum's own, gave a number of idiosyncratic American paintings, notably Edward Hicks' *Peaceable Kingdom.* The importance of the 17-year span of contributions of Sarah Mellon Scaife and her family is without parallel.

In addition to these individual acquisitions, two major private collections have come to the museum as bequests. In 1989, the adjunct curator of Japanese prints **Dr. James B. Austin** bequeathed the museum his collection

Sailing, c. 1911, by Edward Hopper, American; Gift of Mr. and Mrs. James H. Beal in honor of the Sarah Scaife Gallery, 1972.

of more than 2,000 Japanese prints, ranging in date from the 11th century to the 20th, with particular strengths in Ukiyo-e and Buddhist prints. Schools represented in the collection include the Okamura, the Katsukawa, and the Utagawa. Among the artists represented are Hiroshige, Sharaku, Utamaro, Masanobu, Kuniyoshi, Shunko, and Yoshitoshi, as well as such modern figures as Hasui, Koson, Saito, Yoshida, Murakata Shiro, Ito Shinsui, Yumeiji, and François Nakayama. With Dr. Austin's extraordinary collection, The Museum of Art possesses major holdings in a medium so profoundly important in Japanese art.

Over more than 40 years **Mr. and Mrs. James Beal** gave the museum a number of their outstanding collection of American watercolors of the early 20th century, including Arthur G. Dove's remarkable pastel-on-panel *Tree Forms*, and Edward Hopper's early *Sailing*. (The Hopper was attorney Beal's favorite painting but he gave it to The Museum of Art in honor of the opening of the Sarah Scaife Gallery in 1974.) In 1993, at age 95, Rebecca Beal died, activating museum trustee Beal's bequest, bringing to

250 the total in this largest and most important collection of American art owned by The Carnegie Museum of Art.

Rebecca Beal's interest in American painters ranged from Jacob Eichholtz of Lancaster, Pennsylvania, her great-grandfather whose biography she wrote, to Charles Burchfield, whose watercolors she was inspired to collect after seeing his works exhibited in ten *Carnegie Internationals* by 1944. (*Carnegie Magazine*, March/April, 1994, discussed The Beal Collection in detail.)

A third private collection which from 1995 will have a significant presence among the museum's contemporary works is that of **Mr. and Mrs. Charles H. Carpenter, Jr.**, friends who helped "sell" Phillip Johnston on Pittsburgh's Carnegie Museum of Art. As a young chemical engineer with U. S. Steel, Carpenter was the protégé of G. David Thompson, quintessential collector of the work of contemporary artists. With tastes tutored by visits to the *Internationals* and other exhibitions and programs of the museum, Mr. and Mrs. Carpenter collected a major group of contemporary works by Lynda Benglis, Jim Dine, Gilbert and George, Ellsworth Kelly, Kenneth Noland, Claes Oldenburg, Jules Olitski, Ad Rinehardt, Charles Shaw, Richard Stankiewicz, and Jackie Winsor. In addition, a 17th century Connecticut sunflower chest, a rare Tiffany punch bowl of 1906, designed by Louis Comfort Tiffany, and the *Rainforest Table* by contemporary furniture maker Edward Zuzza will join the Decorative Arts collection as gifts from Mr. and Mrs. Carpenter.

In accordance with Andrew Carnegie's original plan, The Museum of Art obtains a number of works, some by purchase and some by gift, from the periodic *Carnegie International Exhibitions*. The previous sections contain more detail on those acquisitions.

The Carnegie Museum of Art Prints & Drawings Collections

Because prints, drawings, and other works of art on paper are vulnerable to light exposure, they are not on permanent exhibition as are oil paintings, sculpture, furniture, and various decorative arts. The Carnegie Museum of Art does, however, have a large and varied collection of prints, drawings, watercolors, pastels, and photographs. By 1995, the total of this collection increased to more than 11,000, of which 7,000 are prints. Represented are outstanding examples from the 15th century to the present, which from time to time are selected by the curators for inclusion in special exhibitions. There are also traveling exhibitions and showings of special interest such as *Mark Rothko: Works on Paper, 1925-1970* which opened for the Founders-Patrons Day in 1984 and *In the Watercolor Tradition: British works on Paper from the Mellon Bank Collection*, shown in 1990, with many other exhibitions in between.

Japan Bridge in the Rain, c. 1835, by Utagawa Hiroshige, Japanese; Bequest of Dr. and Mrs. James B. Austin, 1989.

The Andrew Carnegie Fund in 1917 was largely responsible for The Museum of Art having one of the world's finest collections of works by Charles Meryon, 1821-1868, of Paris. He was the only major French artist of the 19th century to devote himself exclusively to printmaking, having turned to the art of etching when he discovered he was colorblind. The rare series *Eaux-fortes sur Paris*, 1850-1854, consists of 12 large views and 10 accessory items, all printed by the artist on a small press in his apartment. The first image in the series is the most famous: *Le Stryge* or *The Vampire*, 1861. This print is the eighth and final impression by the printmaker and publisher Auguste Delatre, after retouching by the artist.

Edward Duff Balken, a print collector and curator of prints under two directors, Beatty and Saint-Gaudens, bequeathed his considerable collection to the museum. Included were a number of works by Maurice Prendergast. Augmentation of the collections has been aided for nearly 20 years by the Charles J. Rosenbloom Fund for acquiring prints and drawings. By transfer from The Carnegie Library of Pittsburgh, an important group of old master prints, along with well-known images by J. A. M. Whistler, Felix Bracquemond, Jean-Baptiste

Le Stryge, 1861, by Charles Meryon, French; Andrew Carnegie Fund, 1917.

Corot, and Francis Seymour Haden, entered the collection.

Three especially remarkable gifts from private collectors have vastly enriched the museum's holdings: in 1974 the collections of Charles Rosenbloom, centering on early prints and etchings by European masters; in 1978 a collection of Japanese prints which span 800 years of the woodcut technique, given by Dr. and Mrs. James B. Austin; and in 1993 the dazzling collection of watercolors by contemporary American artists assembled by James and Rebecca Beal.

Selections from each of these collections have been exhibited recently. In March of 1993 some of the Rosenbloom gifts were in the *Great Etchings from the Permanent Collection* exhibition. The Austin highlights were shown in the fall of 1993, *The Fifty-three Stages of the Tokaido* (Eastern Sea Highway) by Utagawa Hiroshige (1797-1858) and earlier, *Japanese Prints of the Golden Age*, prints by Hokusai (1760-1859) and Utamaro (1754-1806). And in 1994, a group of 90 works was shown in *Towards Modernism: American Art from the Beal Collection*.

The *Great Etchings from the Permanent Collection* exhibition was enhanced by the inclusion of an etcher's tools, loaned by Pittsburgh-based artist Leonard Liebowitz, who also had several of his own prints in the show. From the Rosenbloom collection there was, among other works, the only known etching by Peter Paul Rubens, *St. Catherine in the Clouds*, 1620-21. The work was created more than a century after the first known print dated 1513. Etching had been a technical secret in the 16th century. This exhibition is worthy of special mention as it highlighted many brilliant etchings from the museum's coffers, among them works by a group illustrative of the evolution of etching: Degas, Dürer, Goya, Picasso, Piranesi, Ribera, Whistler, and Rembrandt. Several other artistic greats were represented, namely the Frenchmen Charles Meryon, Felix Bracquemond, and James

Tissot; and artists Anders Zorn, James Enzor, Pablo Picasso, Edward Hopper, Camille Corot, Kathe Kollwitz, and arguably the greatest of all, Rembrandt with his *Hundred Guilders Print*. An earlier exhibition, in 1982, displayed the museum's series of 22 engravings of the biblical *Book of Job*, interpreted by the British artist and poet, William Blake, 1557-1627.

Aside from the Japanese works, the focus of the print collection is a nucleus of Renaissance and Baroque works by Dürer, Mantegna, Ribera, Pieter Breughel the Elder, Rembrandt, Goltzins, and Lucius von Leyden. They represent some of the finest impressions extant. The modern schools include works by Whistler, Cezanne, Matisse, Picasso, Edward Hopper, and Charles Burchfield. A large number of contemporary prints, many of an innovative or experimental nature, were acquired with various funds. Works by Sol LeWitt, Philip Guston, Jennifer Bartlett, John Graham, Richard Artschwager, Susan Rothenburg, Warrington Colescott, and George Nama of Pittsburgh were among these. Other prints by Felix Buhot and Joseph Pennell were given by Edith and Milton Lowenthal, and a series of 18 wood engravings by the early 20th century American artist Henry Glintenkamp was the gift of Dr. Mark Steele.

In recent years significant additions by contemporary artists Pierre Alechinsky, Jasper Johns, Frank Stella, James Dine, and Robert Motherwell have greatly enhanced the prestige of the collection. *Untitled 1958* by Frank Stella (b. 1936) was the gift of Mrs. George L. Craig, Jr. in memory of her husband.

The latest of the great collections to come to the museum in its 99-year history was the 1993 bequest of The Beal Collection. Added were 250 works of art to those already given to the museum by trustee Mr. and Mrs. James Beal. Along with the oil paintings there are watercolors, drawings, and prints by Winslow Homer, Thomas Eakins, Maurice Prendergast, Edward Hopper, Charles Burchfield, Arthur

Dove, Marsden Hartley, Charles Demuth, Charles Sheeler, Andrew Wyeth, and Rebecca Beal, herself an accomplished artist, all done between 1880 and 1950. There are also lithographs by Philadelphian Benton Spruance (1904-1967). Some of the works in the 1994 Beal exhibition by David Blythe, John Kane's *Bloomfield Bridge*, and Charles Demuth's watercolor *Artist on the Beach* had been earlier gifts by the Beals to the museum.

The drawing collection includes important early works by Tintoretto, Jacopo Bassano, Luca Cambiaso, the School of Leonardo da Vinci and Galli Bibiena, Bibera, and Canaletto, as well as later European works by William Blake, Dominique Ingres, Charles Meryon, and Edgard Degas; and American drawings and watercolors by Benjamin West, Winslow Homer, Thomas Dewing, and James Whistler. Significant artistic developments that occurred at the beginning of the 20th century are reflected in works by Matisse, Modigliani, Klimt, Klee, DuBuffet, Arp, and Chillida.

A collection of 12 drawings, watercolors, and prints by 20th century artists was given by Mr. and Mrs. Sidney M. Feldman. Several contemporary works were acquired through the Leisser Art Fund, including *Acrobat,* a color woodcut by Anne Ryan; *Les Belles et La Bete II,* 1978, an etching and engraving by Peter Milton; and nine etchings and engravings of 1966-76 by Richard Claude Ziemann. Paul Leeman donated 22 prints by contemporary American artists. Six prints by contemporary American and European artists such as James Rosenquist and Jean Helion were presented by Mr. and Mrs. William A. Nitze.

Among the important drawings acquired in 1981: Worthington Whittredge's, *Forest Interior,* 1867, gift of the H. J. Heinz, II Charitable and Family Trust, a masterful pen-and-ink landscape drawing; Theo Wujcik's, *Jasper Johns,* 1980, a large realist portrait of the celebrated painter, gift of The Bryan Foundation; James

Torlakson's, *Southern Pacific No. 3196,* 1980, a photorealist watercolor of a locomotive, purchased with the Patrons Art Fund; Gary Alan Bukovnik's, *Red Tulips,* 1981, a folding screen in watercolor, gift of The Hunt Foundations; and four drawings entitled *Perimeters and Interiors,* 1980, by the British minimalist/conceptualist artist Christopher John Watts, gift of Mr. and Mrs. James L. Winokur.

Other important acquisitions are a watercolor by the British artist Alan Davie, *The Pink Man's Prayer,* 1965, given by the Harry P. Blum Family in memory of Muriel Blum; and a crayon drawing *Les Coureurs* by the Yugoslavian-born Parisian artist Dado, given by Mr. and Mrs. Alexander C. Speyer, III. In 1983 a drawing, *Portrait of a Woman,* 1941-1952, by John Graham, American b. Russia 1881-1961, entered the collection through the Constance Mellon Fund, the William Frew Memorial Fund, and gift of Laura Baer, by exchange.

The Drue Heinz Foundation's gift in 1992 brought the museum a watercolor by famed American industrial designer Raymond Loewy, b. France, 1893-1986, *Pennsylvania Railroad Dining Car Interior . . . ,* 1946. The painting entered the collection and appeared on the menu cover of The Museum of Art Café.

Reference Library
The collection includes art reference books and catalogues on American, European, and Oriental art and architecture; periodicals, bulletins, biographical files, and slides; as well as microfilm of the museum's archives up to 1940. The library of 10,000 volumes is reserved for staff use and purposes of scholarly research by appointment only.

Time Exposed, 1991, by Hiroshi Sugimoto, Japanese; 1991 *Carnegie International.*

The Carnegie Museum of Art Collection of Photographs

The Museum of Art has developed a collection of photographs representing some of the best 19th and 20th century artists in this medium. The works of August Sander, E. J. Bellocq, Julia Margaret Cameron, David Octavius Hill, J. H. Lartique, and Alfred Steiglitz are among those included. The museum also received a large collection of early photographs of Pittsburgh scenes from The Carnegie Library. A group of 10 photographs (1916-1923) titled *Draped Nude* by John Covert entered the collection via the Patron's Art Fund. John Covert is said to be the only artist with a Pittsburgh background to have played a significant role in the development of early 20th century Modernism.

The year 1980 brought a number of important additions: 15 photographs from 1949-1968 by Elliot Erwitt were given in honor of Leon A. Arkus, retiring director of The Museum of Art, by Mr. and Mrs. Eugene Cohen. (Earlier they had given 15 photographs by

Time Exposed, 1991, by Hiroshi Sugimoto, Japanese; 1991 *Carnegie International.*

Manuel Bravo (1902) in honor of Mrs. Cohen's parents, Sarah and David Weis.); 20 photographs by Lewis Hine, many taken in the Pittsburgh area, were given by Mr. and Mrs. Walter Rosenblum. Mr. and Mrs. Leonard Schugar gave four photographic portraits of the Western Pennsylvania photographer Luke Swank, by

Chauncey C. Morley. Mr. Schugar was himself a master photographic artist whose work has been exhibited in The Museum of Art.

Also in 1980 the Joel Greenwald Photograph Purchase Fund was established. Purchases from the Director's Discretionary Fund have included: *Satiric Dancer (Kiki),* 1926, by Andre Kertesz (American b. 1896); three photographs by Harry Callahan (American b. 1912); and a nine-image sequence, *Things are Queer,* 1973, by the Pittsburgh-born artist Duane Michals. Works by Mark Cohen and John van Alstine were also acquired through the Discretionary Fund. A photograph with a double interest to Pittsburghers is the *Self Portrait in Armor,* 1916, by John Covert who was born here, 1882-1960. He was a younger cousin of Walter Arensberg, whose art collection went to the Philadelphia Museum of Art. Covert studied painting here under Munich-trained Martin Leisser, trustee of The Carnegie. This photograph came to Pittsburgh's museum as a gift in 1986 of Covert's uncle Charles Covert Arensberg and his wife.

The Patron's Fund aided the addition of *That Is* by John Baldessari to the collection also in 1986 and, in 1987, two photographs by Ramon Eldzua from his *Loss of Home* series.

Memorable Exhibitions

Photography as an art form and photography as influencing the attitude of a nation were the two themes of the exhibition *American Photographers and the National Parks* at The Museum of Art, the summer of 1982. This major exhibition featured 205 masterworks of American landscape photography by 35 artists from 1870 to the present and traced the development of the national park idea from its genesis to its present spectacular dimensions. Photographs of Yellowstone taken by William Henry Jackson (1843-1942) hung in the Capitol rotunda in Washington, D.C. when the bill was introduced in 1871. When the Yellowstone Act was passed

in 1872, it established the national parks for all the people.

The exhibition included the dramatic, inventive photographs of Eadweard J. Muybridge (1830-1904) whose Yosemite Valley landscapes attracted international attention to the valley and to photography itself in the 1870s. Photographs by George Fiske (1837-1918) who aided noted conservationist, John Muir, in winning national park status for the area in 1880, were also shown. The work of Timothy O'Sullivan (1840-1882) who, in 1873, was the first to photograph the Grand Canyon, was among these photographs which remain the standard against which other photographs of the site are measured.

The works displayed a variety of photographic techniques: vintage albumen prints and controlled black-and-white gelatin silver prints by Ansel Adams (b. 1902) and Edward Weston (1886-1958); cibachrome prints by William Garnett (b. 1916); dye transfer prints by Eliot Portor (b. 1901); and hand-retouched gelatin silver prints by Anne Brigman (1869-1950).

The *Carnegie International Exhibitions* have also been the source of additions to the photography collection of the museum. One notable photograph from the 1985 exhibition was acquired through the Pamela Z. Bryan Fund: *No. 147* (48 by 72 inches), by Cindy Sherman, b. 1954, USA.

Of special interest locally was the excellent survey *Pittsburgh Photography: A New Generation,* exhibited at the museum in 1987.

From the 1991-92 *International,* by gift from trustee Milton Fine, the museum received five photographs: *Arctic Ocean: Nord Kapp; Irish Sea: Isle of Man; Aegean Sea: Pilion; Indian Ocean: Bali;* and *Java Sea: Bali* all from *Time Exposed* by Horoshi Sugimoto b. 1948, Japan.

Other exhibitions have benefited the collection, for example: *Eliza: Elegy for a Mill* was the exhibition in 1986 of the haunting photographs of Mark Perrott, documenting the razing of the Jones & Laughlin blast furnace *Eliza*. The dismantling of the plant, the last steel mill within the city limits, was a visual metaphor for the change that overtook Pittsburgh in the 1980s. These furnaces had stretched along the banks of the Monongahela River in South Oakland since 1859. In 1979 the company decided that the mill would be abandoned, demolished, and the 48-acre plot made the site for high technology firms.

When his request for permission to photograph the demolition process was denied, Perrott assumed the dangerous risk of proceeding on his own, which he did over four years. His photograph *Gloves, 1980* speaks eloquently of the tragedy of abandonment and destruction. "In the detritus the mill hands left behind, the ghostly evidence of past human occupation — gloves, gas masks, salt shakers, upended chairs and tables, trashed files, and graffiti, showed how the workers personalized the spaces and equipment, transforming spots within the industrial workplace into homey sites of respite from noise, heat, and dirt. Without including the image of a single individual at work, Perrott powerfully evoked a feeling for the generations of people who worked the mills and found their version of the American dream." Perrott's *Eliza* photographs underline the unhappy reality that many of the people who counted on the mill economy may never work again. He documented every phase of the demise of the J & L plant.

In the decades of steel's heyday, documentary photographers Lewis Hine and W. Eugene Smith brought the hissing, seething, working mills to life. Smith's extraordinary Pittsburgh project, was originally conceived as photographic documentation for Stefan Lorant's monumental book *Pittsburgh*, envisioned by Edgar J. Kaufmann, president of Kaufmann's department store. Of the 10,000 photographs Smith took for the book, Lorant used only about 60 of them, enraging the volatile Smith.

The dark epic poem Smith created in 1955-56 consisted of approximately 13,000 negatives (among them *Smoky City*, one of the classic American photographs, in the foreground of which appears the J & L plant) and is considered to be one of the great achievements in the art form of the photographic essay.

Both Smith and Perrott endeavored to create bodies of work that would tell an important, revealing story of a unique locale and show an appreciation for the lives that gave meaning to it. Perrott's *Eliza* portfolio of 25 prints was added to the collection of The Carnegie Museum of Art. A book, *Remembering A Pittsburgh Steel Mill*, was published by the Howell Press of Charlottesville, Virginia, with an introduction by John R. Lane, director of The Carnegie Museum of Art when Perrott's images were exhibited here. (Much of this material is from Dr. Lane's introduction.)

Smith's *Smoky City* 1955-57 entered the collection in 1982, by purchase through the Vira I. Heinz Fund of the Pittsburgh Foundation. This photograph brings together two Pittsburgh landmarks: the University of Pittsburgh's Cathedral of Learning and the towers of St. Paul's Cathedral, "the two stand like pillars of hope almost obscured by the smoke of a nearby steel mill." In the opinion of Henry Adams, then curator of Fine Arts at The Carnegie, "*Smoky City* may be the finest photograph Smith took in Pittsburgh. It is as much a part of Pittsburgh's past as is the legacy of Andrew Carnegie."

In 1992, through the Patron's Art Fund, the museum acquired a number of photographs from Mark Perrott's *White* series entitled *Galaxi, Clown, Mad Mouse, Airplanes, Carol, Slide,* and *Scooter Car.*

Exhibits of groups of photographs on a rotating basis are shown from time to time by the museum. Collectors-quality photographs and catalogues of some of the exhibitions are for sale in The Museum of Art Shop.

The Carnegie Museum of Art Department of Film and Video

1995 marks the Department of Film and Video's celebration of its 25th anniversary. The museum's film program was initiated in 1969 by Sally Dixon of the Women's Committee of The Carnegie Museum of Art who began with seasonal weekly screenings and monthly presentations by visiting independent filmmakers. Under William Judson, curator since 1975, the department has grown to become one of the largest museum-based media arts centers in the United States.

In keeping with The Carnegie's goal of representing different cultures and addressing a broad spectrum of the Pittsburgh area community, the department presents a diversity of film series and related programming devoted to issues of cultural perspectives and ethnic identity. One measure of this commitment is the fact that these film programs, from Athens to Zagreb, from Armenia to Zimbabwe, are among the most multilinguistic cultural programs in the region. In a recent 12 month period, for instance, the languages of the films shown by the department included Mooré, Bambara, Wolof, Czech, Slovak, French, Spanish, Danish, Serbo-Croatian, German, Hopi, Lakota, Polish, Russian, and Japanese, as well as English. It is not unusual to hear the audience discussing the film it its own language after a screening.

The Programs: Film

More than 125 series devoted to various aspects of the history of films have been presented since 1970, and the work of nearly 100 important directors from around the world, from Antonioni to Zanussi, has been presented in depth through retrospective series. *The Visiting Filmmaker Series*, which also began in 1970, has developed into one of the most important aspects of the film program, having included artists from countries in Europe as well as from Australia, Japan, China, Iran, the Phillipines, and the United States.

This visiting artist series has had a local component as well: several Pittsburgh film artists like Tony Buba and Paul Glabicki have been invited to show their work, and the 1979 season featured a presentation by the founder of Pittsburgh's Society for Contemporary Crafts, Elizabeth Rockwell Raphael, who showed her collection of experimental films from the 1940s by artists Joseph Cornell and Maya Deren.

In the fall of 1984 the series featured a group of films from New York's underground movement of the 1960s. Jack Smith, actor and filmmaker presented his notorious *Flaming Creatures* (1963) and his recent work. Andy Warhol's *Chelsea Girls* and *Vinyl and/or Loves of Ondine*, of that era were presented by Ondine, one of Warhol's "superstars" who appeared in both films. Later in that fall season the department screened the work of famed controversial director Roman Polanski. The survey began with *Knife in the Water* (1962) and spanned seven of his other films, to *Tess* (1980). (Polanski grew up in Nazi-occupied Poland living under a false identity after his parents had been sent to a concentration camp.)

A 16-mm film *Dog Star Man* (1961-1964) by Stan Brakhage was a gift of the A. W. Mellon Educational and Charitable Trust in 1971. The film is considered a watershed work in the 30-some year career of this prolific artist, recognized as a monumental figure who established a new level of aesthetic ambition and thematic scope in the avant-garde in American films.

A broad variety of films continues to be presented, ranging from examples of the work of important directors, historical films from the early history of the medium, to independently produced contemporary American films and contemporary films from abroad. There are approximately 100 such events each year. Included annually are series of Latin American

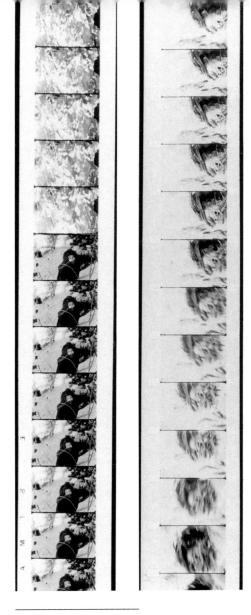

Dog Star Man, 1961-64, by Stan Brakhage, American; Gift of the A. W. Mellon Educational and Charitable Trust, 1971.

and African American films, the latter presented at the Homewood Library as well as at the museum. All the department's showings are accompanied by program notes and, frequently, discussions by special speakers. Quarterly, a brochure with a full schedule of film and video and description of events is widely distributed.

The film programs are usually shown in The Museum of Art Theater, which for evening events is accessible through the museum's Forbes Avenue and Sculpture Court entrances. The video programs are presented in the Video Exhibition Gallery continuously during the museum's regular hours.

Video

One especially memorable video installation in 1985, *Tough Limo* by Francesc Torres b. 1948, utilized a large scale model of a military tank, with live iguanas, folding chairs, and projected videotape. In the video Torres arranged a "house" of playing cards assaulted by an errant toy tank. The central iconographic element in both the video tape and the installation was the military tank. Images showed Russian tanks in Prague in 1968 with sounds of British Field Marshall Montgomery talking to his officers, a heap of chairs recalling the assassination of Egypt's peace-seeking President Anwar Sadat, plus live iguanas as "crew" of the model tank, which also crawls like a lizard. Less specific was the reference to the triune brain theory of neuro-physiologist Paul D. MacLean in which the most primitive layer is called the Reptilian Complex and regulates ritualistic behavior, territoriality, and aggression.

During the summer of 1994, with a subliminal backdrop of the celebrations of World War II's 50th anniversary of D-Day, the department continued to provide a rich menu of film and video. A sampling included two videos: *History and Memory* (1991) by New York-based Rea Tajiri, about the internment of Japanese Americans during World War II, and *Ellis Island*

The Sleep of Reason, 1988, video installation by Bill Viola, American; Gift of Milton Fine and A. W. Mellon Acquisition Endowment Fund, 1988.

(1982) by choreographer/dancer Meredith Monk and Robert Rosen, evoking the traumatic experiences of the turn-of-the-century immigrants. The Museum of Art theater program included a series of French films, all Pittsburgh premieres, including the study of a teenage suicide *Young Werther* by Jacques Dillon and *The Eye of Vichy* by Claude Chabrol, which documents the collaborationist government of Field Marshall Petain from 1940 to 1944. During the same time a series of Chinese films was offered, including the first Chinese film to be nominated for the Best Foreign Language Film Academy Award, *Ju Dou* (1990) by Zhang Yimou, "a complex and factual story of passionate love" which examines the role of women in Chinese society. Another type of love story was *Farewell My Concubine* (1993) by Chen Kaige, spanning the turbulent period of Chinese history between 1922 and 1977.

Cooperation With Other Media

The department has long encouraged and cooperated with the various media arts resources in the region. In 1971, for example, the museum sponsored the establishment of the Pittsburgh Filmmakers as a non-profit equipment access center for the area and over the years has cooperated with the Three Rivers Arts Festival, film and theater arts programs at WQED, the nearby universities, and with other organizations representing specific cultural interests, such as the Holocaust Center and the Thomas Merton Center, and many other ethnic and community groups. Examples of such cooperation have been the screening of films based on Shakespeare's plays during the University of Pittsburgh's Three Rivers Shakespeare Festival, and the screening of *Finnegan's Wake* during the annual Bloomsday celebration of the publication of James Joyce's *Ulysses*.

The Sleep of Reason, 1988, video installation by Bill Viola, American; Gift of Milton Fine and A. W. Mellon Acquisition Endowment Fund, 1988.

Most of the films shown by the museum are rented or borrowed from commercial distributors, independent cooperatives, archives, circulating film series, or the artists themselves. However, the department also has a study collection, begun in 1972 with support from the National Endowment for the Arts' Museum Program and The Carnegie Museum of Art's Women's Committee, containing approximately 200 titles of 16-mm and 8-mm films, and 100 videotapes. In 1990-91, with special grants from the John D. and Catherine T. MacArthur Foundation and the Pennsylvania Council on the Arts, additional works by Pennsylvania artists were added and quality 35-mm projectors were acquired. Films from the museum's study collection are shown in special screenings free to the public. A growing collection of reference materials relating to the film and video collections has been developed, together with

a more general reference library available to the public by appointment. A grant from the Juliet Lea Hillman Simonds Foundation is designed to enhance the film and video collection and to increase its accessibility to the public.

Video Installations

In 1981 the museum, with a grant from the Fisher Charitable Trust for the initial equipment, made an increased commitment to video as an art form, creating permanent gallery space for the continuous exhibition of videotapes. Also, throughout the 1980s the works of performance artists such as Ulrike Rosenbach, Kathy Rose, Spalding Gray, Joan Jonas, and Ping Chong were presented. By 1994, 11 annual one-person video/media arts installation exhibitions had been shown. One especially memorable work was created especially for the Foyer of the Scaife Gallery by James Byrne of

Minneapolis. Seven color screens were hung against the towering glass windows looking to the Sculpture Court showing video images of scenes in the court juxtaposed against the viewer's own visions of the actual scene. Visual cross references were made, for example, between Maillol's sculpture *Night*, a bronze nude woman seated with her head bowed over her knees, and the live figure, also in the sculpture court, of an actual nude male videotaped in a similar location.

The Video Purchase Fund in 1985 bought for the museum *Global Groove* (1973) by Nam June Paik. The artist was born in Korea in 1932, trained as a musician and is generally considered the first major artist to work with the creative possibilities of video. This videotape marked an important moment in his career. The museum since 1986 has acquired the video installations *Will-O'-The Wisp* by Dara Birnbaum, *The Sleep of Reason* by Bill Viola, and *The Big Video Chair* by Buky Schwartz, the New York based Israeli sculptor and video artist.

In 1988 the department organized the major exhibition of video installations, *American Landscape Video: The Electronic Grove*. It was the first exhibition to look at video from a historical prospective, in this instance the tradition of American landscape painting. Following its successful showing, it traveled to the San Francisco Museum of Modern Art and the Newport Harbor Art Museum. In 1991 *Points of Departure: Origins in Video*, organized by Independent Curators Incorporated was presented in Pittsburgh.

Supporters of the Program

Over the years important support for the Film and Video program has been received from the Allegheny Foundation, the Howard Heinz Endowment, the Fisher Charitable Trust, the Pennsylvania Council on the Arts, the National Endowment for the Arts, the A. W. Mellon Educational and Charitable Trust, the John D.

and Catherine T. MacArthur Foundation and the Juliet Lea Hillman Simonds Foundation. Important in another dimension is the praise, encouragement, and attendance of hundreds of loyal viewers. For example the January/February 1992 issue of *Carnegie Magazine* contained a "fan letter" from Gene Levy, of the History Department of Carnegie Mellon University, expressing his appreciation of the Film and Video programming. Special mention was made of the series dealing with censored films such as the American documentary, *Seventeen* and the Polish film *Interrogation*, suppressed in 1982 and only released with the triumph of Solidarity at the end of the decade. The films of Nagisa Oshima, the Japanese director of the controversial *In The Realm of the Senses* in the series of 1985 were lauded. Also praised were films in the *Cutting Edge* series, including *Women's Story*, an exceptional 1988 Chinese film, and *Palombella Rosa* by the Italian filmmaker Nanni Moretti. "Later series dealing with John Cassavetes, Mikio Naruse and Marcel Pagnol remain vivid to me as does a powerful set of films by the Hungarian director Marta Meszaros" . . . a well deserved tribute.

Museum of Art Exhibitions In Addition to the Internationals

As has been mentioned in an earlier chapter concerning the *Carnegie International Exhibitions,* the energies of The Museum of Art earlier this century turned toward exhibiting rather than collecting art. Other exhibitions, as indicative of the changes in emphasis which occurred from the Arkus directorship to that of Dr. Lane, and from John Lane to Phillip Johnston, will be briefly touched upon.

With regard to the major exhibitions orchestrated, if not originated, by The Museum of Art, *The Treasures of Ancient Irish Art* in 1978 and *Shakespeare: The Globe & The World* in the summer of 1980 were stupendous in their scope and the involvement of the community with activities at the museum and the Institute. Each sparked all sorts of lively celebrations, dance, music, theater, bringing the public to the exhibitions, and taking the themes of the exhibitions to the public throughout the area. The exhibitions of each year are listed in the annual report. The 1979 report was Leon Arkus' last as director; the 1980 report was by John Lane but included half a year prior to his taking office, and the 1981 report was of the first full year under his leadership. The exhibitions listed for those three transitional years follow:

1979

· ·

Cliche-verte Prints
Renaissance Prints
Monticelli: His Contemporaries, His Influence
Objects: Modern Design
Fiber Ten
Bunny Goldman/Paper Images
Collection of Mr. and Mrs. Orin Raphael
Collection of Dr. and Mrs. Raymond Goldblum
Downtown at CMU
China Trade Porcelain from the Collection
        of Mrs. James M. Schoonmaker, Jr.
Photographs from the Permanent Collection
69th Annual Exhibition of the Associated
        Artists of Pittsburgh
20th Century French Prints from the Permanent
        Collection
Munakata Woodblock Prints
Photographs by Alan Cherin
Silver in American Life
Anthony de Bernardin: Pittsburgh Naive Painter
French Masterpieces of the 19th Century
        from the Henry P. McIhenny Collection
Josef Albers: Formulation Articulation
Paintings by Harvey Parks
American Printmaking: 100 Years
Art in Modern Handcrafts
Jean DuBuffet: From the Milton D. Ratner
        Family Collection
Bill Haney: Paintings and Drawings

(All below continued into 1980)

Printmaking in Europe: 1600-1700
Pittsburgh International Series: Eduardo

Chillida/Willem de Kooning
Harry Callahan Photographs
Marjorie and Magee Wyckoff Presepio
Christmas Trees 1979 (Presented by the
        Women's Committee, Museum of Art)

1980

· ·

Karen Stoller: Works in Fiber
Etchings and Lithographs by James McNeill Whistler
Luke Swank: Photographs
Sui Generis: Associated Artists of Pittsburgh
        70th Annual Exhibition
Portrait Miniatures in the Collection
        of The Museum of Art
William Blayney and Alex Fletcher: Paintings
Robert Qualters: Paintings
Sonia Delaunay: A Retrospective
Henri Cartier-Bresson: Photographer
Recent Accessions
Kathleen Mulcahy: Works in Glass
American Printmaking: 1900-1975
Shakespeare: The Globe & The World
Textile Fragments from India in the Near East
        in the Collection of The Museum of Art
The Collection of Mr. and Mrs. David Lewis
Frank Dininno: Paintings
Rachel McClelland Stutton: Paintings
Edward Eberle: Sculpture
Dürer and His Contemporaries

(All below continued into 1981)

Constructivism and the Geometric Tradition:
        Selections from The McCrory Corporation
        Collection
Richard Anuszkiewicz: Prints and Multiples,
        1964-1980
Early Pittsburgh in Prints
James Myford: Sculpture
Marjorie and Magee Wyckoff Presepio
Christmas Trees 1980 (Presented by the Women's
        Committee, Museum of Art)

1981

· ·

Utagawa Hiroshige I: The 53 States of the Tokaido,
        Collection of Dr. James Austin
71st Annual Associated Artists of Pittsburgh
Diane Samuels: Sculpture
Daumier: Parisian Characters
In China: Photographs by Eve Arnold
Christopher John Watts: Number and Image

Recent Acquisitions: Prints, Drawings,
    and Photographs
The World of David Gilmour Blythe (1815-1865)
Buky Schwartz: Three Video Works
Herbert T. Olds, Jr.: Drawings
Rembrandt Etchings from the Charles J.
    Rosenbloom Bequest
Gary Bukovnik: Watercolors
Kes Zapkus: Drawing into Painting
Innovative Furniture in America
Jane Ford Aebersold: Ceramics
Artists in Photographs by Arthur Mones

(All below continued into 1982)

Philip Guston: The Last Works
Real, Really Real, Super Real: Directions
    in Contemporary American Realism
William Cronin: Paintings 1969 to 1981
Gordon House: A Print Retrospective
Philip Wofford: Recent Drawings in Color
Robert Cronin: Sculpture in Tin
Christmas Trees 1981 (Presented by the Women's
    Committee, Museum of Art)
Marjorie and Magee Wyckoff Presepio
Lee Hershenson: Photographs

Organized for the Brooklyn Museum by Gene Baro, adjunct curator for Contemporary Art, The Carnegie, was *In China: Photographs by Eve Arnold*. The work of this internationally recognized photojournalist was on view in Pittsburgh after its showing in New York. Also in 1981, two especially outstanding exhibitions were *The World of David Gilmour Blythe (1815-1865)* (see the chapter *Painters with a Pittsburgh Connection*) and in 1982, *Buffalo Bill and the American Wild West*. Each drew thousands of visitors to the museum and reached a broad spectrum of viewers of art.

Real, Really Real, Super Real: Directions in Contemporary American Realism, presented a rich variety of representational painting and sculpture completed in America between 1968 and 1980 by 59 artists including the renowned Pittsburgh-born figure painter Philip Pearlstein. The exhibition was organized by the San Antonio, Texas Museum of Art and sponsored in Pittsburgh by the L. B. Foster Company.

Complementary to *Buffalo Bill and the*

Wild West was the exhibition, *100 Years of Western Art from Pittsburgh Collections*. This was the first time that The Museum of Art addressed, in a major way, art of this genre. Represented in the exhibition were many of the best-known artists of the first generation of Western art: Frederic Remington, Charles M. Russell, and Henry Farny (who lived briefly in Pittsburgh), among others. More recent artists, such as John Clymer, Harry Jackson, and James Bama were also represented, as were works by Doris Lee and Georgia O'Keeffe, from the permanent collection of The Museum of Art.

The exhibition was supported by the Vesuvius Crucible Charitable Foundation and 17 lenders of works of Western art, among whom were Mrs. Henry Oliver, Jr. and William A. Seifert, Jr., each of whom loaned several works. Western art from the collections of Mr. and Mrs. Robert Dickey, III, Mr. and Mrs. Paul Euwer, Jr., Eleanor P. Kelly, Mr. and Mrs. G. Harton Singer, III, and Robert J. Trombetta, director of the Fort Pitt Museum, also was represented. The Vesuvius Crucible Company and its president, T. H. Harley, loaned 15 works from their collections. Art owned by the Duquesne Club, Inc. and Pittsburgh National Bank were included, as well as three paintings by W. H. D. Koerner, famed illustrator for the Saturday Evening Post which in his day had a weekly circulation of more than 3 million copies. The Koerner works were loaned by W. H. D. Koerner, III.

In 1983 the museum mounted *From Vienna to Pittsburgh: The Art of Henry Koerner,* a definitive retrospective exhibition of the work of the Vienna-born Pittsburgh artist, whose paintings and drawings are included in the collections of many Pittsburghers. The Museum of Art, in 1981 acquired Koerner's monumental composite painting *Oh Fearful Wonder of Man,* c. 1962. Although Henry Koerner was not related to W. H. D. Koerner, there is an

Oh Fearful Wonder of Man, c. 1962, by Henry Koerner,
American, b. Austria; The Henry Hillman Fund, 1981.

interesting parallel in that both artists achieved
large national circulation of their works via
popular magazines. From 1955 to 1967 some
54 covers of *Time* magazine were portraits
by Henry Koerner, including those of John
Fitzgerald Kennedy and Maria Callas, (the
opera star linked with Aristotle Onassis before
he married the widowed Mrs. Kennedy). The
Westmoreland County Museum of Art in
Greensburg, Pennsylvania, in 1971 under the
directorship of Dr. Paul Chew, mounted an
exhibition of 231 of Henry Koerner's paintings,
watercolors, drawings, and prints.

An exhibition of special interest to
Pittsburghers in 1984 was *Seven New Artists:
Pittsburgh Today* which showcased the work

of Angelo Ciotti, Jim Denney, Anne Elliott,
Kathleen Montgomery, Phillip Harris, Chuck
Olson, and Peter Stanick. John Caldwell adjunct
curator of Contemporary Art for the museum
selected the 43 paintings, sculptures, and drawings by the artists, all born between 1943 and
1954. The show was made possible by grants
from the Howard Heinz Endowment and the
Pennsylvania Council on the Arts.

In 1985 The Museum of Art and The Carnegie Museum of Natural History combined to
present two simultaneous, dazzling exhibitions:
*Objects of Adornment: 5,000 Years of Jewelry
from the Walters Art Gallery, Baltimore* and
*Masterpieces of the Mineral World: Gemstones
and Jewelry.* In conjunction with the two main

exhibitions there was also a show by 11 outstanding designers entitled *New Visions, Traditional Materials: Contemporary American Jewelry.* At the other end of the arts spectrum was the highly successful 1987 show called *Dr. Seuss From Then to Now,* featuring the whimsical wonderful work of Theodore Geisel, alias Dr. Seuss. An estimated 51,512 visitors came to enjoy it.

The Museum of Art in 1990 selected 24 paintings from the permanent collection for the show *Honest Work: American Realism, 1925-45.* Diana Strazdes, associate curator of Fine Arts, reasoned, "reuniting these works should help us to see something new and valuable in American Realism."

One of the largest exhibitions was the national touring 1992 retrospective: *The Art of Romare Bearden, 1940-87.* It held special meaning for Pittsburgh audiences. Bearden lived in Lawrenceville in 1920 and again in 1927-29. In a sense he was the "August Wilson with a paint brush," using his colorful palette on 110 canvases to conjure up memories of his life in this city. Artist/teacher Jo-Anne Bates and her sister and brother in law, Mr. and Mrs. Milton Washington, with Mr. and Mrs. Ronald Davenport, were instrumental in the museum's obtaining a Bearden painting for The Carnegie (photograph on page 137).

A small group of large paintings by New Yorker Alexis Rockman was shown in the forum gallery in 1993. *Evolution,* eight-feet-tall and 24-feet-long included 214 species of flora and fauna in a diorama-like prehistoric setting, reminiscent of the paintings of the Dutch master Heironymous Bosch, (about 1450-1516). Another Bosch-like work was the enormous four ton sculpture *The Tables* by Tom Otterness loaned by the Lannan Foundation in Los Angeles. More than 100 bronze figures of grotesque animals and unshapely humans populate the 88-foot-long corten steel picnic-type benches, giving the life and death cycle of

today's society. Recalling the themes of Rabelais, H. G. Wells, and Walt Disney, in addition to Bosch, *Tables* is the stuff of nightmares.

Later in 1993, a more civilized, certainly more comfortable, view of the world was the exhibition *Duncan Phillips Collects: Paris Between the Wars.* (Duncan Phillips was born on Wood Street in Pittsburgh in 1886, a member of the Laughlin family of Jones and Laughlin steel fame. Phillips grew up in Washington, D.C. and died there in 1966.) The cultivated taste of this collector was evidenced by this show of 55 works by School of Paris masters such as Bonnard, Braque, Chagall, Derain, Dufy, Gris, Matisse, Modigliani, Picasso, Rouault, and Soutine. The works were painted between 1917 and 1941, and in their day also it took time for the public to learn to appreciate their art. A more recent type of art is that of Jeff Wall whose large realistic photographs record scenes and situations fraught with tension. His work has been shown in the *International* and solo exhibitions at the museum.

Small but beautiful was the 1994 exhibit of *Chinoiserie: Oriental Influences in the Decorative Arts.* Concurrently the museum, for the first time, exhibited pieces of Judaica: a 19th century Hanukkah lamp, ceremonial spice box, and spice tower, all loaned by Sara Abrams of Pittsburgh. As has been indicated, the staff of The Museum of Art presents many exhibitions in addition to the almost overwhelming effort of arranging and mounting the periodic *Carnegie Internationals.* In the opinion of Phillip Johnston, director since 1987, the most important exhibitions organized by the museum during these years were:

John LaFarge
November 7, 1987 - January 3, 1988
John LaFarge, a major retrospective of this artist's work co-organized by The Carnegie Museum of Art and the National Museum of American Art, Washington, D.C., and funded

in part by the Foster Charitable Trust, included paintings, works on paper, and stained glass by one of the most versatile, intellectual, and cosmopolitan 19th century American artists. The beautiful installation coupled with the essay-laden catalogue gave visitors the chance to comprehend the artist's full career.

Lothar Baumgarten
October 31, 1987 - January 31, 1988
The German artist Lothar Baumgarten is deeply committed to the Yanomami Indians of the Amazon rain forest who live in danger of extinction. In his work he attempts to counteract the centuries-long tradition of turning these Indians into objects of exotic fantasies while destroying their societies. Baumgarten painted the walls of the museum's Entrance Gallery – now *Forum* – red, using urucu, a natural pigment, and inscribed on the walls words including: *displaced, collected, depreciated, deceived, exterminated, contained,* and *isolated,* which revealed the meaning of this work. In the Scaife Special Exhibition Gallery Baumgarten hung photographs he took while living among the Yanomami from October 1978 to March 1980. Both shows were organized by Vicky A. Clark.

American Landscape Video: The Electronic Grove
May 7 - July 10, 1988
For the spring of 1988 Bill Judson, curator of Film and Video, organized *American Landscape Video,* the first exhibition to look at video art from a historical perspective — the tradition of American landscape painting. While the museum has had a long-standing commitment to film and video as a serious art form and includes smaller exhibitions as part of a continuing program, *American Landscape Video* represented the museum's first large-scale exhibition in the field. Following its successful showing, it traveled to the San Francisco Museum of Modern Art.

Courts and Colonies: The William and Mary Style in Holland, England, and America
March 18 - May 20, 1989
This exhibition was co-organized by The Carnegie Museum of Art and the Cooper-Hewitt Museum, New York, in celebration of the 300th anniversary of the Glorious Revolution of 1688, which brought William III and Mary II to the English throne. It was the first large-scale international Decorative Arts exhibition to be arranged by The Carnegie Museum of Art. The museum's director, Phillip M. Johnston, curated the American section of the exhibition and contributed an essay discussing the William and Mary style in America to the catalogue.

Impressionism: Selections from Five American Museums
November 4 - January 17, 1987
The next special exhibition, *Impressionism: Selections from Five American Museums,* set a new attendance record of 82,105 visitors in the exhibition's eight weeks. The exceptional quality of the exhibition resulted from an imaginative collaboration of five museums — The Carnegie Museum of Art, The Minneapolis Institute of Arts, The Nelson-Atkins Museum of Art in Kansas City, The Saint Louis Art Museum, and The Toledo Museum of Art. The Ford Motor Company was sponsor for the exhibition and for the museum-published *Art Ventures: A Guide for Families to Impressionism and Post-Impressionism. Art Ventures* was a series of publications written by Bay Hallowell who for 18 years was the museum's creator of art programs for children.

In the Watercolor Tradition: British Works on Paper from the Mellon Bank Collection
November 3, 1990 - January 6, 1991
The exhibition of Mellon Bank's extraordinary collection of 18th, 19th, and 20th century British watercolors was curated by Diana Strazdes,

who also prepared the catalogue. In addition to the 65 works created between 1774 and 1935 there were lectures and demonstrations of the watercolor technique. Readings from letters and poems contemporary with the watercolors were presented by trustee Helen Moore and Charles R. Altman.

In 1990 the *Forum* series of smaller-scale exhibitions of Contemporary Art became a permanent part of the museum's annual program. The first exhibition in the Forum Gallery showed works by Canadian artist Jeff Wall, and was co-curated by Vicky A. Clark and Mark Francis. Free brochures inform about the works, and visitors are encouraged to accumulate them as records of the Contemporary Art shown in the series. (A folder designed to hold a year's set of issues may be purchased in The Museum of Art shop.) In addition, under the aegis of the Department of Education, the museum initiated a program of opening receptions that include an informal talk by the exhibiting artists.

Pittsburgh Collects
February 20 - April 26, 1993
Organized by recently appointed curator of Contemporary Art Richard Armstrong, this exhibition focused on Contemporary Art being collected in this city. It included over 250 works from approximately 40 private and corporate collections and a few from The Museum of Art.

Toward Modernism: American Art from The Beal Collection
April 30 - July 17, 1994
Please refer to the section, "Importance of Individual Collectors," page 115.

Architecture in a Well-Ordered Universe: Lord Burlington's Villa at Chiswick and Thomas Jefferson's Grounds at the University of Virginia
October 29, 1994 - January 8, 1995
Please refer to page 61 in the section "The Heinz Architectural Center."

In addition to the exhibitions the museum has organized in recent years, it should be noted that some of the most important exhibitions of decorative arts produced in the last decade traveled to Pittsburgh. These included: *The Machine Age in America 1918-1944* (1987); *The American Craftsman and the European Tradition 1620-1820* (1990); and in 1995: *Silver in America, 1840-1940: A Century of Splendor.*

Also the museum hosted two highly significant exhibitions of African art, both organized by the Center for African Art in New York City: *Art/Artifact: African Art through Western Eyes* (1989); *Africa Explores: 20th-Century African Art* (1992).

In 1989 the museum co-sponsored publication of the catalogue for the exhibition, *Success is a Job in New York: The Early Art and Business of Andy Warhol* presenting Warhol's early career. In 1989, in less than two months, almost 30,000 visitors came to view the exhibition. ("The Andy Warhol Museum" begins on page 230.)

Carnegie, 1985, by Richard Serra, American; Gift in
memory of William R. Roesch by his wife Jane Holt
Roesch, 1985.

The Carnegie Museum of Art
The Women's Committee, Since 1957

In the early days of Andrew Carnegie's Palace of Culture the Green Room on the balcony of The Music Hall Foyer, was "the ladies withdrawing room where they could smoke in privacy." Now its marble and gold splendor is the meeting and planning place, the smoke-free workshop, of the Women's Committee which has been dedicated to The Museum of Art since 1957, before the Art Department became the museum, before the word "lady" was considered derogatory, and when she was still identified by her husband's name. It came into being with the encouragement of Gordon Bailey Washburn, the first director of the newly designated Museum of Art. Authorized by the Carnegie Institute, the by-laws state that the purpose of the Women's Committee is to further the interests of The Museum of Art and to promote its cultural and educational usefulness in the community.

Not stated but definitely included are chores such as the addressing of hundreds of invitations to many events, as well as the more challenging task of creating a glamorous setting, with beautiful flowers, delicious food, and diplomatic seating arrangements, for special functions such as the annual Founders-Patrons Day Dinner and the festive openings of the *International Exhibitions.*

Not just "the ladies who lunch" the group has included: accountants, educators, doctors, dentists, artists, lawyers, authors, antique dealers, travel agents, photographers, other professionals, movers and shakers, wives of corporate CEOs, and young mothers with full-time family responsibilities at home. All are volunteers for The Carnegie Museum of Art, via the Women's Committee.

The Heart of the World, 1956, by René Magritte, Belgian; Gift of Mr. and Mrs. George L. Craig, Jr., 1960.

Parties with a Purpose

Perhaps Patricia Lowry, Architecture critic of *The Pittsburgh Press*, put it best when she wrote of the Women's Committee of The Carnegie Museum of Art, as a "Band of Angels." The reference was to *The Restoration Gala*, "the party of the decade" (1988) to raise funds for the restoration of the bronze statues: Carnegie's Noble Quartet, Shakespeare, Michelangelo, Bach, and Galileo, and the Muses which adorn the roof of the massive building dedicated to Literature, Art, Music, and Science. For that occasion 35 interior designers transformed the museum halls with elaborate floral decorations plus an indoor garden. The *Gala* raised thousands of dollars and over the years the Women's Committee's efforts have brought many times that to The Museum of Art. The Lowry article mentioned that the restoration project was a high priority of the committee which marked its 30th anniversary that year.

There have been numerous memorable exhibitions and events assisted by this group among which some of the unforgetables are the city-wide *Shakespeare's Birthday Celebration*, and *The Treasures of Early Irish Art* which still holds the record for attendance. As early as 1967 the Women's Committee sponsored the showing of the film *Andy Warhol — Super Artist* in connection with paintings in the *Carnegie International* of that year.

Not a fund raiser but perhaps "the party of this decade" was the marathon, nonstop opening of The Andy Warhol Museum over the weekend of May 13-15, 1994. Women's Committee members Ann McGuinn, Jean George, and Alice Snyder were active workers for the celebration which was supported and attended by many other members and their spouses.

When the Scaife Gallery opened in 1974 it included The Museum of Art Shop, initially sponsored by the Women's Committee. Advisors B. G. Galey and Peggy McGowan "imported" Carole Long, whom they met at the Baltimore Museum, to manage the art shop and the natural history shop. In addition to her taste and flair in stocking the shop with art items, Carole adopted and adapted dinosaurs, marketing them to the financial benefit of The Carnegie.

The tenth anniversary of the Scaife Gallery was observed by the Founders-Patrons Day, November 1984, with a new installation of the collections and an exhibition of Mark Rothko's *Works On Paper 1925-1970*. The Women's Committee, joined by the Fellows Fund and the Patrons Fund, added *Yellow, Blue on Orange*, 1974, by Rothko, American b. Russia, 1903-1970, to the museum's holdings.

Another important painting, *Picnic*, c. 1914-1915, by Maurice Prendergast, American b. Canada, 1859-1924, was acquired through the efforts of the Women's Committee who staged an informal gala to encourage the public to contribute to the museum's acquisition of the painting. The committee also enlisted the aid of the public for the purchase of Kenneth Snelson's *Forest Devil*. The sculpture was exhibited in the Three Rivers Arts Festival of 1977 and is now displayed in Mellon Square in downtown Pittsburgh.

In 1989, the former Heinz mansion on nearby Devon Road, was transformed into a courtly scene, complete with costumed children, a horse tethered under a tree, musicians playing, dancers dancing, and fireworks. The committee's purpose was to benefit the William & Mary exhibition of paintings and decorative arts in the galleries of the museum.

Four past presidents of the Women's Committee (L-R) Rita Coney, Ann Wardrop, Ellen Walton, and Edith Fisher with a detail of *Picnic* by Maurice Prendergast, celebrating the 30th anniversary of the Women's Committee, 1987. Article by Patricia Lowry, *The Pittsburgh Press* March 1, 1987.

Photograph by Andy Starnes

The Public is Invited

Treasure hunters await the biennial auctions for which the members collect the items, polish the silver, arrange the display, stage and staff the event, and keep the computerized records. The auction and, as of 1993, the annual Antiques Show, sponsored by the committee, each raise an average of $100,000 and bring a large new audience to The Carnegie. Forty-some dealers from around the country exhibit their wares in The Carnegie's elegant settings staged by a team of Pittsburgh's top decorators, led by Louis Talotta. (As long ago as 1959 the committee organized the showing of *Treasured Antiques from the Collections of the Region*, held in conjunction with the Pittsburgh Bicentennial celebration. Another early project was the Christmas sale of original prints and drawings, 14th through 20th century.)

Girls and Flowers by Aristide Maillol

Architecture Hall . . . The Christmas Trees

Popular also have been fashion shows dramatically presented in the Hall of Architecture by Kaufmann's department store in cooperation with the Women's Committee. Hundreds of visitors (62,600 in 1989) come to the Hall of Architecture each holiday season to hear the festive musical programs and view the majestic Christmas trees given by Mr. and Mrs. John T. Galey. Since 1961 the trees have been decorated with ornaments handmade by the committee in a different theme each year, ranging from *Fairy Tales* to *Great Cities of History*, each accompanied by a description in hand lettered script. A "portrait" of a garlanded Christmas tree was painted by member Minette G. Bickel, for use by the committee as invitations for the preview parties which help finance the presentation of the trees.

Also in the hall is the annual display of the Neapolitan Presipio, or Nativity scene in an ancient Italian village. The crèche is the centerpiece of the composition which involves hundreds of carved figures (1700-1838) of men, women, children in all walks of life, and their many animals. It was the gift years ago of another member of the Women's Committee and her husband, Mr. and Mrs. George Magee Wyckoff, Jr. A highlight of the season's entertainment around the trees is the party for youthful special guests, many of whom are in wheelchairs. All enjoy the refreshments, the sing-alongs, and talking with Santa Claus.

In spring senior citizens are the honored guests, sometimes more than 300 strong, who come for tea and cookies (250 dozen made by the committee members) and a special guided tour of the galleries with docent members of the committee. The docent program itself was established by the committee and continues to receive annual financial support.

Each fall also there is a different theme for the *Decorative Arts Symposium* at which experts in particular fields speak about their special areas of expertise. In 1988, for instance, the topic was *Louis IV's Versailles*. Another topic was *Pennsylvania Furniture, 1700-1850*, and in 1993 it was *The American Crafts Movement*. This project involves the abiding effort of Mrs. George Ebbert and Mrs. George Berger, Jr., carrying on the decorative arts interests of their mother Mrs. Thomas Wurts, a founding member of the Women's Committee. Mrs. Berger and Carnegie Trustee Mrs. Alan Lehman were founding members of the Junior Council of the Women's Committee in 1957.

Mrs. Wurts and Mrs. John Berdan, with other members of the committee, were staunch supporters of the museum's collection of furniture and decorative art, as attested by their recurring names in the annual list of benefactors.

Activities in the Community

Two other ongoing community activities inaugurated by the Women's Committee are the Three Rivers Arts Festival (1959), directed for years by Mrs. Pierce Widdoes, and the *Man and Ideas* lecture series (1969), chaired by Mrs. Robert Wardrop (see more on page 147). The Arts Festival brings more than a half million visitors to downtown Pittsburgh, and the lectures bring a large audience to The Music Hall. Beginning with the visionary architect Buckminster Fuller the series has featured such diverse thinkers as artist Robert Motherwell, economist Barbara Ward, and anthropologist Margaret Mead. The two projects are mentioned in detail in other chapters, pages 147 and 148.

Another notable achievement in 1969 was the establishment of the museum's film program by Sally Dixon of the Women's Committee. It began with seasonal weekly screenings and monthly presentations by visiting filmmakers. A study collection was formed in 1972 with some 200 titles of 16-mm and 8-mm films and 100 videotapes, with support from the committee and the National Endowment for the Arts.

The Allegheny Landing Sculpture Park near the new Carnegie Science Center also benefited from the input of committee member Alice Snyder as to the selection and placement of the works of art. Her sister, member Mrs. Peter Janetta, as Diana Rose, had statewide influence in her position as head of the Pennsylvania Council on the Arts.

Still Life with Strawberries, c. 1890, by Levi Wells Prentice, American; Museum purchase: Mary Oliver Robinson Fund bequest to the Women's Committee and Women's Committee Acquisition Fund, 1981.

Works of Art for the Museum

The towering weathered steel sculpture *Carnegie* by famed sculptor Richard Serra is a brooding presence near the fountain entrance to The Museum of Art. Created for the *International* of 1991 it was given by committee member Mrs. William Roesch to The Carnegie in memory of her husband, a former president of United States Steel Corporation. (Photograph on page 133.)

A less visible but equally lasting contribution was the establishment years earlier of the photographic library by Elizabeth Mellon Sellers. In her memory members of the Women's Committee gave the Georgia O'Keeffe painting *Gate of Adobe Church* in 1974 to The Museum of Art. In 1978 *Spirit of the Hills* a painting, c. 1925-28, by Pittsburgh-born Augustus Vincent Tack, 1870-1949, was given in memory of Henry Oliver, Jr. by his family and friends. His widow was president of the Women's Committee at the time. Also, in 1982, Mrs. Oliver's generosity was responsible for the

Gate of Adobe Church, 1929, by Georgia O'Keeffe, American; Gift in memory of Elisabeth Mellon Sellers from her friends, 1974.

by his death in March 1983. In his memory they helped purchase a painting from the 1985 *International, Die Verspottung (The Mocking)*, 1984, by Georg Baselitz, b. 1938 in Germany. A ceramic figure group *Flight into Egypt* by the English potter Enod Wood was given in memory of member Mary Read Sutton. In 1990 the museum made its first purchase of an "old master" painting after a 12-year hiatus, *Christ Healing the Blind Man* by Gioacchino Assereto (Genoa c. 1600-1649). It was the gift of Mrs. Thomas S. Knight in memory of her mother, Mrs. George S. Craig, Jr. Mr. and Mrs. Craig had earlier given the museum René Magritte's (b. Belgium 1898-1967), *Heart of the World*, 1960, and in memory of her husband Mrs. Craig gave the museum a work by Frank Stella, *Untitled 1958*.

At the behest of the director of The Museum of Art, Phillip Johnston, in 1991 the

redesign of the plantings at the carriage entrance of The Carnegie as a memorial to her husband, a long-time trustee of the Institute. Included in the new design was a group of stately hemlock trees given in memory of Mrs. Thomas Wurts, by her daughters, Mrs. George Ebbert, Jr. and Mrs. George Berger, Jr. The work was under the supervision of the Garden Club of Allegheny County, with design of the plantings by GWSM landscape architects, in collaboration with Damianos and Associates, consulting architects.

The Women's Committee in 1981 was the recipient of a bequest, from a former member through the Mary Oliver Robinson Fund, resulting in the purchase for the museum of *Still Life with Strawberries*, c. 1890, by Levi Prentice, 1851-1935.

The members of the committee who recalled the dynamic leadership of museum director Gordon Bailey Washburn were saddened

Die Verspottung (The Mocking), 1984 by Georg Baselitz, German; Gordon Bailey Washburn Memorial Fund, Women's Committee Washburn Memorial Fund, and Carnegie International Acquisition Fund, 1985.

Women's Committee donated $50,000 toward the purchase of a work by Lothar Baumgarten on the skylight ceiling of the Hall of Sculpture. It was a site installation for the 1991 *Carnegie International*, titled *Tongue of the Cherokee*. Another unusual work from the 1991 exhibition entering the collection thanks to the Women's Committee is *The Temptation of St. Anthony — the Forms*, 1951 — and 1990/91, by Tim Rollins + K. O. S. (It is made of blood, alcohol, acrylic, and papel linen on wood panel and cost $50,000.)

Other items suggested by Mr. Johnston, previously curator of Decorative Arts, have been a silver chalice and a notable tall clock, among other works of art purchased with help from the committee. (The cost of the clock, $160,000, was shared equally by Mr. Paul Mellon.)

The Carnegie Treasures Cookbook . . .
"A brilliantly planned, highly diverting book"
— *James Beard*

A major undertaking, sparked by the vision and determination of Mrs. James A. Fisher, was the creation of the award-winning *The Carnegie Treasures Cookbook* with introduction by the legendary James Beard, who had briefly attended Carnegie Institute of Technology. The book links imaginative menus with the "Treasures" by including 48 color photographs plus 20 in black and white. Three and a half years of collecting, taste-testing, and arranging recipes and selecting artworks for inclusion preceded the publication of the first 40,000 copies in the summer of 1984. An additional five years of intensive marketing efforts resulted in approximately $150,000 profit which made possible the acquisition by the museum of the drawing of the *Twin Bridges Project Point Park, Pittsburgh*, 1947 by Frank Lloyd Wright. In 1993 this historic work had a place of honor in the opening exhibition of the Heinz Architectural Center in The Carnegie Museum of Art. (The Heinz connection was eminently suitable since a grant from the H. J. Heinz Company Foundation contributed substantially to the development of the book.) Installed in the Center is Frank Lloyd Wright's San Francisco office, a major contribution of the Women's Committee in recognition of the great generosity of the Heinz family to The Carnegie over many years.

Community Outreach
Committee members are also active in the community in different ways: Mrs. Fisher chaired the day-long meeting on specific issues facing museum trustees in conjunction with the American Association of Museums conference in Pittsburgh in 1988. The efforts and single-mindedness of Mrs. Robert Wardrop resulted in the restoration and reinstallation near the former Carnegie Library in old Allegheny of the exedron, Andrew Carnegie's memorial to Colonel Anderson, from whose library young Andrew felt privileged to borrow books.

An important project was *The Family Art Game*, a rotogravure magazine section of *The Pittsburgh Press* May 13, 1992, which by clues and queries interested the public in the paintings and sculptures in the permanent collection of The Museum of Art. The 32-page supplement contained photographs of 52 works of art in the permanent collection, 15 of which were gifts of members of the Scaife family. The imminent demise of the city's evening newspaper fortunately did not prevent the Art Game from raising almost $100,000 for the acquisition fund of the museum, thanks to the 52 advertisers who sponsored the individual works.

Tenth Anniversary, 1967:
Review of Gifts to the Museum
When the Women's Committee observed its tenth anniversary in 1967 an article in the November issue of *Carnegie Magazine* included

photographs of three gifts of the committee namely: *Sculpture*, a bronze by Emil Cimiotti, from the 1958 *International, Grand Ailee* by Alicia Penalba, from the 1964 *International*, and *Abstract Painting, Blue* by Ad Reinhardt, given in 1965. Not photographed but listed were "other major works": *Tarrassa* (pastel) by Adja Yunkers, and *Composition* (oil), by Wolfgang Hollegha, from the 1961 *International*, and *Les Grands Transparents* (oil) by Pierre Alechinsky. The text continued, "during the ten year period, the Woman's Committee has contributed more than $26,000 worth of paintings and sculpture. In addition, more than $10,000 has gone to augment various art-purchase resources, including $5,300 to the G. David Thompson Memorial Fund. Approximately $4,000 has been donated to the Print and Drawing Fund and the Print Rehabilitation Fund, representing a total of just over $40,500. Contributions have been made toward the purchase of the sculpture *Man Walking* by Giacometti, acquired in 1961; five 17th and 18th century miniature portraits, acquired in 1962; and Arp's *Sculpture Classique*, purchased in 1964." The December 1967 issue of *Carnegie Magazine* added another gift of the Women's Committee, namely the painting *The Great Love*, 1966, by Robert Indiana b. 1928 in New Castle, Indiana.

The committee was credited with the organization of 10 major art exhibitions since 1957, one of which was the underwriting of *The Architecture of Louis Kahn* exhibition in 1966. On a smaller scale, arranging the exhibits in the Treasure Room had been a committee responsibility since 1961. In addition acknowledgment was made of the full regular program of educational lectures and the in-depth examination of Contemporary Art provided during the *Pittsburgh International Exhibitions*. This Tenth Anniversary tribute also noted the committee's initiation in 1957 of the Art Resources File, and maintenance of it as a central inventory of art works in the region. The file has been used on occasion by the museum in arranging for exhibitions such as the 1963 *Art since 1900 Privately Owned by the Pittsburgh Area*. One of the most privately owned, and most extensive, of those collections was that of James and Rebecca Beal which came to the museum at Mrs. Beal's death in 1992. She had been a member of the Women's Committee since 1957.

Gifts to The Museum of Art Since 1970

Now, as the centennial of The Carnegie approaches, the computer print-out listing The Museum of Art acquisitions in which the Women's Committee has participated is far too extensive to include here. There are, for instance, in addition to numerous paintings, 40 films, 17 prints, 15 sculptures, and 13 drawings and watercolors as well as a number of miscellaneous items. This is a sampling of some of the pieces important from various points of view, listed by year purchased:

Decorative Arts

1971	French Limoges, Plaque Gramatique
1985	Herter, Gustav, Cabinet with separate mirror, 1860
1990	English, London, Silver Cup, Two-Handled with separate cover and stand, 1659-1660

Film

1977	Brakhage, Stan, *Cat's Cradle*, 1959 Print
1977	Christo (Javacheff) *Not Realized Projects "Museum of Modern Art"*

Sculpture

1972	Italian, Roman *Torso of a Satyr*, First Century, B. C. (This sculpture is used in the ancient civilization tours for school children.)

Pittsburgh Memories, 1984, by Romare Bearden,
American; Gift of Mr. and Mrs. Ronald R. Davenport
and Mr. and Mrs. Milton A. Washington, 1984.

1977 *Owe-Eye-Housepost*, 1930-1950 (This African
sculpture in wood is also used in the art tours
for children.)

Paintings important to the collection:
. . . .

1974 Rothko, Mark *Yellow, Blue on Orange*, 1955

1980 Kensett, John Frederic, *Long Neck Point
from Contentment Island — Darien
Connecticut*, 1870-1872

1983 Avery, Milton, *Dunes and Sea I*, 1958

1985 Kiefer, Anselm, *Midgard*, 1980-1985

This list indicates the wide range of The
Museum of Art's collections, and how the

Women's Committee over the years has helped in their development.

Three members of the Women's Committee were responsible for the 1984 gift to the museum of *Pittsburgh Memories* by Romare Bearden, painted in 1984 just four years before his death at age 70: Jo-Anne Bates, artist and teacher, with Mrs. Ronald H. Davenport and Mrs. Milton A. Washington, and their husbands. Printmaker Bates also designed the 1994 invitations for the Christmas Tree Party — an evergreen bough with a golden ornament in the shape of the logo of The Carnegie. An innovation planned by the committee for the 1994-95 holiday season was a New Year's Eve Party for the young in spirit.

In 1993-1994 alone, as reported by the retiring president, Lu Damianos "the great generosity" and varied activities of the members of the committee resulted in raising some $367,000 for the benefit of The Museum of Art and The Carnegie. The committee has also joined the select ranks of million-dollar pledges to the Second Century Fund of The Carnegie. Even allowing for the effects of inflation, this is a dramatic contrast with the $40,500 contributed by the committee to The Museum of Art over the 1957-1967 decade.

In preparation for a gala celebration of the centennial of The Carnegie Institute in 1995 President Ellsworth Brown appointed trustee and Women's Committee member Janie, Mrs. Harry Thompson, II, chair of the Centennial Committee. Her challenge is to match or surpass the festive opening of The Carnegie Science Center which she orchestrated with imagination and flair.

Early History of the Women's Committee

Many changes have occurred in Pittsburgh in the more than 30 years since the Women's Committee was formed but the goals and dedication to the museum remain the same. It was in 1957 that Director Washburn traveled with

Young Women Picking Fruit, c. 1891, by Mary Cassatt, American; Patrons Art Fund, 1922.

a representative group, Mrs. Verner Scaife, Mrs. W. C. Robinson, Jr., and Mrs. Thomas Wurts, to attend the Conference of Women's Committees at the St. Louis Museum with the idea of establishing a similar support group for the "Art Department" of Carnegie Institute. The information gained at the conference was reported by Mrs. Wurts and Mrs. W. C. Robinson, Jr. at a meeting at the home of Mrs. John B. Rickertson II. Also in attendance were Mrs. John Barkley, Mrs. John Berdan, Mrs. Bernard Horne, Mrs. Henry Oliver, Jr., Mrs. A. L. Robinson, Mrs. John B. Sellers, and Mrs. George Magee Wyckoff. The Women's Committee was then organized with the authorization of Carnegie Institute and the active support of Director Washburn who issued invitations to membership to women active in the community.

Originally there were three classifications of membership: the Advisory Board, the Central Board (these two met together and managed the business affairs), and a Junior Council which met separately had its own officers, projects, and maintained its own funds. In 1966 the committee, under the leadership of Elizabeth Sellers, was reorganized with just two classifications of members, active and advisory.

Presidents of the Women's Committee

. . . .

Central Board		Junior Council
Mrs. Fitch Ingersoll (formerly Barkley)	1957-58	Mrs. George B. Berger, Jr.
Mrs. William C. Robinson, Jr.	1959-60	Mrs. James H. Heroy, Jr.
Mrs. Henry Oliver, Jr.	1961-62	Mrs. T. H. Conderman
Mrs. William D. Bickel	1963-64	Mrs. O. Harry Gruner, III
Mrs. John T. Galey	1965-66	Mrs. Alan Lehman

1967-68	Mrs. John B. Sellers	*Elizabeth*
1969-71	Mrs. George B. Berger, Jr.	*Mernie*
1971-72	Mrs. James H. Heroy, Jr.	*Kate*
1972-74	Mrs. James A. Fisher	*Edith*
1974-76	Mrs. Robert Wardrop II	*Ann*
1976-78	Mrs. A. Reed Schroeder	*Anne*
1978-80	Mrs. Henry Oliver, Jr.	*Emily*
1980-82	Mrs. Charles H. Moore	*Helen*
1982-84	Mrs. W. H. Krome George	*Jean*
1984-86	Mrs. Aims C. Coney, Jr.	*Rita*
1986-88	Mrs. James M. Walton	*Ellen*
1988-90	Mrs. Fred I. Sharp	*Carol*
1990-92	Mrs. George R. McCullough	*Libby*
1992-94	Mrs. Sylvester Damianos	*Lu*
1994-96	Mrs. Karl Krieger	*Janet*

Although the first president of the committee, Mrs. Ingersoll, was a Greensburger, and Sewickley is well represented, it is basically a Pittsburgh-based group with, as of 1994, more than 200 active and advisory members some of whom serve as trustees of The Carnegie, some have been honored as Distinguished Daughters of Pennsylvania. Mrs. Charles Moore, former headmistress of the Ellis School, in 1974 became the first female trustee not serving ex officio as City Council's member for the Carnegie Library. When their term in office is over, these presidents do not "just fade away," they simply take on a new committee responsibility which they carry out with dedication and distinction, while thinking up new ways to raise money to benefit The Carnegie Museum of Art.

The historical notes concerning the establishment of the Women's Committee were written by B. G. Galey and Emily Oliver in 1968. Mrs. Galey presided from 1965 to 1966. Mrs. Oliver, granddaughter and daughter of two presidents of The Carnegie Institute, William Nimick Frew 1896-1914, (the first president), and William Frew 1943-1948, has the distinction of having twice served as president of the Women's Committee, in 1961-1962 and 1978-1980. She is also a life member of the Board of Trustees of Carnegie Institute.

The Carnegie Museum of Art The Patrons Art Fund, Since 1922

Established by Willis F. McCook

"It is a wonderful thing Andrew Carnegie has done for Pittsburgh, and the time has come when some of the people of Pittsburgh ought to show their appreciation of it in a practical manner," stated attorney Willis F. McCook, industrial leader and art collector. It was he who inspired the creation, in 1922, of the Patrons Art Fund by his challenge gift of $10,000, payable over ten years, for the purchase of paintings for the art gallery. His provision was that the president of the trustees, Samuel Harden Church, should get nine others to make similar subscriptions.

Twenty-One Subscribers

Soon after this announcement on Founder's Day, 1922, the number of subscriptions had grown to 21, including the following: Mrs. Edward H. Bindley, Paul Block, George W. Crawford, B. G. Follansbee, Mrs. William N. Frew, Mrs. David Lindsay Gillespie with Miss Mabel Gillespie, Howard Heinz, Miss Mary L. Jackson, George Lauder, Albert C. Lehman, Willis F. McCook, Andrew W. Mellon, Richard B. Mellon, William Larimer Mellon, Franklyn Nicola, Mrs. John L. Porter, Mrs. Henry R. Rea, William H. Robinson, Ernest T. Weir, Emil Winter, and Mrs. Joseph R. Woodwell with Mrs. James D. Hailman (in memory of Joseph R. Woodwell, whose portrait by Thomas Eakins was purchased in 1930 through the fund).

The Carnegie Corporation of New York doubled the first $150,000 subscribed, with that amount being added to the endowment of Carnegie Institute, not to the Patrons Fund. This contribution was mentioned 18 years later in the catalogue for the exhibition in 1940 of the 39 paintings purchased to that time from the Patrons of Art Fund.

The first purchase in 1922 was of Pittsburgh-born Mary Cassatt's *Young Women Picking Fruit*. Sixty years later a group of Cassatt's prints and drawings was exhibited by The Museum of Art, Carnegie Institute. The purchase in 1930 of Thomas Eakins' portrait of *Joseph R. Woodwell*, one of the original trustees of Carnegie Institute, was a far-sighted recognition of Eakins' stature as a master of realism, as well as a tribute also to artist Woodwell. In 1932 two paintings of one individual, by different artists, were purchased: The John Singer Sargent *Portrait of a Boy* and George Luks' portrait *Homer Saint-Gaudens*, at the time director of The Museum of Art. The last painting purchased by the Patrons Art Fund prior to the exhibition was *Georgia Jungle* by Alexander Brook, awarded the first prize in the *International* of 1939.

The 39 paintings in the historic exhibition of 1940 are listed here by the year of their purchase through the Patrons Art Fund. Some of these paintings (marked by an asterisk) were purchased from the *International Exhibitions*. Indicative of the growing contemporary orientation of the purchases through the Patrons Art Fund is the 1980 acquisition of the print by James Torlakson, *Southern Pacific #3196*, a photorealist watercolor of a locomotive. There were also groups of works by individual artists: photographs by John Covert, prints by Günther Förg, and computer animations by Paul Glabicki. All are listed alphabetically by artist's name in the Registrar's records, along with the paintings by Richard Diebenkorn, Alfred Manessier, Joan Miro, Carl Henning Pedersen, Antonia Tapies, and sculptures by Jean Arp, Alberto Giacometti and Dwyane Hatchett . . . to mention just a few.

In 1982 an article in *Carnegie Magazine* noted that this fund had made it possible to add some 60 works from the *International* alone to the permanent collection. The section on the *Carnegie International* mentions some of those purchases, but the limitations of space preclude complete listings of the fund purchases during the 55 year period from 1940-1995.

Patrons Art Fund Purchases, 1922-1940

The following are The Museum of Art's purchases, by year, from the establishment in 1922 of the Patrons Art Fund to 1940, the year of the Retrospective Exhibition. Paintings marked by asterisk were exhibited in the *Internationals* and are now in the collection of The Museum of Art. (Artists' births are indicated by given year.)

1922

Mary Cassatt, American 1845-1926,
  *Young Women Picking Fruit**
Italico Brass, Italian 1870, *The Terrace*, Venice
John C. Johansen, American 1887, *Borderland*
Bernard Boutet De Monvel, French 1844, *Portrait*
Valentin De Zubiaurre, Spanish 1879, *Twilight*

1924

A. J. Munnings, English 1878, *Changing Horses*
Arnesby Brown, English 1866, *A Passing Storm*
Claude Rameau, French 1876,
  Valley of Pouilly on the Loire
Ettore Tito, Italian 1859, Market Place, *San Marc*

1925

George Bellows, American 1882-1925,
  Anne in White
Marius A. J. Bauer, Dutch 1867-1932,
  Interior of a Mosque
Charles Jay Taylor, American 1855-1929,
  A Maine Souvenir
Sir D. J. Cameron, Scottish 1865,
  The Bridge and the City, Berwick on Tweed
Ignacio Zuloaga, Spanish 1870, *Castilian Shepard*

1926

Augustus John, English 1879,
  The Poet, Roy Campbell
Antonio Mancini, Italian 1852-1930,
  Portrait in Red

1927

Rockwell Kent, American 1882, *Annie McGinley*
Robert Spencer, American 1879-1931, *Inland City*
Ambrose McEvoy, English 1878-1927,
  Vicomptesse Henri de Janze

1928

Charles W. Hawthorne, American 1872-1930,
  *Portrait of a Portuguese Gentleman**
Frank Duveneck, American 1848-1919, *Wistful Girl*
Andre Derain, French 1880, *Still Life*

1929

Karl Sterrer, Austria 1885, *Girl with Ships*

1930

Arthur B. Davies, American 1862-1928,
  *At the Chestnut Root**
Thomas Eakins, American 1844-1916,
  Joseph R. Woodwell

1931

Eugene Speicher, American 1883, *Babette*
Felice Casorati, Italian 1886, *Hills*
Gerald L. Brockhurst, English 1890,
  Portrait of Henry Rushbury

1932

John S. Sargent, American 1856-1925,
  *Portrait of a Boy**
George Luks, American 1867-1933,
  Homer Saint-Gaudens

1933

Jose Gutierrez Solana, Spanish 1886,
  Bullfight in Turegano

1934

Colin Gill, English 1892, *The Kerry Flute Player*

1935

Leon Kroll, American 1884, *Morning on the Cape**

1936

Edward Hopper, American 1882,
  *Cape Cod Afternoon**
Felice Carena, Italian 1880, *Midday in Summer*

1937

Bernard Karfiol, American 1886, *Christina*

1938

Cornelius T. M. Van Dongen, French 1877,
  Portrait of E. Berry Wall

1939

Ferruccio Ferrazzi, Italian 1891, *The Tragic Journey*
Alexander Brook, American 1898 (First Prize
  International, 1939), *Georgia Jungle**

Two Models, One Seated on Floor in Kimono, 1980, by
Philip Pearlstein, American; Fellows Fund, 1981.

The exhibition of 1940 was presented as "a
pictorial report" by the director of Fine Arts,
Homer Saint-Gaudens, and in gratitude to the
subscribers "who have become partners of
Andrew Carnegie, as he hoped Pittsburghers
would, in his gift to the City of Pittsburgh."

Fifty-five years have passed since establishment of the Patrons Art Fund and, despite the
escalating prices of art, the totality of the works
acquired for The Carnegie Museum of Art is
indeed impressive.

The Carnegie Museum of Art
The Fellow's Fund

In 1993 the Fellow's Fund of the Carnegie
Museum of Art celebrated its 25 years as an
organization. The fund was initiated by Institute trustee and original chairman James L.
Winokur. The concept was, and is, to help
provide funds for acquisitions which few of the
Fellows could, by themselves, afford. The group
has increased to 90-some members who together contribute about $70,000 annually to
the museum. The idea is "to make the rewards
of patronage within the reach of many who
care about art and our museum."

A 25th anniversary exhibition highlighted some of the 18 works bought solely by or assisted by Fellow's Funds. Two of the specially selected works on view in the Hall of Sculpture were *The Doric Order* (1972) by Alfred Jensen and the large-scale painting *White March* (1970) by Jack Youngerman, American. Jensen was born in Guatemala to Danish parents and this work was organized according to the Mayan calendar.

Acquisitions from other years include: *The Coffee Line*, 1905 *International*, by John Sloan, 1871-1951; *Plain*, 1979, by Philip Guston, 1913-1980; Philip Pearlstein's *Two Models, One Seated on Floor in Kimono*, 1980; *White Top Mountain, New Hampshire*, 1930, by Marsden Hartley, American 1877-1943 bought in 1992; and in the realm of decorative arts, a 1990 purchase *Child's Chair*, c. 1920, by the Dutch architect, Geritt Rietveld, 1888-1964.

In 1984 the Fellow's Fund was joined with that of the Women's Committee to buy Mark Rothko's *Yellow, Blue on Orange*. From the 1985 *Carnegie International*. The Fellow's Fund joined with Kaufmann's department store and the Women's Committee to obtain *Midgard*, 1980-1985, by the German artist Anselm Kiefer, b. 1945. *A Self Portrait*, 1986 by Andy Warhol, 1928-1987, was purchased by the Fellows alone, as was the large sculpture from the 1988 *International*, *Das Nones*, 1988, by Susanna Solano, b. 1946, Barcelona, Spain.

Other artists whose works have been acquired by Fellow's Funds: Antonio Canal, Canaletto, b. Italy, 1697-1768; Shusaku Arakawa, b. Japan; Hiram Powers, 1805-1873 Pedersen, Dewasne, Avery, and an unknown 12th century Indian artist whose carved sandstone relief joins the other works in the permanent collection.

An article concerning the Fellows was written for the July/August, 1993 issue of *Carnegie Magazine* by James A. Fisher, chairman since 1972. He mentioned his co-chairmen, Teresa Heinz and Milton Porter and stated that additional members are welcome.

Carnegie Institute
Man and Ideas
Outstanding Lectures 1969-1994

Carnegie Institute salutes the Pittsburgh corporations and individuals who have had the vision to bring to this city a group of the world's most celebrated people in the arts and the sciences. Originally arranged by the Women's Committee of The Museum of Art, and since 1976 alternately with the Council for Carnegie Museum of Natural History, these lectures have benefited over 50,000 people in our community.

Forerunner, perhaps inspiration for the series, was the passionate debate in the Carnegie Music Hall December 12, 1932. *Does Man Live Again* was the title with the protagonists the famous courtroom spellbinder, 75-year-old Clarence Darrow vs. the 35-year-old, newly elected Pittsburgh Judge Michael A. Musmamo. Moderator was Judge Elder Marshall. According to Cliff Tuttle in *Carnegie Magazine* May/June 1991, every seat was sold and outside were 1,000 people wanting to enter. The police were called.

As part of the *Man and Ideas* series, the following men and women have come to Carnegie Institute to share their ideas directly with their Pittsburgh audiences.

. . . .

1969 R. Buckminister Fuller, Architect

1970 Louis Kahn, Architect
Charles Eames, Designer
Constantions A. Doxiadis, Architect
   and Environmentalist
Isamu Noguchi, Sculptor

1971 Meyer Shapiro, Art Historian
René Dubos, Microbiologist,
   Environmentalist, and Author
J. Carter Brown, Director, National Gallery
James W. Rouse, City Planner

1972   Saul Bass, Graphic Designer and Film Maker
       Philip Handler, Biochemist
       Margaret Mead, Anthropologist and Author
       James C. Fletcher, Administrator of NASA

1973   Barbara Ward, Economist
       John Rewald, Art Scholar
       Sir Rudolf Bing, Director,
           Metropolitan Opera
       Iris Cornelia Love, Archeologist

1974   Jean Mayer, Educator and Nutritionist
       Herman Kahn, Analyst, Public Policies
       Mary McCarthy, Author

1975   Barbara Tuchman, Historian and Author
       Daniel Boorstin, Historian
       Jacques Picard, Underwater Scientist
       Alexander Marshack, Archeologist

1976   Shana Alexander,
           Journalist and Television Commentator
       Robert Motherwell, Artist
       Harold Rosenberg, Art Critic
       John King Fairbank,
           China and Asian Studies Specialist
       Bruce Murray, Space Scientist

1977   Richard Leakey,
           Archeologist and Paleontologist
       George Segal, Sculptor
       Gerald M. Edelman, Chemist

1978   Ada Louise Huxtable, Architecture Critic
       Gerald Durrell, Author and Naturalist
       Jon Lindbergh, Oceanographer

1979   S. Dillon Ripley, Secretary,
           Smithsonian Institution
       Irving Kristol, Journalist
       Joseph Alsop, Art Historian

1980   Henry Kissinger, Statesman
       Lewis Thomas, Biologist, Poet, and
           Medical Administrator
       Barbara Rose, Art Critic

1981   Philip Johnson, Architect
       John Burgee, Architect
       Isaac Asimov, Science Fiction Author
       Alvin Toffler, Futurist

1982   Robert Hughes, Art Critic and Author

1984   Michael Graves, Architect
       Edward O. Wilson, Biologist and Author
       Sir Edmund Hillary, Explorer, Author,
           and Humanitarian

1985   David Hockney, Artist
       Jay Stephen Gould, Scientist and Author

1986   William H. Whyte, Sociologist and Author
       Edgar Kaufmann, Jr., Architectural Historian

1987   Robert Ballard, Scientist, Explorer,
           and Author

1988   August Wilson, Playwright

1989   Vartan Gregorian, Rescuer of the New York
           Public Library

1990   Hedrick Smith, Journalist, Expert on the
           Union Soviet Socialist Republics

1993   J. Carter Brown, Director of the
           National Gallery of Art, 1969-1992

Supporting Carnegie Institute on this gift to the city: Alcoa Foundation, Allegheny International, Inc., Dravo Corporation, Equibank, N. A., Gulf Oil Corporation, H. J. Heinz Company Foundation, Joy Manufacturing Co., Ketchum Communication, Inc., KM & G International, Inc., Koppers, Inc., Mellon Bank, N. A., Mellon Stuart Company, Mine Safety Appliance, Inc., Mobay Chemical Corporation, PPG Industries Foundation, Rockwell International Corporation, Westinghouse Electric Corporation, and Mr. and Mrs. Richard M. Scaife.

The Carnegie's Art in the Community — The Three Rivers Arts Festival Artistic Outreach

The festival, called by the *Pittsburgh Post-Gazette's* art critic, Donald Miller, "the largest, longest, and most popular event in this part of Pennsylvania," was originated by the Women's Committee of The Museum of Art in 1960. Initially an exhibit of painting, sculpture, photography, and crafts by local artists, it has evolved over 35 years to become a 17-day extravaganza of visual and performing arts on an ever-widening basis.

Traditionally there are demonstrations of raku firing, bronze casting, paper making, pewter casting, wheel thrown pottery, weaving, watercolor and oil painting, as well as many

participatory activities for children such as face painting and even free hand decoration of a bus. The Film Festival, which now occurs separately in the fall, was introduced as part of the 1982 Arts Festival with 13 films from seven countries, organized by the Film and Video Department, Museum of Art, Carnegie Institute.

A wide selection of music, dance, theater, poetry, mime, puppets, and strolling troubadours adds lively notes to the scene. The Pittsburgh Symphony, The American Wind Symphony, and The Pittsburgh Youth Symphony Orchestra, as well as Walt Harper and All That Jazz, Nathan Davis and the Tomorrow Band, plus the Trinidad and Tobago Baltimore Steel Orchestra, have performed in the various festivals. The highlight in 1982 was the appearance of Ella Fitzgerald to an audience of more than 100,000 fans, courtesy of KOOL Jazz Festival and KDKA-TV. Another jazz great who performed at the festival was Earl "Fatha" Hines, a true pro. Wearing a leather suit despite the heat, he good-naturedly played on a borrowed piano, propped up on cement blocks, and with missing ivories . . . an impromptu solution to the piano movers strike at the time.

During many of those years Women's Committee member Mrs. Pierce (Babs) Widdoes served as executive director and worked closely with Paula Atlas, administrative assistant, for 23 years. The Carnegie connection has remained strong into the 35th anniversary year with trustee Deborah D. Dodds and Alice R. Snyder as chair and vice chairpersons, with Jeanne Pearlman as executive director. At the time of her retirement, Paula Atlas recalled the strengths each director brought to the festival: Donald Steinfirst, music critic for the *Post-Gazette*, was naturally most interested in the performing arts; Babs Widdoes expanded the festival's range and impact and realized that food would have to become a part of the festival; John Jay brought the performing arts a giant leap forward, and John Brice gave a sense of quality to the arts

and found money for prizes.

Over the decades, the exhibitions have taken place in Gateway Plaza, made available by the Equitable Life Assurance Society, owners of Gateway Center. In the summer of 1982, the 23rd annual festival, threatened by the construction work on the subway, expanded to Point State Park, Station Square, Old Post Office Museum, the United Steelworkers building, the Art Institute of Pittsburgh, the Allegheny County Court House Gallery and the old International Airport.

As a result of a national competition conducted by the festival, with funds from The Pittsburgh Foundation, in 1982 the two-dimensional art was exhibited in handsome new yellow-topped aluminum "display environments." They replaced the 25-year-old ones at a cost of $250,000. The design of Atlanta architect Michael Tych provided optimum protection from the mercurial elements, and improved lighting, while competing least with the works of art shown.

Each festival with a different invited curator has had something special for which it may be remembered. One example was *Modular Wrap III* by noted Pittsburgh weaver Elaina Myrinz, a graduate of Carnegie Mellon University. A giant sculpture was created by wrapping the front 14 stories of the Westinghouse Building in Gateway Center in more than 4,500 square feet of multicolored nylon cloth.

Another CMU alumna, Diane Samuels, now, in 1994, internationally known for her sculpture, collaborated in 1979 with Julie Staelin to produce a gigantic *Sky Sculpture*, and in 1985, independently, *Inflatables*, balloon-filled sculptures of rip-stop nylon.

Smoke Sculpture-The City Above was executed by a skywriting plane in a design by Pittsburgher Christopher Priore. *Pittsburgh Bridge 1982* was a 16-foot high, four-sided painting by architectural illusion artist Hugh Kepets. An enduring presence at the festival is the handsome large sculpture *Pipe Dream IV*, 1970 by Josepha Filkosky, a former nun.

Each year there are favorite and non-favorite works. One of the most controversial was a huge sculpture in 1990, by Louis Jimenez of New Mexico, titled *Hunky, Steelworker*. It was the monumental figure of a laborer in the steel mills. Although clearly alluding to an historical appellation it was perceived as an ethnic insult and caused an outpouring of protest. As a result the word "Hunky" was removed, leaving *Steelworker* as the title of the work.

The 1993 festival presented five special projects, two of which focused attention on artists living and working in Pittsburgh: *Sculpture at the Point, Glass; In the Quest of Being, Degrees of Abstraction; Eight Pittsburgh Artists, Close to Home; Pittsburgh Photographers on Pittsburgh;* and *Veronica Ryan*. The performing arts program included music and dance by Afro-American and Native American groups.

The festival of 1994, under executive director Jeanne Pearlman, continued the multicultural outreach, across all disciplines, featuring in addition, African-influenced, Caribbean and Latino artists for equally diverse audiences.

A favorite in 1994, *Sonic Forest* was the work of Christopher Janney and Geoffrey Pingree. (Fifteen years earlier Janney's piece *Soundstair* began its touring life at the Pittsburgh festival.) *Sonic Forest* in PPG plaza was an evocative arrangement of 24 eight-foot-high aluminum columns (trees) equipped with speakers, lights, and photo-electric cells and planted with flowers at the bases. As people moved through the forest, under the canopy of sky blue and sea green plastic, they triggered the cells activating birds songs and other environmental sounds thereby transforming the empty austere plaza into a lively place.

Another notable commissioned work of the 1994 festival was by Mexico-born Guillermo Gomez-Pena of Los Angeles and his collaborator Roberto Sifuentes. (Gomez-Pena was a 1991 recipient of one of the so-called "genius grants" MacArthur Fellowships). Sheltered in the Wood Street Gallery, *The Temple of Confessions*, was an installation in the form of a chapel for the hypothetical, post-millennial, pop-culture religion based on the teaching of two hybrid saints. Visitors were invited into a "techno-confessional" to speak out their most intimate fears, fantasies, and prejudices about those whose cultural differences make them ill-at-ease.

The ethnic mood was friendlier in well-known Pittsburgh artist Adrienne Heinrich's installation *Grandmothers* in which see-through photographic portraits of six black women were exhibited together with their audio taped commentaries, while overhead, lights were triggered by viewers walking into the environment.

Although sponsored by The Carnegie Museum of Art, and dedicated to its mission of bringing art free to the people, the festival funds are raised separately from corporate, foundation, public, and individual patrons. Proceeds from the sale of works of art, foods, T-shirts, and other items assist the festival, as well as the individual participants. There is now a Winter Artists' Market in addition to the sales booths at the festival which offer works in various media by some 100 artists. The 1982 festival was budgeted at $275,000, lower by $95,000 than the preceding year. By 1994 the budget had ballooned to close to $1 million and it is estimated that more than 600,000 persons annually enjoy this special regional event which has been named by *The Philadelphia Inquirer* as one of the top ten festivals in the Northeast.

Here three great rivers meet and merge
To give this place a name and theme;
And here, as well, those tides converge
Whose source is man's enduring dream:
His hope that what his hands designed,
The surging rhythms in his breast,
The shapes and colors in his mind,
His joys, his griefs, made manifest
In what he carves, or writes, or paints,
Or pours upon the air in song,
Or speaks in dance's eloquence,
May merge and mingle with that strong
Exultant River to the Sea
Flowing from mankind's common heart:
His dream, his immortality,
The holy craft he calls his art.

. . . .

Evocative of the city itself, this tribute to the Three Rivers Arts Festival was written in 1971 by Pittsburgh's poet Sara Henderson Hay (1906-1987).

Pittsburgh's Associated Artists Exhibitions at The Carnegie

Friends of Art for the Pittsburgh Public Schools

The Associated Artists of Pittsburgh is said to be second only to Boston's Copley Society as the oldest continuing association for artists in the United States and Canada, having been established in 1910. In honor of the 75th anniversary, the Associated Artists in 1985 published a comprehensive, nostalgic history of the organization, its members and activities. Some of the highlights of the history were recounted by it's author, Mary Brignano, for *Carnegie Magazine.*

Local artists organized into the Associated in 1910 and held their first exhibition that year in Pittsburgh's Grand Opera House. The all-member jury selected 202 works by 64 artists for the show which coincided with the *Carnegie International Exhibition.* The comparison must have been benign because John Beatty, director of the Carnegie Department of Art, invited the group to exhibit at the Institute the following year . . . a tradition which has remained in effect ever since.

The original annual cash awards gave way in 1958 to purchase prizes, with the winning works being acquired for the permanent collection of The Carnegie Museum of Art.

The AAP 83rd annual exhibition at The Carnegie Museum of Art in 1993 was opened to nonmembers, as advised by juror Richard Armstrong, curator of Contemporary Art at The Carnegie. Of the 289 artists entered, 53 were nonmembers; of the 509 works entered, 104 were accepted; 98 artists were accepted, of whom 12 were nonmembers. The show produced more income and 12 works were sold, an increase over 1992.

Richard Armstrong again directed installation of the Associated's 1994 exhibition, which was also open to nonmembers. A total of 477 pieces by 259 artists were submitted and juried by Beryl Wright, a Chicago-based, freelance curator with an art history degree from Yale University. Many of the artists, 104, exhibited also in last year's show with 115 works.

A group called "Friends of Art for the Pittsburgh Public Schools" also purchases works from these annual exhibitions and has greatly enriched the schools by their gifts. The Friends purchased six works from the 1993 Associated exhibition at The Carnegie: drawings by Cecelia Cortez and James Loney; paintings by Andy Laxton, William Pfai, and Barry Shields; and a photograph by Judy Zimmerman. In addition the Friends gave the schools two major paintings by Marie Kelly and Ruth Selwitz which had been given to the Friends by Mrs. Peter Denby after her husband's death. This brought to 484 the number of works from the Associated's exhibitions at The Carnegie given by the Friends to the Pittsburgh Public Schools since 1916.

It was the idea of John L. Porter, trustee of Carnegie Institute, who served as first chairman of the Friends until 1936. He was succeeded by William Frew, president of Carnegie Institute, then, in 1942, by John O'Connor, Jr., assistant director of Fine Arts at Carnegie Institute. The fourth chairman, who served for 20 years, was professor Walter Read Hovey, of the University of Pittsburgh and director of the Frick Art Museum. He was succeeded in turn by Chairman John H. Cohen, Mrs. Charles H. Moore and currently, John J. Humphrey.

In the late 1920s or early '30s a similar group was established to present artworks to the parish schools of the Pittsburgh Catholic Diocese. Since 1916 Pittsburgh's public schools have acquired a historically significant, valuable art collection with works by such Associated Artists members as A. H. Gorson, Malcolm Parcell, Balcomb Greene, Samuel Rosenberg, Louise Pershing, William Libbey, Virgil Cantini, Marie Kelly, Henry Koerner, Richard Beaman, Wafta Midani, Robert Qualters, Andy Warhol, and many others. In 1984 the collection was valued at an estimated $1.5 million.

Some of the representative artists and their works acquired by The Carnegie Museum of Art for the permanent collection are:

· ·

1958   Leonard Lieb, *Composition*
Joann Maier, *Synonymity*
Larissa Geiss Osby, *A Bridge in the Moor*
Josephine Paul, *Strong is the Light*
Elizabeth Voelker, *Forsythia*

1959   Elizabeth Allison, *Genesis*
Richard B. Beaman, *Fire Wake*
Gertrude Temeles Half, *Related Forms*

1960   Rochelle Blumenfeld,* *Flight*
Virgil Cantini, *Kooster Birds*

Gertrude Temeles Half,*
     Mosaic and Falling Red
Gloria Stoll Karn,* *Night-Blooming Garden*

1961   Jeanne Leger,
     Sense of Shapes, Blue, Mauve, and Ochre
Tom Rowlands, *Blackscape*

1962   Ann Temeles Golomb,* *Accent*
Marie Kelly,* *Animals*
Jack Massey, *Yes*
Russell Twiggs, *White Figure*

1963   Rebecca Berman,* *Essence of Time*
Robert L. Lepper,* *Benign Beast*

1964   Skarlis, *Woman is a Green Wind*
Edwin W. Zoller, *No. 7-64*

1965   Grete Holst Evans,*
The Sea Has Many Voices, collage
Jane Haskell,* *Yaddo*

1966   George Koren, *Icarius*

1967   Joann Maier, *Attractions V*
David Miller, *February*

1968   Charles Jackson, *Aunt Ida's Remark*
     Left us Intragalactic

1969   *Our Environment* show, no awards

1970   Gary L. Jurysta, *Red Trapezoid*
Harry Schwalb, *Spinners Spinning*

1971   Clark Winter, *Celebration*

1972   Roland Gentilcone, *Balance*
Jane Haskell,* *Permutation II*
Troy West, *Soul Tracing*

1973   Marjorie Shipe, *Star Ember*

1974   Joseph Shepler, *Ironic Garden*

1975   Sylvester Damianos, *White Fluid Landscape*

1976   Thaddeus Mosley, *Georgia Gate*

1977   Lloyd Wilson, *Chuco Landscape*

1978   Louise Pierucci, *Paper Ribs*
Jan Zandhuis, *Phase 4, #B*

1979   Jane Haskell,* *Alphabet II*

1980   Herbert Olds, *Collection*
Elizabeth Whitely, *Transparent Birds IV*
Michael Madigan, *Break*

1981   Paula Bogue-Overbay, *Module III*
Teresa Dalla Piccola Wood,
     Mundane Existence Series 3

1982	Charles (Bud) Gibbons, *Maine Landscape*
1983	Robert Qualters, *Hazelwood*
1984	Joel DeGrand, *Allegheny County Courthouse #2*
1985	Robert M. Robinson, *Souvenir*
1986	James P. Nelson, *Back to Pittsburgh*
1987	Jo Leggett, *Untitled II, Untitled I*
1988	Giordano Riccoban, *Sirena II, Yo Hice Mis Unas Por Ti*
1989	Mark Zets, *Under the Broken Rainbow/ The Assumption*
1990	Willy Garver, *Sea Change*
1991	Richard A. Stoner, *Why We Fight, Sept. 18, 1990*
1992	Adrienne Heinrich, *Remember the Children*
1993	Barry Shields, *Uptown View*
1994	Janet Towbin, *Patterns of Chaos II*
1995	Jerry Caplan, *Red Teapot* and *Shack*

* The significance of the asterisks above is in the fact that all these artists, winners of the Carnegie Institute Purchase Prizes in the annual exhibitions of the Associated Artists of Pittsburgh, were pupils of the late Samuel Rosenberg. He was born in Philadelphia in 1896, studied art at the National Academy of Design in New York and at Carnegie Institute of Technology where he taught painting from 1925 to 1966. He directed the Art Department at Chatham College 1927-1945 and taught independently as well. The Museum of Art in 1973 listed three oils by Rosenberg: *Greenfield Hill*, 1932, *Second Avenue*, 1933, and *Time Echoes*, 1952. In 1978 the collection of the museum was enriched by the gift from Murray Z. Rosenberg of 346 drawings and 112 etchings by his father Samuel Rosenberg, who died in Pittsburgh in 1972. Included also in the gift were seven pen-pencil studies by Andy Warhol, who was born in Pittsburgh and moved to New York in 1949. As Andy Warhola, member of the AAP, he had his first exhibiting experience with the Associated in the late '40s. In honor of the opening of The Warhol Museum, in Pittsburgh Friday May 13, 1994, the AAP held an exhibition of multimedia artwork entitled *Andy Mania*, reflecting the influences from Warhol's work conceptually, thematically, and technically on other artists.

A fellow CMU classmate of Warhol was Philip Pearlstein (b. 1924), also a Pittsburgher who moved to New York in 1949. He is represented in the permanent collection of The Carnegie Museum of Art by his *Two Models, One Seated on Floor in Kimono*, 1980, purchased for the museum by the Fellows of The Museum Art Fund in 1981.

Three other "associated" artists also identified with Carnegie Mellon University are represented in the permanent collection. They are Balcomb Greene, who taught History of Art from 1942 to 1952; William Libby, professor of painting and design; and Russell Twiggs, for years massier in the College of Fine Arts. Their works are respectively: *Collage*, 1936, *The Mirror*, 1946-47, and *Abstraction*, 1952, all by Greene; *Lanterns by Libby*, *Unfolding*, 1950, and *The Overseer*, 1953, both by Twiggs; Louise Pierucci, whose *Paper Ribs* was purchased in 1978, was instructor of weaving at Carnegie Mellon University.

Pittsburghers' Support of the Arts
Pittsburgh Art in Other Cities

"Thanks to Andrew Carnegie his memorial has become the home of the oldest gallery of Modern Art, concerning itself with the international scene, in the United States."

— *Gordon Bailey Washburn, 1958*
Director, Museum of Art

Pittsburgh's Bicentennial in 1958
Celebrated Art

Although Pittsburgh has been famed in art circles since 1896, as the home of the *Carnegie International Exhibition of Contemporary Art*, it is remarkable and gratifying that in 1958 the Pittsburgh Bicentennial Association concentrated nearly all its funds on art for the celebration of the city's 200th anniversary. Ignoring the smoky-city image, the association sponsored two exhibitions: *The 1958 Pittsburgh International Exhibition of Contemporary Painting and Sculpture* and *A Retrospective Exhibition of Paintings from Previous Internationals*.

The retrospective spanned more than a quarter of the period of the Pittsburgh Exhibitions. The chairman of the Bicentennial Association was Lawrence C. Woods, Jr. with Adolph W. Schmidt heading the art committee, both of whom were trustees of Carnegie Institute. Mr. Schmidt, former U. S. Ambassador to Canada, was in 1958 chairman of the Allegheny Conference on Community Development. His wife is the former Helen S. Mellon.

Secretary of the Treasury under Presidents Harding, Coolidge, and Hoover, Andrew W. Mellon greatly enriched the collection of The Museum of Art by establishing the A. W. Mellon Educational and Charitable Trust of Pittsburgh.

Mr. Schmidt served as the first chairman of the A. W. Mellon Educational and Charitable Trust, in which he was succeeded by the late Theodore Hazlett, Jr., who had been the first president of the Pennsylvania Council on the Arts. The Council continues to provide important support to Carnegie Institute, The Museum of Natural History and The Museum of Art.

Funds for the International Exhibitions and the collections — Carnegie . . . Mellon

Although the *International Exhibitions* were originally endowed in 1896 by Andrew Carnegie, financial difficulties beset the program quite early. Fortunately, additional generous support was furnished over the years by Andrew W. Mellon, one of the original trustees, and his brother and partner, Richard Beatty Mellon. (Their joint enterprises included investment in such companies as Alcoa, Gulf Oil Corporation, and the Koppers Company in Pittsburgh. Their father Judge Thomas Mellon had early in the century established a bank and, in 1882 on the eve of his 69th birthday, had "given over" the family bank, T. Mellon & Sons, to Andrew, then 27. Five years later Andrew gave half ownership to his younger brother, Richard.)

Aid for the *Internationals* was continued by the A. W. Mellon Educational and Charitable Trust of Pittsburgh enabling resumption of the exhibition. In 1982 the new A. W. Mellon Acquisition Fund established additional support for the purchase program of The Museum of Art.

The National Gallery of Art: 1941

In 1941, the National Gallery of Art was established and endowed by Andrew W. Mellon of Pittsburgh, Secretary of the Treasury under Presidents Harding, Coolidge, and Hoover, and U. S. Ambassador to Great Britain. His own collection was the nucleus and magnet for the addition of other great art collections to the National Gallery, possibly because of

Mr. Mellon's foresight in declining to have the national gallery bear his name. The Andrew W. Mellon Foundation, Inc. of New York and Andrew's son Paul Mellon, gave the nation the splendid $94 million East Wing expanding the National Gallery in 1979.

National Foundation on the Arts and Humanities, 1964

Pittsburgh's William S. Moorhead in 1964 introduced into Congress the bill which established the National Foundation on the Arts and Humanities. In the ensuing years, it has been a powerful influence to assist private, state, and local institutions in encouraging and supporting the arts and humanities in Pittsburgh and across the United States.

The Carnegie's Art Collection: Mrs. Scaife's Influence, 1961-1971

Meanwhile it was Mrs. Alan Scaife, Sarah, daughter of Richard B. Mellon, who sparked the expansion of the permanent collection of The Museum of Art. From 1961 through 1979 more than 40% of the current holdings prior to 1980 were acquired largely as a result of her generosity and influence. In memory of Sarah Scaife, her family and the Scaife Foundation built and endowed the Scaife Galleries of The Museum of Art, completed in 1974.

Mrs. Scaife's brother, General Richard K. Mellon, during his lifetime made many donations, especially to the collections of The Carnegie Museum of Natural History. The foundation bearing his name has continued to assist projects in both museums, as did General Mellon's widow, the late Mrs. Peter Burrell.

Ailsa Mellon Bruce, daughter of Andrew Mellon, continued her father's remarkable generosity to The Museum of Art, sharing her collections, giving and endowing the Ailsa Mellon Bruce Galleries for Furniture and Decorative Arts. Mrs. Bruce's brother Paul Mellon has been for many years a signal benefactor of The Carnegie Museum of Art.

The Mellon descendants have continued their family's generous tradition in support and encouragement of Pittsburgh's cultural life. Richard P. Mellon, grandson of Richard Beatty Mellon, served as Institute trustee. Richard Mellon Scaife, also a grandson of R. B. Mellon, has for years been a moving force on the board, giving enormous support to the Scaife Gallery of The Museum of Art. In 1981, for instance, the large portrait of Andrew Carnegie by Pittsburgh's best-known artist-son, Andy Warhol, was commissioned by the museum through the Richard M. Scaife American Paintings Fund, thereby filling a gap in The Museum of Art's contemporary collection.

In 1979 funds made available by Mrs. Constance Mellon resulted in a significant addition to the growing collection of Italian art: *Christ and the Women of Samaria at the Well* c. 1690-1705 by Francesco Solimena. Other purchases are made possible by funds given by the late Matthew Mellon. The Rachel Mellon Walton Fund of The Pittsburgh Foundation made possible the Walton Hall of Ancient Egypt. Various Mellon relatives are represented in the collections of the museums by gifts from funds and foundations bearing their names or other names such as The Laurel Foundation, The Loyalhanna Foundation, and others. A great-niece of Andrew Mellon, Cordelia Scaife May, established the M. Graham Netting Research Fund in The Carnegie Museum of Natural History. And a great-great-nephew, James Mellon Walton, from 1968 to 1984, served as president of Pittsburgh's Carnegie Institute.

The Carnegie-Mellon cooperative relationship is further evidenced by the nearby university of that name, formed in 1976 by the merger of The Mellon Institute and Andrew Carnegie's Institute of Technology.

Many other prominent Pittsburgh families have for generations given loyal support to Carnegie Institute and are mentioned elsewhere in this brief account, as are the numerous Pittsburgh corporations, companies, organizations, and individuals who, in effect, have become partners of Andrew Carnegie in sustaining and expanding his great museums.

The Art-Interest of Pittsburghers: Important to Carnegie Institute, to Pittsburgh, to Other Cities, and to the Nation

Other cities have also benefited greatly by the contributions of art benefactors who were originally based in Pittsburgh. The late G. David Thompson, voracious collector of "Modern Art," saw his great collections of the oeuvre of Paul Klee, Alberto Giacometti, and other artists find homes in Europe and elsewhere. The late Mr. and Mrs. George R. Hann gathered a splendid collection of Russian icons, which was dispersed by sale in New York. The Museum of Art here received three fine icons in memory of the Hanns: two from central Russia, both of *The Mother of God*, gifts of O. John Anderson, and, from northern Russia, *The Ascension*, gift of Mr. and Mrs. George L. Craig Jr.

Japan's Mountain Tortoise Co. of Tokyo was the destination of at least one important painting which had a Pittsburgh connection. Willem de Kooning's *Interchange*, 1955, was sold in New York in November of 1989, for $20.7 million. The price was a record at auction for a living artist and the highest price paid for a contemporary work. The abstract painting was bought shortly after the artist had completed it in 1955, by Edgar Kaufmann, Jr., who had it in his home until his death in July of 1989. Also included in the collection which was auctioned by his estate were major pieces by Piet Mondrian, Picasso, Paul Klee, de Kooning, Claude Monet, and Joan Miro.

New York City boasts the Frick Museum which displays the collection of Impressionist paintings and art objects in the home of Henry Clay Frick. Washington, D.C. has the collection of Duncan Phillips. The Cubist paintings collected by Walter Arensberg, who also was born in Pittsburgh, may be seen in the Philadelphia Museum of Art. In Hagerstown, Maryland there is the Washington County Museum of Fine Arts, the gift of Mr. and Mrs. William Henry Singer, Jr. Singer (1868-1943), of a Sewickley steel family, was an accomplished post-Impressionist landscape painter who lived much of his life in Norway and the Netherlands. His wife was a Hagerstown native. The Singer Collection is another which escaped our city. The Singers left art to Bergen, Norway, Laren, Holland and Hagerstown. Singer's own handsomely done paintings are shown along with works by Homer, Church, Rodin, Moran, Metcalf, Sully, Sloan, Inness, Henri, and Hassam. (Recent work exhibited there has included that of Paul Warhola, as reported by Donald Miller in the *Pittsburgh Post-Gazette*, August 28, 1993.)

Yale University New Haven, Connecticut, was the beneficiary of Paul Mellon's collection of works by English artists, masterpieces representative of an entire era, from the birth of Hogarth in 1697 to the death of Turner in 1851 — the richest period in British art. Mr. Mellon was born in Pittsburgh, son of his English mother and Andrew W. Mellon.

When USX announced in 1989 the intended sale at New York auction of 64 choice works from the corporation's art collection the reaction was public dismay. Compounding the consternation was the fact that USX is the descendent of Andrew Carnegie's own company which led to the implication that the art should come to Carnegie's art museum in Pittsburgh. There were conjectures as what Carnegie himself would have thought about the proposal. The art was collected by the corporation over 20 years with the advice of Leon A. Arkus, the former director of The Carnegie Museum of Art.

From a business standpoint the sale was made when market conditions were most favorable and was expected to bring an estimated $4 million. Although USX's right to convert the art into cash was acknowledged, there was editorial and individual regret that the collection would be leaving town. Of the artists whose works were included, 15 were Pittsburgh natives, and of the total number most had participated in Pittsburgh exhibitions over the years, so the works were familiar to the city's art lovers. The collection was particularly strong in Contemporary Art, with works by Hans Hoffman, Adolph Gottlieb, Morris Louis, Robert Motherwell, Jules Olitski, Joan Mitchell, and Frank Stella.

A selection of 19th century American paintings included work by: Mary Cassatt, Marsden Hartley, Childe Hassam, and John Henry Twachtman, and sculpture by Harry Jackson. In addition, there were works by Impressionists Paul Signac, Fernand Leger, Sonia Delauney, Edouard Vuillard, and Eugene Delacroix and an Abstract painting by Pierre Alechinsky. The art was sold in separate specialized auctions without a total tally but the proceeds did not quite match the estimates.

Robert Wilburn, president of The Carnegie, gave a measured reply to the criticism of the corporation, recalling the generous support USX had extended over the years: $1 million to the capital campaign, $1.5 million for the Second Century Fund, corporate sponsorship for the 1985 *Carnegie International,* and underwriting the travel for The Museum of Art's *American Drawings and Watercolors* exhibition to Edinburgh, Scotland, for the sesquicentennial celebration of the birth of Andrew Carnegie.

Man with Pipe, c. 1912, by Jean Metzinger, French; gift of G. David Thompson, 1953.

Cubism in Pittsburgh, 1913

"What we can say with certainty is that in 1913, Pittsburgh, a city known for its artistic conservatism, was exhibiting some important examples of the latest style of Cubism."

— Aaron Sheon, *Carnegie Magazine*, 1982

Boggs & Buhls Sponsors Cubist Art Show — How It Came to Be

Remarkable in its far-reaching effect was an art event sponsored more than 80 years ago by Boggs & Buhl, then *The* Pittsburgh department store, which in 1963 was demolished for the building of Allegheny Center on the North Side. How this avant-garde exhibition came about was detailed by art historian Aaron Sheon. In an article in *Two Museums*, the publication which accompanied the then 50-some-year-old *Carnegie Magazine*, the University of Pittsburgh's Professor of Art History wrote: "the only connection Pittsburgh had with Cubism was through Walter Arensberg." Born in Pittsburgh, educated at Harvard, Arensberg became a writer for the New York Post. He visited the famous

Armory Show in New York in 1913 which exhibited over 1,100 works, many experimental, created in Europe. "The paintings by the Parisian Cubists caused the most consternation and controversy." Arensberg purchased several of the most controversial works and became a close friend of artist Walter Pach, who had relatives associated with New York department stores, and with Arthur B. Davies, artist and chief organizer of the Armory Show, both of whom had paintings in that show.

News Editorial Calls for Pittsburgh to Rival Armory Show

Although neither Pach nor Davies was a Cubist, the paintings of Davies, reclining nudes entitled *Sleep*, submitted to the *International* of that same year, were "viewed with alarm" by Pittsburgh art critic Marion Brunot. But an editorial in the *Pittsburgh Chronicle Telegraph* called for a Pittsburgh exhibition of Modern Art to rival the Armory Show. An art instructor at Carnegie Tech, Charles J. Taylor, knew many of the exhibitors in Armory Show and admired Cubism. According to the Carnegie Tech newspaper, *The Tartan*, he inaugurated the newly completed Fine Arts Building with Pittsburgh's first Cubist exhibition, a show of his students' work in that style. One of the artists included in the Armory Show was Henry J. Keller, who had taught at Pittsburgh's Art Institute from 1902 to 1908, later moving to the Cleveland Institute of Art. Keller, whose work was exhibited in the *Carnegie International* in 1910, knew many local artists. The Armory Show occurred in February of 1913 in New York. On June 30 an important exhibition of French Cubist paintings opened in Cleveland, at the Taylor Department Store (no relation to Professor Taylor).

Display in Boggs & Buhl's Rug Department, 1913

Then on July 10, it opened for a week's display in the Rug Department of Boggs & Buhl's Department Store, in Pittsburgh. Billed as "direct from Paris," the exhibit included works of Pierre Demon, Albert Glees, APR, Fernand Leger, Jean Metzinger, Gustav Miklos, and Jacques Villon. There were also some paintings by Pittsburgh artists John Hawthorne, James Bonar, A. H. Gorson, Will Hyett, Fahilla Jameson, John Kaye, Charles Kemper, Mary AcAuley, Elizabeth Robb, and Adele Williams.

The show was well-advertised and well-attended and caused quite a stir. Boggs & Buhl included announcement of the Cubist exhibition in their newspaper advertisements, mentioning that Pittsburgh art critic Arthur Burgoyne had praised the show. Printed in the ad was also a "cubist" passage from Pittsburgh-born Gertrude Stein's essay *Matisse*. Through the Buhl Foundation this early support of the arts continues into the 21st century to the benefit of the Carnegie Institute and other Pittsburgh institutions.

Cubist Exhibition at The Carnegie Museum of Art, 1913

After the Boggs & Buhl exhibition, the Pittsburgh Art Society asked Director Beatty to exhibit some of the contemporary paintings by American artists affiliated with the Armory Show. As a result, in December 1913, 40 Cubist-inspired paintings were shown at The Museum of Art, selected by Arthur B. Davies, for the Pittsburgh Art Society. Davies showed six of his latest works, and there were three or four paintings each by ten other artists: Walter Pach, William Glackens, Walt Kuhn, Elmer McRae, George Of, Maurice Prendergast, Morton L. Schamberg, Charles Sheeler, Allen Tucker, and Joseph Stella. Stella showed three versions of his *Battle of Lights*, (Coney Island), his important Cubist-inspired work, one of the most experimental works by an American artist in 1913. This exhibition in Pittsburgh was the first one after New York's Armory Show to include American artists influenced by Cubism.

Carnegie Museum of Natural History Directors, 1896 to 1995

Mr. Frank H. Gerrodette
Ethnologist
June - September 19, 1896

Dr. William J. Holland
Minister, Paleontologist, Entomologist
March 18, 1898 - May 21, 1926

Dr. Andrey Avinoff
Artist, Entomologist
August 1, 1926 - June 15, 1945

Dr. O. E. Jennings
Botanist
October 22, 1946 - December 31, 1948

Mr. Wallace Richards
Civic Planner
January 1, 1949 - December 31, 1953

Dr. M. Graham Netting
Herpetologist-Ecologist
January 1, 1954 - March 31, 1975

Dr. Craig C. Black
Paleontologist
May 1, 1975 - September 1, 1982

Dr. Mary R. Dawson, Acting Director
Paleontologist
September 1, 1982 - June 1983

Dr. Robert M. West
Paleontologist
June 1983 - 1986

Dr. David A. Watters, Acting Director
Anthropologist
January 1, 1987 - August 31, 1987

Dr. James E. King
Geologist, Paleobotanist
September 7, 1987 - present

The Carnegie Museum of Natural History Establishing the Collections

Director of the Museum, Dr. Holland First Annual Report, 1898

The simple heading of the first annual report of Dr. W. J. Holland, as director of The Carnegie Museum in Pittsburgh, April 1, 1898, was *Historical.* Although titled *Publications of the Carnegie Museum: No. 3*, this was the first annual report. The roster of the board included politicians, industrialists, scientists, educators, clergymen, leading citizens of the time, several of them boyhood chums of Andrew Carnegie, and a number of forebears of today's important supporters of Carnegie Institute.

William J. Holland, Ph.D., D.D., lepidopterist, paleontologist, chancellor of the Western University of Pennsylvania (forerunner of the University of Pittsburgh), had been a member of the Board of Trustees of The Carnegie Fine Arts and Museum Collection Fund before being called upon to assume the directorship of The Carnegie Museum. His predecessor in the post, Harvard-trained Frank H. Gerrodette, had resigned after just three months, as a result of controversy arising because of his energetic pursuit of his scientific duty in the authorized excavation of the Indian Burial Mound at McKees Rocks.

One Pittsburgh newspaper, now defunct, had attacked the disturbance of alleged recent burials of named individuals. The storm of unfavorable publicity made it impossible to continue, even after other Pittsburgh newspapers disproved the charges and exposed the story as having been fabricated in a local bar in McKees Rocks. Although vindicated, Gerrodette resigned, and the museum was run, from September 1896 to March 1898, by a committee of the trustees until the appointment of Dr. Holland.

Truly a Renaissance man, Dr. Holland was pastor of the Bellefield Presbyterian Church,

Throughout the 84 years of his life, Dr. William J. Holland was pastor of Bellefield Presbyterian Church, naturalist for the U.S. Eclipse Expedition to Japan, Chancellor of the University of Pittsburgh, Director of Carnegie Museum of Natural History, and an authority on natural history, world law and entomology. Here Holland holds a page from the revised edition (1931) of his publication, *The Butterfly Book*, a popular guide to the butterflies of North America (1902). In 1903, *The Moth Book*, also by Dr. Holland was published.

Photograph courtesy of Carnegie Library of Pittsburgh

naturalist for the U. S. Eclipse expedition to Japan, and was an authority on natural history, world law, and entomology, especially butterflies. Dr. Holland's authority as a paleontologist was further enhanced in later years by the discovery that his opinions, which differed from other experts over the decades, were correct. He was right as to which head belonged to a certain dinosaur, he was correct as to the proper placement of another dinosaur in time sequence with other discoveries.

Dr. Holland was also far ahead of his time in planning, in 1903, an expedition to Alaska to investigate a possible former bridge of land connecting the continents of North America and Asia. Two Carnegie paleontologists, John B. Hatcher and his brother-in-law, O. A. Peterson, had researched the same theory with regard to the southern hemisphere. They had excavated a ton and a half of fossils in Patagonia, while working for Princeton University. Hatcher's skill at poker helped fund the arduous expeditions which sought to prove that there had been a single southern land mass of Africa, Australia, Antarctica, and South America, called Gondwanda. Before The Carnegie's planned 1904 return expedition to Patagonia and Antarctica could take place, Hatcher died. After surviving the earlier hardships of the Patagonian winters, he died of typhoid fever, contracted from Pittsburgh's untreated drinking water.

It was not until 1912 that Alfred Wegener propounded the theory of continental drift, and the 1960s before the theory of plate tectonics became well established. Work by Carnegie's paleontologist Dr. Mary Dawson and research associate, Dr. R. M. West, in the Arctic starting in 1975, helped to verify the theory.

Policy Established

The declared policy was, "to develop collections representative of the Appalachian region, illustrative of the natural history and resources of the region of which Pittsburgh is the metropolis; of the early history of the region; of its prehistoric inhabitants; of the arts: graphic, textile, fictile design, etc.; and collections representing the materials employed in the various industries of the region and cooperation with the Academy of Science and Art, with volunteer aids and others in frequent courses of popular scientific lectures."

These policies were energetically pursued under the beneficent eyes of Andrew Carnegie. When the appropriation originally made was found inadequate, it was supplemented, after the Founder's Day, November 3, 1896, by an additional grant of $5,000. The total for the year was then $12,000, of which $2,752 was for salaries. A striking comparison may be made with the fact that in 1993 The Carnegie Museum of Natural History received direct financial support of $1,544,096.34 from 450 individual organizations.

The Camel Driver Attacked by Lions was exhibited at
the Paris Exposition in 1867 and won a gold medal for
60-year-old taxidermist Jules Verreaux. The American
Museum of Natural History purchased the exhibit for
several thousand dollars but later decided that it was
too sensational. Their curator contacted Carnegie's
preparator Webster, and for $50 plus shipping costs,
The Camel Driver came to Pittsburgh in 1898. In 1994
it was restored, thanks to a Second Century grant from
the Pittsburgh Chapter of the Safari Club International.
Standing at the entrance to the Hall of African Wildlife
it shows two examples of a subspecies of Barbary lion
now extinct.

Photograph courtesy of Carnegie Museum of Natural History

Preparation of Exhibits

Dr. Holland's report goes on to note the importance of the engagement, as preparator, of
Frederic S. Webster, "one of the ablest and most
widely known artists of his class." During his
tenure, to 1908, this outstanding taxidermist
pioneered in the development of habitat groups,
many of which are today among the most popular in the entire Museum of Natural History. A
photograph of the exhibit of American flamingoes was included in this first report. The report

The Museum of Natural History lent 10,000 spectacular
butterflies to PPG's Wintergarden in a traveling exhibit
developed for the corporate community.

Photograph by Steidl/Blazer

of the following year included the Zuni pottery makers, and, in a glimpse into the preparation department, there was a view of *The Camel Driver Attacked by Lions*, a display which had won the gold prize in the Paris Exposition of 1867. Another perennial favorite, the Indian braves in the *Moki Snake Dance*, appeared in the report of 1901.

That early report also contained a detailed account of the general housecleaning, successfully concluded by means of, "the skillful invention of a machine for using compressed air, designed by the superintendent of the building." Dr. Holland had observed that, "the preservation of such collections in good condition necessarily involves considerable labor in a city in which the importance of the consumption of smoke is not as thoroughly appreciated as we trust it will ultimately come to be." The report also thanked Mr. George Westinghouse, Jr. for the donation of an electric motor which supplied power to the laboratory, "thus greatly facilitating the work of preparation."

Assembling the Collection

"Old Smoky" was Andrew Carnegie's affectionate term for Pittsburgh as he described his indebtedness to this city for his material success. His interest in the museum and, "the picture gallery" was generous and personal. Each year the reports, in the alphabetical lists of accessions, under, "Carnegie, Andrew," included a veritable catalogue of items, beginning, in 1896, with, "two mummies, with cases, from Egypt."

In acknowledged fact, the nucleus of the inaugural collections was obtained by transfer from the Academy of Science and Art of Pittsburgh, through the good offices of Andrew Carnegie. Also appreciated were the 51 reproductions of the bronze statues discovered at Pompeii, a series of sculptural and architectural models, a collection of 12,000 specimens of 3,000 species of moths from British India (transferred from the custody of Dr. Holland),

plus models of fish, frog, snail, leech, etc.

Botanical models of sweet pea, primrose, daisy, potato blossom, grape bloom, wheat blossom, grain of wheat, etc., were obtained, as well as models, "of man complete," including models of heart, brain, eye, and ear sections. Models of gorilla, horse, turkey, ear of bird, ear of fish, serpent, silkworm, etc., with complete synoptic table of each and models of comparative anatomy of the organs of various animals, were also all carefully listed, as received by the museum, and all thanks to Andrew Carnegie.

Comparative Anatomy

The museum purchased a large series of osteological specimens to which was added, by the

"George," a resident of the Pittsburgh Zoo for 12 years, until 1979, is now at home in the Hall of African Wild Life exhibit in The Carnegie Museum of Natural History.

Photograph courtesy of Carnegie Museum of Natural History

generosity of Mr. Carnegie at a cost in the neighborhood of $5,000, a magnificent collection of anatomical models made in Paris. "This collection has already proved itself one of the most interesting features of the museum, and its value for educational purposes can hardly be overestimated."

After the heading *Historical* came *Mammals*, which noted a variety of acquisitions. Purchased from Lieutenant Robert Peary were several Atlantic walruses captured on his latest Arctic expedition. (Peary, as Admiral Peary, reached the North Pole in 1909. He was born in Cresson, Pennsylvania in 1856 and died in 1920.) A "superb specimen of gorilla," collected in the valley of the Ogove in tropical Africa, was obtained through Dr. Holland. A number of additional specimens of mammals in the collection of F. S. Webster were obtained from him for the museum. The museum also received animals which died at the Zoological Garden, now the Pittsburgh Zoo.

Birds

The Western Pennsylvania Sportsmen's Association's collection of game birds was transferred from the Academy of Science and Art to the museum. A collection of over 200 birds was given by a donor in Youngstown, Ohio, and a group of more than 1,000 specimens was purchased from Mr. Webster. He was also credited in the memorable first report with setting up the aforementioned group of flamingoes and the group of California condors and turkey buzzards. "The latter group challenges comparison with anything of like character in the museums of this country, or Europe." This exhibit is still, almost a century later, one of the most popular.

Reptiles and Batrachians (Amphibians)

A collection of the reptiles of Western Pennsylvania was loaned by the Pittsburgh High School Naturalists, indicating that then, as now, young people are tremendously interested in snakes.

Some other specimens were obtained live from Florida, and the famous Mr. Webster succeeded in making a cast representing a rattlesnake in the act of striking. This was made from a living specimen, "which was subjected to the influence of chloroform." Also noted was the gift from the proprietor of the Klondike Museum in Pittsburgh, "of a number of alligators in the flesh which have been prepared for mounting by Mr. Webster."

Fishes and Mollusca

It was hoped in the coming summer to secure specimens of the fishes known to inhabit the waters of Western Pennsylvania. "The collection of mollusks in the possession of the museum is already considerable, and represents nearly one-third of the species which have been named and catalogued by naturalists." An early benefactor of The Museum of Natural History was George H. Clapp, for whom Clapp Hall of the nearby University of Pittsburgh was named. He gave a number of collections of shells, fresh water from Allegheny County, as well as marine shells, more than a thousand specimens as of 1898. In addition, Dr. Clapp was interested in collecting insects, which he added to the collection of the museum. A fund in his name continues to benefit The Carnegie Museum of Natural History.

In 1909 the collection of fresh water mollusks was further expanded by specimens in an ancient riverbed, unearthed in the excavations for Forbes Field, which was for 70 years the scene of Pittsburgh's professional baseball games. The site is now the Forbes Quadrangle of the University of Pittsburgh.

Crustacea and Marine Vertebrates

The collection of crustacea was still small, and that of marine vertebrates, "still in its infancy" despite the purchase of a large collection of corals from the Great Barrier Reef of Australia.

Insects

Beetles and butterflies abound in this section of the report of 1898. Dr. John Hamilton, of Allegheny, a leading coleopterist of this country, gave his entire collection of beetles, one of the largest and most accurately determined, plus all his library on the subject, by will to Dr. Holland for proper disposition. Dr. Holland added his own entomological collection, one of the largest and most perfect of its kind, including the entire collection which formed the basis for the monumental work *The Butterflies of North America* by William H. Edwards. There were in all over 25,000 species represented in the collection by nearly 300,000 specimens from Japan, Switzerland, Africa, as well as from North America and other parts of the world. This was in addition to the large collection of East Indian butterflies and moths purchased by Andrew Carnegie in 1893 and given to the museum.

Paleontology

Collections were comparatively small, but through, "the kindness of the British Museum" Pittsburgh secured a singularly perfect specimen of the Irish Elk. It was the first fossil skeleton mounted at Carnegie Museum and in some respects finer than the one in the national collection in London. Also, "through the kindness of Mr. F. Mansfield, who for a small sum consented to reopen and pump out an abandoned coal mine, which is very rich in fossils, and which had once been resorted to by the Geological Survey of Pennsylvania, we have been able to obtain a very large collection of the fossil plants of that portion of the coal measures represented in the Pittsburgh district."

Botany

The collections of the Western Pennsylvania Botanical Society, the second oldest in the country, was made accessible to the curator of Botany. The large collection of the late Professor Gustave Guttenburg, curator of the Academy of Science and Art was purchased. The curator prepared for publication a list of all the plants known to be or which had been indigenous to Allegheny County.

Minerology and Geology

The geological collection was comparatively small and unimportant. The nucleus of the mineralogical holdings was the entire collection of Professor Guttenburg, purchased at his death, Dr. Holland hoped that, during the summer of 1898, it would be possible to make a nearly perfect collection of flint spear and arrow heads found near the junction of Deer Creek and the Allegheny River.

Ethnology, Ancient and Medieval Art, Modern Arts and Manufacturers, and Historical Collections were subjects next touched upon. When discussing the museum library, Dr. Holland stressed the urgent need for the museum to acquire its own working library of scientific publications, such as a complete set from the United States National Museum. To encourage the interest of young scholars in the museum there were programs such as The Prize Essay Contest and Andrew Carnegie's Naturalists Club which met in the museum's laboratory for practical experiments and instruction. Also there was increased cooperative exchange of collections with schools and colleges in the teaching of anatomy and zoology. By 1900 a circulating collection had been developed to assist teachers in utilizing the resources of the museum as a teaching aid. The attendance from November 1, 1897 to January 15, 1989 was recorded at 2,172 pupils, accompanied by 52 teachers — quite a record, even today.

Each annual report since the beginning may be mined for interesting facts, figures, and fancies. One can see the budgets and collections growing, directions changing. This brief overview can only express amazement at the things which have NOT changed in the ensuing years since the 1890s . . . the popularity of the ancient exhibits such as *The Camel Driver Attacked By Lions* which are now extinct, the Egyptian mummies, the Indian Rain Dancers, the reptiles, vultures, and other habitat groups of animals and birds. The dinosaurs have retained their preeminent popularity over all the years. The Carnegie Museum of Natural History is renowned the world over as their home.

The Carnegie Museum of Natural History The Collections Rated Outstanding Major Center for Scientific Research

The Carnegie Museum of Natural History is one of the great natural history museums, ranking among the six largest in the United States and famous throughout the world as the, "home of the dinosaurs." In that area it is foremost but other areas are also important. The entomology collection includes one of the most important butterfly collections in the world. Pittsburgh's museum has the fifth or sixth largest groupings of birds in the country, fourth or fifth largest groupings of amphibians and reptiles, and one of the ten most extensive collections of mammals. In the ultra specialized realm of the endangered Yanomami Indians of Brazil, the museum's collection of artifacts is regarded as the best in the world.

The museum has established itself as a major center of scientific research. Behind the exhibition and public spaces of the museum, scientists and staff members care for and study the 17 million anthropological, archeological, biological, and geological specimens and artifacts in the collections. The visiting public sees only a small percentage of the work that goes on to identify, analyze, prepare, catalogue, and store these myriad items. Each section's scientists also honor requests for loans of specimens, reprints, and information. Of the millions of specimens only about 10,000 are displayed at any one time.

The museum occupies some 290,000 square feet of space of which, approximately three acres, or 130,680 square feet, is devoted to public exhibit halls and classrooms. The remainder is used for offices, laboratories, collection storage, and construction and design areas. There are 75 full-time and about 75 part-time staff members including exhibits personnel, educators, scientists, scientific preparators, and assistants, the administrative staff augmented by an army of loyal volunteers.

Research, field expeditions, and the assembling and conserving of the major collections are carried out by the museum's three scientific divisions: Earth Sciences, Life Sciences, and Anthropology.

The Division of Earth Sciences includes the sections of Vertebrate and Invertebrate Paleontology, Minerals, Geology, and Paleobotany. Deciphering over four billion years of earth history is their goal. The Division of Life Sciences studies how the biosphere is changing and includes the sections of Amphibians and Reptiles, Botany, Birds, Mammals, and Invertebrate Zoology. The Division of Anthropology includes archeology and ethnography. The Section of Conservation which tends the collection of artifacts is within the Division of Anthropology.

The Division of Exhibit Design and Production creates the visual embodiments of the research of the scientific divisions in dramatic displays for the enjoyment and enlightenment of visitors to the museum. The outreach of the museum to the general public, as well as to the visitors, is the role of the Division of Education. There is also the Natural History Library, the data services, an archival collection, and the collection of Nature Portraits. Each of these sections and the exhibit halls will be considered in more detail.

In a series called *The Elements of Greatness, Carnegie Magazine* between 1979 and 1984 featured histories of all the scientific sections of The Carnegie Museum of Natural History.

Section	Vol.#	Date
Intro	53	June 1979
Botany	53	June 1979
Education	53	September 1979
Vertebrate Fossils	53	October 1979
Animal Portraits	53	November 1979
Data Services	53	December 1979
Minerals	54	April 1980
Mammals	54	June 1980
Invertebrates	54	September 1980
Section of Man	54	November 1980
Vertebrate Preparation	54	December 1980
Amphibians & Reptiles	55	March 1981
Invertebrate Fossils	55	April 1981
Section of Birds	55	Summer 1981
Exhibit Design/ Production	55	November 1981
Entomology	57	Jan./Feb. 1984

The Museum Specialist Program, a form of *Carnegie International*, established in 1963 by the Richard K. Mellon Foundation, provides for Museum Specialists in Residence and for a number of visiting experts from foreign countries such as Argentina, Brazil, Uruguay, Canada, Czechoslovakia, England, France, Netherlands, Rumania, Switzerland, Mexico, and South Africa. From around the world they come to study the collections, the techniques, and the accumulated research data. This scientific exchange has enriched the visitors and the museum alike, resulting in a massive updating of the collections and opportunities for our museum scientists to conduct research in foreign countries.

Bringing the museum into the 21st century as far as research facilities are concerned is the Biosystematics Laboratory for the Life Sciences Division. The Fisher Scientific Corporation of Pittsburgh presented the museum with the latest in laboratory furniture and equipment and the laboratory space was renovated through the generosity of Trustee J. Judson Brooks.

The annual report of The Carnegie Museum of Natural History records in impressive detail the service the Carnegie staffers perform as members of national and international professional organizations in addition to the publication of the results of their research. Mentioned also are their contributions to educational outreach as judges or panelists of competitions, seminars, and similar activities designed to inspire youthful participants.

The 1993 annual report of The Carnegie Museum of Natural History announced that for the sixth year in a row The Museum of Natural History was awarded a $75,000 general operating support grant from the Institute of Museum Services. The museum was one of only 17 Natural History museums in the nation to receive this award, which in 1990 was presented to the director Dr. James E. King by the then First Lady, Barbara Bush, at a White House ceremony.

An annex facility off Baum Boulevard, acquired in 1978, houses the Division of Anthropology and the Section of Mammals. In 1992 it was named the Edward O'Neil Research Center celebrating the museum's benefactor and trustee. The Carnegie Museum of Natural History also maintains Powdermill Nature Reserve, a 2,200-acre biological research center in the Ligonier Valley, 50 miles east of Pittsburgh.

The Second Century Fund

Thanks to the support of the Second Century Fund established in 1988, The Museum of Natural History opened a number of new halls, refurbished various older exhibits, and received endowments for some of the research sections. Specifically, the Hall of African Wildlife, Walton Hall of Ancient Egypt, and the Discovery Room for Children were opened, and the Hillman

Foundation endowed the Hillman Hall of Minerals and Gems. The Alcoa Hall of Native Americans is scheduled to open in 1995. Each is discussed in some detail in later chapters.

The Carnegie Museum of Natural History Library, a Major Resource

Director William J. Holland in the early 1900's stressed the urgent need for the museum to acquire its own working library of scientific publications. The museum library is now the major natural history library resource in Western Pennsylvania as well as serving the research and education needs of the staff. In 1986 the museum library qualified as a major research library under guidelines of the United States Department of Education which, in 1988, funded the retrospective cataloguing and conservation of botanical monographs with a grant of $108,142. More than 2,200 botany titles were recorded on a national library database in 1989, 133 of which had not been recorded previously by any member library. That year also conservation was stressed as more than 600 volumes received technical treatment. In 1993 the library was awarded $124,000 from the same federal program to catalog its foreign monographs and rare books. In this project, over 1,500 titles were added to the database and conservation treatments were performed on over 500 of these volumes.

An important project was the obtaining of oral history interviews with long-time senior members of the museum staff: James Swauger, curator of Anthropology, Mary Dawson, curator of Vertebrate Paleontology, Kenneth Parkes, curator of Birds, and Juan Parodiz, curator of Invertebrate Zoology.

From Borrower to Lender

The Carnegie Museum of Natural History has gone from being a major borrower in the interlibrary loan system to being a major lender. In 1994, more than 450 requests were filled from institutions throughout the country, almost three quarters of which were university and college libraries and 20% involved foreign-language publications. The museum's research library houses 120,000 books and annually receives 2,000 scientific and educational periodicals from over the United States and around the world.

The library is cooperating with about 20 institutions in the United States by sending issues of the museum's Annals and Bulletins to 17 institutions in Latin America as part of a five-year pilot project. Another project initiated in 1988 was the creation of an index to a collection of news clipplings assembled by Director Holland. This will result in a computerized index to oer 50,000 articles between 1892 and 1919.

Data Service Division Serves The Carnegie

The installation of data processing equipment was made possible in 1978 by a grant from the Richard K. Mellon Foundation. Within the year the Section of Mammals alone catalogued data on 54,438 specimens and the total number of records at the end of the year reached 213,143. A record includes the complete history of an object, specimen, or activity. Through the reports of each section in The Carnegie Museum of Natural History, work on the computerization of the accumulated data has been a persistent theme.

With funding by the National Science Foundation in 1992, the museum is participating with seven other large museums and botanical gardens in a study of their computer systems, leading to the sharing of data about their collections.

The Carnegie Museum of Natural History Publications

A most important aspect of the work of the scientists in all sections of The Carnegie Museum of Natural History is the publication of the results of their investigations on field trips and their studies within the enormously varied collection of the museum's own holdings and those of other museums. As more and more international, national, and regional meetings are held and attended, the reports of these meetings add to the material studied and published. The curatorial members of The Carnegie Museum of Natural History frequently serve as officers of the many professional associations in the fields of their particular interests involving the publishing of other reports, papers, and newsletters.

An especially noteworthy publication in 1985 of The Carnegie Museum of Natural History was *Species of Special Concern in Pennsylvania*. It was the first product of the then-recently-enacted Pennsylvania Wild Resource Conservation Act which authorized a check-off on one's state income tax return to support the Commonwealth's Conservation efforts. The 430-page volume identifies the endangered species.

Exchanged with over 600 libraries, museums, and universities around the world, the three publications series of The Carnegie Museum of Natural History include:

Annals of Carnegie Museum — published continuously since 1901 and as a quarterly since 1989. . .

Bulletins of Carnegie Museum of Natural History — a monographic series, begun in 1976 and published irregularly. Bulletin 31, covering the skull and atlas-axis complex of *Camarasaurus*, was published in 1995. (There were also scientific papers published as *Memoirs* between 1901 and 1936.)

Special Publications of Carnegie Museum of Natural History — begun in 1976 with variable content and format, designed for scientists and interested laymen. The *Identification Guide to Pennsylvania Snakes* is perennially popular.

On April 30, 1991 the museum issued the continuously updated *Catalogue of Scientific Publications of The Carnegie Museum of Natural History*. It is chock-full of fascinating and challenging titles, approximately 1,120, covering the period of almost 90 years. Of the hundreds of publications listed, the most expensive at $120 is about birds. One of the special publications in 1988 was the 52-page *Field List of the Birds of Western Pennsylvania and Adjacent Regions* issued by Powdermill's birdbander Robert C. Leberman. In 1994 *Advances in the Biology of Shrews*, edited by Joseph F. Merritt et al., was published. The annual report of each section contains a record of the year's scores of scientific publications. This reference is only an indication of their scope.

In addition, the museum has an active publishing program for the general public. Published in 1982, *Carnegie's Dinosaurs*, by Helen McGinnis, discusses the collections in Dinosaur Hall, many of which are not dinosaurs!

The museum prepares beautiful catalogues for special exhibitions and the opening of each new exhibit hall. The popular Discover Series of activity books for children currently has five titles, with *Discover Life Through the Ages* being the most recent.

Several times each year, colorful magazine-type brochures are issued by the School of the Carnegie describing the many courses available to students, children, and adults. Also, issues of *Carnegie Magazine* contain interesting articles by members of the different sections. The museum also provides a diversity of print pieces written for visitors, both adults and children. Included are games, scavenger hunts, brochures, and teacher resource packages covering museum exhibits, collections, and research.

The Carnegie Museum of Natural History Powdermill Nature Reserve

The Powdermill Nature Reserve as a natural laboratory for long-term scientific studies was conceived by M. Graham Netting, director from 1954 to 1975 of The Carnegie Museum of Natural History. Located between the Chestnut and Laurel ridges of the Allegheny Mountains near Rector, Pennsylvania, the reserve was established in 1956 on land donated by the families of Richard K. Mellon and his sister, Sarah, Mrs. Alan M. Scaife. Their foundations, with other philanthropists, have made important gifts over the years, bringing the area of the reserve to approximately 2,200 acres.

Least Bittern at Powdermill Nature Reserve.
Photograph by Robert Mulvihill

Bird-Banding

Powdermill is the country's busiest and longest continuous inland banding station for non-game birds, and is the third largest bird-banding station in the nation. Modern bird banding traces its roots to an experiment by the great wildlife artist John James Audubon. Born in Haiti in 1785, he spent his boyhood in France. At 18 he came for two years, 1804-1806, to supervise his father's estate, Mill Grove, in Montgomery County, Pennsylvania. There the abundant wildlife inspired the hunter to become the artist. In 1805, discovering a nest of phoebes, he attached "silver threads" to

their legs, to see if the birds would return the next spring, and he observed that they did!

The bird banding project, which attracts hundreds of visitors each year to Powdermill, began in 1956 and since then more than 335,000 birds of some 183 species have been banded with bands supplied by the Fish and Wildlife Service of the U. S. Department of the Interior. In 1990 alone close to 14,000 birds of 120 species were banded. In other years, 1988 for example, as many as 176 different species were banded. The most distant place from which bands have been recovered is in the jungles of Peru, where a tribesman, with a blow gun, killed a thrush which had been tagged at Powdermill. The records compiled provide better understanding of the migration, distribution, and life span of birds.

Environmental Research

The woodlands, fields, thickets, ponds, streams, nature trails, herb and butterfly gardens, make Powdermill a natural laboratory in summer and winter for long-term, interdisciplinary scientific research, combining the efforts of specialists in botany, ornithology, mammology, entomology, and soil sciences. Twelve regional colleges and universities have programmed activities there. The *Guide to the Mammals of Pennsylvania*, by Joseph F. Merritt, Powdermill's director, provides a ready reference to the 63 species of wild animals in the state. After four years of research, it was published for the museum by the University of Pittsburgh Press and was featured in an article by Louise Craft in the November/December 1987 issue of *Carnegie Magazine*. It includes information about the specialized mating habits of porcupines and an anecdote about a dead skunk capable of transmitting rabies even after two years in a freezer!

Research has been pursued since 1985 to determine the long-range effects of logging, acid rain, and the gypsy moth infestations on forest regeneration. It was in 1889 that Medford,

Massachusetts became the first American town to experience an outbreak of the moths. A French entomologist, Etienne Leopold Trouvelot in 1869 had imported live moth eggs, hoping to crossbreed them with a species of American silk worm, to create a hybrid resistant to the disease which had almost totally destroyed the silk industry in Europe. When the moths escaped it was reported by the scientist but little notice was taken of the incident.

The studies at Powdermill are far-ranging. Aquatic organisms, peepers and frogs in local streams, and the biology of the gypsy moth in nearby forests are examined. Radio-telemetry is used to check on the winter survival of the Siberian dwarf hamster, in cooperation with scientists from the former Soviet Union. In May of 1989 NASA, the National Aeronautics and Space Administration, sponsored a workshop at Powdermill on geologic applications of Remote Sensing.

The Florence Lockhart Nimick Nature Center
The Nature Center was established in 1983 by a grant from Thomas H. Nimick Jr. The small museum of plants and animals has become an attraction which in 1992 had 10,035 visitors. Year-round weekend programs range from Pennsylvania's black bear management program to stream ecology workshops to nature printing on clay. In 1993 a 1,350 square foot classroom designed by architect Jules Labarthe was added for $120,000. It is dedicated to M. Graham Netting, trustee John T. Galey and William Rea and his wife Ingrid, a Carnegie trustee. The Rea's five children in 1986 honored their parents' 50th wedding anniversary by a gift for the Rea Natural History Exhibit in which an audio-visual program and habitat dioramas show the flora and fauna of the Laural Highlands.

The May/June 1991 *Carnegie Magazine:* article on Gypsy Moths by Anatole Wilson; January/February 1994 issue: The Nimick Nature Center.

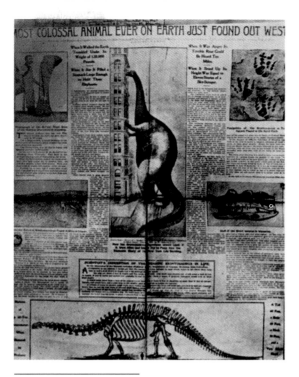

Article in *New York Journal*, November, 1898. Seeing this, Andrew Carnegie sent a note to Director Holland, saying "Dear Chancellor, Buy this for Pittsburgh," thus beginning the Museum's famed fascination with dinosaurs.

Photograph courtesy of Carnegie Museum of Natural History

The Carnegie Museum of Natural History Becomes World Famous

Andrew Carnegie's Dinosaurs
"The wealth of dinosaurs and other fossils collected by the Department of Vertebrate Paleontology can largely be attributed to the driving force of one man — Andrew Carnegie."

— Helen J. McGinnis
Carnegie's Dinosaurs, 1982

"Most Colossal Animal Ever on Earth Discovered Out West" was the headline in an issue of *The New York Journal* in November, 1898. When Andrew Carnegie saw this he sent a note to Dr. Holland: "Dear Chancellor, buy this for Pittsburgh." He later sent a check for $10,000. Thus started the decades of paleontological work of The Carnegie Museum of Natural History.

Dr. Holland traveled to Wyoming to see

William H. Reed, the discoverer of the dinosaur described in *The New York Journal* article. Reed signed a contract with Carnegie Museum and presented Holland with a bone from the upper part of a dinosaur limb. Later, after a tortuous trip of several days from Medicine Bow, Wyoming, by horse-drawn wagon, the paleontologists and crew labored for several more days without discovering a single bone. Reed then confessed that the bone he had given Holland was the only dinosaur bone he had ever found at the site; therefore, *The Journal's* trumpeted discovery of, "The Most Colossal Animal" was based upon a single bone!

Although discouraged, the searchers continued, and two months later, 30 miles from the original site, they made the first discovery, July 4, 1899, of a dinosaur skeleton, practically intact. A. E. Coggelshall, the preparator who had accompanied Curator Jacob Wortman, suggested that the find might aptly be called the, "Star Spangled Dinosaur," but it was officially identified as *Diplodocus*, meaning, "double beamed." ("Dinosaur" means, "terrible lizard" which covers a large and varied group of long-extinct creatures of two distinct types: the reptile-hipped and the bird-hipped.) The new species, *Diplodocus carnegii*, was named in honor of the Museum's benefactor. A few parts of the skeleton had deteriorated, and so a composite

was prepared from other bones which were found, making the a mounted skeleton. Measuring 84-feet-long it could not be mounted until the original museum building was expanded to its present size. Mr. Carnegie's namesake became a star attraction and remains so to this day. Mrs. Carnegie also had a namesake, *Apatosaurus louisae*.

The campaign of excavations continued, by horse, mule, wagon, sledge, pick, and shovel in the sweltering badlands of Wyoming. Important discoveries were also made by Carnegie prospectors in Nebraska and Utah, site of the swampy Jurassic riverbed of 160 million years ago, now Dinosaur National Monument. Of the hundreds of tons of dinosaur fossils shipped to the museum, some have still to be uncrated by the preparators.

The transition from 86 feet of solid rock in Wyoming into the dramatic skeleton in Pittsburgh involved eight years of arduous work. In the interim King Edward VII of Great Britain, while lunching with Andrew Carnegie at his Skibo Castle in Scotland, admired an artist's drawing of the proposed reconstruction. The royal hint that the British Museum might like to obtain such a specimen resulted in Carnegie's donating exact copies of his *Diplodocus* to museums in nine capital cities of the world. From his early 1898 first major

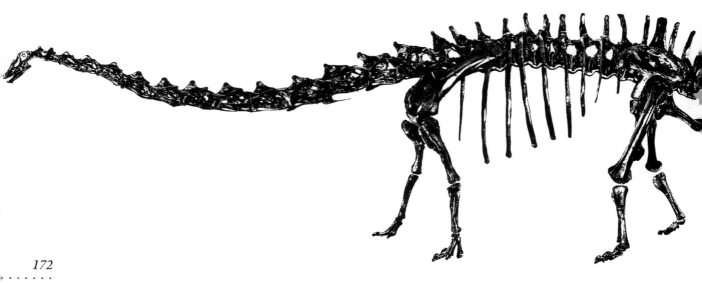

fossil purchase, (a nearly complete skeleton of an American mastodon found in Indiana), until his death in 1919, Andrew Carnegie was personally interested in the museum's program of fossil gathering. For the paleontological expeditions he contributed over $250,000, exclusive of his endowment of the institution. Without the patron, the funds were greatly reduced and the number of expeditions curtailed. An early assistant at the dinosaur quarry, J. Leroy Kay became curator of vertebrate fossils in 1941 and held the post until his retirement in 1957. During those lean years the generosity of Dr. Childs Frick helped keep Kay afield in the Tertiary fossil beds of Montana, Utah, Colorado, Wyoming, Idaho, and British Columbia. Frick was himself a vertebrate paleontologist and former Pittsburgher, son of Henry Clay Frick, Carnegie's early business associate and, later, adversary.

Carnegie's Influence —
Dinosaur National Monument

Two of the most famous fossil quarries in the United States were discovered by the scientists of Carnegie Museum and became national monuments within the National Parks system. In 1909 Earl Douglass discovered the dinosaur fossils in northeastern Utah in a quarry which was named Dinosaur National Monument in 1915. Some time after Douglass' discovery

the land was opened to homesteading. To prevent a speculator from filing claim on the quarry property, Dr. Holland instructed Douglass to file a claim for mineral rights to the land on behalf of the museum. This was disallowed by the government on the premise that dinosaur bones cannot be considered minerals in the usual sense. The ruling was appealed. Dr. Holland traveled to Washington, D.C. to confer with his old friend Dr. Charles D. Walcott, secretary of the Smithsonian Institution and former director of the U.S. Geological Survey. As a paleontologist of international repute, Walcott recognized the timeliness and importance of Holland's concern. He then convinced President Woodrow Wilson of the significance of the matter and, on October 14, 1915, the president signed an order designating 80 acres surrounding the quarry a national monument.

Holland explained the transaction to Douglass: "Under date of January 8th I have received from the Secretary of the Interior a permit allowing the Carnegie Museum to carry on the work of investigation at our quarry, now designated as the Dinosaur National Monument, for the year 1916." Successive applications by the museum to continue the excavations were approved for 13 more years. Douglass' repeated urgings contributed to the eventual construction of a unique museum

The first and longest dinosaur discovered by Carnegie Museum of Natural History, *Diplodocus carnegii*, 84-feet-long, established the Museum as a center for collecting and studying dinosaurs.

Photograpgh by Vincent Abromitis, courtesy of Carnegie Museum of Natural History

where the public may view these gigantic fossils exactly at the site where they perished millions of years ago.

At about the time when Douglass was digging in Utah, O.A. Peterson was opening a series of quarries in western Nebraska where hundreds of skeletons of extinct rhinoceros and many other fossil animals were preserved. In the mid-1960s these quarries were also taken into the National Parks system as Agate Springs National Monument. Thus, the museum's early research interests have enriched the lives of millions through the discovery and preservation of these remarkable fossils.

Controversy Over a Head

As other types of the enormous extinct beasts were exhumed and added to the collection, a dispute arose among the experts as to which head belonged on the body of the *Brontosaurus*, correctly called the *Apatosaurus*. The question lay between the short-snouted skull, favored by distinguished authorities at Yale University, and the longer, *Diplodocus*-like one advocated by Dr. Holland. Yale seemed to win that contest, but during Dr. Holland's lifetime, even for ten years after his retirement, the giant creature remained headless.

After Dr. Holland's death in 1932, the controversial head was installed, where it was until 1979 when the curators decided that Dr. Holland was right after all! So with full news coverage, the *Apatosaurus* received a new head, and skeletons in four other museums in the United States promptly did also.

Dinosaurs continue to be as good copy for the newspapers as they were when discovered. The sensational story of November 1898 carried an artist's sketch with the caption, "How the *Brontosaurus* would look if it were alive and should try to peep into the 11th story of the New York Life Building." Other captions were, "When it walked, the Earth trembled under its weight of 120,000 pounds. When it

Ottmar F. Von Fuehrer, chief staff artist at Carnegie Museum of Natural History, 1922-1965, with the preliminary chalk sketch of his 24' by 36' mural of *Tyrannosaurus rex*, completed in 1950.

Photograph courtesy of Carnegie Library of Pittsburgh

ate, it filled a stomach large enough to hold three elephants." "Footprints of the *Brontosaurus* a yard square found in solid rock." "Photograph of the 8' thigh bone of the monster discovered in Wyoming." The news article specified, "A Tall 60', a Body 40', a Neck 20' and a Very Small Head," and continued, "When it was angry, its terrible roar could be heard 10 miles." How did the writer of the newspaper article almost 100 years ago know that the dinosaur could produce a loud roar? He did not explain, but decades later an article in *Carnegie Magazine* stated, "most had a well-developed cochlea (organ of hearing) implying vocal communication."

The Pittsburgh Press, October 28, 1979, outlined the debate among scientists as to whether dinosaurs were hot-blooded, like birds and mammals (endotherms), or cold-blooded, like snakes (ectotherms). The roster of the different types of dinosaurs is mind boggling, but it is clear that the subject of these enormous creatures and the mystery of their extinction continues to fascinate layman and expert alike.

In the 1995-1997 $3 million redesigning of Dinosaur Hall, *Tyrannosaurus rex* will be displayed having two instead of three claws and no longer standing upright (as shown here) but in the correct crouched position, with head forward and tail lifted in the air.

Photograph by Vincent Abromitis, courtesy of Carnegie Museum of Natural History

From *Carnegie Magazine*, March 1978 by Leonard Krishtalka, associate curator, Section of Vertebrate Fossils, "the great variety of dinosaurs precluded a collective statement about their hot- or cold-bloodedness or any other aspect of their mode of life . . . trackways show they roamed the Mesozoic forests in herds, with the younger animals protected in the center of the group. Most dinosaurs had structures such as horns, crests, sails, plates, domed-heads, and claws that were used against sexual rivals and predators in courtship displays and combat. This diversity in form, physiology, and behavior makes their extinction all the more difficult to explain."

In the September, 1982, *Carnegie Magazine,* Dr. Krishtalka disputed the versions of dinosaur extinction based on alleged global catastrophic effects of an asteroid/comet explosion. He pointed out that according to paleobotanists a gradual long-term cooling, "over a few million years," could have caused the demise of the dinosaurs, other reptiles, and some invertebrates. Krishtalka argued that at this point the fossil record implies the pattern was mosaic, the magnitude large but selective, and the timing gradual ". . . the steady death and birth of species is the rule, not the exception and not catastrophic."

In any case the giant skeletons on display in Dinosaur Hall in The Carnegie Museum of Natural History make believable the paleontologists' assertion that, for approximately 125 million years, dinosaurs were the dominant land dwellers of the earth. Yet none survived past the end of the Mesozoic Age, around 65 million years ago. "Why?" is the question still puzzling the scientists and the public who wonder how the dinosaurs moved, ate, slept, procreated, parented, lived, and died.

Field Expeditions: Carnegie Research

The schedule of field work undertaken by the curators and others on the roster of Carnegie Museum of Natural History evidences the variety of their research and the diversity of the locales: expeditions have ranged from archeological excavations in North Park, Pittsburgh, through the Appalachian region for Ice Age fossils; to New England on the trail of the evolution of the short-tailed shrews, and thence to South Carolina and Florida, still checking on shrews; to Alabama and Mississippi to learn more about fresh water turtles' community ecology; to Missouri, Arkansas, and Oklahoma for clam-like brachiopods; and to seek fossil mammal remains from Eocene deposits in Uruguay and New Mexico of about 50 million years ago; and also to New Mexico seeking fossils of fish, reptiles, and amphibians from Early Permian Age, about 280 million years ago.

Other expeditions have gone to the Pacific Northwest to collect mammals for studies of comparative structure, to Quebec to excavate bone-bearing deposits in a cave on the Gaspé Peninsula to gain information about environmental changes in the wake of the receding Ice Age glaciers; to Ellesmere Island in Arctic Canada for the collection of Eocene fossils.

The importance of the Eocene fossils is that they may provide proof of the Tectonic Plate Theory that the continents of Europe and North America were once linked by a bridge of land. Animals migrating across this strip of land and dying there would leave bones, now fossilized, to attest their long ago journeys. Even without evidence of migration, clues indicating similarities between flora and fauna on each side of the theorized, "bridge" would prove its former existence.

Fossil seeking expeditions to Ethiopia have led to the discovery of the skull of a human-like creature, hominoid, which may predate earlier findings and push back the probable date of man's appearance on the earth.

Specialized studies of birds have led Carnegie Museum of Natural History scientists to various islands of Mexico, Baja California. The mammalian fauna of Colombia have been studied, as have the small mammals of Surinam, to obtain data on environmental changes from human disturbance of tropical forests. In South Africa mammal studies have given information of the evolutionary radiation of bats . . . on the Island of Samos, Greece, remains of late Tertiary fossil mammals have been the subject of study and so on and on.

. . . .

Geologic Time Scale

Era	Period	Length in Millions of Years	Beginning Millions of Years Ago
Cenozoic	**Quaternary**		
	Holocene	.01	.01
	Pleistocene	1.59	1.60
	Tertiary		
	Pliocene	3.40	5.00
	Miocene	19.00	24.00
	Oligocene	13.00	37.00
	Eocene	21.00	58.00
	Paleocene	8.00	66.00
Mesozoic	**Cretaceous**	78.00	144.00
	Jurassic	64.00	208.00
	Triassic	37.00	245.00
Paleozoic	**Permian**	41.00	286.00
	Carboniferous		
	Pennsylvanian	34.00	320.00
	Mississippian	40.00	360.00
	Devonian	48.00	408.00
	Silurian	30.00	438.00
	Ordovician	67.00	505.00
	Cambrian	65.00	570.00
Precambrian		3,930.00	4,500.00

These scientific journeys and other activities have been sponsored by the Alcoa Foundation, the National Geographic Society, the National Science Foundation, the O'Neil Field Fund, the W. L. and M. T. Mellon Fund, the Rea Natural History Endowment Fund, and the M. Graham Netting Research Fund, endowed by the Cordelia S. May Charitable Foundation.

Cenozoic Hall

The most recent 65 million years of the history of life on earth is known as the Cenozoic Era or, more popularly, the Age of Mammals. Mammals had evolved much earlier, during the early part of the Mesozoic Era, but became extremely numerous and diverse during the Cenozoic. With the disappearance of the dinosaurs, mammals dominated life on land.

Displayed in Cenozoic Hall are fossil representatives of some Cenozoic plants, fishes, and mammals. The exhibits are arranged in a semicircle chronologically according to shorter time intervals of the Cenozoic Era called epochs. Actual skeletons accompanied by reconstructions of how each fossil mammal appeared in life illustrate the various life forms that flourished during five consecutive epochs, up until two million years ago. Other exhibits demonstrate anatomical changes in the evolution of two families that were originally North American natives: the camel and the horse.

The last two million years of earth history are the Pleistocene Epoch, known popularly as the Ice Age. At least four times during this epoch, ice sheets advanced and retreated over much of the northern hemisphere. The fluctuating climatic conditions strongly affected plant and animal evolution and distribution. Extreme anatomical modifications are shown by the gigantic antlers of the Irish Elk and the large size of the moa, a flightless bird from the Pleistocene of New Zealand.

Paleozoic Hall

Some 575 million year ago the earth's surface was dramatically different than it is today. Water covered much of its surface and land masses were slowly shifting. Throughout the following 325 million years, known to us as the Paleozoic Era, the surface of the earth underwent many changes, and plant and animal life became both diverse and profuse. Most notably, during the Paleozoic Era, the first amphibians emerged from the sea and, somewhat later, reptiles began to populate the land.

Geologist have divided the Paleozoic Era into seven shorter intervals called periods. These periods vary in the amount of time encompassed. Each was typified by particular forms of plant and animal life.

Paleozoic Hall illustrates, with dioramas, some of this diversity. Reconstructions of communities of primarily marine life from the Paleozoic's seven time periods line the hall, portraying some of the plants and animals that lived during each period. In cases below each diorama are actual plant and animal fossils on which the reconstructions are based.

The Carnegie Museum of Natural History Natural History Exhibition Gallery and The Changing Exhibits Gallery

The Visitor Center was installed in 1976 to showcase the work of the curators in each of the many scientific sections within The Carnegie Museum of Natural History. In 1991 it made way for the creation of a 3,000 square foot Natural History Exhibition Gallery for changing displays of photographs, paintings, and artifacts of special interest. Designed by Charles B. Froom, the sparkling white area is equipped with special climate control and security. (Benefactors were the Allen and Selma Berkman Charitable Trust, Mellon Bank, and Robert S. Waters.)

Sparked by the 100th anniversary of the American Kennel Club the, "dog days" of 1984 featured intense activity at the museum. The exhibit: *The Natural History of the Dog*, spanned from fossils of wild canines and archeological evidence of the dog in other cultures to live demonstrations of numerous breeds and the effect of domestication on the size, shape, and character of the animal.

In conjunction with the exhibition *Carnegie Magazine* July/August issue contained a veritable mini encyclopedia about dogs. The curator of Vertebrate Paleontology, Dr. Mary R. Dawson, wrote *Dogs and Man: A Long Partnership* and Leonard Krishtalka, associate curator, authored *A Breed Apart.* Of the estimated 400 breeds of dogs worldwide, the American Kennel Club recognizes 125. (Dr. Dawson raises and shows Bernese Mountain Dogs from Switzerland). The artist's conception of the dog's ancestor, *Miacis* of 42 million years ago, looks remarkably like a long-tailed, extra-hairy rat!

Among the first exhibitions in the new gallery were *Spirits of the Rain Forest, Pretty Deadly: Poisonous Plants of Forest, Field & Garden,* and *Portraits of Nature: Paintings of Robert Bateman. The Spirits of the Rain Forest* highlighted the life of the Yanomami Indians of Brazil. Their leader, Davi Kopenawa Yanomami, spokesperson for the 9,000 of his people spoke movingly about their plight. A news article in the August 20, 1993 *Pittsburgh Post-Gazette* reported the slaying of 15 of the Yanomami by hostile gold miners seeking to drive them out of the forest. Ten of those killed were children. Scores more of another Yanomami village, according to a news article the following day, also perished.

Other exhibitions, in 1992, included, *Making Waves: The History of Broadcasting in Pittsburgh, Islands of the Blest: Peoples of Egypt's Oases,* and *The Art of American Livestock Breeding.* The latter exhibit featured portraits of European and American farm animals from

Early ancestor of the dog, *Miacis gracilis*.

Illustration by Jim Senior, courtesy of Carnegie Museum of Natural History

more than a 100 years ago that are no longer being raised. Many of the these breeds are in danger of becoming extinct and some have already done so. The danger of extinction is not confined to animals in remote places like the rain forest; it is an issue on American farms at this very time. As part of this exhibit, more than 25 breeds of rare farm animals were brought to the museum for a, "Rare Breeds Alive" day. This presentation attracted some 1,500 visitors.

Plans for Centennial Exhibition

The Carnegie Museum of Natural History plans for the Centennial an exhibition of a kaleidoscopic selection of things strange, odd, historic, or beautiful. From the archives will come objects old but new to the public. They range from the curious: the two-headed calf (stuffed) to the intriguing: the Chinese oracle bones, "the oldest writing in the world," (6,000 years) used in fortunetelling. General George Washington's travel desk, gift of the Rae family in the 1920s,

is here as is the sterling silver and gold scale-model of a Pullman sleeping car, specially made as a gift to Andrew Carnegie from George Pullman. (An investment in a newly created sleeping car company was an early foundation of Carnegie's fortune.)

There are brass cannon captured at the battle of Fort Ticonderoga, May 10, 1775, and a belt buckle which belonged to "Mad" Anthony Wayne. There is beauty in the carved jade from Costa Rica, Central America, and charm in the solid gold animal figures also from Costa Rica. From The Carnegie's own Netting Collection of Nature Portraits there are beautiful paintings from various eras of the celebrated century.

The Carnegie Museum of Natural History Council, chaired by Carole Kamin and assisted by more than 150 volunteers, plans for a 1996 *Centennial Safari,* celebrating 100 years of scientific research to be highlighted by vignettes suggesting field research camps of past decades.

Changing Exhibits Gallery

The Changing Exhibits Gallery offers, for instance, the winning photographs of the (1993) *16th Annual Natural World Photographic Competition and Exhibition*. Another popular exhibition featured the rings and trophies of the football heroes, Pittsburgh Steelers and San Francisco 49ers, the only two professional teams to have won four Super Bowl Championships.

The all-time champions of The Carnegie Museum of Natural History are the dinosaur fossils. The Changing Exhibits Gallery in spring of 1986 displayed photographs of the excavation work of the museum's vertebrate paleontologists at their digs in the west under the title *Revealing the Past: 50-Million-Year-Old Life in Wyoming*. In the summer of 1993 the gallery featured *Dinosaur Families: The Story of Egg Mountain*. The lives of these prehistoric creatures were interpreted through life-like robotic dinosaurs, reconstructed fossil skeletons, egg clutches, and models of mother dinosaurs guarding their nests.

A grant from The Hillman Foundation, Inc. created an endowment for the development of exhibitions for the long-established Changing Exhibits Gallery.

The Carnegie Museum of Natural History Nature Portraits: The M. Graham Netting Collection

In the 1960s some plant and animal illustrations done by staff artists, along with a few purchased or donated items, accumulated in The Museum of Natural History. Director Netting was interested in nature portraits and encouraged the budding collection. The works sometimes appeared in publications and exhibitions but they were uncataloged, unmatted, stored in various niches, and in need of conservation.

A grant from the Allegheny Foundation in 1972 enabled the museum to begin organizing the collection to which were added five watercolors by Ned Smith, whose paintings were featured on covers of *Pennsylvania Game News*. The next year a grant from the Scaife Family Charitable Trusts funded further development of the collection and stipulated that it be named the M. Graham Netting Animal Portraiture Collection.

Now numbering more than 4,000 portraits, the collection includes paintings, pastels, drawings, etchings, engravings, sculpture, prints, photographs, even a sizable number of cave pictures. Represented are such well known natural history artists as Jay Matternes, Carl Rungius, and John Sutton in addition to Ned Smith. Also added were two prints by Thomas J. Hirata: *A Christmas Carol* which depicts a cardinal and *Fishing the Summer Marsh*, a bittern, which the artist painted from specimens borrowed from the museum. Several works in the collection were acquired through similar exchange agreements.

All 200 Andrey Avinoff watercolors that appear in *Wildflowers of Western Pennsylvania & The Upper Ohio Valley Basin* are in the collection, as is a group of unpublished Avinoff watercolors. A scientist as well as an accomplished artist, Avinoff served as the fourth director of The Carnegie Museum of Natural History, from 1926 to 1945. His wildflower paintings were all done during the spring, summer and fall of 1941 and 1942.

The Showy Lady 's Slipper is a rare orchid that at the time could only be found in swampy areas of Crawford County, near the Ohio border. These particular blossoms were on the property of a farmer who was protecting the valuable plants. Contacted by Otto E. Jennings, the museum's botanist, he donated a plant which Jennings took directly to Avinoff, "never mind that it was already late at night." Foregoing sleep to capture the freshness of the flowers, the artist

Showy Lady's Slipper by Andrey Avinoff is one of 200 Avinoff watercolors that appear in the book *Wildflowers of Western Pennsylvania & the Upper Ohio Valley Basin.*

A detail of this watercolor is on the cover of *Carnegie Magazine*, March/April 1995. The cover story "Andrey Avinoff Remembered" is by his nephew, Nicholas Shoumatoff, for more than four decades a research associate of The Carnegie Museum of Natural History.

Photograph courtesy of Carnegie Magazine

stayed up all night to complete his painting.

Some of the finest pieces were shown in the museum's Changing Exhibits Gallery in the summer of 1991, for the first time an exhibition of all original works from the Netting Collection. Dr. Netting, as curator, continues his interest in the collection which is housed in the Museum Annex under the supervision of Greta Holst Evans, artist and collector of orchids.

The Carnegie Museum of Natural History Division of Education

The Division of Education, as currently organized, was formed in 1975. It creates a learning experience for visitors of all ages to the museum and to the subject of natural history. The guided tours led by specially trained docents are enjoyed by many thousands (48,038 in 1994) of school children, adults, and families each year. The exhibits themselves, plus the multitudes of specially designed publications, brochures, games, etc., create indelible impressions on the viewer. The division also offers the Natural Science Academy, the In-School Program, the Educational Loan Collection, Museum on the Move, adult programs, popular publications, and new programs: Teen Docents and a school assembly program called Science on Stage. The division also sponsors an annual intern to work with the various programs.

Guided Tours, Educational Programs for Children

The guided tours program has been one of the museum's educational mainstays for many years. During the 1993-94 school year of the 48,038 individuals, 32,655 were students, visiting the musuem's natural history and anthropological halls with museum docents. The Children's Program became the Natural Science Academy in 1983. The NSA offers formal instruction to children ages 2 $^1/_2$ through 14. There are also adult-child classes and family workshops.

In-School Program and In-Service Courses

The In-School Program was the division's first effort in recruiting and training volunteers. With the continued support from the Roy A. Hunt Foundation, it enlists a corps of volunteers to take interpretive presentations to kindergarteners through sixth graders in regional schools.

In 1991 the In-School Program reached 11,534 students through 480 programs in elementary classrooms in 124 different schools. Carnegie staff also worked with the Pittsburgh Board of Education to develop an expanded school-museum program, funded by the Richard King Mellon Foundation. Within the museum the Educational Resource Room was completed in 1991 with support from Trustee Paul G. Benedum, Jr., to provide a space for audio-visual and hands-on student orientation. In addition to student orientations, the Division of Education conducted a number of accredited in-service courses for teachers which in turn extend the outreach of The Carnegie Museum of Natural History. The subjects covered include dinosaurs, geology, insects, and wildlife habitats.

The development and opening of each new hall engages the Division of Education in preparing especially applicable programs and publications. A grant from the Pennsylvania Historical and Museum Commission supported the Benedum Hall of Geology in 1988. The educational focus of the Hall of Ancient Egypt in 1990 was made possible by a grant from the National Endowment for the Humanities.

The exhibition *Dinosaurs Alive* in 1988 branched out into *Dinosaur Den*, a hands-on activity room for families, initiating an entirely new direction in programming. By the end of the 14-week exhibit, over 50,000 visitors had entered the den. This success led to the creation of the Discovery Room with only six months of planning. *Dinosaurs Alive*, enlarged and updated, made a highly successful repeat appearance at The Carnegie Museum of Natural History in the summer of 1993.

There are also special theme parties that teach, like the Polar World, Dinosaur, and Safari Birthday Parties for youngsters. Special events occupy the division as well: the Natural History Egg Hunt; Dinosaurs and Dragons; the Pet Week Poster Contest; Member's Night at the Museum and the ever-popular *Annual Natural World Photographic Competition and Exhibition*.

Learning Museum Program

The Learning Museum Program, 1979-1982, served as the foundation for adult programs, which continue today. A grant of $327,748 from the National Endowment for the Humanities established The Carnegie Museum of Natural History as a center for formal education in the humanities and natural sciences for the general public, with the Learning Museum Program. The resultant three-year series *Becoming Human: The Bio-cultural Journey* covered man's interaction with the natural and man-made environment from the, "Primordial seas" to the present and beyond. In 1981 two highly successful lecture series *By the Year 2000* and *The Twenty-First Century: Our Human Future* brought major speakers, including *Omni* magazine editor Ben Bova, popular science and science fiction writer Isaac Asimov, and astro-nomer Carl Sagan. Over 500 adults participated in evening courses taught by museum and university scientists.

Educational Loan Collection

The Educational Loan Collection since 1898 has provided regional educators with natural history specimens reaching many thousands of children and adults. Important additions to the Loan Collection in 1989 were more than 50 birds and mammals salvaged by the Pennsylvania Game Commission Wildlife Conservation officers, plus the 15 mounted Pennsylvania mammals donated by the West Overton Museum of Scottdale, Pennsylvania (the birthplace of Henry Clay Frick). The collection has grown to 694 portable cases on natural history and archeological study specimens under glass and 8,000 individual specimens: mounts of reptiles, amphibians, birds, mammals, and fish preserved in life-like poses. There is a nesting pair of sunfish and a group called, "Undertakers of the Forest" (decomposition of a red squirrel). Available are 29 different cases of bird groups. Insects and invertebrates may also be borrowed for study. A major reorganization and rehabilitation of the collection was accomplished with generous support from the J. M. Hopwood Charitable Trust. The record year so far was 1994 when 15,041 loans were provided, reaching an estimated audience of over 133,000 individuals.

Museum on the Move

In cooperation with the Child Life staff of Children's Hospital of Pittsburgh, and with funding from Geyer Printing Company, in 1982 a pilot project was developed to take programs to the young patients at Children's Hospital. Designed to engage the children's interest and participation, the program uses, "Museum on the Move" carts which take the materials to the patients' bedsides. Dinosaurs were the subject of the pilot project, and when the volunteers from The Carnegie Museum of Natural History completed their session, each child had a red dinosaur tote bag (donated by Kaufmann's) filled with a stuffed fabric dinosaur, a balloon dinosaur, a clay dinosaur in an egg, a cast of a dinosaur fossil, a dinosaur activity book, and a dinosaur hunting license!

A similar program for older children concerned Native Americans and had the addition of native music, plus instruments available for the children to play. In 1988 Museum on the Move collaborated with the Western Pennsylvania School for Blind Children and Frick Park Nature Center in combined classroom bird study with outdoor bird walks in Frick Park.

When the Museum on the Move program began, two institutions serving 793 children were visited regularly. In the twelfth year of serving audiences with special needs, 50 trained volunteers visited 33 different agencies with 533 programs reaching 6,101 children — and five of the volunteers had been involved since the program started. This nationally recognized outreach program continues to be funded by the Friends of Geyer Printing Company, Inc.

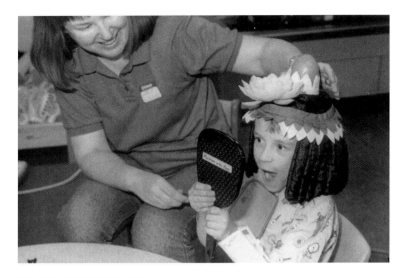

Museum on the Move at Children's Hospital, Pittsburgh.

Photograph by Melinda McNaugher, Carnegie Museum of Natural History

and and by the end of 1993 had reached more than 52,000 children without their having even come to the museum! The dedicated volunteers have given almost 40,000 hours of their time to bring this traveling treat to the children in 40 Pittsburgh area schools, hospitals, and institutions.

The Leonard S. Mudge Environmental Education Program

This outreach program, established in 1976, developed cooperative projects with environmental organizations such as the Western Pennsylvania Conservancy, resulting in a popular series of nature field trips, Out-of-Doors Days, and the annual *Natural World Photographic Competition & Exhibition*. In addition, the Mudge Program co-sponsored the conference *Species of Special Concern*, bringing together professional scientists and interested members of the public in a series of discussions concerning the status of various endangered species of fauna and flora in Pennsylvania. Many educational activities at Powdermill Nature Reserve

were also assisted by the Martha Edwards Lazear Fund as well as by the Mudge Program.

Benefactors

The support of the Buhl Foundation was important in the formative years of the Division of Education, 1977-84. The Scaife Family Foundation and the Claude Worthington Benedum Foundation under the Benedum Endowment for Education support the production of information sheets and booklets on vairous aspects of the collections and exhibits, distributed free to the general museum visitor, as well as full-length books for the general public. The Scaife Family Foundation also made possible the Discovery Room The Benedum Foundation also supports the Eductional Loan Collection. Other support for the division comes from the Consolidated Natural Gas Company Foundation, the Friends of Geyer Printing Co., Inc., and The Hunt Foundations of Pittsburgh.

Carnegie Magazine, September 1979, Volume 53, Number 7, Pages 24-29.

The Carnegie Museum of Natural History Division of Exhibit and Design Production

The work of the division is the creation of magic! Instead of pulling the proverbial, "rabbit out of the hat" the artists, designers, preparators, taxidermists, carpenters, and other craftsmen make magic by creating wondrous places such as the sparkling Hall of Minerals and Gems (1980). They take the visitor across the frozen tundra into the white Arctic of Polar World (1983) or into the dessert to the hidden world of the tombs of the pharaohs of ancient Egypt (1990). Their artistry makes us almost smell the animals living in the many different habitats in the Hall of African Wildlife (1993)! In brief they make us feel we are there! Each of these great halls is described in detail in other chapters. Closer to home the division was also involved with the award-winning exhibit *Pieces of the Past* featuring archeological relics unearthed during excavation for the PPG building (formerly Pittsburgh Plate Glass Company), discussed further in the Division of Anthropology.

From the presentation of the original idea to the completed work, whether it be an entire new hall or part of a display incorporating refurbished exhibits from earlier eras, many intricate steps are involved. An important but unseen function of the division is cost analysis of a project and helping with grant proposals. The drawing and building of detailed scale models requires close cooperation with the curators in the other relevant sections such as botany, zoology, mammals, etc. It may take years to bring the concept to reality. Other creative accomplishments of the division are described in the information on Natural History and Changing Exhibits Galleries.

For The Carnegie Centennial Celebration in 1995-1996 the division is preparing a walk-in tropical rain forest and the Alcoa Hall of Native Americans. Meanwhile, there are the many changing exhibits prepared throughout the year

Moon Rise, Zabriskie Point, Death Valley, CA, by Kerik Kouklis from the *Natural World Photographic Competition & Exhibition.*

which also engage the creative talents of the Exhibit and Design Division of The Carnegie Museum of Natural History.

Carnegie Magazine, November 1981, Volume 55, Number 9, Pages 16-25.

The Carnegie Museum of Natural History
Division of Earth Sciences
Section of Vertebrate Paleontology

The Division of Earth Sciences includes the Section of Vertebrate Paleontology which deals with the fossilized remains of a multitude of creatures with backbones or vertebrae, from the smallest rodents to the largest crocodile and the tallest dinosaur, as well as flying reptiles as small as robins or larger than eagles. Paleontology is the science that deals with these questions concerning the life of past geological periods. Paleontology is at the center of natural history and at the focus of evolutionary theory in the biological scene. A paleontologist looks at the central theme of how plants, animals, insects, and their current associations came into being, and how they changed over millions of years.

A computerized database contains all of the collection's locality information based on the museum's collecting of fossil vertebrates for more than 90 years. New dimensions were added to the research projects by the acquisition of Bioquant, a computerized imaging process, via a grant from the National Science Foundation. In addition to the famous dinosaurs The Carnegie Museum of Natural History has an outstanding collection of later Paleozoic fishes, including a major donation of some 500 specimens of Permian fishes from Texas.

Many of the section's curators hold adjunct appointments in the Department of Geology, University of Pittsburgh, advising graduate students and presenting courses on Vertebrate Paleontology. The staff is also active in numerous national and international professional organizations. Dr. Mary R. Dawson, chief curator of Earth Sciences and Vertebrate Paleontology, received recognition and an award by the National Geographic Society for her years of paleontological work in the Canadian Arctic, on Ellesmere Island only 500 miles from the North Pole. She was further honored in 1988 when named a Distinguished Daughter of Pennsylvania.

Expeditions to the Canadian Arctic, Ethiopia, China

The expeditions of Dr. Dawson and Dr. Robert West, formerly of the Milwaukee Public Museum, and director of The Carnegie Museum of Natural History (1983-1986), began in 1973. They produced fossil evidence of the theory that North America and Europe were once joined by a land, "bridge," across which animals traveled from one continent to the other. (The theory had been proposed by the museum's director, Dr. Holland, in the early 1900s). The $4,000 award shared by Drs. Dawson and West was established as a memorial to Arnold Guyot, a distinguished paleontologist, geologist, explorer, and author who taught at Princeton University.

The activities of the associate curators in 1981 ranged from work at Ghost Ranch in New Mexico to the expeditions to the Arctic, and in addition Curator Krishtalka was searching for fragments of bones in the barren hills of Ethiopia. He came upon a momentous find — pieces of a hominoid skull of an animal-like man predating, "Lucy," another hominoid which had been discovered some years before by the famous Louis and Mary Leakey. The results of their researches helped date the earliest man known on Earth up to that time. The Leakeys' son, Richard, continues their work and came to Carnegie Institute to lecture in the *Man and Ideas* series in 1977.

The international stature of the section and the museum, as well as the collections, was further enhanced in 1981 when new acquisitions included fossils and casts from the People's Republic of China. This resulted from a U. S. State Department sponsored expedition to China by a delegation of seven American museum officials, led by Dr. Craig C. Black, then director of The Carnegie Museum of Natural History

Dr. Mary Dawson's name on a Chinese letter stamp.
It was presented to her on her scientific expedition to
China in 1983.

and president of the American Association of
Museums. (In 1907, as a fledgling organization,
the American Association of Museums held
its second annual meeting at The Carnegie
Museum in Pittsburgh.)

The reciprocal benefits of the museum's
international exchange program were under-
scored in 1983 when Dr. Mary Dawson was
received in The Peoples Republic of China as a
distinguished foreign visitor. She was met and
accompanied on her scientific expedition in
search of the evolutionarily important fossils
of small mammals by fellow paleontologists
Li Chuan-kuel and Ting Su-yin, both of whom
had conducted research in The Museum of
Natural History. As the first foreigner, except
for Japanese troops, to visit the region of Shanxi
province since 1942, Dr. Dawson was the subject of great interest. It was her being under the
auspices of the distinguished Chinese scientists
that provided the three-Jeep convoy, photographer, and special cook and maids, as well as access to a variety of, "fossiliferous" remote areas.
As a result of this field research Dr. Dawson
was caused to rethink previous concepts of the
history of vertebrates. The trip, subject of a
delightful article by Dr. Dawson in *Carnegie
Magazine*, January/February issue, was made
possible by the Edward O'Neill Fund of the
Section of Vertebrate Fossils and with the permission of the Academia Sinica.

Expeditions in North America, Wyoming

Carnegie Institute president Robert Wilburn,
in a timely letter to members, proudly reported
that, "The discovery in 1985 of the best preserved site of 50-million-year-old fossils by two
of our paleontologists, Dr. Leonard Krishtalka
and Dr. Richard Stucky, in the badlands of
Wyoming's Wind River Basin has attracted
national and international attention, and much
coverage in the world media. While researchers
have been working in the area for more than
40 years, this discovery is one of the most important ever made and rivals the significance of
work done by Carnegie's own dinosaur hunters
in the early years of this century."

The specimens recovered from the site
date to the Eocene Epoch (58 to 37 million years
ago), a transitional phase between the earlier age
of primitive mammals and animal life as we now
know it. During the Eocene Epoch most of the
world was a subtropical forest with a rich wildlife and many streams and marshes in which the
creatures became buried and preserved. At that
time the Gulf of Mexico covered most of the
south east coast of the United States, extending
as far north as Cairo, Illinois. The Eocene was
also an era of change. There was much less varia-
tion in climate, but the earth was becoming
dryer. Seasons, if any, were wet and dry instead
of hot and cold, and in North America a much
more temperate climate was prevailing. The first
ancestors of modern man would not appear for
about 46 million more years.

During this period most ancient groups
of mammals became extinct, while many modern
mammal families appeared. Fossils provide scientists with their first actual look at what many of
these species were like during this critical time
in the evolution of life on earth. Continuing
exploration of the fossils in the Wind River area
turned up the small skull of the, "dawn horse,"
which was three-toed and about the size of a
collie dog. The series of prehistoric animals
which were the ancestors of the modern horse

is on display in The Museum of Natural History.

Among the discoveries of Krishtalka and Stucky was the tiny skull of a tarsier relative, a small monkey-like animal, a prize that scientists have been seeking for 150 years. This fossil and those of other small species like bats, lizards, snakes, and rodents lived about 15 million years after the last dinosaur had died.

Tiny fossilized bones give paleontologists valuable clues about the environment in which the small creatures lived, their diets, habits, relationships with one another, and why they may have become extinct. Many times the bones have been preserved because of the activities of owls and pack rats which hide their catches in caves, thus providing natural protection from the elements and from destructive land traffic of various kinds. Piles of semi-digested and other fossil-bearing debris accumulate in uninhabited caves and may suddenly drop thirty-some feet into a "sinkhole" which then becomes a death trap for larger animals, leaving more information for paleontologists.

Explorations in the Pittsburgh Area

As early as 1910, the museum's collections included plant fossils, reptile, and amphibian bones from Pittsburgh rocks dating from the Carboniferous Age, some 300 million years old, as well as bones of tapirs, ground sloths, and forest musk-oxen, Ice Age bones only a few tens of thousands of years in age, from a cave near Altoona, Pennsylvania. Some of these fossils were of extinct mammals, new to science, but before radioactive dating techniques became available scientists had no way of accurately dating such sites. From the 1950s the section has maintained an active program of both exploration and research on the bone deposits in the hundreds of caves in the Appalachian Mountains, from Quebec's Gaspé Peninsula south through Pennsylvania to Tennessee.

The Section of Vertebrate Paleontology has had help from many sources during the long years of research in our Appalachian backyard. An early interest in the project by Mrs. Adolph W. Schmidt resulted in an initial grant from the A. W. Mellon Educational and Charitable Trust. Additional backing was furnished by the National Science Foundation, the Netting Research Fund and the National Geographic Society.

The linkage between fossils and rocks resulted in the staff of the section being occupied during 1987 and 1988 with preparations for the opening of the Benedum Hall of Geology. Other activities included the popular temporary exhibit of robotic dinosaurs, *Dinosaurs Alive!* which, expanded and updated, returned to entrance a new group of visitors in 1993. Associated with the original exhibit, five public lectures on dinosaurs were presented by nationally recognized paleontologists. Dinosaur Hall was used by the British Broadcasting Corporation, for part of a television series in preparation for which the dinosaurs received their bi-annual cleaning. The American mastodon skeleton purchased by Andrew Carnegie in 1898 was remounted with preparatorial and curatorial assistance.

Acquisitions

In 1985 Princeton University discontinued its paleontological department and transferred its fossil collection to Yale. The Scott-Sinclair-Jepsen Library from the Department of Geology of Princeton University was a major acquisition in the late '80's. This historically important collection of over 15,000 separate reprints covering all aspects of vertebrate paleontology was donated to the museum through the efforts of Research Associate Donald Baird of Princeton and alumnus Carnegie Trustee John T. Galey.

One of the most unusual additions to the section's holdings was 200 tons of cannel coal from northeastern Ohio, purchased with help from the National Geographic Society. This coal contains a remarkable record of Pennsylvanian age vertebrates, including bony fishes, sharks, and amphibians.

Among the outstanding specimens collected that year were the oldest known Eocene fossils showing sexual dimorphism in the mammalian order Primates. The canine tooth of the female is short and conical; the male canine is long and stabbing. The degree of difference implies that males competed aggressively for females during breeding season. Successful males probably kept harems.

Dogs

The word, "canine," referring above to teeth, is used also with regard to dogs. Articles in *Carnegie Magazine*, July/August 1984 by curators Dawson and Krishtalka, traced the North American ancestry of *Canis familiaris* back 38 million years.

The oldest undisputed fossil dog came from a 14,000 year-old cave in Iraq. Since dogs evolved from wolves 14,000 years ago they have served as helpful hunter, herder, draft animal, guardian, police partner, detector of narcotics and explosives, Seeing Eye or Hearing Ear, therapist, and, of course companion, which includes being a blanket for some Aborigines in regions of Australia. In North America fossil dogs from 11,000 years ago were found in Jaquar Cave in Idaho, which humans also inhabited.

Dinosaurs, Models, Postage Stamps, Films and Relics

Dinosaurs continue to star as attractions for visitors. The Carnegie's scale models of the museum's dinosaurs have proven to be popular in museum shops around the world. An exhibition of dinosaurs developed by the Section of Vertebrate Paleontology opened in Tokyo, Japan in July, 1992 and was seen by more than 311,000 visitors during its first three weeks. The exhibit traveled to seven other cities in

Skull of *Triceratops brevicornus*, a horned dinosaur of the Cretaceous. Three horns grew from the snout and above each eye. In life, the bony neck frill may have been fringed with spines. Such armament helped ward off *Tyrannosaurus rex* and other predators.

Photograph courtesy of Carnegie Museum of Natural History

Japan before closing in September 1993. What a finale!

Paleontologists, philatelists, and politicians took the U. S. Postal Service to task in 1989 for misnaming a postage stamp honoring Dinosaurs. The scientifically correct (1874) appellation *Apatosaurus* was ignored in favor of the more popular name Brontosaurus (1878). Both names were proved in 1903 to be of the same creature. The oldest valid name first used is considered the scientifically correct one.

Having invested a quarter of a million dollars in printing the 60 million stamps depicting four types of dinosaurs, (painted by Alexandria artist John Gurche) the Postal Service acknowledged its deliberate inaccuracy but stood by it, expecting to make a bonanza selling the stamps, t-shirts, etc. to children. It was Christine Harbster, an 8-year-old first grader in Chandler, Arizona, a true dinosaur buff who first publicly pointed out the erroneous nomenclature.

Dinosaurs were still a marketing marvel in 1993 with the block busting success of the movie *Jurassic Park*, which to the spring of 1994 had grossed well over $300,000,000. Not just a historical horror film, the theme is up-to-the-minute science, dramatizing the potential ability of man to recreate gigantic living dinosaurs by the use of DNA derived from their fossilized remains. Also in 1993, the museum presented the exhibit, *Dinosaur Families* attracting twice the usual summer attendance.

Meanwhile fossilized dinosaur eggs and pieces of alleged fossilized dinosaur droppings brought high prices at auctions in London, England.

See *Carnegie Magazine*, December 1980.

The Carnegie Museum of Natural History Division of Earth Sciences Section of Invertebrate Paleontology

The Bayet Collection, Five Days to Inventory

The reports of this section of the museum refer to the job of cataloguing a variety of specimens from the Bayet Collection of European fossils, which was given in 1903 to the museum by Andrew Carnegie. Portions of the Bayet Collection are in this section, in the Section of Vertebrate Paleobotany, and the Section of Paleobotany. The assembling of the collection was the life work of Baron Ernest de Bayet of Brussels, secretary to Leopold II of Belgium. Over a period of 40 years, the Baron amassed one of the largest private collections of fossils in Western Europe. It occupied an entire three-story house which de Bayet had to sell when, at age 65, he married a much younger woman who wanted a chalet on Lake Como, Italy.

It took an official from the British Mu-seum of Natural History five days in 1898 to make an inventory of the collection. When The Carnegie Museum of Natural History learned, in 1902, of the impending sale, the competition was already keen, including the Imperial Museum of St. Petersburg, Russia,

England's British Museum in London, Harvard University, and the American Museum of Natural History. A German dealer notified the museum's curator of Paleontology who appealed to Director Holland who wrote Andrew Carnegie on May 9, 1903, at Skibo Castle, his retirement home in Scotland. Carnegie replied promptly, approving the purchase of the Bayet Collection in its entirety. The price asked was $25,000. The price paid was $20,500 including packing and shipping the fossils. Dr. Holland took a ship to Brussels to oversee the packing, reporting later that he never worked harder in his life! All 259 cases arrived in Pittsburgh in September 1903.

Because of lack of space in the museum at that time, the collection was sent to a warehouse, which later suffered a fire. Fortunately, although the cases were dampened, their contents were undamaged. After the completion of the enlarged Carnegie Institute building in 1907, the collection was moved to The Museum of Natural History. A portion of the collection is exhibited in Dinosaur Hall, while much was stored in the Section of Vertebrate Paleontology, as well as in the Section of Invertebrate Paleontology. Andrew Carnegie's purchase was an invaluable addition to the holdings of the museum, numbering in the tens of thousands, especially rich in invertebrate fossils, representing various eras, found in Europe. Many specimens are irreplaceable because the sites from which they came have been destroyed by fire or war, filled in, or covered with buildings. When the curator, Dr. John L. Carter, joined the museum in 1972, he was surprised to see in the Bayet Collection several thousand fossils from European quarries he had found ruined for collecting when he had visited them the previous year.

Quarry in Germany, Worked Since Roman Times

One of the most famous sites is the Solnhofen

quarry in southern Germany, quarried since Roman times. Here was preserved a remarkable record of late Jurassic animal life which had perished in the sub-tropical lagoons which had extended across Europe. The pure, fine-grained limestone that was laid down in these shallow seas has already yielded more than 600 species of fossil animals. Some show impressions of soft parts that are rarely seen in fossils: dragon-flies with out-stretched wings; prawns and lobster- and crab-like crustaceans with legs and delicate antennae exquisitely preserved; and squids and cuttlefish with the outlines of the tentacles, their ink sacs still containing ink! Several specimens of this collection, which is probably the largest collection of Solnhofen invertebrates in North America, can be seen in Dinosaur Hall.

Pterosaurs and Arthropods

The Bayet Collection of The Carnegie Museum of Natural History also includes many fish, several of which are displayed in Dinosaur Hall. The skeletons of reptiles that lived in shallow seas that covered parts of Europe during the Mesozoic Era can be seen along one wall of Dinosaur Hall as well. Another priceless part of the Bayet Collection, the pterosaur ("winged reptiles"), consists of eleven specimens. Four of these are displayed along the back wall of Dinosaur Hall. These fossils are especially valu- able. With these eleven pterosaurs, Carnegie Museum has the fourth largest collection of Jurassic pterosaurs in the world, outranked only by museums in Munich, Eichstatt, and London.

Collected in 1948 by a group from The Carnegie is a huge slab of sandstone on display near the entrance to Paleozoic Hall. Preserved on its surface are the appendage and body im- pressions of a gigantic arthropod. It is one of a group of over 800,000 discovered species such as spiders, insects, crabs, lobsters, etc., comprising about eighty percent of all known animal species. Arthropods, among the animals without a backbone, have developed the most

successful adaptation to life on land and in the air. This large fossil had never been catalogued because its exact biological affinities and geo- logical age were uncertain. In 1981 two British paleon-tologists came to Pittsburgh to study it, with the result that the fossil could be identified by its own special name.

Millions of Shells

The collection was established with a nucleus of "fishes and mollusca" dating from 1878, representing nearly one-third of the species which had been catalogued by naturalists. One hundred years later the significant achievement was the completion of a new arrangement of the land shells of the world. Not including the large number of American shells, it took 300 drawers to accommodate the nearly 4,000 specimens. Basically a study collection, it is measured not by individual specimens but by lots — 75,000 in all, ranging from one shell to several hundred, housed in 66 cases. The total number of shells is in the millions. The section has 1,500 type collections, that is holotypes: species that were new when first identified. A group of scientifi- cally important Tertiary shells from Peru, col- lected more than 100 years ago, was received by exchange from the British Museum.

Threat to Our Water Supply

Of perhaps more general interest is the fact that the section has collaborated with the con- servation agencies concerning the Asiatic clam. After introduction into the southern states more than 20 years ago it has proliferated even into the Allegheny River, where it has clogged water intake systems. Involved is assessment of the biological fresh water resources in Western Pennsylvania. Water problems are not new to the scientists at The Carnegie Museum of Natu- ral History. In the early 1900s the waters of Pittsburgh and the area were seriously affected by pollution, causing fatal outbreaks of typhoid fever and the disappearance of aquatic life.

The waters unfit for life were identified by the museum's curator of invertebrate zoology, in *The Destruction of Fresh-Water Fauna in Western Pennsylvania* (1909).

Collections Increased By 50% In One Year

Other noteworthy additions include two very large contributions to our local Pennsylvanian age collections: from John Anderson over 22,000 snails (more than 180 species) from the tri-state area, and Field Associate Alan Saltsman added over 11,000 invertebrates from several local formations. Virtually all of approximately 49,000 specimens are of late Paleozoic age and the majority of them originated in Western Pennsylvania. Besides staff collections totaling about 3,400 specimens, gift collections were received from David Brezinski, including over 45,000 conodonts and trilobites of Pennsylvanian age and Mississippian snails. Also received were rare Pennsylvanian starfish, a rare Pennsylvanian cephalopod beak, and Oligocene insects.

More than 1,000 specimens of land, fresh water, and marine mollusks were added to the collections, the major portion of which was the gift of Dr. William E. Clench, curator emeritus of the Museum of Comparative Zoology, Harvard. After 29 years of service to The Carnegie Museum of Natural History, Juan Jose Parodiz became curator emeritus. His book *Darwin in the New World* was published, and the *Bulletin of The Carnegie Museum of Natural History* has his article on his research on non-marine mollusks of Ecuador, several brochures were released, especially on *Collecting Land Shells.*

The work of the section has mainly focused on fresh water and land mollusks, which constitute the strength of the collection. The section is also concerned with the increased number of endangered species of fresh water shells, especially from the eastern regions of the country.

Staff Activities

Curator John Carter and Research Associate

Thomas Krammer completed a monograph describing for the first time fauna of the Price Formation in West Virginia. Carter also completed two additional works, one a biostratigraphic subdivision of the Mississippian system in North America based on the brachiopod record, and the other comprising descriptions of new genera and species of branchiopods from the Keokuk and Warsaw formations in Iowa, Illinois, and Missouri.

Fieldwork in 1990 continued in Missouri, Indiana, Kentucky, Kansas, Oklahoma, and New Mexico and involved examining the middle Mississippian stratigraphy and collecting fossils. Specialized research includes a two-part study to define and propose a new phylum of invertebrates, Phylum Conulariida, meriting special mention.

The section has hosted several international visitors from the Royal Institute of Natural Sciences, Belgium, the University of Bordeaux, France, and Chulalongkorn University, in Bangkok, Thailand and other countries. In 1990 at the 2nd International Congress on Living and Fossil Brachiopods held in Dunedin, New Zealand, Curator John Carter's scientific research on brachiopods was honored. He was entrusted with a monumental task: the revision of all or part of seven super-families of brachiopods, including well over 300 genera, for a new edition of the *Treatise on Invertebrate Paleontology.* As part of this project, Carter completed systematic papers on new and previously misinterpreted genera of brachiopods.

Curator Carter spent two weeks in Moscow and St.Petersburg (formerly Leningrad) studying spiriferid brachiopods. He was in Moscow during the aborted coup of August 1991, which attempted to overthrow President Gorbachev. This dramatic event did not delay his research, he admits, however, that the experience of being there at that time was, "interesting."

Carnegie Magazine, April 1981

The Carnegie Museum of Natural History
Division of Earth Sciences
Section of Paleobotany

Paleobotany involves the study of fossilized plants. In 1986 the collection numbered 13,000 which had been lumped together, "at the back of the Big Bone Room." Thanks to a full roster of research and collection improvements grants, plus 13 months of effort, these fossils were more suitably housed, arranged according to geologic age and locality by 1990.

In opening crates purchased in 1903, the section was delighted to discover some of the best examples of Eocene palms ever reported from the Monte Bolca quarry of Italy. Included among the 22 specimens are entire plants, some over four feet in height. These specimens were all part of the Bayet Collection. Fortunately, it was discovered that some of these specimens were being attacked by pyrite deterioration, a problem that has been addressed.

National Park Service funded research projects in the Yellowstone/Grand Teton region involving the climate and vegetation history of Grand Teton Park since the retreat of glacier ice about 13,000 years ago. The history of prehistoric fires in Yellowstone and their role in altering vegetation development is to form the basis for evaluating the long-term effects of the 1988 fire in the park. Fossil pollen and other plant remains are under study from several lake cores located in remote parts of Teton Wilderness. Coring was done during a seven-day packtrip involving four people and 14 horses. Pollen changes during the last 200 years are showing the effects both of elk overgrazing and fire suppression. Members of the section also hiked, skied, and traveled by snowmobile to remote lakes in the park. To collect sediment samples from the lake bottom for pollen analysis, it was necessary to auger through four feet of surface ice.

Under a contract from Rockwell Hanford Operations, a quality assurance plan was drafted for forthcoming paleoclimate research at the Hanford Reservation, part of the selection procedure for a national nuclear waste repository. Other research projects have included an analysis of the pollen in 22-million-year-old lake sediments from Devon Island in Arctic Canada. A study of the vegetation history at the Newton Mammoth Site in Bradford County, Pennsylvania was completed in 1986 and the results presented at the Smith Symposium at the Buffalo Natural History Museum in 1987. Pollen from an archeological site in coastal Maryland has indicated to Carnegie scientists the effects of human disturbance on the ancient vegetation.

The first major acquisition of plant fossils since the purchase of the Bayet Collection for the museum by Andrew Carnegie in 1903 occurred in 1988. The museum received a gift of over 4,200 superb plant fossils from the Anthracite region collected by the late John Oleksyshyn of Philadelphia. It took two people 18 months just to catalogue these specimens which show plant evolution and the formation of coal.

Donations of specimens from Montana, Ohio, West Virginia, and Pennsylvania, including a gigantic lycopod trunk and root system excavated near Pittsburgh, were added to the collections.

The section's superb collection of about 20,000 fossil plants was being curated and rediscovered, a deliberate, patient, often painstaking process. Over 4,000 specimens were catalogued, bringing the total number of curated specimens to 11,200 and leaving about 9,800 yet to be identified and conserved as of 1990. Rich fossils of Carboniferous age, especially those from the Pennsylvanian Period, were collected in Allegheny, Schuylkill, and Luzerne counties, Pennsylvania. Roughly half of the fossil plants are now identified to the generic level, and nearly half of these are seed ferns. The remainder are mostly true ferns, articulates, lycopods, and cordaites, all of which were particularly prolific in the coal swamps of the Pennsylvanian Period.

The Paleobotany Section is active in educational programs and has assisted with parent/child classes offered by the Division of Education: "Behind the Scenes in Paleobotany" and "Pittsburgh, 300 Million Years Ago."

The Carnegie Museum of Natural History Division of Life Sciences Section of Amphibians and Reptiles

Pennsylvania Collection Most Extensive
Living amphibians and reptiles are relics of groups that flourished during earlier geological times. Amphibians evolved from primitive fish and first emerged on land some 350 million years ago. From about 225 million years ago onward for approximately 160 million years, descendants of the amphibians, the reptiles, including dinosaurs, ruled the world.

Although amphibians and reptiles are zoologically distinct groups, they share several common characteristics. Both groups are vertebrates (have backbones), are ectotherms (cold-blooded), and usually have four limbs with digits. With over 3,000 living species, amphibians include frogs, toads, and salamanders. Reptiles, with about twice as many living species, include turtles, crocodiles, lizards, and snakes. Several endangered species include the Nile crocodile, the American crocodile, and the Galapagos tortoise. A museum display does provide a comparison between amphibians and reptiles.

In the museum, most of the snakes, lizards, frogs, and salamanders on display are casts of living animals made of latex or plastic which are painted realistically as in life. In some cases the actual skin is used in a mounted display but it must also be painted since the colors of

amphibians and reptiles are in their skin, a living organ, whereas colors of mammals and birds are in non-living structures, feather and fur, which survive after the creature no longer lives.

The scientific research collection started by the Pittsburgh High School Naturalists in the early part of this century has grown to more than 190,000 computer-catalogued specimens. In 1989 alone the section received 125 specimens from Madagascar and 8,000 reptiles donated by the Virginia Herpetological Survey. Judged on size, diversity, and number of type specimens (holotypes), the collection ranks among the ten most important in the United States. Sixty percent of the collection is of U. S. origin, with large collections from Pennsylvania, West Virginia, Virginia, and Maryland.

Snakes of Pennsylvania Identified
Popular guidebooks, *Poisonous Snakes of Pennsylvania* and *Identification Guide to Pennsylvania Snakes*, have been published by the section under the Benedum Resource Project. Even more ambitious was the completion of the Pennsylvania herpetology inventory, a manuscript checklist, bibliography, and distribution atlas of Pennsylvania amphibians and reptiles, incorporating data collected during the first 60 years of section history. (The latest field find in Pennsylvania was the rediscovery in Franklin County of the mud salamander which had not been seen in Pennsylvania in this century.

Voucher Maps Important
Geographic distribution maps are important in the identification of species in danger of extinction and the determination of their level of jeopardy. The entire museum has several million voucher specimens which document the existence of a species at a given time and place and provide a retrospective picture of a species' distribution as well as a starting point for field studies of present ecological situations. This ecological history must be continually supplemented by

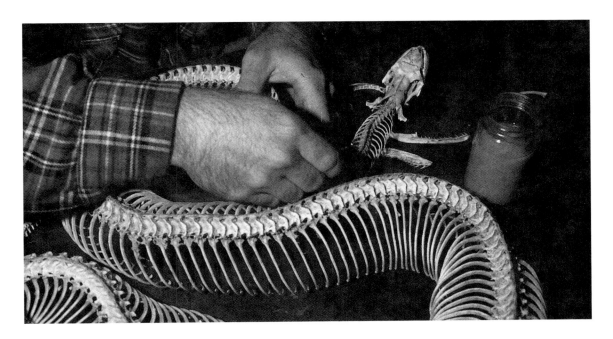

Python skeleton in preparation for exhibition.

Photograph by Vincent Abromitis

vouchers that will portray the flora and fauna of today to future generations. The collecting of vouchers minimizes the use of the actual specimens of endangered species being documented. Photographic vouchers have been used to record the locations of burrows, dung, and fragments of shell found where the tortoises had been slaughtered for food.

Field Work
Reproductive Biology of Sea Turtles

Field work in the section has been and will continue to be very diverse. Over the last several years extensive field work has been done on the Caribbean island of Anguilla, initially supported by the National Geographic Society, concerning the endangered endemic iguana and other ground lizards of the Lesser Antilles. Beginning in the late 1980s and continuing into the 1990s the Wild Resources Conservation Fund has supported research on endangered and threatened amphibians and reptiles of Pennsylvania. The mid-1980s saw two trips to Belize, Central America, to survey the herpetofauna of this country. One extensive, future project is planned in Paraguay which will be are visiting of trips taken to this country in the early 1980s.

In the late 1970s five years of intensive research on freshwater turtles produced about 10,000 specimens. One aspect of the field work of the section was discussed in *Carnegie Magazine* of September, 1982: the study of the reproductive biology of sea turtles. Sea turtles, once abundant in tropical oceans, have been decimated by humans for food. All species of sea turtles are endangered. Studies have shown that the temperature experienced by the developing sea turtle egg at a critical phase of incubation determines the sex of the hatching turtle. Since one male turtle can fertilize the eggs of many females, deliberate production of a majority of females could greatly speed the replenishment of depleted breeding populations. Field work in Costa Rica by members of The Carnegie in the 1980s provided eggs used to determine the "sex switch" temperature of one sea turtle species.

The research and field work of the section continues to investigate turtle biology. Expeditions to southern Mexico, Alabama, Tennessee, and Wisconsin, as well as donations by research associates, have made The Carnegie's the largest freshwater turtle collection in the world. Over 25,000 turtles provide a base for study to many researchers around the world.

Publications and Professional Activities
The study of the distribution, conservation, and historical biogeography of the Bolson tortoise in Mexico involved investigation in some of the most remote and inaccessible desert country in North America, and was published in the *Annals of Carnegie Museum*. Also published was the comparative study of female reproductive cycles in tropical snakes, completed in 1987. A book-length, popular account of the Pennsylvania amphibians and reptiles is being published in 1995. (It was begun in 1989 by the curator C. J. McCoy, who started with the museum in 1964 and died July 7, 1993.)

The section's reprint collection, consisting of close to 50,000 scientific articles on amphibians and reptiles in now accessed by a computerized index, making it possible to quickly locate scientific articles on amphibians and reptiles by

title, name, geographic location, or 38 other subject categories.

Section staff continued to take active roles in many professional organizations locally and nationally. In 1989 members of the section attended the first World Congress of Herpetology at the University of Kent in Canterbury, England. Work continues on the herpetology project in South India, as a joint undertaking of The Carnegie and the National Museum of Natural History, New Delhi, funded by the Smithsonian Office of International Programs.

Carnegie Magazine, March 1981, Volume 55, Number 3, Pages 25-33.

The Carnegie Museum of Natural History Division of Life Sciences Section of Botany: Botany Hall

Knowledge of Botany Important
Botany, the science and study of plants, is of vital importance because plants photosynthesize life substances from the raw elements, forming the first link in the chain of life upon which the existence of all other living things depends. Animals use plants for food and shelter; humans adapt plants into clothing and medicine, and of course, food.

Dioramas in the Hall
Botany Hall, through realistic dioramas, highlights an amazing diversity of plants depicting four different biomes found in the continental United States: a Florida Everglade jungle, a Mt. Rainier alpine meadow, a Sonoran desert in Arizona, and a Pennsylvania valley area. All illustrate how varying conditions of temperature and water affect plant life. Other dioramas depict seasonal variations at some of Pennsylvania's unique and highly valued natural habitats: Presque Isle during summer, a Warren

County bog in the fall, and the Allegheny National Forest in spring.

Presque Isle did not exist 10,000 years ago. Sand and gravel have been deposited at a rate of one-half mile per century to form the peninsula. This exhibit demonstrates vividly the natural succession of plant communities, from the grassy sand dunes to the Bearberry Heath to the Cottonwood Ridge to, eventually, the Red Oak Forest. Additional exhibits in Botany Hall feature plants that have been used for food, as medicine, or in industry.

Herbarium – Library

Botany was one of the original sections endowed by Andrew Carnegie in 1896, and aided by the Botanical Society of Western Pennsylvania, the second oldest in the country which celebrated its 100th anniversary in 1986. A biosystematics laboratory for plant classification became a reality thanks to gifts in kind from the Fisher Scientific Company of Pittsburgh. The section now includes an herbarium (the central plant collection) and a supporting botanical library of 10,000 volumes and periodicals plus dozens of volumes from the 18th century, including those of Linnaeus. Linnaeus is the latinized version of the name Karl von Linné (1707-1778), the Swedish naturalist who established the system of binomial nomenclature of plants in his *Systems Natural* (1753).

An herbarium is an unbound library of dried plants in which each "page" contains a pressed plant specimen that has been identified and filed. The oldest here, dating back to 1738 is that of the Englishman William Paine. With regard to the library, botanical books with type description never go out of date, because, beginning in 1753, the first correctly published botanical name has priority. These three botanical resources are utilized to show how the flora of Western Pennsylvania is closely related to that of Eastern Asia, especially that of Japan and China.

National Regional Depository — Value of Duplicate Specimens

The Carnegie's herbarium is a designated National Regional Depository, ranking 19th among the more than 1,100 institutions in the United States with herbaria. The botanical collection contains more than 450,000 plant specimens from all the major plant groups over the world and includes more than 2,500 types, that is, specimens which were new to science when collected. Duplicates are still of great importance as well, even for insurance if something should happen to the original cited type. For example, the section's 200 isotypes from the Philippines, and from British Borneo collected in the early part of this century, have a significant status since the herbarium in Manila, where the cited types were stored, was totally destroyed during World War II. An isotype set

This flowering vine *Centrosema virginianum*, a member of the bean family, was collected during field work in the Dominican Republic conducted by the Sections of Botany and Invertebrate Zoology.

Photograph courtesy of Carnegie Museum of Natural History

in Berlin was also destroyed. The section has the first and most complete set of an early collection from Colombia, which contains approximately another 1,000 types.

For years the section coped with a backlog of some 20,000 unmounted specimens, some 70-years-old in their original newsprint folders. During the Cold War specimens sent to or received from the Soviet Union and the People's Republic of China had to be surrounded by blank newsprint, newsprint without news! A grant from the National Science Foundation assisted in improving the collection.

Collection Answers Many Questions

The botanical collection is of use to other sections of the museum, such as those which study various creatures who feed on plants. The identification of the plants ingested provides many clues concerning the animals and their interaction with their environment, thus helping date the time of their existence.

Botany in effect pervades most of the newer exhibits throughout the museum which show animals and the plants native to their habitats. For the Hall of African Wildlife which opened in 1993, the exhibits staff relied on the botany curator to identify the types of plants to be included in each of the biomes displayed.

With a more general application, poisonous mushrooms and flowering plants are held for comparative purposes in the event of an emergency. Specimens in the collection document the spread of new species and weeds into our area. Medicinal plant specimens from the tropics, collected by the drug companies in their search for new, "green medicines," are deposited in the herbarium as a reference of their activities. Other specimens which directly support technical and evolutionary studies dealing with plant natural history, such as pollination ecology, hybridization experiments, and chemical, anatomical, and chromosomal analyses, are deposited in the Carnegie Herbarium to

document for the future exactly what botanical materials were used.

Growth of the Collection

Of the 8,837 total specimens added to the collection in 1980, approximately 60% were from Asia, with 30% from North America. In 1981 the section divested its collection of 22,500 specimens of plants which produce neither blossoms nor seeds, such as fungi, mosses, lichens, etc., obtaining in exchange some 4,000 vascular plants from areas in which the section already has a collection strength and research interest.

In 1987 the section purchased 4,370 botanical species from the discontinued herbarium of the Catholic University in Washington, D.C. and in 1991 acquired the herbarium of the St. Vincent College in Latrobe, Pennsylvania.

During the period 1990-1994, a total of 58,733 specimens were added to the Carnegie's herbarium, of which 24,144 were staff collections.

In the early 1990s a major contribution was the private herbarium of Jacob Walle, grandfather of Dr. William Holland, the Museum's Director, who also added to that collection.

Field Work, Research, Publications

In 1990 joint field work with the Japan Ministry of Education resulted in multidisciplinary study of plant species common to Eastern Asia and Western North America. Focusing on the lily family of North America the Japanese collected specimens from 24 states with the living plants to go to research gardens at Kyoto and Hokkaido Universities for use in cellular and genetic studies. In other field work, deep in the tropical forests of Ecuador, a botanist studied the temperature of flowers using a special thermometer, gathering information to explain the insect-dependent pollination process of plants in the aroid family.

Research in the herbarium and lab has centered around two projects. Work on a

Distribution Atlas of the Vascular Plants of Western Pennsylvania required the preliminary mapping of the 200,000 specimens which represent the 1,800 species in our region. The other project has involved biosystematic research on the lilies of the Northern Hemisphere, the life history of the lilies of Pennsylvania, and a specimen-based flora of Powdermill Nature Reserve. The section cooperates closely with the Hunt Institute for Botanical Documentation, Beechwood Farms Wildflower Sanctuary, the Phipps Conservatory, and the Western Pennsylvania Conservancy.

Exemplifying significant publications of the section are several books by Dr. Otto E. Jennings, curator of botany, head of the Biological Sciences at the University of Pittsburgh, and from 1946 to 1948, director of The Carnegie Museum of Natural History. Dr. Jennings' *Mosses of Western Pennsylvania* underwent two different printings (1913, 1950), his *Botany of the Isle of Pines* (Cuba), published in 1917, remains a classic for the island, and his two-volume *Wildflowers of Western Pennsylvania and the Upper Ohio Basin*, which includes reproductions of the lovely plant watercolors by Dr. Andrey Avinoff, then the museum's director, is the major floristic reference for our region. Jennings would range the woodlands, wetlands, and meadows and rush his discoveries to Avinoff, who would work far into the night to capture the freshness of the flowering plant. From the spring of 1941 through the flowering season of 1942, this collaboration produced 296 watercolors, illustrating 351 native or naturalized wildflowers . . . earning Avinoff, the Russian émigré, a reputation as the Audubon of botany.

Carnegie Magazine, June 1979, Volume 53, Number 6, Pages 6-13.

The Carnegie Museum of Natural History Division of Life Sciences Section of Birds: Bird Hall

Birds — 9,000 Species, Others Extinct

The study of birds, ornithology, has a long and distinguished history at The Carnegie Museum of Natural History. Within the museum Bird Hall contains exhibits of dioramas which show a small sampling of the more than 9,000 species of birds existing throughout the world. Birds obtained by past Carnegie expeditions to various parts of the Americas are displayed realistically as to pose and habitat.

Birds have lived on earth for over 100 million years but some species have become extinct like the famous dodo, and more recently, the passenger pigeon. In one of the dioramas the ivory-billed woodpecker exhibited was collected in Florida in 1894 when they were still common. The California condor is shown with several other examples of species of extinct or endangered birds. Carnegie also has, because it is a relatively old museum, a number of specimens of extinct species such as the Stephens Island wren, which already was extinct when science learned about it in the 1890s. Not yet extinct in the 1890s, the passenger pigeon was so prolific that its mass migratory flights would darken the sky for hours but it, too, in a few short years ceased to exist as a species. These birds were slaughtered in droves and shipped to fine restaurants in the east to be served as delicacies to the gourmets and gourmands of the day.

The Collection and Library, Outstanding

Over the years, museum scientists have built the collection into one of the largest and richest in this country. The Section of Birds has around 1,000 birds on display, plus about 6,000 skeletons, and 9,000 sets of eggs. The 4,000 alcohol specimens have been used for dissecting tissues in research from early in the 20th century. Birds stuffed with cotton, 160,000 of them, were stored in wooden drawers in huge metal filing cases until 1986. The storage capacity was increased by 60% with the installation of a state-of-the-art compactor storage system made possible by a grant of $250,000 from the National Science Foundation. The required match of $50,000 was satisfied by The Carnegie's contribution of materials and labor. All in all, as of 1990, the section held about 185,000 bird specimens and egg sets.

A formula and method of measuring bird's eggs was devised by Dr. Frank W. Preston who also designed the needed instruments and subsidized the measuring of thousands of eggs in the Carnegie collection. When Dr. Preston died in 1989 at age 93, his eulogy was given by Dr. Graham Netting, director emeritus of the museum.

Annual reports acknowledged that over the years the section's collections were greatly increased by the donation by interested people of birds salvaged after their deaths when hitting picture windows, TV towers, and automobiles. It is now illegal for an individual to salvage dead birds without a permit. The section lends birds to recognized professional artists and carvers as models. The wings from birds destined to become skeletal specimens, are often spread for artists' use as acknowledged by master carver Larry Barth. His *Forbesway Drummer,* lifelike depiction of a ruffed grouse, is resident in the Nature Center at Powdermill, the gift of Thomas H. Nimick, Jr.

The museum's ornithological library, already one of the finest in the country, was greatly enhanced in 1981 by the generous gift of 583 volumes from John P. Robin of Pittsburgh, (aptly named) civic leader and former right-hand-man of David L. Lawrence, mayor of the city (1946-1959) and governor of Pennsylvania (1959-1963).

Birds as Predators or Victims

The long tradition of distinguished ornithological research continues with expeditions to the Philippines, Argentina, and Mexico, and many other areas for the study of living birds as well as the classification of and relationships among species of the world. Research covers the divergent views of birds as predators and birds as the objects of predation. In 1980 studies were made of the bird predation on the incredible wintering concentration of Monarch butterflies in Michoacan, Mexico. The next year in an expedition to Isla Socorro, Baja California, it was discovered that doves known only there and formerly abundant and tame, are now extinct in the wild. This tragic loss of bird life is probably due to the introduction of domestic cats, now feral, when the Mexican government established a small military base on Socorro in 1957 and families were permitted to bring domestic animals to the island. A full report on the results of the two expeditions is in *The Wilson Bulletin* of early 1982.

Much of the museum's research in bird activity recognized by the public occurs at Powdermill Nature Reserve and is discussed in more detail beginning on page 166.

Carnegie Magazine, Summer 1981, Volume 55, Number 6, Pages 8-16.

The Carnegie Museum of Natural History
Division of Life Sciences
Section of Mammals

Count Noble — Canine Centenarian

Less exotic but special is life-like Count Noble, the prize-winning English setter who died in 1891. Eight years later his mounted skin was donated to the museum and famed preparator Webster remounted it and exhibited Count Noble with quail in a habitat group. The exhibit was refurbished in 1961 with a new background by Ottmar von Fuehrer and plant models made by his wife Hanne. This century-old canine represents the breed of the oldest gun-dog in America, the English setter. Count Noble was imported from England in 1880 by David Sanborn of Michigan, and from 1881 had a highly successful career in field trials and as sire of 28 field trial winners. After Mr. Sanborn's death the Count passed to Mr. B. F. Wilson of Pittsburgh whose relative, S. R. Wilson gave the dog, as a mounted skin, to the museum in 1899. (Dr. Mary R. Dawson, *Carnegie Magazine* July/August issue, 1984).

Collector, Conservationist Phillips

Some of the mammal specimens displayed in this hall were collected for The Carnegie by the consummate conservationist and sportsman Pittsburgher John M. Phillips (1861-1953). He was responsible for the Pennsylvania Game Laws and campaigned in 1905 to establish a resident hunting license. (He did not hunt for sport but to photograph or collect specimens for the museum.) Only a few months before his death at 92 he brought a private law suit to prevent the cutting of timber in Cook Forest State Park. His 20-year tenure on the State Game Commission ended when he refused to obey the order of Governor Gifford Pinchot requiring each of his appointees to personally pledge to observe the Volstead Act (Prohibition) of 1924.

Tadarida brasiliensis from Tol Sou Eul Cave, Dominica, confirming the largest known maternity roost site for this bat in Lesser Antilles.

Photograph courtesy of Carnegie Museum of Natural History

The Collection

The staff of the Section of Mammals curates the collection, performs laboratory research, conducts field work, assists in the training of international visitors, and organizes meetings. With approximately 80,000 specimens the collection of the Section of Mammals in 1980 was the eighth largest in North America. Included were 42 holotypes of various species of mammals. Collection care and conservation research in the section changed focus in 1988. A major research emphasis on the effects of various chemicals, both fumigants and preservatives, on natural science specimens was begun with funds provided by the Institute for Museum Services and Westinghouse Electric Corporation. Collection activities for that year, which was fairly typical, included seven accessions of 2,911 specimens. In 1990 alone, the section identified, verified, reorganized, installed, and catalogued over 18,000 specimens of insectivores, rodents, and bats. By 1992 the collection had passed the 100,000 mark.

Activities

Foreign specimens and 42 domestic loans of specimens were sent. Eighty-seven requests for specimen data, with computer print-outs, were honored, involving 15,333 specimens in the research collection. The seven-year field survey of West Virginia mammals was concluded while a survey of mammals of New York continued in collaboration with the New York State Museum.

Five members of the staff served on 26 committees and held two offices in professional societies, such as the American Society of Mammalologists of which Carnegie's curator Dr. Hugh H. Genoways was president in 1986. Staff members also served as judges for regional science competitions.

The section works with the Pennsylvania Game Commission to identify confiscated trophies and other specimens of endangered species for the Division of Law Enforcement of the U.S. Fish and Wildlife Service, and operates as a repository for voucher specimens of small mammals used in epidemiological studies of human diseases at the U. S. Army Medical Research Unit laboratory in Seoul, Korea.

The preparation laboratory and environmental chamber were refurbished after 12 years of heavy use. Work on the curation backlog resulted in a significant increase in the collections. Data on more than 20,000 specimens were either added or enhanced by curation efforts in 1991 alone. Exhibit development trips to Africa in 1991 were made for the Hall of African Wildlife. Exhibitions staff studied the bat fauna of the French West Indian Islands of Guadeloupe. Research in Ghana on African mole rats, an agricultural pest in much of Africa, continued.

The influx of visiting international mammalologists is a recurring theme in each of the section's annual reports. Two international scientists completed extended visits during 1991. Santiago Reig returned to Madrid, Spain, after spending over two years as a post-doctoral student working on North American weasels.

Christian Chimimba of the Museums of Malawi, Africa, completed a six-month visit to the museum, studying tropical bats and a group of African rodents.

New Frontiers in Molecular Biology

An article in *Carnegie Magazine* in 1991 recounted the finding in the Austrian Alps of the body of a man from the Copper Age (4000 -2200 B. C.) frozen, mummified, hidden in the ice for 5,300 years. Entombed in ice with the man were remnants of a grass cape and tools. That dramatic occurrence, and the scientific opportunities it presented, led into a description of a new frontier in molecular biology using frozen tissue in preserving information about animal species. For $10,000 in 1986, the Section of Mammals acquired an ultra-cold freezer which holds its contents at -80 degrees Celsius or -112 degree Fahrenheit. Inside, as of 1992, are approximately 40,000 small vials of tissue from some 13,000 animals, such as rabbits, raccoons, bats, and moles, from North and South America, the Caribbean, Asia, and Africa. These tissues are of interest to the National Institutes of Health in Washington, D.C. because they include samples from rodents native to the area of Africa where the AIDS virus is believed to have originated and may help develop a laboratory rodent model for AIDS research in place of primates presently used.

Carnegie Magazine, June 1980, Volume 54, Number 6, Pages 30-36.

The Carnegie Museum of Natural History Division of Life Sciences Section of Invertebrate Zoology — formerly Entomology, Insects, Spiders, and Malacology

The Section 1895 - 1995

The Section of Invertebrate Zoology concerns the most varied and successful animals on earth: the insects. During 350 million years insects have evolved into an incredible number of species. Some 1,500,000 species are already known, and an estimated 10,000,000 remain to be discovered. The first curator of the section was William J. Holland, who as a youthful collector in the 1860s aspired to have in his collection, "a specimen of each known genus of moth and butterfly." By the time of his appointment as curator of the new museum in Pittsburgh in 1895, Holland had already assembled a collection of international importance. Dr. Holland became director of the museum in 1898 and served until 1926.

Significant early holdings of the museum were Dr. Holland's lepidopteran collection — which included the priceless Edwards butterfly collection — and a vast amount of exotic material from the rain forests of Africa and South America, as well as a collection purchased by Andrew Carnegie in 1893 — the Knyvette Collection of Indian Butterflies.

The Collection

From the beginning Holland intended that The Carnegie Museum of Natural History collection of insects should be international in scope and outstanding in all insect orders. Even before the inauguration of the museum, Holland obtained the extensive beetle collection of Dr. Hamilton, and in 1901 he purchased the historic beetles of Henry Ulke, many of which were captured during federal government surveys and pioneering expeditions to our western territories. Vast collections of wasps, beetles, dragonflies, and grasshoppers were brought in from the forests of Africa and South America, often from remote areas no longer accessible or now stripped of native plants and animals.

(A fascinating article about Henry Ulke, *The Man and His Collection* by George E. Wallace, curator of the Section Insects and Spiders, was featured in *Carnegie Magazine*, February 1978.)

Private collections too numerous to name here came to the museum containing specimens from all parts of the world; many were collected by distinguished hobbyists and museum professionals. Today the Carnegie insect collection contains some 6.5 million specimens. Research, in this section and Botany, received an endowment bequest in 1989 from Mary Wible, a long-time supporter of their work.

New Insect Cases

Hundreds of insect specimens, collected from locations extending from Pittsburgh to the Congo Basin of Africa and the Amazon of South America are newly displayed. The diversity of insects includes a 15-inch-long walking stick, beetles the size of baseballs, butterflies of every color, and pests that we see every day. The cases are divided into themes dealing with insect diversity, variations, Pennsylvania insects, butterflies and moths, and butterfly colors and wing patterns.

The six new insect cases were made possible in 1994 through a gift from Paul Benedum to The Carnegie Second Century Fund.

Publication of Popular and Scientific Research

Research publications have been a major concern of most entomologists at The Carnegie Museum of Natural History. Several library shelves of entomological literature have been produced by staff curators and their associates. Butterflies and moths are a primary subject throughout the history of the scientific publications, reflecting a trend started by Dr. Holland,

Handmaiden moth from Africa: An extremely rare species *Balacra rubrostiriata* whose caterpillars do not eat plants, but prefer algae and lichens growing on tree branches or on rocks.

Photographed in northern Malawi in 1988 by Dr. John Rawlins, Curator, Invertebrate Zoology, Carnegie Museum of Natural History

whose books and journal articles still stand as foundation literature for the study of North American and African lepidoptera.

Among the other insects important research has been published on the dragonfly fauna of the Isle of Pines in Cuba, on North American flat-footed flies, minute parasitic wasps, and on the classification, natural history, and evolution of checkered beetles.

An in-depth study of the Section of Entomology completed the *Carnegie Magazine* series *The Elements of Greatness* on the history of the scientific sections of the museum.

Carnegie Magazine, January/February 1984, Volume 57, Number 1, Pages 22-29.

Firefly beetle on lantana flowers: A species of the family Lampyridae from Texas and related to our Pennsylvania fireflies.

Photographs by Dr. John Rawlins, Curator, Invertebrate Zoology, Carnegie Museum of Natural History

Holotype female specimen of *Carnegia mirabilis* Holland, an African species of wild-silk moth described in the genus *Carnegia* by Dr. Holland in 1896 in honor of Andrew Carnegie.

The Carnegie Museum of Natural History Division of Anthropology

Study of Human Adaptation to Conditions

Anthropology is the study of man, and in the museum that science has many facets: archaeological research within the collections and in the field, expeditions, excavations, acquisitions, and exhibitions, as well as obtaining the funds and working with the design experts and artisans to bring the results of the work "alive" to the museum visitors, children and adults alike.

From the earliest human beginnings about four million years ago to the present, each culture continuously expresses a special versatility in response to ever-changing conditions. Thus, people living in the Sahara Desert have a lifestyle very different from those inhabiting the jungles of Brazil or the frozen tundra of the Arctic. Even under the same environmental circumstances, two cultures may develop quite differently, as in the case of the Pueblo Indians and the Apaches.

Creation of Halls and Exhibitions

Creation of the Great Halls, such as Polar World and Ancient Egypt were the ultimate challenge and triumph shared by the Divisions of Anthropology and Exhibit and Design Production. (They are treated in some detail in other chapters.) The seven-year preparation for the Hall of Ancient Egypt was the focus of the division in 1988. Conservation research on the 3,900 year-old timbers of the funerary boat continued, as well as studies of post-pharonic textiles. The painting in accurate detail of the vivid designs decorating the reproduction of an ancient Egyptian tomb was an artistic challenge.

The largest undertaking of the division to date is the Alcoa Foundation Hall of Native Americans which includes Northwest Coast, Southwest Central Plains, Northeast Amazon Basin ethnology as well as Western Pennsylvanian archaeology. The Carnegie is one of the few major museums actively pursuing archaeological

Native American boy, Andrew Soeder, dancing at the Council of Three Rivers American Indian Center Powwow on September 27, 1992 at Dorseyville, PA.

Photograph by Dr. James B. Richardson III, Carnegie Museum of Natural History

research in the Amazon Basin. During the past 15 years, over 2,000 objects have been added, making the collection among the largest in the country. Over 800 Native American objects added to the collections in 1991 lend great strength to the development of the Hall of Native Americans. A 900 pound bronze statue by the Navajo artist R. C. Gorman was also a gift from Alcoa. When completed the hall will feature approximately 2,500 objects from native peoples.

Exhibitions are the most accessible facet of the work of the division. In 1986 *Mr. Carnegie's Museum* included views of his original *Palace of Culture* plus exotic artifacts such as a carved whale's tooth depicting the whaling ship *Wiscasset,* which brought young Andrew Carnegie and his family to New York in 1848. John A. Inches in 1986 gave the museum a gold ring which his grandfather had received from Mr. Carnegie. A smoking jacket of Andrew Carnegie's was received in 1990 from Pat McArdle, also added to the collections were 14 Hero medals of the type presented by the various Carnegie Hero Funds throughout the world.

Excavations in the Pittsburgh Area and Beyond

Pittsburgh local history was unearthed during the excavation for the glass neo-gothic PPG building (formerly the Pittsburgh Plate Glass Company) in downtown Pittsburgh. The 1987 exhibition *Pieces of the Past: Archaeology in Pittsburgh* displayed a selection of the numerous pottery shards, glass bottles, and relics which came to light. Funded by PPG Industries Foundation, the Carnegie researchers documented 30 wells and cisterns and a number of building foundations dating across the 19th century, in addition to an extensive documentation of the Pittsburgh bottle-making industry which flourished in the mid-1800s.

A full range of ceramic and metal objects, as well as normally perishable remains of cloth and leather, comprise the site inventory; even eggshells, seeds, fruit pits, animal bones, and fish scales were salvaged. Curiously, a handgun, a harmonica, a watch, an artist's brushes, and a can of paint pigment were found together. The former site of Pittsburgh's first Natural History Museum was discovered situated along Market Street between Third and Fourth Avenues.

For many years the museum's Division of Anthropology has been the official recording station for 22 counties in Western Pennsylvania as part of a Pennsylvania History and Museums Commission archaeological survey system. A two-year inventory project catalogued 62,715 items, and for the 22 Western Pennsylvania

counties the total of archaeological sites was 6,527. The total number of sites recorded at the museum since 1952 reached 8,387, including 1,860 from other northeastern states.

Albert Miller and the Meadowcroft Foundation donated the archaeological collection from the famous Meadowcroft Rockshelter near Avella, Pennsylvania. From excavations at Crawford-Roberts historic site in Pittsburgh's Hill District 2,397 artifacts came to the museum from The Urban Redevelopment Authority. Fifteen thousand historic artifacts from excavations conducted during the construction of the East Street Expressway, Pittsburgh, were donated by the Pennsylvania Department of Transportation. Staff and volunteers processed over 20,000 archaeological specimens into the museum collections. The division also studied how Pittsburgh's munition industries affected the city's participation in local, national, and international conflicts.

The archaeological survey of the Upper Ohio Valley, which began in 1950, continues and data was computerized in 1988. The earliest Pennsylvania inhabitants, the Paleo Indians, were studied, and 167 new archaeological sites, added to the survey files in 1986, led to a revised prehistory of the Upper Ohio Valley. For the fourth season, excavations continued at the Wylie site, a late prehistoric Monongahela Indian stockaded village in Washington County.

Various items of island peoples were recovered from sites on Martha's Vineyard, Antigua, Montserat, and the Leeward Islands and other areas in the Caribbean. Stone tools dating from 8,650 B.C. were excavated in Peru.

Coins and Stamps

The museum's 17,500 coins were inventoried preliminary to the 1989 exhibit *Coins from The Carnegie,* and the documentation of postage stamps was begun. This was in accordance with a court order of December 20, 1980, the result of a lawsuit brought by The Historical Society of Western Pennsylvania. Public controversy arose when the museum announced a decision to auction the stamps and most of the 200,000 coins, (described by the president of the auction house as one of the most important collections in the world and valued then at $1,250,000) because they were underutilized and there were problems with security. The proposal was to transfer the libraries on those topics to The Carnegie Library of Pittsburgh, which was done, and to retain certain rare and ancient coins. The court order provided for the sale of the entire collection of stamps with the exception of a master collection of United States and foreign stamps which are to be exhibited at the museum from time to time. Early in 1982 the Board of Trustees decided to sell the U. S. silver dollars and six U. S. proof sets, approximately 275 coins, with plans during the next two years to dispose of all but "a representative collection" of the rare and ancient coins.

Growth of the Anthropology Collections

Collection growth kept pace with the division's various research and exhibit programs. Donations to the collection in 1986 were wide ranging. Among hundreds of items from Central and South America were a Peruvian blow gun and quiver. Nineteenth century American pieces included 51 Indian baskets, bringing the collection to well over 1,000. In addition the division received a collection of Plains and Northwest Coast Native American artifacts from the Lackawanna Historical Society. A group of Australian Aborigine materials was also received. A major collection of artifacts from the tribes of Irian Jaya, Indonesia, was given by Dr. Andrew J. Strathern the Andrew Mellon Professor of Anthropology at the University of Pittsburgh.

There were also items from St. Vincent College in Latrobe, Pennsylvania. Betty J. Meggers of the Smithsonian Institution donated her collection of ethnic dolls bringing The Carnegie doll collection to more than 5,000.

Miss Kochi, the Japanese doll from the city of Kochi, one of 58 Japanese and over 12,000 United States Friendship dolls exchanged between American and Japanese children in 1929, to promote peace between our two countries.

Photograph by Melinda McNaugher, Carnegie Museum of Natural History

Japanese-American Relations, Dolls as Ambassadors

In 1927 before World War II, the Federal immigration laws and those of California discriminated against Japanese-Americans and other Asians. A former missionary in Japan for 20 years, Dr. Sidney Lewis Gulick conceived a good-will project — American children sending dolls to Japanese schools as Ambassadors of Friendship. By year's end 12,739 dolls were gathered from all 48 states (the U.S.A. total in 1927) and sent to Japan where they were honored in the annual Doll Festival on the third of March. Among the thousands of dolls was

"Alice Johnston," named for a Wilkinsburg school teacher. Alice went to a school in Kamiyama, Japan. The Japanese sent the doll, "Miss Kochi" to Pittsburgh where she was displayed in The Carnegie Museum of Natural History.

Sixty-six years later, but not looking a day older, Alice Johnston and Miss Kochi again were ambassadors of good-will between the school children of Japan and Wilkinsburg, U.S.A. The *Pittsburgh Post-Gazette* October 9, 1993, reported that during World War II many of the dolls were destroyed, but Miss Kochi was safe in The Carnegie and Alice Johnston was concealed in a box in a janitor's closet in the Japanese school. Three years ago Mr. Shinya Ominami of Kamiyama wrote Wilkinsburg asking for information about Alice's donor. Mayor Robert Pitts asked his administrative assistant Robin Hurt to respond. She did so and founded "Friendships are Forever" to renew the doll exchange. As a result a Japanese delegation brought Alice Johnston here for homecoming and The Carnegie sent Miss Kochi to Japan for her homecoming. The efforts of Carnegie Museum of Natural History Research Associate, Terry Hiener, expanded the goodwill doll exchange project to the Pittsburgh area schools and each year the people of Kochi donate artifacts for the "Friendship Ambassador" project. More dolls and more delegations are showing that, "Friendships truly are Forever."

Ethnographic Policy Established by Law
A museum policy on human remains and sensitive objects was approved by the Board of Trustees in response to the movement for respect of the cultural mores of indigenous peoples and other ethnic groups with regard to the retention and display of their ancient customs and ancestral artifacts acquired and researched decades ago. By law, museums of all kinds holding any ethnographic or archeological objects of Native American or Hawaiian

The Fall of the Sky by Hone (1981). This depiction of the Yanomamo creation myth shows people, rocks, and trees falling through the hole in the upper sky.

Illustration courtesy of Carnegie Museum of Natural History

materials are required by the Native American Graves Protectional and Repatriation Act of 1990 to report them by tribe, with the summaries sent to the Departmental Consulting Archeologist, National Park Service, by November 16, 1990.

Although, "No extensive research is required, copies of inventories should be provided all Indian tribes likely to be affiliated with museum collections. The information will be of interest to potential claimants for the returning of objects, including human remains, to tribes."

A detailed list of human remains and/or associated grave goods is to be compiled and reported by November of 1995.

Activities
Along with their intensive research, members of the division are prominent in the areas of education and public service, holding leadership posts in many professional and inter-agency organizations. A first for the division was the formation of an archaeological field school in

cooperation with Gannon University, and 54 participants attended that inaugural year. Another first was the traveling exhibition *The Spirits of the Rain Forest* concerning an endangered tribe in the remote jungle of Brazil which opened in The Carnegie and traveled to museums in other cities in the United States.

James L. Swauger, curator emeritus after 47 years with the museum, continues his research on petroglyphs from eastern United States, on dolmens in Israel and Jordon, and completed work on the Ashdod site in Israel.

Curator David A. Watters and Daniel H. Sandwer's initiated a cooperative international scientific endeavor with archaeologists in Cuba.

Headquarters for Anthropology and Mammals is an annex at Baum Boulevard, acquired in 1978 to contain material transferred from the Meridian Anthropology Center. Only about 10% of the specimens are on display in the museum with the rest secured here. In 1992 the annex was named the Edward O'Neil Research Center celebrating the museum's longtime benefactor and trustee.

An article in the *Pittsburgh Post-Gazette*, October 9, 1993, by Barbara White Stack is the source of the information concerning the doll exchange between the United States and Japan.

The information about the law of 1990 regarding potential repatriation of Indian relics was contained in an article by Donald Miller in the *Pittsburgh Post-Gazette*, August 28, 1993.

The Carnegie Museum of Natural History Conservation Laboratory

Conservation is the repair, restoration, and caretaking of the multi-various artifacts in the numerous collections of the different sections of The Museum of Natural History. Caretaking, whether of objects uncovered during excavation for the Pittsburgh Plate Glass Building in downtown Pittsburgh or of ancient Egyptian coffins, includes a wide variety of techniques and skills. "Stabilization" is an important concept that means doing minimal work on an object so its integrity is not compromised by modern chemicals. Conservation includes cleaning and mending of specimens which are also described, photographed, sketched, and prepared for exhibition.

In addition to knowledge of organic materials, it is necessary to have specialized knowledge of the treatment of inorganic materials such as ceramics, faience and jewelry, and bronzes. Conservation of the Egyptian items in preparation for the opening of the Hall of Ancient Egypt ranged from textiles to the funerary boat, which included study of the planks, cross beams, and paddle. At the other end of the scale the temporary exhibit *Spirits of the Rain Forest* encompassed Yanomami objects made of delicate organic materials such as feathers, wax, shell, and wood as well as some stone and metal. The proper level of light and climate control in the gallery was also a concern of the Section of Conservation.

An example of the versatile creativity of conservator Joan Gardner was the design and construction, in 1986, of temporary support systems for each of the museum's Egyptian mummies (26 animals and 4 humans), so they could be safely x-rayed at the Forbes Metropolitan Health Center in Wilkinsburg. The work on the Egyptian objects covered several years.

A grant from the Institute of Museum Services was received in 1988 for a general conservation survey of the holdings of The Carnegie Museum of Natural History. This was the first Institute of Museum Services Conservation Survey Grant awarded to a major natural history museum in the country. Six consulting conservators reviewed the museum's collection in 1989 evaluating all scientific sections, exhibits, education, the library, animal portraiture, security, building and grounds. Their reports are the basis of a long range conservation plans for The Carnegie Museum of Natural History submitted in 1990.

The Carnegie Museum of Natural History
The Council for the Museum

Purpose

The Council for The Museum of Natural History is a service group organized to support the goals and projects of the museum and to enhance its contributions to the community. Council was founded in 1976 to provide a support group for The Museum of Natural History, as the Women's Committee serves for The Museum of Art.

Goals

To participate, as needed, in the planning and execution of ongoing in-house events at the museum; to sponsor programs which will enhance community awareness of the resources and assets of the museum, making it more accessible to the people of all ages; to raise funds for the museum through various means, such as organizing a main event alternate years and to arrange programs designed to educate members of the Council in topics of natural history.

This statement of purpose and goals was adopted by the Executive Committee March 18, 1992, after circulation to the membership. All of the goals listed reflect Council philosophy from the beginning in 1976. An additional goal of the founders was for Council to be a channel for people entering volunteer work at the museum.

Members of the first Executive Committee in 1976 were:

Stewart Steffey, *Co-Chairman*
Farley Whetzel, *Co-Chairman* *
Craig Black, *Museum Director*
Barbara Thorne, *Recording Secretary*
Florence Nimick, *Membership*
Ingrid Rea, *Program* *
Cleveland Rea, *Treasurer*
Mary Tankersley, *Family Members Night*
Ed Brueggman, *(Treasurer of Carnegie Institute),*
    Assistant Treasurer
Joseph Van Buskirk, Esquire, *By-laws*

* *Member, Women's Committee, Museum of Art*

The by-laws were adopted at the initial Council meeting, February 7, 1977. Membership was 131 persons. Meetings then, as now, are held three or four times a year with speakers from the museum.

The newsletter of the Council for The Natural History Museum first appeared in the fall of 1985, edited by Eloise Ruffing with special credit to Jane Konrad and Fraser Foster for its inception. In 1989, after Mrs. Ruffing's death, Elizabeth Mertz became editor. News and notices of Council and museum events and other activities of interest are covered. The Council helps with special museum events, especially *Family Members Night*, with behind the scenes tours of the museum for all members. It also arranges receptions in connection with the opening of new temporary and permanent exhibitions.

The Council, alternatively with the Women's Committee of The Museum of Art, sponsors lectures in the *Man and Ideas* lecture series. This involves a dinner before the program, for sometimes as many as 125 people and often a reception as well, for as many as 500.

The inaugural Council program, February 18, 1976 was part of the *Man and Ideas* series, a lecture by Richard Leaky, with a reception afterwards, sponsored by Rockwell International Corporation. Loudspeakers were provided for the expected and actual overflow audience at the

Invitation cover for "Night on the Nile," a fundraising event sponsored by The Council of the Carnegie Museum of Natural History in 1991.

Carnegie Music Hall. Council organized and provided the reception when the popular Mr. Leakey returned two years later and sold out the Music Hall again as keynote speaker for a program on the *Origins of Man*, sponsored by the National Endowment for the Humanities.

Most recently, in 1992, Suzanne Wilkinson arranged the reception for the opening of the Hall of African Wildlife. Council organized the following *Man and Ideas* lectures in addition to the 1976 Leakey program:

1980 • **Lewis Thomas**, *The Role of Error in Biology*, sponsored by Koppers Company.

1981 • **Isaac Asimov**, *By the Year 2000*.

1981 • **Alvin Toeffler**, sponsored by the Joy Manufacturing Company.

1984 • **Edward O. Wilson**, *The Origin of Human Nature*, sponsored by Mobay Chemical Company.

1984 • **Sir Edmund Hilary**, climber of Mt. Everest, sponsored jointly by Allegheny International, Ketchum Communications, and Mine Safety Appliance Company.

1985 • **Stephen Jay Gould**, *Hens Teeth and Horses Toes*, cocktail reception by Council and Mr. and Mrs. Arthur Scully.

1987 • **Robert Ballard**, explorer of the wreck of the oceanliner Titanic, cocktail reception by Council and Mr. and Mrs. Thomas Nimick, Jr.

1991 • **Robert Bateman**, *Art, Nature and the State of the Earth*, (joint effort with the Women's Committee), sponsored by Mr. and Mrs. Torrence M. Hunt, Sr. and Mr. and Ms. Thomas Nimick, Jr.

1992 • **Walter Lewis and Memory Elvin-Lewis**, *Medicinal Plants Used by the Amazonian Jivaro*, with support from the Hunt Institute for Botanical Documentation, Carnegie Mellon University.

Other fundraising projects have been varied and imaginative:

1984 • *Auction.* Tom and Libby Schmidt co-chaired a live auction of donated objects of interest to Council members, raising over $30,000 for the exhibit and program fund of The Museum of Natural History.

1986 • *Gem Spectacular.* Council member Fraser Foster used the *Gem Spectacular* logo to silk screen shopping bags as favors for this spectacular event at which gems, stones, and jewelry worth more than $3 million were displayed. Sotheby's, auction house of New York, brought 40 pieces of rare and important jewelry, Aurora Corporation showed 60 carats of naturally colored diamonds that were currently featured in *Town & Country* magazine. Amba Gem Corporation displayed a collection of rare Burmese rubies and Kashmiri sapphires and member D. A. Palmieri's company provided a master comparison stone display. The largest intact gold nugget in North America was also on view. Refreshments and tours of the Hillman Hall of Minerals and Gems preceded the raffle drawing for more than $2,000 worth of jewelry and services.

1987 • *Gem Spectacular II.* The collection of rare and unusual gems and jewelry included a pink Burmese sapphire, a faceted topaz of 10,000 carats and other pieces that had never before been seen in Pittsburgh. The exhibition was high-lighted by nine superb floral arrange-ments, designed around minerals in the

Hillman collection, created by members of the Pittsburgh Civic Garden Center. There was also a brunch and fashion show with a drawing for a rainbow bracelet and a diamond ring. The committee was chaired by Fraser Foster assisted by Donald Palmieri, Susan Utech, Suzanna Wean, Richard Souza, Andy Hungerman, David Watters, Suzanne Wilkinson, Libby Schmidt, Mary Louise Gailliot, Connie Black, and Dr. James E. King.

1991 • *Night on the Nile* was chaired by Susan Utech with the help of some 150 volunteers during the year-long planning and the evening of the event. The theme related to the newly opened Walton Hall of Ancient Egypt. There were about 500 guests, mostly in costume, who visited the Hall, enjoyed Egyptian food, shopping in the bazaar, having their picture taken, playing Egyptian games, admiring mideastern gems, and viewing the newly acquired and restored Sphinx, the gift of the Haber family. Belly dancers circulated everywhere, even to the front steps where they attracted quite an audience from Oakland. The festivities netted almost $25,000 to fund the video theater in the Hall of African Wildlife which was open for a preview.

1992 • The reception for the official opening of the **Hall of African Wildlife** was arranged by Suzanne Wilkinson.

1992 • *American Indian Dance Theater.* Suzanne Wilkinson organized a Council theater party to see an excellent Native American dance program at the Fulton Theater. Council members were also invited to attend the Festival of Native American Culture after the dance program.

Holiday Displays

1989 • *Natural History Christmas Trees.* Fraser Foster and Diane Grzybek inaugurated a tradition. Parents and Council members help children make special ornaments to decorate trees in various places in The Museum of Natural History.

1993 • Libby Schmidt and Diane Grzybek coordinated the Christmas Tree project in which children assembled paper peacocks with tails of feathers as decorations for trees at the carriage entrance of The Carnegie.

Information, 1994, by Council President Louis A. Cutter.

Drawing for an invitation by the Council of the Carnegie Museum of Natural History.

The Carnegie Museum of Natural History Division of Earth Sciences Benedum Hall of Geology

Section of Minerals

The scientists of this section are involved with Geology Hall and the Hall of Minerals and Gems. Geology Hall opened on Earth Day April 7, 1980, and in 1990 celebrated the 10th anniversary of Earth Week. Geology is the study of the earth's composition and its history as recorded in rocks. As dwellers on the earth we are aware of the many environmental concerns confronting us now and into the future.

In Geology Hall the exhibit *Our Changing Earth* features a six-foot revolving globe that illustrates the earth and oceans with mountains and low lands. The exhibit answers questions about the earth and the forces that continuously modify it. The actions of water, ice, and wind as they alter the surface of the earth and the processes within the earth that lead to mountain building, volcanoes, and crustal movements are documented through photographs, specimens, and visual programs. A seismograph, operating constantly, records earthquakes and other movements as they occur inside the earth.

The Time Tower in the Benedum Hall of Geology.

Photograph by Tom Barr

The Stratavator takes visitors on a simulated journey down through 16,000 feet of rock layers under Pittsburgh. They watch a miner (via videotape) explain what they observe on their seven-and-a-half minute trip. Benedum Hall also has computer programs called Radiometric Dating and The Pittsburgh Area's Rocky History. Still impressive is the massive wall of layers of rock, tilted to the diagonal through millions of years of pressure and upheaval.

The installation of Geology Hall was initially supported in part by gifts from Mr. and Mrs. Albert Shoemaker and Consolidation Coal Company. As of 1990 the hall had been retitled, updated and expanded, funded by the Claude Worthington Benedum Foundation. The Section of Minerals also worked closely for decades with the Division of Exhibit and Design Production in preparation for the *Hillman Hall of Minerals and Gems* (discussed in detail beginning on page 213). Their joint effort culminated in the creation of both halls.

The Carnegie Museum of Natural History Discovery Room

Planned especially for children "of all ages" is the Discovery Room in the lower floor of the Natural History Museum. It is a treasure-house of horned, hoofed, webbed, and winged creatures, some like the great brown bear, mounted and life-like in their presence. They may be patted, stroked, or touched, "with just two fingers, please" as the eager visitors examine the feathers, fur, wool, and skin of different animals. Shells and rocks in profusion may be handled while other mysteries may be viewed through a microscope. Featured is a Tree for all Seasons — which is changed periodically to depict the seasons — with birds and animals and insects that live in trees and among the roots. Also in due season the brown bear disappears, presumably to hibernate, and a big white polar bear stands tall on his hind feet, dominating the space. Then there are the living creatures lurking in their aquarium homes — waiting to be glimpsed — while overhead a giant turtle hovers, safely, observing all.

In 1994, 79,357 visitors were welcomed to the Discovery Room by 77 volunteers who contributed 5,284 hours of their time to the museum.

The Discovery Room was funded by a Second Century Fund gift from the Scaife Family Foundation.

Carnegie Magazine, September/October 1991 contains more about the Discovery Room and refers to an article in the September 1933 issue of the magazine.

This diorama of the Rocky Mountain Elk depicts a
ritualistic bout between bull elk on the edge of Hayden
Valley overlooking the Yellowstone River.

Photograph courtesy of Carnegie Museum of Natural History

The Carnegie Museum of Natural History The Mellon Hall of North American Mammals

In 1981 the museum received a grant of $1.5
million from the Richard King Mellon Foundation for the complete renovation of the North
American Mammal Hall and the establishment
of a North American Mammal Research Institute. Named in honor of the late Lieutenant
General and Mrs. Richard King Mellon, the
new hall exhibits the mammals by the ecological
units (biomes) of the continent so visitors can
see which animals share the same turf and the
same environment. The North American Mammal Research Institute provides for continuing
research to keep the exhibits and educational
programs up to date.

Starting at a point on the shore near Point
Barrow, Alaska, on floe ice with polar bears
and walruses in the tundra biome, the exhibit
progresses south through: Mountain tundra
(the Rocky Mountains), Dall's sheep and mountain goats; coniferous forests (southern Canada
and northern United States), moose and a
beaver pond; deciduous forests (such as around
here), black bear and white-tailed deer; grass-
lands (the Great Plains), pronghorn antelope, a
bison display; and deserts (the Southwest), the
jaguars and javelina (wild pig) exhibit. Smaller
biomes are included, too, the woodlands between the Rockies and the Sierra Nevadas
(bobcat and hog-nosed skunk), the chaparral
of Southern California (kangaroo rats and brush
rabbit), and the subtropics of Florida (the
Manatee), mammals all!

The Carnegie Museum of Natural History
The Hall of African Wildlife

The Hall of African Wildlife became a reality in 1993 because of the combined visions and generosity of Torrence Hunt, Sr. and Willard F. Rockwell, Jr. It was in 1980 that a gift from Mr. Hunt of the Hunt Foundations of Pittsburgh made possible the display of "George" in the museum. A 350-pound silverback gorilla in the prime of life, he came from Gabon in the 1960s. George was obtained from the Pittsburgh Zoo in 1979, after he died unexpectedly of natural causes at the age of 14. When the Hall of African Wildlife became a project of Carnegie's Second Century Fund, the Rockwell Foundation and the Hunt Foundations of Pittsburgh gave additional funds for the construction of the 3,500 square foot gallery. And George may now be seen in his natural habitat.

Among Africa's over 800 mammal species are some of the largest animals in the world, many of which are found on the continent's savannas. Estimates of the continent's total biological diversity indicate over 57,000 species of plants, 2,000 species of amphibians and reptiles, and 1,900 species of birds. The total number of insects is undetermined, but it is well over one million. Represented in the hall are Africa's four major life zones or "biomes:" savanna, rain forest, mountain, and desert. Each biome has its own climatic conditions and a distinctive plant and animal life.

The black rhinoceros standing at the entrance to the Hall of African Wildlife is an epoxy replica of an animal shot in 1909 by the former

Replica of the Rhinoceros shot in 1909 by former President of the United States, Theodore Roosevelt.

president of the United States, Theodore Roosevelt. His safari for the Smithsonian Institution, Washington, D.C. crossed paths with that of young Childs Frick (1883-1965) who was collecting for The Carnegie Museum of Natural History. Childs Frick was the son of Pittsburgh industrialist Henry Clay Frick, an associate of Andrew Carnegie. Young Frick made two safaris to East Africa from 1909 to 1911. In those days a safari was a huge and dangerous undertaking, with guides, pack animals, and bearers to carry all the provisions needed for a trek of many months. Largely as a result of his expeditions the museum has an excellent collection of large African mammals in family groups that were gathered and prepared many years ago. It would be impossible to create the collection today because strict regulations now protect wildlife in Africa. The black rhinoceros is an endangered species, having been nearly poached to extinction due to the demand. In Yemen the horns are used to make dagger handles and in the Far East are sought for their alleged qualities as an aphrodisiac.

The Section of Mammals has provided the most dramatic specimens in the hall but expertise and specimens have also been drawn from the sections of amphibians and reptiles, birds, botany, entomology, or invertebrate zoology. Some of the animals obtained were prepared and exhibited more than 70 years ago and are being seen again for the first time in decades. They are still among the best in the world, the work of the Santens brothers from Belgium who raised their taxidermy technology to high art in the realistic reproduction of animals in life-like poses. Their artistry included surface details indicating blood vessels, tendons, and realistic touches such as mud on the buffalo's head and saliva in the mouth.

Ten different species from the Santens' original mounts are displayed — all collected on the Childs Frick expeditions. Salted and dried,

the specimens arrived into the hands of the Santenses, recognized as among the best taxidermists of their day. Rather than going to Africa, the Santens brothers made regular trips to the Bronx Zoo to observe the animals' movements. They then treated and stretched the hides over lifelike models made from wood, metal and clay.

The Hall of African Wildlife developed from work in Kenya by Carnegie scientists under the O'Neil Field Research Fund. It was established in the early 1970s by Edward O'Neil, friend and trustee of The Carnegie Museum of Natural History. Mr. O'Neil, 84, died in his home on October 3, 1993.

The taxidermy crew led by Remi Santens (on ladder) places skin on a giraffe mannequin circa 1910. Anna Dierdorf is assisting. The Carnegie giraffes were the first full mounts ever displayed in the United States.

Photograph courtesy of Carnegie Museum of Natural History

Calcite from the Joplin Mining District in Missouri.

Photograph courtesy of Carnegie Museum of Natural History

The Carnegie Museum of Natural History Division of Earth Sciences Hillman Hall of Minerals and Gems

"Minerals" covers a wide spectrum — from table salt (for which the South American natives traded gold!) to the 500 pound section of an amethyst geodite from outer space which landed in Brazil.

The sparkling 5,400 square foot hall was the gift of the Hillman Foundation and the creation of the Division of Exhibit and Design Production in consultation with the scientists in the Section of Minerals. A decade of cooperative effort culminated with the opening in 1980. This spectacular exhibit hall acquaints the viewer with basic facts about crystals, minerals, and rocks. The seven crystal systems, for example, are described and illustrated. Some are distinguishing properties of minerals such as fluorescence, phosphorescence, radioactivity, cleavage and fracture, which are examined through

Beryl, variety aquamarine; Nagar, Hunza, Pakistan.

Photograph by Harold and Erica Van Pelt

"hands-on" demonstrations. In yet another area, over 350 minerals are grouped systematically according to chemical composition. Pennsylvania's mineralogical diversity is exhibited with information on coal and other minerals that have been important to the state's economic development.

The original collection had been augmented by a bequest of precious carved jade and ivory from Henry J. Heinz, who, at his death in 1919, was honorary curator of the section as well as a trustee of Carnegie Institute.

In the inaugural year of the hall a total of 219 specimens were received by 40 gifts and nine purchases. Included in this group are a set of seven carvings of Russian nobility and peasants by Manfred Wild in the style of his grandfather, who was master carver for Fabergé in the mid-1800s; a carat diamond gem from India; a masterpiece specimen of tennantite on white blades of crystalline quartz; various special types of crystal from Morocco and Afghanistan; a large platinum nugget from Russia; and a carving of two monkeys in a tree, in gem quality red crystal opal.

Regrettably, the magnificent diamond disappeared from its supposedly secure case the next year, leaving a vacuum filled in 1982. Insurance coverage made possible replacement of the gem with a light yellow, round, brilliant cut diamond weighing 15.5 carats. The following year the Hillman Foundation donated a significant collection of gold to the museum.

Through the support of the Hillman Foundation, the section currently has one of the most active and successful minerals acquisition programs of any major American museum. Among the 1986 acquisitions are the largest and finest cluster in existence of powellite from India; a superb golden topaz crystal from Brazil; and one of the largest hibonite crystals from Madagascar. In addition, a donation of a 90 carat, deep amber-colored calcite gemstone is the finest example of its kind.

The birthstone display created in 1985 was extended into 1987 and beyond, because it proved to be extremely popular with the public. The section assisted the Natural History Council in the 1986 first Carnegie *Gem Spectacular* show. For the show, the museum borrowed the, "largest single North American gold nugget currently in existence." An excellent collection of jewelry from Sotheby's, New York, joined the exhibit arranged by Donald Palmieri, gemnologist and research associate of the section. He also held a series of informative lectures concerning purchasing gemstones and jewelry.

International Mineralogical Award Created

In 1988 as part of the Second Century Fund campaign the Henry L. Hillman Foundation established an endowment fund for the Section of Minerals and Gems and created a new international award — *The Carnegie Mineralogical Award*. It is given annually to a recipient recognized for major contributions to the preservation, conservation, and educational use of minerals. The award carries a bronze medallion, a certificate of recognition, and a cash prize of $2,500. In 1988, the Tucson Gem and Mineral Society was selected as the inaugural recipient for its 35 years of dedication in presenting the annual Tucson Gem and Mineral Show, the largest public minerals-related event in the world. Each year at that show *The Carnegie Mineralogic Award* winner is announced. Recipients of the award in successive years were: Dr. Frederick H. Pough, John Sinkankas, Paul E. Desautels, (former curator of minerals for the Smithsonian Institution) and, in February 1994, Cornelius Hurlbut, Harvard professor, author of, "the standard textbook on minerals."

Participation by The Carnegie in national mineral exhibitions dramatically increased in 1989 and the section was represented for the first time in the 21-year history of the Denver Gem and Mineral Show. In addition to the two top national shows, items from the jewelry collection were loaned to the Philadelphia Academy of Science, and gold specimens went to the opening of California State Mining and Mineral Museum in Mariposa, California. Meanwhile, a major inventory of the collection was completed, covering 20 years of historical and accession recording, reexamining over 2,700 specimens and producing a computer-based catalogue of the collection. A portion of the Thomas McKee Mineral Collection was acquired in 1988, bringing superb crystals of vivianite from Idaho to the museum. In fact, of the 45 items acquired in 1988 seven were of masterpiece quality. Each annual report describes in scientific nomenclature and detail the acquisitions and donations of specific gems and minerals from around the world — too numerous to list but suffice it to say that the collection has doubled since the opening of the hall in 1980.

The period from 1983-1988 was one of tremendous growth in the exhibit, educational programming and utilization of the section and its collection. Eighteen exceptional items were acquired, including 11 important Bolivian specimens by purchase, and by gift, a remark-able Art Deco jewelry piece designed by Andrey Avinoff, director of The Carnegie Museum of Natural History, 1926-1945.

The former Collection Manager, Richard A. Souza, co-authored *Minerals of The Carnegie Museum of Natural History* which had wide distribution as a special supplement to The Mineralogical Record of September/October 1990. Written in honor of the hall's tenth anniversary the article contained an overview of the section's history and a photographic essay on some of its outstanding mineral specimen. The *Anniversary Celebration* was an exhibit of rare gems and minerals in observation of the hall's brilliant decade, expanded and enhanced by the continuing interest and generosity of the Hillman Foundation. A traveling exhibition displayed highlights of the collection at the 1990 mineral

shows in Tucson and Denver. Acknowledged as one of the finest mineral exhibition halls in North America it has fulfilled the original idea of Henry L. Hillman, its donor, to provide an exhibit of, "minerals in the manner of sculpture and shown for their beauty as well as physical properties and economic uses."

Carnegie Magazine, April 1980, Volume 54, Number 4, Pages 13-18.

Rhodochrosite; Sweet Home Mine, Alma, Park County, Colordo.

Photograph by Debra Wilson

This scene of a 19th century snowhouse interior is included in Carnegie Museum of Natural History's "Polar World: Wyckoll Hall of Arctic Life" exhibit. A woman and child can be seen on the sleeping platform where they are preparing a fox skin for use.

Photograph courtesy of Carnegie Museum of Natural History

The Carnegie Museum of Natural History Polar World: The Wyckoff Hall of Arctic Life

From 1902 to 1980 The Carnegie Museum of Natural History mounted 38 expeditions to the Arctic and sub-Arctic. Their collective achievements are incorporated into Polar World which opened in 1983, the first major anthropologic hall in the museum since 1913. It is named for George W. Wyckoff, Jr., a long-time friend of the museum with an active interest in the Arctic. The results of the years of field work and design preparation are evident in the dioramas and exhibits, especially *Arctic Adaptations: The Ever-Changing Eskimo.* It focuses on cultural change through 4,500 years of time and the influence of the harsh environment and social contact with foreigners on the native way of life

in the central Canadian Arctic. They now are properly known as Inuit, "the people" rather than Eskimo, "eaters of raw flesh," a name given them by other peoples.

Polar World captures the atmosphere of the frozen North along with one's imagination. At the entrance a caribou and a musk ox nearby seem to be observing the visitor. There is a sense of the vast emptiness and stillness even in the presence of the life-size human figures in the acts of harpooning a walrus and spearing fish in the icy water. One may enter the snow house or igloo and observe native family life in their winter home on the ice during the walrus hunting season. In summer they lived in a caribou-skin tent on land.

A series of films with chilling sounds of the wind and the howling of wolves gives further insights into the way of life of these Arctic people. "How to build a snow house" is just one of the things a visitor learns. The small theater is named for Mr. Wyckoff, who filmed the original footage for a documentary of Peungitoo, perhaps the last of the self-sufficient Inuit following the traditional way of life.

Displayed is the amazingly inventive array of tools like the snow shovel carved from whale bone or the little pouch made from birds feet sewn together. There is a case full of scrimshaw, the carving on ivory, often the work of sailors on their long voyages.

The intrusion of foreigners is also documented in the model of the sailing ship H. M. S. Erebus which was trapped in the ice September 12, 1846 while seeking a northwest passage to the Orient. Shown are the men making a sledge from a longboat to carry the provisions unloaded from the vessel in preparation for the long winter there. The sister ship aptly named the H. M. S. Terror was also locked in the ice and both were abandoned in April of 1848. All 129 men from the two ships were lost. History records that the search for the northwest passage was pursued as early as 1576 by Sir Matthew Forbisher of England.

The large collection of modern Inuit art, including paintings, sculptures, carvings in soapstone, bone, and ivory, and other artifacts was given by Mrs. Adolph Schmidt, née Helen Mellon, with additions from the Harry M. Price Collection. The hall and related interpretive materials and programs were made possible through the generous support of over 220 individuals, 14 Pittsburgh foundations, and the National Endowment for the Humanities.

As one leaves Polar World, a full-color photograph of a life-sized polar bear on the wall above gives the visitor the sense of having actually been to the North Pole.

The Offering Diorama, located at the entrance to the new Walton Hall of Ancient Egypt show Sety I, a New Kingdom pharaoh, making an offering of two alabaster jars to the falcon-headed god Horus.

Photograph by Melinda McNaugher

The Carnegie Museum of Natural History
The Walton Hall of Ancient Egypt

The Walton Hall of Ancient Egypt opened in February, 1990, as a project of the Second Century Fund, almost 100 years after the museum acquired the first of its Egyptian antiquities.

The coffin of an Egyptian mummy was given by Andrew Carnegie on June 1, 1896, establishing the collection which, by 1980, had grown to more than 4,900 ethnographic and historic items. Many of these came originally through the efforts of international teams of researchers sponsored by the Pittsburgh Chapter of the Egyptian Exploration Society, which was formed at the turn into the 20th century.

A 2,000 year old Ptolemaic stone sphinx, weighing about a ton, now outside the Walton Hall was given by the Haber family in 1989, in memory of Dr. Richard E. Haber. The sphinx, recovered from the harbor of Alexandria in Egypt, was purchased and brought by Henry J. Heinz to adorn the garden of his home in Pittsburgh some 75 to 100 years ago.

Displayed in the hall is a 3,900 year old funerary boat, one of only two in the United States. It was excavated near Dashur and dates to the 12th dynasty of pharaoh Senwosret III. Andrew Carnegie gave it to the museum in 1901. By purchase in 1934 from Muenchener Gobelin Manufaktur in Germany, the museum acquired an extensive collection of Coptic textiles. Although not exhibited, all of the items were thoroughly researched and conserved. In the process, an X-ray analysis by the Forbes Health System of one of the museum's Egyptian mummies from Abydos revealed that it is that of an eight- or nine-year-old child. Boy or girl was a question not answered. In any case a number of educational games on Egyptian themes were developed for children visiting the hall.

An interactive information-reference system supplies information that complements exhibit labels and graphics nearby. A video gives ten six-minute presentations on topics such as mummies, temples, etc. using high quality film images from various sites in Egypt. The interactive technology, developed at Carnegie Mellon University, shows real artifacts in relation to original contexts, with moving images, digitalized still images, ancient text translations, and accompanying modern analyses and commentaries.

The artists of the Division of Exhibit and Design created the colorful nine foot tall statues of the Egyptian god Horus and Pharaoh Seti I as well as the life-size mannequins of Egyptian craftsmen. The ceremonial burial vault of a mid-level functionary was recreated in vivid color and detail based on careful scientific research by Lynn Holden, artist and associate dean of the College of Fine Arts, Carnegie Mellon University.

The architectural design of the hall gives one the sensation of being in an underground labyrinth of chambers similar to those in the actual tombs carved beneath the Egyptian desert. The hall was seven years from concept to completion. It was funded by $900,000 from the National Endowment for the Humanities plus a generous $500,000 grant from the Rachel Mellon Walton Fund of the Pittsburgh Foundation, in honor of her son, James Mellon Walton and his sixteen years as president of The Carnegie (1968-1984).

Carnegie Magazine September/October, 1991, by Lynn Holden; "New Light on Ancient Egypt: Using Computers to Understand Traditional Cultures"

The Carnegie Science Center
The Buhl Planetarium and Institute of
Popular Science, 1939

Original photograph by Ken Balzer, photograph enhancement/special
effects by Jeff Boyd; photograph courtesy of Carnegie Magazine

The Carnegie Science Center.

Photograph courtesy of The Carnegie Science Center

The Carnegie Science Center which opened October 20, 1991 could be likened to a galaxy which is composed of many stars. A major "star" is the new Henry Buhl, Jr. Planetarium and Observatory. It is the direct descendant of The Buhl Planetarium and Institute of Popular Science which opened on the North Side of Pittsburgh in 1939. This was the gift of the Buhl Foundation in memory of Henry Buhl, Jr. (1856-1927) who used his $11 million estate to establish the foundation in honor of his wife, Louise. His fortune was derived from the fine department store Boggs & Buhl which served the carriage trade in old Allegheny for many years. Twelve years after his death, The Buhl Planetarium was considered a marvel in 1939. The fifth planetarium built in the United States, it featured a Model II Zeiss Star Projector (the only modified one still in use) which could project the skies as they appeared tens of thousands of years in the past, or in the future.

During World War II, 1939-1944, the Buhl trained the military in celestial navigation. It opened the Junior Space Academy in 1958 as a local response to the dawning of the Space Age with the launching of the space-craft SPUTNIK by the Union of Soviet Socialist Republics. (A bit of The Carnegie in the form of a six-foot banner reading, "1991 — A banner year for Jay Apt and The Carnegie Science Center" accompanied Pittsburgh's first shuttle astronaut into space. The banner is displayed in The Science Center in acknowledgment of the former Buhl Planetarium's role in sparking Jay Apt's interest in becoming an astronaut.)

The Carnegie and The Buhl Science Center

In the late 1970s, after 30 years of service to the science-thirsty public in Allegheny County, planning began to update the planetarium by bringing the new technology of an Omnimax Theater to Pittsburgh. By 1982 the newly renamed Buhl Science Center was operating independently of the supportive Buhl Foundation and the new president Joshua C. Whetzel, Jr. was exploring specific expansion plans. Various sites were considered before the most dramatic was made possible by a unique partnership.

Hailing the Carnegie-Buhl merger, an editorial in the *Pittsburgh Post-Gazette* July 15, 1986 said, "Joshua C. Whetzel, Jr. in four years as president of Buhl has changed it from a sleepy planetarium on the North Side to a showcase for the latest in science and technology, including computers and robots. His latest achievement and a coup for Pittsburgh was garnering $13.8 million from the legislature for a new center with a 300-seat Omnimax large-screen theater, expected to be a major tourist attraction."

Since Mr. Whetzel is the son-in-law of Rachel Mellon Walton, his successful diplomacy was historically reminiscent. It was the public-private partnership of the democratic mayor of Pittsburgh David L. Lawrence and republican banker Richard King Mellon (cousin of Mrs. Walton) which resulted in cleaning the city's smoke-filled air in the late 1940s. Decades later the politically democratic city of Pittsburgh and Allegheny County offered riverfront land on the Ohio River as the site for a new science center plus essential financial support. Republican governor of Pennsylvania Dick Thornburgh sponsored a commitment from the Commonwealth, and the trustees of the Buhl Foundation tripled their gift to $3 million for the Henry Buhl, Jr. Planetarium and Observatory to be located in the new science center. Also necessary was the agreement of the Pennsylvania Department of Transportation to reroute North Shore Drive to accommodate the great building on the shore of the river.

In 1987 The Buhl Science Center merged into The Carnegie. By 1991 Carnegie's Second Century Fund had designated $40 million from government and private resources for The Carnegie Science Center (so named in 1989). By mid-1994, commitments from 91 donors, individuals, families, corporations, foundations, and government totaled $40.4 million, with an additional $1 million needed to be raised.

When ground was broken for the new building on October 5, 1989, more than 800 volunteers formed a living wall to outline the structure. The original Buhl Planetarium, renamed The Carnegie Science Center, Allegheny Square Annex, continued during the construction phase as a fully-developed education facility for the outreach activities of The Science Center, giving Pittsburgh one of the largest public science programs in the country. In addition, The Carnegie in 1992 purchased the Miller Printing Company's building on the North Side for $3,293,602.74, to provide for further space needs of The Science Center.

The Carnegie Science Center opens in 1991

The pre-opening sneak preview of this gigantic, magical Science Center was, "Black tie and Sneakers" a highly successful $200 per ticket gala "celebrity preview," which engaged the efforts of volunteers from throughout the Carnegie complex. A new STAR was born with the formation of a Steering and Resource Committee, "to promote, enhance, and support The Carnegie Science Center as it educates, excites, entertains, and inspires the widest possible audience through interactive public exhibits and programs in science technology; as it provides for excellence in science among highly motivated children, adults, and educators; and as it positions Pittsburgh as a major tourist attraction." Suzy Broadhurst was succeeded by Mary Jo Winokur as chairperson of STARS as of 1994.

During the first 30 days of operation, more than 65,000 visitors discovered how fun and exciting science can be. Featuring more than 250 hands-on exhibits and 1,000 seats in four theaters, The Science Center lets visitors see the big picture in film on the Rangos Omnimax Theater's gigantic domed screen; visit children's discovery areas; figure out the physics of a curve ball; get a taste of the science of eating; discover a tornado in the refrigerator; tour the galaxies in the world's most technologically sophisticated planetarium; and delight in the view and menu in a cafe with a river front terrace.

Carnegie Magazine, September/October 1991 issue was devoted to an article by the editor, R. Jay Gangewere, about the new Science Center designed by Pittsburgh architect Tasso Katselas whose body of work includes Greater Pittsburgh International Airport. The history and development of the center is detailed and the complex is vividly described. This is a condensed excerpt: "A walking tour of the science complex starts with the giant-size bronze and stone compass set in the ground in front of the main entrance. Inside is the interactive

Aquabatics Fountain a 'water machine' which rises almost 30 feet into the air, demonstrating different hydraulic principles and allowing visitors to control the flow of water. It was made possible by the contributions and efforts of Mr. and Mrs. Quentin C. McKenna and the Pittsburgh High Technology Council and others."

Rangos Omnimax Theater
Traveling exhibits are shown in the four-story-high atrium gallery which is surrounded by a spiral network of sunlit ramps from floor to floor linking the 40,000 square feet of exhibition space. A two-ton projector and giant spools of film rise by elevator from the ground floor lobby to produce the thrilling sight and sound experience of the, "ultimate trip" offered in the Rangos Omnimax Theater. It is named for donor John C. Rangos, Sr., chairman of the Chambers Development Charitable Foundation whose $5 million gift was the largest private donation to date — in 1991. The screening of *Grand Canyon: The Hidden Secrets* in 1993 broke attendance records as it was viewed by almost a quarter of a million people. *Yellowstone,* an exciting adventure in history, geography, and geology at the Omnimax Theater the second half of 1994 may well test that record.

The Buhl Planetarium & Observatory, New in 1991
The new 156-seat Henry Buhl, Jr. Planetarium & Observatory incorporates the most advanced technology available. The old Zeiss projector has been replaced by Digistar, a computerized projector which is capable of showing a whole list of non-astronomical simulations as well, including chemical reactions, the human brain, and a 3-D trip through downtown Pittsburgh and up the USX building. Beneath the 50-foot aluminum dome, no two shows are exactly the same because of the interaction by the audience with the programs.

The Science Center in 1993 produced its first planetarium show *Cosmic Perceptions*, selected for its excellence by the International Planetarium Society to show at their 1994 conference. Also produced in Pittsburgh by an international team led by the planetarium staff at The Carnegie Science Center, *Seven Wonders of the Sun* takes viewers on a flight through the solar system to the sun.

Health Science Theater
The Blue Cross Health Science Theater, with 300 seats, extends from the first level to the second and presents programs dealing with human biology, health and medicine, and contemporary advances in biomedical disciplines.

Special Exhibits
Continuing up the ramp the visitor reaches the Science Way where scientific principles behind ordinary objects and familiar scenes are illustrated, while in the nearby Gallery of Illusions nothing is what it appears to be. Live sky shows take place in the evenings and are fed to the planetarium from the rooftop observatory. Thus visitors can enjoy using the observatory which has a 16-inch, "university grade" telescope.

On the third level is Ports of Discovery, a three-part, water-related area consisting of the Aquarium, Early Learners' Landing, and Science Pier. The Aquarium, a low-maintenance, balanced coral reef ecosystem, consists of four large tanks representing the distinct environments of more than 100 species of ocean inhabitants.

Children ages three to six learn science and technology concepts through enjoyable activities in Early Learners' Landing. For example, they may travel to the bottom of the ocean in an Exploratory Submersible, where they can operate the ship's controls, climb into a make-believe seascape, and identify ocean creatures. The Interactive Watertable encourages experimentation with water. Children may change the water's flow by operating gates, dams, and paddle wheels or draw water from one pool to another by using an Archimedes screw.

Magnetics and Optics

An array of hands-on activities stimulates sensory awareness in Magnetics and Optics. Young scientists experiment with magnetic mitts, kaleidoscopes, lenses, mirrors, and more. Children from seven to 13 are challenged by activities on a higher level in Science Pier. In Laser Lab colorful exhibits reveal facts about lasers which have a variety of uses, including holograms, telephone technology, surgery, and light show. Biosphere encourages children to explore the diversity of life. Waterscape is a 20-foot-long watertable featuring a large reservoir, working lock, water wheel, and river velocity station. Up-to-the-minute information about the conditions of the Ohio River as it flows past The Science Center is shown in the Riverscope display. HyperSpace features four computer work stations within modern triangular truss walls where children operate laser videodiscs.

Exhibit of H. J. Heinz Company

The Eating Exhibit of the H. J. Heinz Company Foundation presents the entire range of food-related activities: food acquisition; food processing; preservation and packaging; body processes and nutrition; plus cultural, ritualistic, and social aspects of eating. Learn also about the latest agricultural advances that make it possible for only 3% of the U. S. population to feed the entire nation, compared to 70% in agriculture at the start of the 19th century. The Body Walk is the 21-foot-long mechanized model of the human digestive system. Topics such as feeding a rapidly growing world population, the bioengineering of plants and animals, and the safety of food preservatives are graphically explained.

The Discovery Hive — a honeycomb of cells with activity boxes for children.

Photograph courtesy of The Carnegie Science Center

Electronic Exhibit Theater

Set in an environment rich with industrial flare, The Works is actually an Electronic Exhibit Theater showing how the properties of natural phenomena — energy, matter, and information — have been applied to industry through technological innovation. The Works also transforms into a dramatic theater for the presentation of SCIENCE SPECTACULAR, a 20-minute, multi-media extravaganza that focuses on each of the five stages individually. Through sound, lighting, fog, and other special effects, the entire space comes alive and involves the audience in an adventure into the unknown.

Changing Exhibits

The changing scientific treats at The Carnegie Science Center range from hi-tech to home-on-the-range tech as described by Suzanne Martinson in the *Post-Gazette* article December 1, 1993. Chemistry is the secret ingredient in *Chocolate Decadence*, a cake made without flour, baking soda, or baking powder. It was a hit with the full-house crowd at the demonstration kitchen in the Heinz, "Eating" exhibit. Created by chef Gregory Rollins of Christopher's restaurant on Pittsburgh's Mount Washington, the culinary recipe was described in terms of chemistry. Others of the changing exhibitions are equally, "visitor friendly" in translating scientific terms for the enlightenment and enjoyment of most of us but just don't taste as good. New for the second half of 1994, *Star Trek: Federation Science* updates the old *Star Trek* series which first aired 30 years ago and combines today's real science technology with the fantastic vision of the future. More than 30 interactive exhibits focus on space travel and the scientific principles which are a challenge for the future.

The Miniature Railway

An enduring favorite with the public is the Miniature Railway, for years a magnet attraction at the original Buhl Planetarium. Charles Bowdish, a hobbyist from Brookville, Pennsylvania, began construction of the railroad in 1917, and first displayed it to entertain guests during a Christmas wedding in 1920. By 1952, the display had grown so much in size and popularity that Bowdish's insurance agency was reluctant to cover the thousands of guests who passed through his home. Therefore, a new location was sought, and the first "Christmastown Railroad" debuted at The Buhl Planetarium in 1954. The railroad remained at Buhl for 37 years.

Since that time, the railroad has moved to The Carnegie Science Center and has expanded 60 percent to occupy 2,300 square feet of exhibit space. Hundreds of staff and volunteers have dedicated thousands of hours to the improvement of the ever-changing display. This animated journey through 1920s Western Pennsylvania celebrated its 40th season in 1994. There are more than 2,000 handpainted figures, 100 animations, and dozens of historical replicas, including the birthplace of Rachel Carson,

Pittsburgh's Monongahela Incline, and a ferris wheel, in honor of the ride's 100th anniversary. Night turns into day and back to night again by computer-controlled, updated switches, signals etc., installed in time for the holiday season of 1993.

The educational outreach programs attracted 105,000 students and teachers in five states and the overall attendance at The Carnegie Science Center reached 606,000 in 1993. A new, permanent, interactive exhibit is *The Science of Baseball*. It was created at The Science Center, with the assistance of the Pittsburgh Pirates, and the cooperation of AT&T which donated its 1993 Airports, Science, and Technology vignettes. Little Leaguers and big leaguers may test their reaction times, pitching speed, etc. . .a sure winner.

An additional challenge for the future was met with the appointment of Seddon L. Bennington of Perth, Australia, to head The Carnegie Science Center, starting August 17, 1994. He was chief executive officer and funding director of Scitech Discovery Centre in Perth and succeeds Al DeSena who directed the $40 million Carnegie Science Center for its first 18 months.

World War II Submarine

The Science Center extends beyond it's dramatic building to the river's edge where there is moored a, "vintage" World War II submarine, the USS Requin, now a four-star attraction as an adjunct to The Carnegie Science Center. Launched January 1, 1945 in Portsmouth, New Hampshire, the Requin, named after a voracious species of sand shark, was sent to Guam in the South Pacific but saw no naval action as the war against Japan ended August 15, 1945. In 1959 the conning tower was replaced by a larger one of fiberglass, with a silhouette similar to nuclear submarines in order to mislead potential enemies. The Requin was in active duty for 23 years, finally as a Naval Reserve training ship.

The *USS Requin*, the WWII submarine moored in front of The Carnegie Science Center, has had more than 118,000 visitors since arriving in Pittsburgh in the fall of 1990.

Photograph courtesy of The Carnegie Science Center

Based in Tampa, Florida, by 1968 as a tourist attraction, it was unappreciated and out-of-place there. In April 1990 President Bush signed a bill transferring the USS Requin from the city of Tampa to The Carnegie. With approval of the Secretary of the Navy, the late Senator John Heinz (republican from Fox Chapel, Pittsburgh) had sponsored the legislation expediting the transfer.

The trip to Pittsburgh was ignominious for the 312-foot submarine. Held in a giant sling, towed backwards by four barges, from Tampa across the Gulf of Mexico to New Orleans, up the Mississippi and the Ohio it reached the North Shore of the Allegheny River. Dredges had to clear the mud to provide a proper berth for the submarine. Dedication ceremonies were held October 20, 1990, preceding the opening of The Carnegie Science Center by one year. In the six weeks, "sneak preview" more than 16,200 visitors toured the non-submersible submarine. It had been repaired, refurbished, repainted, and cleaned by 95% volunteer effort, primarily given by members of the various labor unions within the Pittsburgh Building Trades Association. Naval ROTC students

from McKeesport helped, other Naval groups donated signal flags and welding and electrical expertise. A video of the ship was produced by Carnegie Mellon graduate students who had the idea while waiting in the line to view the submarine.

The last official captain of the USS Requin was Rear Admiral Leroy Collins who attended the dedication. The day-to-day skipper is Thomas Flaherty, a, "fresh out of the Navy" sailor.

The proper pronunciation of the vessel's name varies depending on the authority: Ron Baillie of The Carnegie chooses RECK-QUIN, Al Regits who served on the sub in the early 1950s says RAY-QUIN, and Webster's 3rd International Unabridged Dictionary selects RECK-INN.

Special edition of *Carnegie Magazine*, September/October 1991; "The Carnegie Science Center" by Editor R. Jay Gangewere.

Carnegie Magazine, July/August, 1994 "Star Trek: Federation Science" by Abby Mendelson.

Articles about the USS Requin:
Pittsburgh Post-Gazette:
February 23, 1990 by Tom Barnes
September 6, October 19, and December 10, 1990, all by Gabriel Ireton.

The Pittsburgh Press: April 15, 1990 by Dwight C. Daniels.

Andrew Carnegie, 1981, by Andy Warhol, American;
Richard M. Scaife American Paintings Fund, 1981.

The Andy Warhol Museum, located on the North Side at Sandusky and General Robinson streets, just across the 7th Street Bridge from downtown Pittsburgh, is one of the museums of Carnegie Institute and is a collaborative project of Carnegie Institute, Dia Center for the Arts, and The Andy Warhol Foundation for the Visual Arts, Inc.

Photograph © 1994 Paul Rocheleau

Opening and Dedication

Almost 100 years after three days of dignified festivities marked the opening of Andrew Carnegie's Palace of Culture, housing The Carnegie Library, The Museum of Natural History, and the Department of Art, Andy Warhol, Prince of Pop, Pittsburgh's other poor boy turned mega-rich, also rated a three-day extravaganza. His museum opened Friday May 13, 1994 and joined the pantheon of The Carnegie.

The three-day weekend of "raucous revelry" included a 24-hour marathon open house from midnight of the 14th to midnight of the 15th "free to the people" on a space-available basis. Bus tours to view Andy's birthplace, schools, church, and grave-site cost $10. One visitor, Regis McGuigan did not go inside the museum that night and was not among the 113 persons taking the tour. He was the artist with Donatelli Memorials who had carved the simple inscription on Andy Warhol's black granite tombstone.

Among the 10,000 invitees, those in attendance vying for photo-ops were far fewer than the number of celebrities expected. One who did show was Warhol film star Ultra Violet, born Isabelle Collin Dufresne, in Isere, France. Dennis Hopper, another star who rose from the underground to fame in *Easy Rider* attended, as did filmmaker John Waters and Pittsburgh artist J. S. G. Boggs, subject of the film *Money Man*. Fellow Pop artist Roy Lichtenstein found the galleries "spectacular." Fashion designer Mary McFadden was photographed with Stuart Pivar, Andy's companion on his daily shopping sprees. His friend and biographer Bob Colacello was also present. Fresh from hosting a Warhol Museum pre-opening bash in his New York restaurant frequented by Warhol cronies, Michael Chow was on hand for the real thing. The man credited with masterminding the promotion and merchandising of Andy Warhol's art, Fred Hughes was prominently present.

A big white tent sheltered the 2,200 invited guests at the seated dinner Friday, ($300 each), catered by the exclusive Duquesne Club and Saturday evening's buffet, ($125), catered by the also exclusive Pittsburgh Golf Club. Meanwhile nonstop variety acts entertained the crowd of 5,000 waiting patiently to be admitted to the museum, no more than 1,000 at a time. Then, in a reversal of the Cinderella theme, at midnight the sky over the Allegheny River was alight with fireworks, including a profile image of Andy Warhol. The doors opened, the people thronged in, and at 5 a.m. there were still hundreds hoping to enter.

Inside the museum, in a white room containing one of the most popular exhibits, *Silver Clouds* with dozens of free floating pillow-shaped mylar balloons, some visitors were having pillow fights, popping the balloons and keeping the tattered remnants for souvenirs. Workers filled fresh balloons for awhile but it was a losing battle, to the consternation of guest artist Billy Kluver, the Bell Labs scientist who had collaborated with Warhol on the work in 1966.

On Sunday afternoon families with children were on hand for the street fair, to enjoy the music, balloons, and the special attractions from other branches of The Carnegie. Among those present were creatures from The Carnegie Science Center, in cages of course, including a boa constrictor and a colony of two-inch-long "giant hissing cockroaches from Madagascar." Children ogled them and moved on to the next table of The Museum of Art where they could crayon different colored visages of Andy Warhol. The Museum of Natural History featured a smorgasbord of bones — from shin bones to skulls — which travel to schools and hospitals in the Museum on the Move program. Meanwhile, weary parents listened to the music and sat at the round tables, which on Friday night were centered with neon Warhol profiles (available for $400), and were now graced by Heinz Ketchup bottles, symbolic of one of the most generous sponsors of the blockbuster event.

Also on Sunday afternoon the official dedication ceremonies were held amid the towering white flower arrangements in the entrance lobby of the museum. Returning for the occasion were Teresa Heinz, widow of the late Senator John Heinz, Governor Robert Casey, looking fit with his new heart transplant, Senator Harris Wofford, local political and other dignitaries. Pittsburgh's Mayor Tom Murphy, with his silver hair and youthful physique, good-naturedly posed to be photographed with the large look-alike self-portrait of bewigged Warhol which dominates the space.

The *New York Times* in an article titled *Warhol Museum: A Shrine for an Iconoclast* observed, "Its remarkable, singularly appropriate new home. . . its austere, open spaces and contrasts of quietly sensuous materials: tinted plaster, galvanized iron, brushed aluminum, and etched glass, as well as cork and concrete, also make it one of the best looking and most comfortable museums to come along in some time."

"Housed within this structure are extensive holdings of Warhol Art and Warholiana . . . an amazing sweep of innovation, of subjects, media and even history . . . Warhol helped open art to a new power of the everyday — that not quite real reality that played in the media, in advertising, and the movies — and he drew its beauty and strange packaged isolation into his art."

" . . . missing are many crucial examples, especially from the 1960s which would elucidate his contribution more completely . . . full-sized examples of the electric chair paintings, and early self portraits, a good representation of his Oxidation series and a painting from his 1964 series using images of racial violence in Birmingham, Alabama."

"Nevertheless, the opening exhibition touches in some way on nearly every aspect of Warhol's frenetic activity as artist, entrepreneur and social figure, as well as his artistic evolution."

"It is especially moving to encounter this material which brims with precocious talent and a longing to be big-time in the city where Warhol's dreams began" this, concerning the gallery devoted to his efforts in the 1940s as a student in Pittsburgh and in the 1950s as a successful commercial artist in New York.

In addition to the art on the walls, it is all there: every memo, photo, bill, invitation, every object, every item, new or old, bought or salvaged, including even the famous silver, almost animate, wigs . . . in scrapbook-like arrangements in wall and table vitrines . . . a masterpiece of organization.

Why a Museum?

Andy Warhol was more than a cult figure; he was a seminal figure in an important era in American art. Respected art critic Donald Miller in the May 13, 1994 *Weekend Magazine* of the *Pittsburgh Post-Gazette* wrote about The Andy Warhol Museum, "The museum reveals a protean talent that not only found artistic substance in the power of American advertising art but expanded the boundaries of what the Western World today regards as Contemporary Art — i.e. idea-oriented and conceptual in content."

His work is prized by other museums. The Baltimore Museum of Art owned 23 of the artist's works, including his famous paintings of Campbell's soup cans. In 1994 the Baltimore museum paid $1 million for 15 Warhol paintings and three drawings, making it second only to Pittsburgh in Warhol holdings.

The Andy Warhol Museum was created by a unique triumvirate to showcase the life work of America's most eccentric, most controversial, most successful contemporary artist, Pittsburgh's Andy Warhol. The man, his life, his work and now his museum are inextricably intertwined. And so this account weaves in and out of the Warhol biography, his art, his mystique, his critics, and the legal controversies continuing after his death. Since his death he has been the

Marilyn (Three Times), 1962, by Andy Warhol, American, 1928-1987); The Andy Warhol Museum, Pittsburgh; Founding Collection, Contribution: The Andy Warhol Foundation for the Visual Arts, Inc.

Photograph by Richard Stoner

subject of three biographies with more to come, a voyeuresque diary, several books of photographs, numerous articles and seminars, a major retrospective at the Museum of Modern Art and a multi-million dollar sale of his collections of fine and decorative art and flea market collectibles.

His Life

The youngest of three sons of Carpatho-Rusyn immigrants Andrej and Julia Warhola, Andy was born August 6, 1928 at 73 Orr Street, Pittsburgh, near the present Birmingham Bridge. The family moved in 1934 to another rental at 3252 Dawson Street close to Holmes Elementary School, which Andy attended. His father was a coal miner and construction worker. His mother made and sold paper flowers and eggs decorated with traditional designs. She encouraged her son Andy's early efforts to draw and paint. He was tutored in the Saturday Tam O'Shanter art classes offered free at The Carnegie Museum. He and his fellow students were inspired by the teaching of Professor Joseph C. Fitzpatrick who died April 29, 1994, just days before the opening of the museum named for one of his famous pupils. While attending Pittsburgh's Carnegie Institute of Technology (now Carnegie Mellon University) Andy worked as a window dresser at Horne's department store. One of his college professors, Robert L. Lepper, had labeled him the "student least likely to succeed" while his other instructor in pictorial design, Harold L. Worner, called him "the only student with a salable product." With degree in hand Andy became a New Yorker in 1949 and about that time dropped the final "a" from his name. By 1959 he had become successful as a commercial artist but was unrecognized by the New York art elite until the fall of 1962. In the interim he succeeded in transforming his shy but egocentric persona into a certified celebrity, appearing at innumerable "openings," instantly identified by his silvery Raggedy Andy wig, several of which are now on display in his museum.

His Death

Dubbed the Pale Prince of Pop, Andy Warhol died at New York Hospital, unexpectedly, February 22, 1987, age 58, after an operation for a gangrenous gall bladder. Under the terms of his will the bulk of his vast estate established the grant-making Andy Warhol Foundation for the Visual Arts. The only other bequests were $250,000 each to his brothers John and Paul Warhola and to Frederick W. Hughes, his long-time front man, business manager, and commissioned sales agent, who was made sole executor of the estate and president of the foundation. (Hughes had saved the artist's life when he was shot by Valerie Solanas, a disgruntled wannabe member of Warhol's Factory June 3, 1968, the day before Robert Kennedy was assassinated. These events changed Warhol's life dramatically. He no longer was front and center at every publicity event but continued to work at a frenetic pace and to attend Mass regularly.)

His Estate

In April 1988, in ten days of "Andy Warholmania" Sotheby's auction house in New York attracted an estimated 60,000 people and realized $25.3 million from the sale of more than 10,000 items owned by the late artist. Along with the sale's proceeds, the estate included the artist's collection of works by others and his own paintings and prints and a multi-million dollar business empire of film, video, and publishing, especially *INTERVIEW* magazine. There was $1 million in cash plus $4.5 million in insurance, and stocks and bonds valued at $13.5 million. The Warhol real estate included an acre of beach front and other property in Montauk, Long Island, land in Colorado, and, in New York City, two townhouses and the Warhol Factory. The factory was a former Con Edison 24,000 square foot substation close to Fifth Avenue, between East 32nd and 33rd Street.

The townhouse on Lexington at 89th Street had been the home of the artist and his mother. In 1974 Fred Hughes occupied it as tenant, and after his friend's death he purchased the residence from the estate, for $593,500. The "baronial" six-story townhouse at 57 East 66th Street, where the artist lived for years prior to his death, was crammed with his art, artifacts, furniture, and "general cultural detritus." (His collection of cookie jars brought $250,000 at Sotheby's auction.) Except for the kitchen and his bedroom, it was one vast storage facility, even the stairs were cluttered with boxes. In addition, the estate reportedly received $5 million to $7 million in settlement resulting from

Joseph C. Fitzpatrick

Mr. Fitzpatrick, the famous art teacher who taught the Tam O'Shanter and Pallette Saturday art classes at The Carnegie for nearly 50 years, died on April 9, 1994, at the age of 85. Beginning in the 1920s he influenced thousands of Pittsburgh's most gifted young artists, including Andy Warhol, Philip Pearlstein, Mel Bochner, and Jonathan Borofsky.

In a March/April 1987 *Carnegie Magazine* interview, Fitzpatrick recalled the techniques which led to his success, and about a year later there was a reunion at The Carnegie at which many hundreds of his former students showed up to honor him.

Donald Miller, art critic for *Pittsburgh Post-Gazette*, was one of his students, and recalled in 1987 that Fitzpatrick not only had charm, but, "He was the first person of style we knew who could discuss aesthetics." He was kindly: "Gentleman to the bone, he had no time for harshness. We would have walked through fire for him."

a malpractice and wrongful death suit brought by the estate against the hospital in the New York Supreme Court in December 1991. Most of these proceeds went to the Warhola brothers, as did Andy's pension funds of $430,000 to John and $330,000 to Paul.

The Warhol Foundation and The Carnegie

After a year of negotiations, a formal agreement, signed October 2, 1989, established a joint venture committee composed of members of The Carnegie Museum of Art, The Andy Warhol Foundation for the Visual Arts, Inc., and Dia Art Foundation. Inspired by Fred Hughes, the Dia was the creation of Philippa de Menil, a Schlumberger heiress, and her German husband Heiner Frederick. Hughes had been a protégé of the de Menil family since his college days in Houston, Texas. (In the late 1970s Dia bought 80 of Warhol's *Shadow* paintings for $1.6 million, no doubt at Hughes suggestion).

On the committee from The Carnegie Museum of Art: Trustees Milton Fine, Richard M. Scaife, and Museum Director Phillip M. Johnston; representing the Dia Art Foundation: John C. Evans, Dia's Chairman Ashton Hawkins, and Charles Wright; for The Andy Warhol Foundation for the Visual Arts: Vincent Fremont, who had helped Hughes run the Warhol business for 20 years, and attorney Edward W. Hayes. According to Mark Francis, curator of The Warhol Museum, it is clear what these three partners bring to the project: "The Carnegie gives its museological, encyclopedia, one-of-everything approach. The Dia supplies the thinking behind its sizable but non-encyclopedic collection of such artists as Joseph Beuys, Barnett Newman, and Warhol. The Warhol Foundation supplies the final approach, the museum as a cabinet of curiosities."

The committee met for the first time March 7, 1990 with at least four meetings a year scheduled while overseeing operations during the museum's first years. The museum and its

programs were funded through The Carnegie and operated originally in conjunction with The Museum of Art. The Andy Warhol Museum is now one of the museums within Carnegie Institute. An early grant of $165,000 from the Henry Luce Foundation, established by the founder of *TIME* magazine, was in support of the archives program to help preserve and make accessible to scholars Warhol's art from 1950-1987.

Warhol Museum Director Appointed

In spite of the acrimony which developed between Hughes and attorney Hayes, members of the board were unanimous in their choice of Thomas N. Armstrong III, director emeritus of the New York's Whitney Museum of American Art, to head The Andy Warhol Museum. John Warhola, by his brother's will one of three directors and vice-president of the foundation, was instrumental in the choosing of Pittsburgh as the location for this, the largest American museum devoted to the work of a single artist, perhaps the largest in the world. Not only is this fitting because Andy Warhol was a native Pittsburgher, but also because it will fill a gap in Pittsburgh's arts collections — that of the 1960s pop-art era that he did so much to generate.

The Collection

After visiting the *Andy Warhol: A Retrospective* exhibition in Venice, Italy in March 1990, *Pittsburgh Post-Gazette* editor John S. Craig, Jr. was impressed: "The totality of the exhibition — 36 rooms over three floors — is extraordinarily compelling, including as it does not only the familiar paintings and silkscreens, but also motion pictures, wallpaper, at least 100 black-and-white photographs from the 'Factory,' a silver-painted New York City loft where Warhol worked and performed, and four video documentaries on Warhol's life shown simultaneously on banks of TV sets."

"Much of this art is from the Warhol

estate and the Dia Collection leaving no doubt about the dimensions of the motherlode coming to Pittsburgh. On the basis of this evidence alone, it is beyond argument that the local museum's collection will be definitive."

Definitive indeed! Arguably the most comprehensive artist's archive in the world, The Andy Warhol Museum contains 613 "Time-Capsules," dated boxes Warhol filled with junk mail, reviews, random objects, souvenirs, etc. of his almost daily shopping sprees. His entire business records, 40,000 Polaroids, video and audio tapes plus a full run of his *INTERVIEW* magazine from 1966 are included. (By 1986 the magazine with a circulation of 180,000 and 1,177 ad pages annually had begun to show a profit. It was sold in May 1989 to newsprint magnate Peter Brant for $12 million, but as of June 1994 there are still unresolved legal questions about the transaction.)

The pre-opening collection consisted of some 800 paintings, 77 sculptures, 42 drawings, and 23 prints. Under discussion with The Andy Warhol Foundation was a list of 1,500 drawings, prints, photographs, film, and video.

Andy's Early Drawings: Shoes
Andy Warhol's drawings, especially of shoes for I. Miller ads which appeared in the *New York Times* in the mid-1950s, launched his career as a commercial artist. They were featured in *The New York Times Magazine* in the special report on a half-century of fashion of the times entitled *How Fashion Broke Free*, October 24, 1993. "Warhol, it is sometimes said, couldn't draw. But his commercial style . . . fitted perfectly the taste of the time — linear, loose-limbed, and lightheaded." Of the nearly 30 Warhol drawings unearthed from *The Times'* "morgue" some had the lettering done by Julia Warhola in her old-world script, in furtherance of her son's career. A *Warhol Footnote* article also mentioned his exhibitions at the Bodley Gallery of New York of fantastic portraits of famous people as shoes.

Actress Zsa Zsa Gabor was a silver-and-gold-plated high heel, and cosmetic tycoon, Helena Rubenstein, was a mule (slipper) with a feather at the tip, like a pompadour. And there was more on Warhol's early drawings in a squib in the *Pittsburgh Post-Gazette* November 18, 1933, reporting that 42 of them had vanished from the Museum of Modern Art, having been last seen in April, 1988. (A case in the Warhol museum contains some of the famous shoes and others saved, perhaps for inspiration.)

The Museum Building
This major new art museum occupies a seven-story structure at 117 Sandusky and East General Robinson streets on Pittsburgh's North Side. In construction from 1911-1913, it was originally a warehouse for Frick & Lindsay Co., industrial suppliers. (The Frick of the company was a distant relative of Henry C. Frick). Designed by an architect whose name is not recalled, the building was a tour de force of classical ornamentation with garlands, leaves, fruit, and heads of lions and Greek gods, all in cast terra cotta. The ornate cornice was crumbling and had to be removed when the building was enlarged in 1920. It was occupied by the Volkwein Music Company for 30 years before it was sold to Carnegie Institute in the spring of 1990 for $967,572.38. The transformation of the building into The Andy Warhol Museum cost $15.4 million.

Richard Gluckman Architects, New York
The Carnegie engaged Richard Gluckman Architects, New York, a firm whose work includes renovation of Boston's Museum of Fine Arts Foster Gallery. Gluckman "Alchemist of Light" is "the architect of choice to the art world" since his 1977 work on the townhouse of Philippa de Menil and her husband Heiner Friedrick, two of the most influential patrons of Contemporary Art. This success led to a series of commissions for the Dia Center for the

Arts of which Friedrick was founding director. Especially notable as forerunner of the Warhol commission was Gluckman's renovation for Dia of a four-story, 19th century warehouse in the Chelsea section of Manhattan. For the Warhol, associate architects were the Pittsburgh-based firm UDA. Mellon Stuart Construction Inc. was the general contractor, with a budget of $8.26 million. Of the $20 million goal, $15 million was initially raised by The Carnegie, including $6 million from the Commonwealth of Pennsylvania and $9 million from foundations.

The planning process included close attention to appropriate types and levels of light not injurious to the various kinds of artwork. Discarded fragments from the artist's silkscreens were tested to determine whether the art would suffer fading or damage from exposure to ultraviolet light, filtered daylight, or simulated daylight. Conducted for The Museum of Art, the tests by the Carnegie Mellon Research Institute investigated the potential effects of almost one hundred years of exposure to different kinds of light.

The elaborate cornice was recreated by the use of modern technology and computer imaging and substituting fiberglass for the heavier, more expensive, terra cotta. In addition to mechanical updating, an eight-story tower, encasing new passenger and freight elevators, and a new stairway help transform the warehouse into a showcase. As in the Guggenheim Museum in New York, visitors generally go by elevator to the top floor and move to the lower floors as they view the exhibition. The ceiling height of 10 feet was doubled in areas between the fourth and fifth floors to provide for very large paintings. In all, there are 16 spectacular, spacious galleries. Near the entrance is the museum shop stocked with Warholiana. A theater with 100 seats (designed by Marcel Breuer and saved from a French theater) is part of added construction in the back quadrant. The basement houses educational facilities, sponsored

by Mellon Bank, and the Underground, a small cafe, seating 35. The renewed, refurbished, and expanded building is now a $12 million facility for the display of Warhol art and artifacts, some 40,000 pieces in all. Of the more than 80,000 square feet, about half is exhibition/public space.

Paintings

Among the initial donations from The Andy Warhol Foundation to the museum were the first pop series of hand painted images (1960-62), classic silkscreen paintings of, *Flowers*, *Campbell's Soup Cans*, *Liz Paintings* (Elizabeth Taylor), *Elvis* (Elvis Presley), *Disaster Series*, *Electric Chairs*, *Most Wanted Men*, and a large grouping of major later works such as portraits of *Mao* (China's dictator), *Skulls*, *Oxidations* (urine as an ingredient), and *Last Suppers*.

One of the artist's biographers, Victor Bockris, in his book *The Life and Death of Andy Warhol* asserts that the soup cans and flower paintings were based on his past. "What Andy was painting was his mother's kitchen: the soup cans. And the flowers she made and sold. His interest in movie stars goes back to the Shirley Temple photographs he had as a child. His disaster paintings are directly related to his ideas on religion. The black and silver colors of the Factory are the coal and steel colors he knew in Pittsburgh."

In addition to his self portraits, which are shown in the museum, Andy Warhol was also the subject of works by several other artists. His Carnegie Tech classmate Philip Pearlstein in 1950 painted an 8 x 10-inch oil portrait which Warhol gave to the Whitney Museum in New York. Jamie Wyeth also painted a portrait of his fellow artist but has retained it in his own collection.

Films

Of the Warhol films available to the museum, *The Life and Times of Andy Warhol* opened the 1991 Three Rivers Film Festival in Pittsburgh.

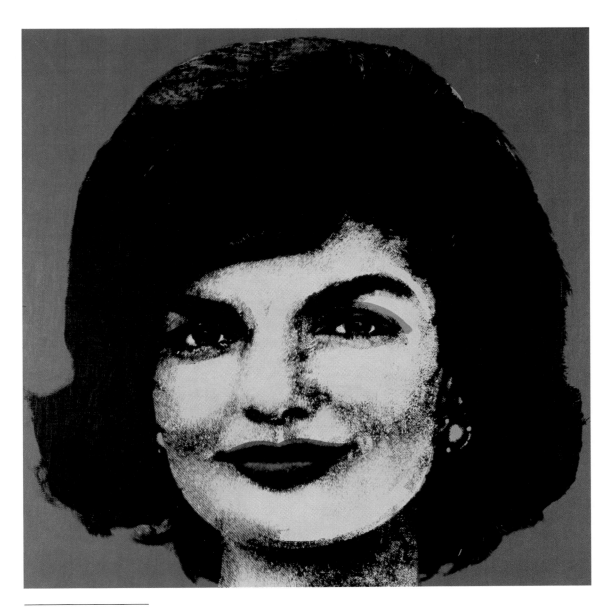

Jackie, 1963, by Andy Warhol, American, 1928-1987);
The Andy Warhol Museum, Pittburgh; Founding
Collection, Contribution: The Andy Warhol Foundation
for the Visual Arts, Inc.

Jacqueline Bouvier Kennedy Onassis (1929-1994)

Photograph by Lockwood Hoehl

Also shown in that series were *Nude Restaurant*, *Vinyl*, and *Lonesome Cowboys*. The video *Songs for Drella* by Lou Reed, singer, songwriter with the Velvet Underground, and John Cale, Sere/Warner Brothers is a 15-song album celebrating Warhol's "migration from the obscurity of Pittsburgh to the fear and loathing of the New York Art world." (As early as 1967 the Women's Committee of The Carnegie Museum of Art sponsored a showing of the film *Andy Warhol — Super Artist* in connection with paintings in the *Carnegie International* of that year.) As part of the celebration opening the museum in 1994, two Warhol films, *Empire* and *Kiss*, played continuously.

Early Sales and Successes

Fueling the Warhol ambition was the lack of interest in him artistically or socially by contemporary artists, movers and shakers in the New York art world whom he admired, especially Robert Rauschenberg and Jasper Johns. It was their friend filmmaker Emile de Antonio who is credited with aiding Warhol's acceptance by giving him artistic advice and introducing him to Eleanor Ward, owner of the Stable Gallery. In the fall of 1962, his show there of some of his now famous images was a sensation and a sell-out to collectors and museum directors. Architect Philip Johnson bought *Gold Marilyn* for $800 and the Museum of Modern Art bought another *Marilyn* for $250. Twenty-seven years later the painting *Shot Red Marilyn* (1964) of Marilyn Monroe with a bullet hole above an eyebrow, sold at Christie's for $4.1 million. This dark side of Warhol's art often depicted gore and death in violent car crashes, suicides, race riots, electric chairs, and the assassination of President John F. Kennedy.

Executor Hughes vs. Attorney Hayes

Credited with being the builder of Andy Warhol's financial empire, it was Fred Hughes who instigated Warhol's lucrative, commissioned silk-screen portrait business. Beginning with Hughes' patron Dominique de Menil (mother of Philippa), Rothschilds, Agnellis, and other luminaries were charged $25,000 and up. From 1972 until his death in 1987 the artist and his assistants produced 50 to 100 society portraits a year. Hughes also established a network of Warhol dealers in European capitals and cultivated an assembly of international notables as collectors of Warhol art.

The day after Andy Warhol's death, executor Hughes hired attorney Edward Hayes to represent the estate and secure the properties. Said to be the prototype for the lawyer in Tom Wolfe's *Bonfire of the Vanities*, Hayes' fee was to be 2.5%, later reduced to 2%, of the value of the estate. Hayes was dismissed by Hughes July 6, 1993, having already received $4,850,000, far less than the $14 million he claimed based on his evaluation of the value of the estate. Hughes, himself embroiled in legal battles, was awarded $5.2 million in a settlement reached by The Andy Warhol Foundation for the Visual Arts, the New York state attorney general's office and executor Hughes. The foundation was in court again in November of 1993 seeking to close to the public all record of its huge inventory of Warhols. The judge refused the request. The legal contests and consequent hemorrhaging of cash from both the estate and the foundation still continue even after The Andy Warhol Museum has become a reality. The three-way litigation among Hughes, Hayes, and the foundation continues with no end in sight. There are those who advocate that the foundation turn over all its holding to the museum and go out of business. This position is based on the report that administration, legal, and other expenses of the foundation consume more than 90% of each dollar available as awards to grantees.

Warhol Foundation Reorganized

Within the year of his friend's death, Hughes' health, due to multiple sclerosis, declined and he became confined to a wheel chair. Andy Warhol's will in 1987 gave him total power over the foundation, but in 1990 he appointed the former head of the John Hay Whitney Foundation, Archibald L. Gillies, to succeed him as president. Hughes held the title chairman of the board until February, 1992 when he resigned, being replaced by Brendan Gill of *New Yorker* magazine. Hughes' new title became co-founder and chairman emeritus. The by-laws were amended in 1990 to permit expansion of the board by adding "professionals" — Gill and Agnes Gund, president of the board of the Museum of Modern Art and Anthony S. Soloman, former president of the New York Federal Reserve Board. In December of 1990, Vincent Fremont quit the board to become the exclusive agent for Andy Warhol paintings and Gillies succeeded him on the board. The board was expanded further and, as of 1994, now includes Kinshasha Holman Conwill, director of the Studio Museum in Harlem; and Kathy Halbreich, director of the Walker Art Center in Minneapolis.

The Andy Warhol Foundation for the Visual Arts has given out more than $18 million since the spring of 1989 when the first 58 grants were announced, totaling $1.9 million to art, film, video, educational, and preservation institutions. Since its inception it has given $23 million to some 600 groups, while incurring $21 million in expenses.

Warhol Art Appraised

The value of the art has been estimated to be more than $500 million or as little as $120 million. The question seemed to be finally settled July 20, 1993 with the valuation set at "approximately" $220 million by agreement of the foundation, Hughes as executor and the New York state attorney general's office. The $220 million evaluation was established mainly from an estimate prepared by Christie's of the artist's own work in the estate. Christie's estimates continued to be challenged in court in December

1993 as the two sides skirmished. Lawyer Hayes sought to maximize the value of the Warhol art works in order to enlarge his 2% fee. The foundation was trying to minimize the value because of the 5% it is required by law to distribute in grants each year.

The $220 million valuation did not hold and in April, 1994 Judge Eva Preminger of the Surrogate Court in Manhattan ruled that the art appraisals were off by a factor of four, and that, combined with other assets, the estate was worth $509 million. In June of 1994 the foundation appealed the higher valuation and asked that the judge disqualify herself from the case because of being a "social acquaintance" of attorney Hayes.

Appraisals Challenged

The appraisal methods of Christie's were scrutinized as it was shown that in the case of a group of Warhol's Polaroid photographs used for his society portraits, the original appraisal of five cents each was raised to $1.00 and later to $100 apiece. His collection of almost 20,000 black-and-white photographs was valued at $107,000 by Christie's but Hayes was willing to take the lot in settlement of his claim based on his expert's valuation of the photos at $11.6 million. Hayes' lawyer also brought out the fact that Christie's appraisal of the Warhol portrait of *Andrew Carnegie* for gift purposes was $250,000 while a comparable work, a portrait of Golda Meir, sold at auction for $49,500.

The work of other artists collected by Warhol (said to rival the holdings of The Museum of Modern Art) was appraised by Sotheby's also of New York; the films and videos, by Michael Fried, curator of the Academy of Motion Picture Arts & Sciences in Los Angeles.

In addition to the stupendous cost of the ongoing litigation, the main reason for the large discrepancy between high and low estimates of the value of the estate was due to the escalating prices which had been commanded by works of Andy Warhol. It was one record-breaking price after another until May of 1993 when Fred Hughes, because of massive medical and legal fees, put 10 of his 100 or so Warhols for auction. Sotheby's already had two Warhols from other consignors. The art market was shocked when only two of the lots sold, both offered by Hughes — *Old Telephone*, from the early 60s, and a 1982 portrait of Britain's Princess Diana — bringing in about $600,000. These works were signed while others, said to be of lesser quality, were not.

Interestingly, Warhol's old nemesis Jasper Johns and Robert Rauschenberg did well . . . Johns' *Untitled, 1980* which failed to sell at the height of the art boom, went at Christie's for $607,500, while Rauschenberg's *Nettle* fetched $717,500. Just one year earlier a 1962 Andy Warhol study of full, empty, and half-empty Coke bottles sold for $2,090,000.

Andy Warhol Remembered

Prior to his death Warhol had exhibitions of his work, notably the showing of his portraits in 1971 at the Whitney Museum for American Art in New York. But, it was not until his death that he was recognized with a retrospective by The Museum of Modern Art in New York. In the summer of 1989 Pittsburgh's Carnegie Museum of Art held an exhibition called *Success is a Job in New York: The Early Art and Business of Andy Warhol.* The title was derived from the first piece Warhol illustrated for *Glamour* magazine shortly after he arrived in New York in 1949, a 20-year-old graduate of Pittsburgh's Carnegie Tech. In less than two months, 29,905 visitors came to view the exhibition, a fitting tribute to the artist whose early instruction was in the Tam O' Shanter Saturday morning art classes at Carnegie Institute.

Although Andy Warhol, the man, has gone, his mystique is still magnetic. More than 25,000 people attended the museum's weekend

Andy Warhol (1928-1987)

Photograph by Patrick McMullan, courtesy The Andy Warhol Museum

opening celebrations, including the 22,000 who came to the free 24-hour open house. For the weekend alone the museum's bookstore sales totaled $23,964.42. When the museum opened Monday, May 16, for its first official day of business, 50 people were waiting at the door. After Allegheny County commissioner Tom Foerster purchased the first ticket, the second and third were bought by two European exchange students who had traveled to Pittsburgh from Dallas and Columbus to visit the museum. They were included among the 4,156 who visited during the inaugural week. From May to December, 1994 some 95,500 visitors came to The Andy Warhol Museum. Tom Armstrong, director since April 1, 1993, was credited by The Carnegie's President Ellsworth Brown with having performed "a powerful job overseeing design and getting the museum running." It was admitted that Armstrong's decision to leave as of March 1, 1995 was a surprise to The Carnegie, The Dia Center for the Arts, and to the Andy Warhol Foundation for the Visual Arts.

Farewell to Andy Warhol

Andy Warhol's memorial service April 1, 1987, was held at St. Patrick's Cathedral in New York, drawing 2,000 people to the church on Fifth Avenue. The April Fool's Day farewell was arranged by his old friend and executor, Fred Hughes. Now, in the Warhola burial plot in the Greek Catholic cemetery in Bethel Park, Pennsylvania, there is — in those "Pittsburgh" colors — a plain black and grey marble tombstone incised simply, "Andy Warhol." Here visitors come, leaving offerings such as a box of Brillo pads and torn pieces of a Xerox image scattered at the base of the monument in silent tribute to this most commercial of American artists.

Sources include:

Carnegie Magazine:
The Carnegie's special edition May/June 1994
July/August 1994

Pittsburgh Post-Gazette:
Special magazine sections May 8, and May 13, 1994, including articles by Diana Nelson Jones, Patricia Lowry, Georgia Sauer, Barry Paris, Leslie Rubinkowski, Tony Norman, Harry Kloman and Donald Miller (superseding *Post-Gazette* articles by these and other writers from 1988 through 1993.)
March 7, March 15, 1994, by Donald Miller
May 14, 1994, articles by Donald Miller and Scott Mervis

Reuters News Service:
May 6, 1993, by Dan Cox

Carnegie Mellon Magazine:
Volume 9 Number 3, Spring 1991, feature article by Patricia Lowry, art and architecture critic for the *Pittsburgh Press*
Volume 12 Number 4, Summer 1994, feature articles by Bernard B. Perlman A'49 and Ann Curran

Pittsburgh Magazine:
May 1994

The New York Times:
July 21, 1993, article by Carol Vogel
December 2, 1993, article by Carol Vogel
December 21, 1993, article by Carol Vogel
May 1, 1994, article by Grace Glueck
May 16, 1994, article by Carol Vogel
May 26, 1994, article by Roberta Smith
June 12, 1994, article by Alison Leigh Cowan and Carol Vogel
June 17, 1994, article by Carol Vogel

The New York Times Magazine:
October 24, 1993, A Warhol Footnote by Michael Kimmelman

New York Post:
November 3, 1993, article by Richard Johnson

The Village Voice:
New York, May 24, 1994, article by Elizabeth Hess and Guy Trebay

New York Magazine:
February 22, 1988, article by John Taylor
January 27, 1992, article by Paul Alexander
November 30, 1992, article by Christopher Byron
May 2, 1994, article by Paul Alexander

Vanity Fair Magazine:
July 1993, article by Bob Colacello, former editor Warhol's magazine (Author of 1990 memoir *Holy Terror: Andy Warhol Close-Up*)

Harper Bazaar Magazine:
January 1993, Richard Gluckman by Christine Pittel

The brochure of The Andy Warhol Museum
The Carnegie Museum of Art 1993

The Carnegie — General Information

The Carnegie includes the Library of Pittsburgh, the Museum of Art, the Museum of Natural History, the Music Hall, the Science Center, and the Andy Warhol Museum, and is dedicated to the understanding and enjoyment of literature, art, science, and music.

The Carnegie collects, preserves, interprets, and exhibits objects from natural history and our cultural heritage, and makes its collections and resources available to the widest possible audience. The Carnegie is committed to providing public programs that educate, excite, entertain, and inspire.

As one of America's great cultural centers, The Carnegie services all the residents of its region as well as national and international audiences.

Maintaining Carnegie Institute

"In the Carnegie Institute the great rooms, with their freight and plunder of the past, seem to float, as it were, above a multitude of workshops and laboratories; they are upraised, supported and maintained by a marvelously active little city that is essential to the structure's very existence."

> — James D. Van Trump (1907-1995)
> *An American Palace of Culture*, 1970

Carnegie Institute needs a small army of security officers, custodians, mechanics, engineers, carpenters, painters, plumbers, plasterers, and cement makers to maintain it year round, in addition to the scientists, curators, conservators, other museum specialists, and administrators who run the enormous institution to serve the public. In 1993, there were 928 jobs filled by 873 persons.

The 1993 Budget: Financial Data

Andrew Carnegie's dream was that the Institute should be "free to the people" and his philosophy was: public funds to support the library, which is separate, and private contributions to maintain The Museum of Natural History and the Art Gallery. His 1896 gift of $6 million to endow the complex "in perpetuity," in 1994 provides just 33.5% of the operating budget of $17,965,000.

The facts of economic life led in 1973 to a suggested admission contribution. In 1994 members and children under three are admitted free, and the contribution suggested is $5.00 for adults, $4.00 for children and students. Admissions in 1993 accounted for 21.3% of the Institute's Funding Income. Attendance was approximately 1,346,000. Nearly 35,000 individual, family and corporate memberships supported 15.3% of the cost of its annual operations. Gifts and grants added 9.2%; Government sources 8.6%; interest 2.4% and other sources 9.7%. Board designated funds and restricted funds provided $24,640,000 to be expended in 1993 for additions to collections, building renovations, major equipment purchases, research activities, and special programming, including educational projects, temporary exhibitions, and film programs.

The Second Century Fund capital campaign was launched in 1988 and surpassed its original goal of $125.5 million. In 1994 the overall endowment was more than $150 million, with approximately $20 million of that amount designated for art acquisitions. The campaign also provided for the following capital projects: The Carnegie Science Center, the Oakland parking garage, air conditioning and climate control of the Oakland facility, and the creation, renovation, and refurbishment of many exhibition halls and galleries throughout the complex.

Inestimable Service of Volunteers

In 1993 approximately 1,256 volunteers contributed 109,334 hours working as docents, salespersons in the gifts shops, serving as information volunteers and staffing the Discovery Room in The Museum of Natural History. They also prepared specimens for scientific study, assisted with public education programs, worked in administrative offices, and helped to raise money. Volunteer support groups whose hours are not recorded are the Women's Committee for The Museum of Art, the Council for The Museum of Natural History, the STARS for the Science Center and Friends of the Performing Arts for The Carnegie.

Auxiliary Activities at the Carnegie

Auxiliary activities include the Continuing Education Programs, Music Hall, Special Events, museum shops, food services, and parking lots. The Travel-Adventure Series for members had an attendance of 78,768 in 1993 and has for years been managed by volunteer Juliette Grauer.

Special Events had an aggregate attendance of 138,496 at performances in the Music Hall, The Museum of Art Theater, Scaife Foyer and Galleries, Hall of Architecture, Outdoor Sculpture Court and other areas in the Oakland complex. The Science Center and Andy Warhol Museum also have areas available for rental.

The Museum Shops and Food Service

The shops and dining facilities are an important source of income to the Institute and are attractions to the visiting public, who may patronize them without an admission fee. Food service: at The Carnegie in Oakland, the Cafeteria and the Café; at The Science Center, the Riverview Café; and at The Andy Warhol Museum, the Coffee Shop, called *Underground.*

The Nature Shop in The Museum of Natural History, given in 1948 by the Junior League of Pittsburgh, features dinosaur items, kits to make your own models, skeletons, books, cards, mazes, pencils, and T-shirts. The Museum of Art Shop, established in 1974 by the Women's Committee, sells contemporary gift items, jewelry, handmade clothing items, art posters, cards, books, some even of the early *International Exhibitions,* plus many of the publications of The Museum of Art and more. The Carnegie Science Center's Discovery Shop sells gyroscopes and Jacob's ladders, science kits, astronomy oriented gifts and books, astronaut food, T-shirts, and more. The Andy Warhol Museum Shop carries books, postcards, T-shirts, etc., all featuring work of the artist. Merchandise from Warhol's contemporaries may be added.

General Information about The Carnegie

Ellsworth H. Brown, since 1993, is president of Carnegie Institute which includes three museums, the Science Center, and Music Hall.

The Museum of Art, Museum of Natural History, and Music Hall are under one roof at 4400 Forbes Avenue, Pittsburgh, Pennsylvania 15213, telephone: (412) 622-3131.

The Carnegie Museum of Art includes the Sarah Scaife Galleries, housing permanent collections of paintings, sculpture, and prints; the Heinz Galleries for special exhibitions; the Heinz Architectural Center; the Ailsa Mellon Bruce Galleries for furniture and Decorative Arts; and a nationally recognized film section. Phillip M. Johnston is director since June 1988 (acting director January 1987-May 1988).

The Carnegie Museum of Natural History, known as the "home of the dinosaurs," houses Benedum Hall of Geology; Hillman Hall of Minerals and Gems; Polar World: Wyckoff Hall of Arctic Life; Walton Hall of Ancient Egypt; Hall of African Wildlife; Mellon Hall of North American Mammals; Alcoa Hall of Native Americans; and many more permanent exhibits. More than 10,000 objects are on display in its numerous halls and millions more are available for research. Dr. James King is director since September 1987.

The Carnegie Institute's complex also contains the Music Hall, Lecture Hall and Museum of Art Theater for a full program of drama, music, poetry, films, and lectures. Memberships with benefits are offered to families, individuals, and corporations.

The Carnegie Science Center is located next to Three Rivers Stadium at One Allegheny Avenue, Pittsburgh, Pennsylvania 15212, telephone: (412) 237-3400. The center serves the public with, "more than 250 hands-on exhibits covering nearly every scientific field." Permanent exhibitions include: Science Way; The Great Miniature Railroad and Village; Eating; Sea Life Aquarium; and Aquabatics. Also featured are the U.S.S. Requin (the WW II submarine); the Rangos Omnimax Theater; the Henry J. Buhl, Jr. Planetarium and Observatory; and more. Seddon L. Bennington is director since August 1994.

The Andy Warhol Museum is located on Pittsburgh's North Side at 117 Sandusky Street, Pittsburgh, Pennsylvania 15212, telephone: (412) 237-8300. The world's largest one-artist museum, it houses more than 3,000 works of art and an extensive archive, all "dedicated to the art and life of Andy Warhol." One of the most influential artists of the 20th century, he grew up in Pittsburgh, attended classes at The Carnegie and received formal training at the Carnegie Institute of Technology (now Carnegie Mellon University). Thomas N. Armstrong, III, formerly of the Whitney Museum in New York, served as director from April 1, 1993 through the Museum's opening in May 1994, until March 1995.

CARNEGIE INSTITUTE, a non-profit organization, was founded in 1896. It is governed by a 66-member Board of Trustees re-organized in the 1980s into components. The board includes elected officials from the city and county governments and an official from the Board of Education along with members of the community.

Facilities

- Carnegie Institute: 1,293,530 square feet (about 38 acres).
- Powdermill Nature Reserve: 2,200 acres field research facility; research station for plant/animal population studies; and field station for nature programs for area youth.
- The Edward O'Neil Research Center, Carnegie Museum of Natural History, 5800 Baum Boulevard, Pittsburgh. Offices, labs, storage in 33,000 square feet of additional space for Section of Man and Mammals.

Collections

- Carnegie Museum of Art — Over 27,800 works of art.
- Carnegie Museum of Natural History — Over 17 million specimens.
- The Carnegie Science Center — More than 250 hands-on exhibits.
- The Andy Warhol Museum — Over 3,000 works of art and an extensive archive.

Tours

In 1993 school and general tour groups, totaling 42,600 visitors, came from 21 counties in Pennsylvania, 8 in Ohio, and 7 in West Virginia. Tours also came from New York, Ontario, and elsewhere.

Privileges of Membership

Three different types of membership are now available to The Carnegie, with benefits varying depending on the category of membership.

- Unlimited free admissions to museums
- Free admission to the Institute's Travel-Adventure Film Series
- 10% discount in the gift shops
- Members-only events and previews
- Free admission to 150 Science Centers nationwide
- Free admission to 27 art and natural history museums
- Two free tickets to Rangos Omnimax Theater
- Guests privileges (up to four guests per visit)

And much more.

The Carnegie

Visitor Orientation Map —
Museum of Art and
Museum of Natural History
1995

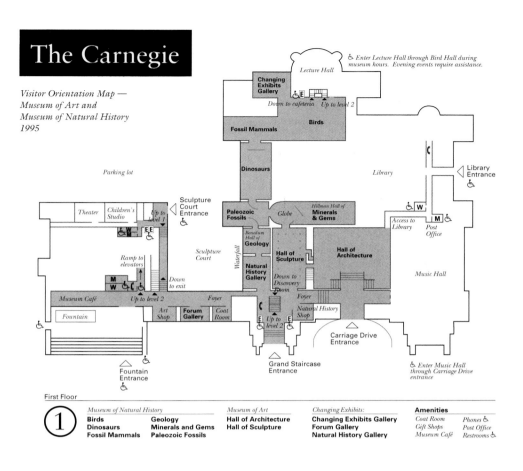

&. Enter Lecture Hall through Bird Hall during
museum hours. Evening events require assistance.

&. Enter Music Hall
through Carriage Drive
entrance

First Floor

	Museum of Natural History		Museum of Art	Changing Exhibits:	Amenities	
①	**Birds**	**Geology**	**Hall of Architecture**	**Changing Exhibits Gallery**	*Coat Room*	*Phones* &.
	Dinosaurs	**Minerals and Gems**	**Hall of Sculpture**	**Forum Gallery**	*Gift Shops*	*Post Office*
	Fossil Mammals	**Paleozoic Fossils**		**Natural History Gallery**	*Museum Café*	*Restrooms* &.

Key to Symbols

M *Men's Restroom*

W *Women's Restroom*

E *Elevator*

&. *Wheelchair Accessible*

C *Telephone*

▨ *Museum of Art and Natural*
History areas open to the public

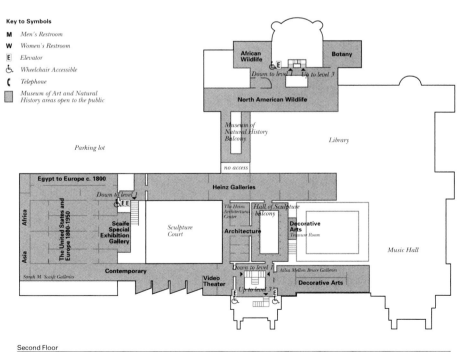

Second Floor

	Museum of Natural History	Museum of Art		Changing Exhibits
②	**African Wildlife**	**Architecture**	**Contemporary**	**Heinz Galleries**
	Botany	**Africa**	**Egypt to Europe c. 1800**	**Scaife Special Exhibition Gallery**
	North American Wildlife	**Asia**	**The United States and Europe**	**Decorative Arts Treasure Room**
		Decorative Arts	**1800-1950**	
		Video Theater		

Ampere, Andre Marie | Aristotle | Audubon, John James | Bach, Johann Sebastian | Bacon, Roger | Beethoven, Ludwig van | Berlioz, Louis Hector | Bizet, Georges | Brahms, Johannes | Bramante, Donato d'Agnolo | Buffon, Georges Louis | Chaucer, Geoffrey | Chopin, Frederic | Cicero (Marcus Tullius) | Columbus, Christopher | Copernicus, Nikolaus | Cuvier, Georges | Daguerre, Louis | Dana, James Dwight | Darwin, Charles | DeCandolle, also Candolle, Augustin de | Dickens, Charles | Donatello (Donato di Niccolo di Betto Bardi) | Donizetti, Gaetano | Dvorak, Antonon | Emerson, Ralph Waldo | Faraday, Michael | Franklin, Benjamin | Fulton, Robert | Galileo, Galilei | Galvani, Luigi | Glinka, Michail Ivanovich | Gluck, Christoph Willibald von | Goethe, Johann von | Goldsmith, Oliver | Gounod, Charles | Gray, Asa | Guttenberg (also Gutenberg), Johann | Handel, George Frederick | Harvey, William | Hawthorne, Nathaniel | Haydn, (Franz) Joseph | Henry, Joseph | Herodotus | Herschel, Sir William | Homer | Hooker, Sir William Jackson | Humboldt, Alexander Baron von | Ictinus | Irving, Washington | Jonson, Ben | Kepler, Johannes | Lamarck, Jean Baptiste Pierre Antoine de Mont, Chevalier de | Laplace, Pierre | Leidy, Joseph | Leonardo da Vinci | Linnaeus, Karl von Linne | Liszt, Franz | Livingstone, David | Longfellow, Henry Wadsworth | Lowell, James Russell | Lyell, Sir Charles | Macaulay, Thomas Babbington | Magellan, Ferdinand | Mendelssohn, Felix | Meyerbeer, Giacomo | Michelangelo Buonarotti | Milton, John | Moliere (Jean-Baptiste Poquelin) | Morse, Samuel F. B. | Mozart, Wolfgang Amadeus | Newton, Sir Isaac | Owen, Sir Richard | Palestrina, Giovanni Pierluigi da | Phidias | Pliny the Elder (Plinius Secundus) | Pope, Alexander | Praxiteles | Priestly, Joseph | Purcell, Henry | Pythagoras | Raphael (Raffaello Sanzio) | Rembrandt van Rijn | Rossini, Gioacchino | Rumford, Benjamin Thompson, Count | Saint-Saens, Camille | Say, Thomas | Schubert, Franz | Schumann, Robert | Scopas | Scott, Sir Walter | Shakespeare, William | Stephenson, George | Straus (Strauss), Richard | Tasso, Torquato | Tennyson, Alfred Lord | Thackeray, William Makepeace | Thomas, Theodore | Titian (Tiziano Vecellio) | Tschaikowsky (Tchaikovsky), Peter Ilych | Verdi, Giuseppe | Veronese, Paolo Caliari | Velasquez, Diego de Silva y Rodriguez | Virgil (Publius Vergilius Maro) | Voltaire, Francois-Marie Arouet de | Wagner, Richard | Watt, James | Weber, Carl Maria von | Wren, Christopher | . . . . .

Glossary of the Names on the Cornice of The Carnegie

Ampere, Andre Marie (1775-1836). French physicist, mathematician, and natural philosopher noted for exploring the relationship between electricity and magnetism. The measure of electrical current strength, the ampere, is named for him.

Aristotle (384-22 BC). Greece's most influential philosopher. His most popular works today are *Nichomachean Ethics* and *Poetics*. His logic and scientific methods, revealed in a collection of treatises titled *Organum*, were unquestioned for centuries. Aristotle believed the universe to be made of discrete substances which could be enumerated and categorized.

Audubon, John James (1785-1851). A painter and naturalist, he supplied the drawings and narrative and descriptive background for his masterwork *Birds of America* (4 volumes, 1827-38).

Bach, Johann Sebastian (1685-1750). This German master, like Mozart, was regarded by his contemporaries not as a great composer, but rather as a keyboard virtuoso. Bach's works for the keyboard, and his chamber music, passions, and the stupendous *Mass in B minor* are among the sublime creations of art.

Bacon, Roger (1214?-94). This Franciscan friar was renowned as an English scholar, scientist, and philosopher. His anticipation of modern scientific methods was his most remarkable achievement.

Beethoven, Ludwig van (1770-1827). His rigid self-discipline and innate genius for improvisation surfaced during his childhood in Bonn. Gradually becoming totally deaf, he relied on remarkable imaginative powers to compose his last and greatest works. Sonatas, concertos, chamber music (above all the string quartets), and nine symphonies are among his enduring monuments.

Berlioz, Louis Hector (1803-69). Composer, music critic, author, he was the leading figure of French romanticism. A master of colorful, sometimes gargantuan orchestration, he favored program music, as in his quasi-autobiographical, *Symphonie fantastique*.

Bizet, Georges (1838-75). French composer whose first opera was written when he was only sixteen. Best known for *Carmen*, he wrote other operas, incidental music for Daudet's *L'Arlesienne*, and a charming youthful symphony.

Brahms, Johannes (1833-97). This great German composer wrote in almost every form but opera. His range extends from songs, piano, and chamber music works, to concertos and symphonies, and the massive choral *German Requiem*.

Bramante, Donato d'Agnolo (1444-1514). Among the greatest architects of the Italian Renaissance, he was selected by Pope Julius II to redesign St. Peter's in Rome. Although little had been built by the time he died, the colossal scale and crowning dome of the present building derive from his plan.

Buffon, Georges Louis (1707-88). French naturalist best known for his 44-volume *Histoire naturelle, generale et particuliere*, a comprehensive survey of the animal kingdom.

Chaucer, Geoffrey (c. 1343-1400). The first English poet to write in ten-syllables, a form later to become the heroic couplet, he also experimented with a variety of elaborate verse forms. His major works are *Troilus and Criseyde* (1385) and *The Canterbury Tales* (1387 ff.).

Chopin, Frederic (1810-49). Polish composer and virtuoso pianist identified with France, where he spent much of his life. His compositions, written almost exclusively for piano, include preludes, nocturnes, etudes, mazurkas, waltzes, sonatas, and concertos.

Cicero (Marcus Tullius) (106-43 BC). Roman orator, philosopher and statesman remembered for his letters, his orations against Catiline, and for a series of quasi-philosophical tracts. *De Amicitia (On Friendship)* and *De Senectute (On Old Age)* are among the latter.

Columbus, Christopher (1451-1506). Credited with the discovery of America, this Italian navigator and merchant was stalwart in the face of adversity. Sailing westward across the Atlantic in 1492, his discovery of the West Indies resulted in the first permanent European settlements in the New World.

Copernicus, Nikolaus (1473-1543). Polish astronomer who laid the foundation for modern astronomy with his *De revolutionibus orbium coelestium*, which described the sun as the center of the great system and the earth a planet revolving around it.

Cuvier, Georges (1769-1832). The father of paleontology, this French naturalist and comparative anatomist was the first to dissect existing animals in order to gain insight into extinct ones. He developed a new and advanced classification of the animal kingdom.

Daguerre, Louis (1789-1851). French. The father of commercial photography, he invented the daguerrotype, a process that produces an iodine-treated photograph on a silver or silvered plate.

Dana, James Dwight (1813-95). The official geologist and mineralogist for the U. S. government expeditions of the South Seas and coastal Pacific Northwestern United States. His textbook, *The Manual of Geology* (1862), was long a standard work of many editions.

Darwin, Charles (1809-82). A five-year cruise as official naturalist on a British naval expedition marked the beginning of a career of investigation and observation which led to the development of the theory of evolution by natural selection. His thoughts were presented in the *Origin of Species* (1859).

DeCandolle, also Candolle, Augustin de (1778-1841). Authored a history of succulent plants and a natural system of botanical classification. Though Swiss, he made an extensive botanical and agricultural survey of France which lasted much of his life.

Dickens, Charles (1812-70). English novelist and short story writer, noted for novels published in serial editions, about early industrial England. An immediate popular success, his appeal has endured through such novels as *The Pickwick Papers* (1836-7), *David Copperfield* (1849-50), *Bleak House* (1852), *A Tale of Two Cities* (1859).

Donatello (Donato di Niccolo di Betto Bardi) (c. 1386-1466). Perhaps the greatest artist of the Early Renaissance in Florence, Donatello's works both define the Renaissance and move beyond it. His outstanding contribution is the profound sense of humanity conveyed by his works (*David, Penitent Magdalene, Judith, Gattamelata, St. Mark*).

Donizetti, Gaetano (1797-1848). Italian composer of several durable operas including *Lucia di Lammermoor, The Elixir of Love* and *The Daughter of the Regiment*.

Dvorak, Antonon (1841-1904). During a three-year stay in the United States, this Bohemian (Czech) composer gathered impressions for the most popular of his nine symphonies, *From the New World*.

Emerson, Ralph Waldo (1803-82). American poet, essayist, philosopher, lecturer, and editor, his home in Concord, Massachusetts, became the center for discussions among the major transcendentalist thinkers. Notable among his works are, "Nature" (1836), "The American Scholar" (1837), *Essays*, 1st and 2nd Series (1841; 1844), *Poems* (1847), and *Representative Men* (1850).

Faraday, Michael (1791-1867). English scientist known for his discovery of electromagnetic induction. He researched the transformation of electrical energy to mechanical, work which helped to develop the electric generator.

Franklin, Benjamin (1706-90). American scientist, statesman, and writer. Having established his success as a printer, he decided in 1848 to devote more time to scientific study and in his famous kite experiment identified lightning as electricity.

Fulton, Robert (1765-1815). American engineer concerned chiefly with canal engineering and machinery. His anticipation of the use of steam power led to his design of the *Clermont*, the first commercially successful steam boat in the United States.

Galileo, Galilei (1564-1642). Italian astronomer and physicist whose work established the foundation of modern experimental science. He constructed telescopes which he used to study the heavens and was first to observe the mountains of the moon and the Milky Way. He also established many gravitational principles and demonstrated that objects of different weights fall with the same velocity.

Galvani, Luigi (1727-98), Italian physicist and physician known for his chance discovery of electric current.

Glinka, Michail Ivanovich (1803-57). A versatile composer, "The Father of Russian Music" is best known for his opera *A Life for the Tsar*.

Gluck, Christoph Willibald von (1714-87). German composer who reformed opera along the lines set forth in the preface to his *Alcestis*. Other notable works include *Orpheus and Eurydice* and *Iphigenia in Aulis*.

Goethe, Johann von (1749-1832). A popular and prolific poet, novelist, and dramatist who bridged the eras of Classicism and Romanticism, he became known as Germany's premier romantic for works such as *The Sorrow of Young Werther* (1774), *Wilhelm Meister* (1795), and *Faust* (1808).

Goldsmith, Oliver (1728-74). English friend of Dr. Johnson and other great men of the eighteenth century, his enduring works are *She Stoops to Conquer* (1773), a sentimental comic drama, and *The Vicar of Wakefield* (1776).

Gounod, Charles (1818-93). Apart from *Faust*, this French composer is known for the operas *Sappho, Le Medecin malgre lui*, and *Romeo et Juliette*. His other works include religious choral pieces and a *Petite Symphonie* for wind instruments.

Gray, Asa (1810-88). Harvard botanist internationally known for his studies of biogeography and the classification of plants, particularly those from the Eastern United States and Eastern Asia.

Guttenberg (also Gutenberg), Johann (1397-1468). Credited as the first European to print with movable type, this German printer's Mazarin Bible is a masterpiece.

Handel, George Frederick (1685-1759). A German composer who progressed through Italian opera to English oratorio, his artistic destiny. Renowned for the *Messiah*, he wrote many outstanding vocal and instrumental works.

Harvey, William (1578-1657). This English physician's research determined the function of the heart as a pump and traced the circulation of the blood through the body.

Hawthorne, Nathaniel (1804-64). American novelist and short story writer, New England regionalist in subject but universal in symbolic reference, he wrote *Mosses from the Old Manse* (1846) (including "Young Goodman Brown"), *The Scarlet Letter* (1850), *The House of the Seven Gables* (1851).

Haydn, (Franz) Joseph (1732-1809). Austrian composer known as "The Father of the Symphony," he was a major figure in the development of classical forms. His astonishing productivity includes 104 symphonies, 68 string quartets, two great oratorios, and the familiar *Austrian Anthem*.

Henry, Joseph (1797-1878). An American physicist, his experiments with electromagnetism laid a foundation for the development of the telegraph, telephone, radio, and the electric motor.

Herodotus (c. 484-25 BC). Greek. "The Father of History," he recorded the conflict between Greece and Persia in the fifth century BC in his *History*.

Herschel, Sir William (1738-1822). German-born English astronomer who as the king's astronomer discovered the planet Uranus and determined the rotation period of Saturn and its seventh moon. He catalogued over 800 double stars and 250 nebulae. He was the first to suggest that our solar system moves through space.

Homer (c. 850 BC). A great Greek epic writer and the first European poet, his verses formed the basis of Greek literature and education. The *Iliad* and *Odyssey* are attributed to him.

Hooker, Sir William Jackson (1785-1865). A leading botanist in his day, he developed the Glasgow and Kew botanical gardens. His writings include *Flora Scotica* and *British Flora*.

Humboldt, Alexander Baron von (1769-1859). German naturalist who conducted botanical and astronomical studies during South and Central American expeditions. His *Kosmos* (1845-62), a description of the physical universe, is among the world's greatest scientific writings.

Ictinus (second half of the fifth century BC). One of the most celebrated Greek architects, he collaborated with Callicrates on the design and erection of the Parthenon in Athens.

Irving, Washington (1783-1859). He was the first American to be recognized as a professional man of letters. His work tends to be light, among the best examples being *Knickerbocker's History of New York* (1809), *The Sketch Book* (1819) (including "Rip Van Winkle" and "The Legend of Sleepy Hollow").

Jonson, Ben (1573-1637). Classical English poet, dramatist, and critic, ranked by some as the equal to Shakespeare in comic drama, his major plays include *Every Man In His Humour* (1599), *Volpone* (1605-6), and *The Alchemist* (1610).

Kepler, Johannes (1571-1630). Influenced by the teachings of Copernicus, this German astronomer formulated several important scientific laws. He was also the first to determine that a relationship existed between the tides and the moon.

Lamarck, Jean Baptiste Pierre Antoine de Mont, Chevalier de (1744-1829). French. The founder of invertebrate paleontology, he introduced several evolutionary theories. He believed that life forms evolved over long periods of geologic time and that characteristics acquired by the parent animal during its lifetime were transferred to its offspring.

Laplace, Pierre (1749-1827). French astronomer who studied the motion of the moon and its effect on the Earth's orbit. With the aid of a fellow astronomer, Lagrange, he established beyond a doubt the correctness of Newton's hypothesis of gravitation.

Leidy, Joseph (1832-91). A physician, his knowledge of comparative anatomy allowed him to take an early lead in American vertebrate paleontology. He authored three landmark monographs on fossil studies in the American West. His *Elementary Treatise on Human Anatomy* was long felt to have been the best American text in the field.

Leonardo da Vinci (1452-1519). The most widely accomplished artist of the Italian Renaissance. He traveled extensively pursuing his interests as a painter, sculptor, architect, musician, inventor, and scientist. Although he never finished many of his works, the *Last Supper* and *Mona Lisa* testify to his genius. The brilliant fertility of his mind is best revealed by his notebooks.

Linnaeus (Karl von Linne) (1707-78). A Swedish botanist, he originated the modern binomial system of naming plants and animals. He wrote 180 books, including *Species plantarum* (1753) and *Genera plantarum.*

Liszt, Franz (1811-86). A phenomenal Hungarian piano virtuoso, he influenced Wagner and later composers. He wrote many works and transcriptions for piano and twelve symphonic poems, a form which he invented.

Livingstone, David (1813-73). Scottish missionary and explorer of Africa. He discovered the Victoria Falls and the source of the Nile.

Longfellow, Henry Wadsworth (1807-82). A professor at Harvard, he compiled the first anthology of European poetry and was among the first to teach modern languages and European literature. Among his major poetic works are *Evangeline* (1847), *The Courtship of Miles Standish* (1850), and *Hiawatha* (1855).

Lowell, James Russell (1819-91). American poet, essayist, and diplomat, Russell published in one year (1848) *The Vision of Sir Launfal, The Bigelow Papers,* and *A Fable for Critics.*

Lyell, Sir Charles (1797-1875). British geologist influential in shaping popular ideas about science in the 19th century. One of his major contributions to geology was the division of the Tertiary period into Eocene, Miocene, and Pliocene epochs.

Macaulay, Thomas Babbington (1800-59). English. Popular in his time as the poet-author of *The Lays of Rome* (1842), his major work was the five-volume *The History of England from the Accession of James II* (1849-61).

Magellan, Ferdinand (c. 1480-1521). This Portuguese navigator confirmed the existence of a water passage from the Atlantic to the Pacific Ocean through straits that now bear his name. His ships were the first to circumnavigate the globe.

Mendelssohn, Felix (1809-47). German composer of symphonies, concertos, chamber music, oratorios and other forms of music. A precocious youth, he conceived some of the music for *A Midsummer Night's Dream* at seventeen.

Meyerbeer, Giacomo (1791-1864). German composer of grand opera who influenced Wagner and Verdi. His activity in Paris is reflected in *L'Africaine, Le Prophete,* and *Les Huguenots.*

Michelangelo Buonarotti (1475-1564). The most famous of Italian Renaissance artists, within his own lifetime he became known as, "Il Divino" (the Divine). Active as a sculptor, painter, and architect, he created masterpieces in all three areas. His best known works are the *Pieta, David,* and the Sistine Ceiling frescoes.

Milton, John (1608-74). English Puritan poet and prose writer, he composed a defense of free press, *Areopagitica* (1644), and many unexcelled sonnets. After the return of the monarchy, he wrote his masterpieces, *Paradise Lost* (1667), *Paradise Regained* (1671), and *Samson Agonistes* (1671).

Moliere (Jean-Baptiste Poquelin) (1622-73). French dramatist excelling in the comedy of manners with unusual depth of psychological insight, his major plays include *Tartuffe* (1664), *The Misanthrope* (1666), and *The Miser* (1668).

Morse, Samuel F. B. (1791-1872). A successful American artist, Morse's interest in electricity was rekindled after hearing the lectures of James F. Dana. He conceived of the telegraph in 1832, perfecting it for twelve years.

Mozart, Wolfgang Amadeus (1756-91). This Austrian developed from an amazing child prodigy to the most versatile composer of all time. Outstanding among his abundant works are three symphonies and three operas: *Don Giovanni, The Marriage of Figaro,* and *The Magic Flute.*

Newton, Sir Isaac (1642-1727). English mathematician and natural philosopher. He formulated the law of gravity and is also known for his laws of motion and for his studies of visible light.

Owen, Sir Richard (1804-92). British comparative anatomist and zoologist famous for his studies of both extinct and existing animals. He was instrumental in founding the British Museum (Natural History).

Palestrina, Giovanni Pierluigi da (c. 1525-94). Regarded as the greatest 16th century composer of Roman Catholic church music, he served as choirmaster of the Julian Chapel at the Vatican.

Phidias (active fifth century BC). An Athenian sculptor, he is believed to have designed the great ivory and gold cult statues of Athena and Zeus which adorned their temples at Athens and Olympia. Now lost, they were greatly praised in antiquity. He is also thought to have designed the marble metopes, freize and pediment sculpture of the Parthenon.

Pliny the Elder (Plinius Secundus) (23-79). A Roman statesman, warrior, advocate and naturalist. He penned the 37 books of the *Historia naturalis*.

Pope, Alexander (1688-1744). English. Waspish satirist and brilliant versifier, he raised the heroic couplet to its most refined level in such works as *The Rape of the Lock* (1712), *The Dunciad* (1728), and *An Essay on Man* (1733-34).

Praxiteles (active fourth century BC). Athenian sculptor whose relaxed and sensuous style characterizes Greek 4th century sculpture. It is debated whether the *Hermes* at Olympia is his original sculpture or a fine copy. Otherwise, his works are lost and known only through copies.

Priestly, Joseph (1733-1804). English theologian and scientist whose discovery of oxygen was a landmark in chemistry.

Purcell, Henry (1659-95). Rising from organ tuner to organist at Westminster Abbey, this prolific English composer wrote much varied music. His best known work is the opera *Dido and Aeneas*.

Pythagoras (582 - c. 507 BC). Greek. The central doctrine of Pythagoras concerned the recognition of the real and objective existence of numbers. His theories had useful applications in the discovery of the relationships of musical tones and in the determination of the earth's spherical shape.

Raphael (Raffaello Sanzio) (1483-1520). Italian Renaissance painter who, influenced by Perugino, Leonardo and Michelangelo, evolved a simple and grand new style which helped define the High Renaissance. For Pope Julius II he painted the famous *Stanze* in the Vatican Palace. His compositions of Madonna and Child are among his popular works.

Rembrandt van Rijn (1606-69). The greatest Dutch painter and printmaker. His prolific output includes portraits, landscapes, and genre scenes as well as subjects from mythology and the Old and New Testaments. The profundity of his understanding of human character gives his work universal appeal.

Rossini, Gioacchino (1792-1868). Italian composer who virtually retired from composing at 37, after writing 39 operas and a *Stabat Mater* in operatic style. *The Barber of Seville* and various overtures are established in the repertoire.

Rumford, Benjamin Thompson, Count (1753-1814). American-born physicist and administrator known for his observations on the weightlessness of heat (at a time when heat was thought to be a material substance). He helped establish the American Academy of Arts and Sciences.

Saint-Saens, Camille (1835-1921). French composer and pianist who began as a child prodigy. His many works include various concertos, the *Third Symphony* (with organ), *Danse macabre* (a symphonic poem), the *Carnival of Animals* and the opera *Samson and Delilah*.

Say, Thomas (1787-1834). Explorations of the Rocky Mountains, the Mississippi and the rivers of Minnesota provided this American naturalist with a wealth of information for his most valuable publications: *American Entomology* (1824-28) and *American Conchology* (1830-34).

Schubert, Franz (1797-1828). Incredibly productive Viennese composer of sonatas, chamber music, symphonies, masses, operas, and over 600 songs. Among symphonies of the highest rank are his No. 8 in B minor *(Unfinished)* and No. 9 in C major *(The Great)*.

Schumann, Robert (1810-56). His music, reflecting his literary proclivities, expresses a depth of feeling and drama which places him among the greatest of German Romantic composers. He is noted for his many songs and for piano, chamber music and symphonic works.

Scopas (active fourth century BC). A Greek sculptor whose works, all now lost, were noted by ancient writers for their dramatic vigor and realism.

Scott, Sir Walter (1771-1832). A Scottish novelist and poet whose works were for more than a century a classroom staple, he wrote the long narrative poem *The Lady of the Lake* (1810) and the Waverley novels of which *Ivanhoe* (1819) and *Kenilworth* (1819) are especially well-remembered.

Shakespeare, William (1564-1616). Generally regarded as one of the world's greatest dramatists, his famous history plays include *Henry V* (1598), his romantic comedies *A Midsummer Night's Dream* (1595), his tragedies *Hamlet* (1600), his problem plays *All's Well That Ends Well* (1602), and his later ethereal comedies *The Tempest* (1611).

Stephenson, George (1781-1848). English developer of the locomotive, he designed an engine to propel coal cars in the mines where he worked as a young man. He was consulted on the building of railroads in England and elsewhere.

Straus (Strauss), Richard (1864-1949). Bavarian composer of symphonic poems *(Don Juan, Till Eulenspeigel)* and operas *(Salome, Der Rosenkavalier)*. Ed. note This seems to be a mistaken inclusion instead of Johann S. Strauss, (1825-1899), Austrian composer, especially of waltzes. However Richard Strauss may have been an intentional exception to the no-living-person criteria because he had appeared in 1904 as guest conductor with the Pittsburgh orchestra.

Tasso, Torquato (1544-94). Considered by some to be Italy's greatest epic poet, his major work, about the first crusade, was *Jerusalem Delivered* (1581).

Tennyson, Alfred Lord (1809-92). English Poet Laureate (1850-92) and poetic voice for Victorian England, he published collections of poems every eight or ten years throughout his life. Among the best-known are *In Memoriam* (1850), *Idylls of the King* (1854), *The Charge of the Light Brigade* (1854), and *Enoch Arden* (1864).

Thackeray, William Makepeace (1811-63). A rival of Dickens in popularity, his works have lasted less well. Among the best are the novels *Vanity Fair* (1848) and *The Memoirs of Barry Lyndon* (1844).

Thomas, Theodore (1835-1905). Noted for his efforts in forwarding musical culture in the United States, this German-born violinist and conductor founded the orchestra which was to become the Chicago Symphony.

Titian (Tiziano Vecellio) (c.1487-1576). Venetian painter whose prolific works include idyllic Madonnas, profoundly psychological portraits, and erotic mythological pictures. He developed a new style of oil painting characterized by free and loose brushwork and brilliant color accents. Among his greatest works are the *Assumption of the Virgin* in Venice and the so-called *Venus of Urbino* in Florence.

Tschaikowsky (Tchaikovsky), Peter Ilych (1840-93). Russian composer of many popular ballets, concertos, operas, symphonies and symphonic poems. Well-known pieces include the *Nutcracker Suite*, *Romeo and Juliet*, and the *Symphonie pathetique*.

Verdi, Giuseppe (1813-1901). The foremost 19th century Italian composer of opera. *Rigoletto, La traviata,* and *Aida* are old favorites. Non-operatic items include his great Requiem and four choral works.

Veronese, Paolo Caliari (c. 1528-88). North Italian painter whose style is highly decorative. His splendid paintings of magnificent pageants adorned both private villas and monasteries.

Velasquez, Diego de Silva y Rodriguez (1599-1660). Spaniard who served as court painter to King Phillip IV from 1623 until his death. He specialized in portraits of the royal family *(Les Meninas)*, but he also painted mythological and other subjects *(Rokeby Venus, Las Hilanderas)*.

Virgil (Publius Vergilius Maro) (70-19 BC). The dominant figure of Latin literature, his influence was profound through all later Western literature. His best-known work, the *Aeneid*, an epic relating the founding of Rome, places him among the first rank of world poets.

Voltaire, Francois-Marie Arouet de (1694-1778). French philosopher, novelist, and historian, notable as the major representative of The Enlightenment, his major works include the philosophical *Letters Concerning the English Nation* (1737), the novella *Zadig* (1748), the *Philosophical Dictionary* (1764), and the satire *Candide* (1779).

Wagner, Richard (1813-83). German composer, who in revolutionizing opera, created the music drama. He wrote texts and music, designed the staging and even a theater for the production of such monumental works as *Ring of the Nibelung*.

Watt, James (1736-1819). This Scottish inventor's improvements produced a more efficient steam engine.

Weber, Carl Maria von (1786-1826). The founder of German Romantic opera. Prolific and versatile, he is best known for *Der Freischutz*.

Wren, Christopher (1632-1723). An English scientist, he practiced as an amateur architect until the Great Fire of London (1666) provided him with the challenge to redesign St. Paul's Cathedral and some 51 smaller parish churches. His classicizing style greatly influenced early American religious architecture.

Compiled by Robin Mager

On view at the 1988 *Carnegie International, Das Ende des 20. Jahrhunderts (The End of the 20th Century)* 1983-1985 by the German sculptor Joseph Beuys. The work is made of 31 basalt stones, clay, and felt, the dimensions of each stone being 16" x 67" x 16". Courtesy of Galerie Bernd Kluser, Munich.

Photograph by Howard P. Nuernberger

Additional Bibliography

My Own Story, by Andrew Carnegie, Houghton Mifflin Company from *The Autobiography of Andrew Carnegie*, copyright 1920 by Louise Whitfield Carnegie.

Andrew Carnegie, by Joseph F. Wall, Originally printed by the Oxford University Press 1970, Reprinted by the University of Pittsburgh Press, 1989.

The Carnegie Nobody Knows, by George Swetman and Helene Smith, McDonald/Swärd Publishing Company, 1989.

An American Palace of Culture, The Carnegie Institute and Carnegie Library of Pittsburgh, by James D. Van Trump, published by Carnegie Institute and the Pittsburgh History & Landmarks Foundation, Pittsburgh, Pennsylvania, copyright January 1970.

Annual Reports of The Carnegie Museum, 1898, 1899, 1900, 1901 and later years, and Annual Reports of Carnegie Institute for 1978, 1993.

Carnegie Magazine, edited by R. Jay Gangewere, published since 1927, 10 issues per year prior to 1982, bi-monthly thereafter.

Art:

- *Tastemaking in Pittsburgh: The Carnegie International in Perspective, 1986-1905*, by Gabriel Weisberg.
- *Interview re International*, Caldwell-Lane, November/December, 1985.
- *Postmodernism in the '88 International*, Vicky Clark, July/August, 1989.
- *Phillip Johnston on The Carnegie Museum of Art*, March/April, 1990.
- *One Hundred Year History, State of Art Today*, Vicky Clark, September 1991.

Assorted publications, brochures, etc. of Carnegie Institute, including *The Catalogue of Painting Collection, Museum of Art, Carnegie Institute*, 1973.

Catalogues of the *Carnegie Internationals* and *The Catalogue of the Retrospective Exhibition of Paintings from Previous Internationals*, Carnegie Institute, 1973.

The Museum of Art, Carnegie Institute, *Collection Handbook*, 1985.

American Painting and Sculpture to 1945 in The Carnegie Museum of Art, 1991.

Carnegie's Dinosaurs by Helen J. McGinnis, Carnegie Museum of Natural History, Carnegie Institute, copyright 1982.

The Carnegie, Ellen Wilson, 1992.

1985 Carnegie International, Museum of Art, Carnegie Institute, 1985.

1988 Carnegie International , Museum of Art, Carnegie Institute, 1988.

1991 Carnegie International, Museum of Art Carnegie Institute, two volumes, 1991.

Pittsburgh Post-Gazette, Donald Miller on Art.

The Pittsburgh Press and *Rotogravure Sections*, especially November 15, 1981, and May 13, 1992, and articles by Patricia Lowry on art related topics.

Art Ventures by Bay Hallowell, The Carnegie Museum of Art, 1987

Typeset in ITC Galliard
Typesetting: Kacsuta Parks Design
Cover stock: Kromekote Gloss Coated Cover
Text stock: White Sterling Gloss Text

Design/Production Management: Kacsuta Parks Design
Publication Design: Dolly Kacsuta Parks
Production Assistance: Sharon Smith

Printed by Hoechstetter Printing Company, Pittsburgh, PA

Cover images: The Carnegie Hero Medal, photograph courtesy of Carnegie Library of Pittsburgh; *Tyrannosaurus Rex*, photograph by Vincent Abromitis, courtesy of The Carnegie Museum of Natural History; Globe illustration by Jeffrey Boyd, courtesy of *Carnegie Magazine*; *Andy Warhol*, photograph courtesy of The Andy Warhol Museum and *Thousand and One Nights* by Henri Matisse, courtesy of The Carnegie Museum of Art.